Gender in Performance

Gender in Performance

THE PRESENTATION OF DIFFERENCE

IN THE PERFORMING

ARTS ❦ Edited by LAURENCE SENELICK

TUFTS UNIVERSITY

Published by University Press of New England / Hanover and London

TUFTS UNIVERSITY
Published by University Press of New England, Hanover, NH 03755
© 1992 by Trustees of Tufts University
All rights reserved
Printed in the United States of America 5 4 3 2 1
CIP data appear at the end of the book

Jill Dolan's essay "Gender Impersonation Onstage:
Destroying or Maintaining the Mirror of Gender Roles?"
was originally published in *Women & Performance* 4 (1987).
Reprinted with permission.

Contents

Editor's Acknowledgments

❦ The origins for this anthology are to be sought in a Salzburg Seminar on Gender and the Humanities held in 1988. Cocooned by the baroque splendor of Max Reinhardt's Schloss Leopoldskron, my ideas benefited from lively exchanges with the seminar's leaders, Alberta Arthurs, James Boon, Joan Scott, Elaine Showalter, and Jeffrey Weeks. More stimulation came from discussions with Josine Blok, Frances Finnegan, Mario Klarer, and Marty Knepper.

The potential usefulness of such an anthology bore in upon me when I tried to organize my own graduate seminar in Gender in the Performing Arts at Tufts University. The students in that experimental symposium deserve my gratitude for their animated discussions and probing questions. Once this project was under way, it profited from the advice, encouragement, and suggestions of Henry Akina, Sally Baines, George Chauncey, Jr., Rhonda Cobham-Sander, Chris Durang, David Greenberg, Peter Jelavich, Dorothy Keyser, Teresa de Lauretis, John Lithgow, Emily Mann, Elizabeth Natalle, Yvonne Noble, Mark Oshima, Patrice Pavis, Joel Schechter, Martha Vicinus, Andrzej Wirth, and Masao Yamaguchi. Rose Marie Whiteley, public relations officer of the Omaha Magic Theatre, provided needed material. My fullest thanks go out to the contributors themselves, who enthusiastically responded to my appeals and diligently revised at my behest; and to Jeanne West, humanities editor of the University Press of New England, who cheered on the book from the beginning and patiently bore with it to the end.

L.S.

Introduction

❦ Gender *is* performance. As a cultural construct, made up of learned values and beliefs, gender identity (if one can posit such an absolute) has no ontological status. Whatever biological imperatives may order sexual differentiation, whatever linguistic patterns may undergird it, it is outward behavior that calibrates the long scale of masculinity and femininity in social relations. Like a Berkeleian universe, gender exists only in so far as it is perceived; and the very components of perceived gender—gait, stance, gesture, deportment, vocal pitch and intonation, costume, accessories, coiffure—indicate the performative nature of the construct. Even when the projection of gender becomes second nature, it can, like any performance, vary in plausibility, verisimilitude, and persuasive power. What Erving Goffman calls "The Arts of Impression Management,"[1] the avoidance of inopportune or ambiguous signals, is crucial to the performance of gender in everyday life.

A variable charged with protean potential, the gendered body's performative aspects engage continuous re-examination and reassessment. Before the critic and historian can interpret these tokens as symbols, they must ask in Joan Scott's words, "Which symbolic representations are invoked, how, and in what contexts?"[2] The unpuzzling of performance raises another crucial question—How and under what circumstances is the symbolic representation received? Only when these questions are satisfactorily answered can one proceed to such speculative issues as the meaning, especially the political meaning, of the performance.

The performance of gender is doubly fraught with implication when it moves from the everyday sphere onto the stage, where presentation invariably entails representation. To begin with, the actor is concerned with conveying not a personal code of gender but a set of signals that are at once more abstract and more graphic than those transmitted in standard social intercourse. A spectrum of such ordinary signals can be found in Marianne Wex's book on "feminine" and "masculine" body language.[3] To support her contention that the ways men and women move, stand, sit, lie have been imposed not by biology but by patriarchal (specifically Christian) authority, she adduces hundreds of pictures, from ancient Egyptian sculpture to modern snapshots, of human beings in these homely postures. These illustrations are organized to prove that in the remote past men and women shared the same physical deportment, but that, by the Middle Ages, men had already adopted the splayed legs and upper-body expansion that fill space and claim territory, forcing women into the knees-together, upper-arms-welded-to-upper-torso constriction that spells self-effacing submission. Centuries of social pressure, says Wex, have frozen men and women into these physical classifiers of gender. They are equipped with a limited stock of signifiers because the official colors are black and white, male and female; intermediate shades do not receive the Good Housekeeping Seal of Approval.

These sweeping conclusions are more polemic than proven, but Wex's picture gallery is a useful conspectus of the common- or garden-variety performance of gender in life. It should be contrasted with an eighteenth-century treatise on acting, such as that of J. J. Engel or Henry Siddons, in which specific emotions are attributed to given poses and gestures. Wex's pictures tend to lack context: Often the only message conveyed is the stark one of gender, and the subjects are presumed to send this same message on a regular basis throughout their lives. But in the acting manuals, the pose efficiently transmits to the spectator the affective content of the role at any given moment; stage performance is not so much a continuum as a series of discrete instants, each with its own statement to make. The actor's portrayal of gender is an essential conveyance of the affect, manipulated and subordinated to an artistic rendering of something else.

In cultures where a code of gender is universally accepted and easily legible, the social arts of impression management—a man sustaining his virility by keeping his hands away from his face or a woman promoting her ladylikeness by refusing to cross her legs—work as a telegraphic statement of the individual's chosen gender identity. But when such social behavior is put on stage, it takes on an iconic value, heightening and drawing attention to the conventional or overlooked aspects of the behavior. How these signs of gender are to be read may or may not be the authorized method, just as their transmission may or may not employ a body identical to the body represented. The willed "masculinity" or "femininity" of hands-away-from-face or not-crossing-legs comes across as a larger statement about both the character and the contexture that ordain this sort of identity constraint.

The formal or professional performer is highly aware of the conventional sign language, because it has to be further refined and codified for representational use. Particularly in non-naturalistic theaters like those of Asia, the "extra-quotidian" techniques of the actor, labeled by Eugenio Barba "pre-expressiveness" (*pré-expressivité*),[4] are sedulously learned, a physicality that precedes psychology. (Even in the naturalistic theatre, the basic needs of visibility and vocal projection tend to enforce this precedence.) Working within a conventional frame, the performer does not have to worry about adapting spontaneously to given circumstances in order to maintain a chosen gender role. The body and voice of such a performer are wielded to convey the necessary messages, and irrelevant or contingent information is edited out to prevent the message from blurring.

Consequently, gender roles performed by "performers" never merely replicate those in everyday life; they are more sharply defined and more emphatically presented, the inherent iconicity offering both an ideal and a critique. Cross-dressing, for instance, is a basic technique in this procedure. As Judith Butler points out, "In imitating gender drag implicitly reveals the imitative structure of gender itself—as well as its contingency."[5] The clearest example of this revelation may be the *onnagata* or female impersonator of the classical Kabuki, whose stylized bearing derives not from observed behavior but from an abstract concept of allure (*irokē*), and in turn projects an impression of *das Ewig-Weibliche*. The performance may influence social codes of gender, but the relationship is oblique.

Theatrical gender is not only more perspicuously intelligible than the behavioral kind, it is also more variegated in its possibilities. The performer is freer to move in and out of gender roles: Even when the *onnagata* actor was expected to act like a woman offstage, this behavior was sanctioned conduct not available to a "civilian" transvestite. One might compare the modern Indian *hijra,* a transvestite eunuch whose prostitutional activities are covered by the mantle of religion owing to his castration, while an intact male whoring in drag is contemned by *hijras* and Hindu society alike. The performer's special status, beyond lay constraints, authorizes dangerous games.

Historically, the theatre has been a safe-house for unconventional behavior. Although its public nature has required it to endorse norms, its space is specially licensed to harbor unorthodox individuals and otherwise inadmissible conduct. Commonly accepted reality may be inverted or parodied within this space, a practice natural in the rituals of simpler societies but conducive to anti-theatrical prejudice in later periods. The discrepancy between the acceptance of gender diversity in early theatre and hostility to it in later periods may be accounted for by Victor Turner's now-famous distinction between the "liminal" and the "liminoid";[6] for Turner, the distinction pivots on the notion of play. In tribal societies, liminal activities, no matter how ludic, ultimately confirm or reassert the society's structure: The alternatives they present are meant to function only within the temporal-spatial confines of the ritual. The activities themselves feed back into the society in a clearly teleological way. In complex, industrial civilizations, on the other hand, leisure and cultural pluralism foster a more widespread and diverse play, which is pseudo-liminal or liminoid. It often satirizes the values of its society and apes the liminal, but, being relegated to leisure, fails to be deterministic. However, because heterogeneous societies are more porous in their absorption of ideas, the play does not stay circumscribed within its event but colors and motivates the rest of our lives.

To adapt this idea to the performance of gender, one might say that an initiatory rite in which the male warriors-to-be dance disguised as women is liminal. The transsexual performance is used to enhance their future virility by contrast and perhaps to exorcise any "feminine" alloy in their nature. The rite condones the temporary aberration for a greater end, the forging of warriors. The result of the ritual is to change the participants from a transitional state to a completed state. An evening of lip-synching at a drag bar, however, is a liminoid performance: Some of the performers may have adopted drag for the evening, others may wear it in "real life." They may be heterosexual, homosexual, or bisexual, amateurs or professionals, closeted or declared, even men or women. The performance itself is no guarantee of a permanent transformation in either participants or spectators, however much perceptions may alter in the process. Performing another gender does not define one's "true" gender, either by confirmation or contrast.

Another important distinction derives from the erotic pervasion of the theatrical space. Of course, many liminal rituals are sexualized: mating dances, fertility rites, ecstatic movement to stimulate erethism. But again, there is an essential teleology that is critical to the survival of the society on a physical or psychological plane. The liminoid erotics of theatre becomes, as part of a leisure activity, a more personal interchange of desires. To appear on stage is to display one's body to strangers: A commodity available to the gaze may, in given circumstances, be vendible in its entirety. The inscription of gender as allure, in a more blatant manner than society condones, becomes one of the theatre's most potent attractions and, to the authorities, one of its most dangerous features. Since the object of desire is traditionally Woman, the actual deployment of women and the use of surrogates, such as boys and young men, become problematic; but in both cases, the gender signals sent from the stage are more powerful than those available in ordinary life. The prostitutional aspect of the theatre makes its performance of gender especially dynamic.

In the West, the growing predominance of written drama over non-literate forms, the gradual legitimation of theatres as a branch of court, government, or social service, and the increase of women in the audience—

in short, the rise of respectability—also meant a shrinking of gender variants played out on the stage. Most of the avant-garde movements of the modern Western stage have been attempts to reclaim the anti-social and disruptive elements of peformance that confront and overthrow norms, gender norms among them. As Elin Diamond puts it, "Experimental theater can be, occasionally is, a laboratory for interrupting signification, for marring the icon's reception, and thus alienating the spectator's processes of reading and being."[7] French audiences were quite content with traditional theatrical cross-dressing—clowns playing old women and female beauties encased in tight trousers—when Guillaume Apollinaire launched the first surrealist drama, *Les Mamelles de Tirésias* (1917), in which husband and wife switch genders to the degree that husband procreates unendingly and sprouts balloon breasts. This farcical trope, capable of being traced back to the *commedia dell'arte,* spelled subversion to a wartime public encouraged by the government to breed prolifically. Similarly, in the 1960s and 1970s, an American public accustomed to glamor drag was assailed by gender-fuck: rock musicians and fringe performers in sequins and net stockings who did not bother to shave their moustaches or chests. Such critical techniques have become s.o.p. for feminist theatre. At the WOW Café in New York's East Village, a woman's company of mixed ethnic background and sexual preference subjects the lesbian roles of "butch" and "femme" to comic dissection alongside standard heterosexual poses for a primarily female audience. When the game of gender impersonation becomes too tame, the deck has to be reshuffled.

Offending the audience is, however, primarily a modernist ploy. Performance, particularly outside the West where the association between ritual and theatre is more intimate, has traditionally been a medium of reconcilement and mediation rather than one of rejection and alienation. Enactment of liminoid elements is a means of integrating them within an otherwise antagonistic system. What seems at first sight unacceptable, extreme, and outlandish can be subsumed into conventional categories. The representational clarity of the stage and its license to be different allow, paradoxically, for a show of ambiguity. Oppositions and differences, which in everyday life might arouse anxiety, tension, or hostility, are given a hearing that often resolves the conflict or at least provides a fresh alternative.

These contradictions and paradoxes, the historical and cross-cultural diversity of the performance of gender, are demonstrated in this anthology's contents. The focus here is not so much on drama, the literary artifact, as on live performance, from Islamic passion plays to Wild West shows. Much recent writing on performative gender has been concerned with analyzing written texts and consequently with "legitimate" theatre; popular entertainments and folk theatre are often overlooked as vital signifiers of ingrown attitudes. Some of this writing has been culture bound, narrowly concerned with the current American scene; its historical references tend to be cavalier, hiccupping from Euripides to Hroswitha to Aphra Behn. Without pretending to be comprehensive, this anthology offers a spectrum of cultural manifestations, from high to low and from obsolete to state-of-the-art. Several of the contributors are anthropologists, others are theatre historians, still others are engaged in the practical realization of gender concepts in the theatre. The concentration is on analyzing observed or researched data rather than on articulating new theories. Too much of what presently passes for theory is a kind of abstruse speculation unsupported by hard evidence or close attention to detail. The material presented here provides grist for further study without, I hope, mangling it on a Procrustean bed of foregone conclusions.

The image of woman dominates this book, because, in most cultures until very recently, to be human meant to be male. Man was taken as the generic form, and woman as a subspecies, a somehow imperfect version or soluble problem. Since women have often been barred from public performance and their roles relegated to men or youths, this impersonation required special handling. The causes of this ban are ostensibly dictated by social prescripts but may originate in deeply rooted traditions of religious taboo or magical practice.

The investigation of such conventions raises questions such as: Why are women not allowed on stage? How is their essence understood, interpreted, and communicated by men? (To play a "female role" does not necessarily mean to play a female.) What effect does this convention have on the perception of femininity offstage? Who is doing the perceiving? What resonances and repercussions occur beyond the performance arena? What happens when the situation is reversed and women portray men?

To complicate matters, the proscription against female performance often co-exists with a notion of performance as being within Woman's sphere. Although women themselves are not allowed to take part, men might perform a male conception of the feminine to experience vicariously an emotional plenitude perceived to be inherent in women and, through this alterity, transcend socially defined roles and achieve a wholeness not otherwise available. Discussing classical tragedy, Froma I. Zeitlin points out that, for the Greeks, mimesis or role-playing was essentially feminine. In Greek thought, Woman had a dual nature; so

by virtue of the conflicts generated by her social position and ambiguously defined between inside and outside, interior self and exterior identity, the woman is already more of a "character" than the man, who is far more limited as an actor to his public social and political roles. Woman comes equipped with a "natural" awareness of those very complexities men would resist, if they could. . . . Hence the final paradox may be that theater uses the feminine for the purposes of imagining a fuller model for the masculine self, and "playing the other" opens that self to those banned emotions of fear and pity.[8]

The first section of this book, which examines the trying-on of alternatives, is therefore called "Assuming Gender" to imply both the assumptions made about the gender to be performed and the way in which such roles are undertaken. Jill Dolan's seminal (if such a word is not out of place) essay has, as she grants, the semblance of an historical document: It is a relatively early statement of feminist wariness of such impersonations. Dolan regards the traditional definition of the theatre as *speculum mundi* with distrust. A mirror, after all, makes claim to a certain objectivity, and if the reflection does little more than cast back prevalent abuses and inequities, it is of scant value to reformers. For her, conventional impersonation is a means of propagating and endorsing the *status quo,* especially in the case of gender. The purpose of studying it is to disclose the ways in which the performing arts accomplish this reinforcement, and how they contribute to the power relations of gender within a given society.

Dolan's afterword notes how current perspectives have broadened and lost some of their polemical edge. If one approaches the subject with the preconception that all such gender impersonations are merely variants of the same recurrent and ubiquitous patriarchal oppression, the answers tend to be formulaic and identical. A call for change has to presume the possibility of change: Gender is not so inflexible, after all, and performance may serve to reveal repressed potentials.

A preoccupation with the patriarchal repression and distortion of women is in fact borne out by William Beeman's study of Muslim passion plays. Rigid definition and the avoidance of experimental possibilities characterize the female impersonation of Iranian performance. Because Islam regards women's ability to ignite desire as dangerously automatic, their presentation in a dramatic context is fraught with difficulty. In religious drama, they must be played by men "non-mimetically," through purely semiotic devices. In secular comedies, the masculinity of the actor is apparent through the thin disguise, a contradiction that contributes to farce. But when female sexuality is represented, either by a biological woman or a young man, the actors take pains to distance themselves from what they are portraying.

The stasis of a traditionalist society is thus maintained by the mimicry. In twentieth-century America, on the other hand, stage transvestism has been used to mediate social awareness, as I try to demonstrate in my essay on female impersonation in American popular theatre of the Progressive Era. The creations of Julian Eltinge and Bert Savoy neutralized and humanized the New Woman and the fairy, types of gender intermediacy that were impinging upon public consciousness. Radical change demanded rapid shifts in the definition of gender, and these performances served to disarm an otherwise threatening reality.

A similar but less disinfecting process is observed by Jennifer Robertson in contemporary Japan, where a new type of male impersonation has supplemented the accepted modes of female impersonation and has created a troubling duality. The traditional *onnagata* of Kabuki, man playing woman, creates an ideal female without reference to reality and, in our age at least, is not expected to transmit such traits to private life. But those young women of the popular Takarazuka revue who play men are expected to adopt actual markers of socially defined masculinity. Their art, while admired, is seen to provide a subversive subtext, encouraging an "abnormal life-style." Traditional concepts of unmarried womanhood are affronted by the *Takarasienne,* provoking widely divergent responses, depending on the sex of the viewer. The clash of sanctioned performance, unsanctioned behavior, and the projection of desire contribute to the Takarazuka's extraordinary impact in a society that is sharply divided between old and new, male and female.

In Moe Meyer's view, the authority to attribute gender has, in the West, become vested in the medical community, which insists on either/or choices and precipitates sex-change operations in lieu of fostering a more androgynous model. Meyer's description of a striptease act as a metaphor for the transsexual's clinical progress suggests that performance recapitulates ontology. When performed by a transsexual, the folkloric drag show becomes a Pirandellian probing for some putative core identity. The speculum that Dolan distrusts splits into a whole hall of distorting mirrors.

Given such scientific directives, is it possible to transcend gender? In Robert Wilson's Frankfurt production of *King Lear,* casting an elderly actress in the title role was neither an arbitrary choice nor a statement of sexual politics. For Wilson, as Erika Fischer-Lichte explains, dying is a rite of passage, and death is indifferent to gender: Marianne Hoppe's grandmotherly Lear moves through a transitional phase to the final transfiguration—her incorporation in all being. Wilson's utopia is characterized not by androgynes or conflations of gender but by the cancellation of difference. It might be remarked that such a staging makes stronger claims to universality than did the concurrent *King Lear* directed by Lee Breuer. Breuer consistently reversed sexes and turned the Fool into a neutered drag queen, but also opted for a Dogpatch-like milieu. By adding all sorts of modern American signifiers of class and race, he hopelessly confused the issue, muddying the reversal of gender with other signifiers that were occasionally apt but more often irrelevant. Breuer cast as his Lear Ruth Maleczech, a strong (that is, "masculine") actress of impeccable avant-garde credentials who brought to the role the toughness long associated with American stage matriarchs. Wilson's casting was more radical, since Hoppe had, since pre-Nazi times, played the young heroines of classical drama and critics have noted a ladylike strain (*Damenhaftigkeit*) throughout her work. It was Cordelia playing Lear, but a Cordelia who had grown to be her father, her conventional "femininity" submerged in her great age.

"Femininity" or "femaleness" becomes a central issue when women declare women, that is, when actresses take to the stage and wrest back the portrayals of gender from male performers. The next group of essays presents a variety of ways in which women have historically taken advantage of this opportunity to expand permissible gender boundaries or else have been hemmed in by conventions devised to control their troubling presence.

As Virginia Scott points out, in the increasingly conservative society of seventeenth-century Paris, the Comédie-Italienne, that offshoot of the *commedia dell'arte*, featured actresses in roles of capable, independent women, resistant to unsuitable matches or importunate suits. The popular stage set up not a reflection but an option for its audience. Whether Victorian imagery of Woman as victim reflected or misconstrued reality is debated by Joseph Donohue. Theatrical iconography may signal a two-way traffic between life and art, as in the case of Ellen Terry who lived up (or down) to literary and artistic models presented for her incarnation. The illusions of desire fed from the stage often had to be played out behind the scenes. Beyond the legitimate theatre, more unorthodox means were available. Tracy C. Davis presents the sharpshooter Annie Oakley as a mass of contradictions: a woman demonstrating skill in a traditionally masculine field of action but projecting the image of the perfect lady, a wife firing guns at her husband while maintaining an idyllic marriage, a domesticated Amazon, a thaumaturge wielding appliances found around the house.

The multiversatility expected of the modern American woman and prefigured by Oakley's virtuosity is repeated in the manifold redefinitions of women in early Soviet society. Spencer Golub examines how icons of the female were reshaped by postrevolutionary requirements. Performance, itself equated with femininity, generated brave new models, such as the gynoid, which retarded or outstripped the actual changing roles for women within the society. The ideal continually outstripped the real, leading to a frustration of genuine progress.

In his discussion of Ariane Mnouchkine's Asian cycle, Adrian Kiernander takes up the theme of the identification of woman with the Orient. Orientalism has commonly been a way to reduce Asia to "feminine," subservient status, to subjugate the dangerous Other. The topos recurs throughout this book: Moe Meyer touches on the pseudo-Oriental trappings of the *femme fatale*—the transsexual stripper as down-market

Salome; and Megan Terry discusses how in her play *Viet Rock* the Viet Cong were played by women to suggest vulnerability and victimization. Mnouchkine consciously retained this stereotype but avoided the depiction of desire to lessen the sense of sexual differentiation. By so doing, she was able to present an overlapping of opposites and the possibility of a poly-centric world. In this respect, I might add, Mnouchkine is poles apart from David Henry Hwang and his popular play *M. Butterfly*. Based on an actual case, it related the infatuation of a French diplomat for a beautiful Chinese actress, who was in fact a male spy. Hwang was eager to conflate Western fantasies about the East with male fantasies about femininity, but for all the trading back and forth of gender roles, the American playwright denies the viability of gender multiplicity. For him, loss of strict gender identity entails the collapse of self.

Dance, dependent on the body for its expression, offers a particularly fertile field for studying the definition and presentation of gender. Differ-ence is encoded by primarily, sometimes exclusively, physical means. In Ba-linese culture, ordered by antinomies, well-established performance codes in dance-drama sanction gender play and inversion. John Emigh and Jamer Hunt explore the nexus between Balinese fears and fancies and their ex-ploitation in performance. Liminal roles like the androgyne, highly revered in the divine world, are seen as dangerous and anarchic in the human. But as performances evolve from sacred to secular, they lead to sexual contact: Gender switching becomes riskier as it becomes more eroticized and arous-ing. The pressures of modern life scramble the code and proliferate the messages.

A similar proliferation can be seen in modern Western dance with the breakdown of traditional positions of weakness and strength in the cho-reographic distribution of roles. Judith Lynne Hanna summarizes the his-tory of modern dance as an object lesson in victimization and counsels that educational reform can aid in eliminating discrimination. She catalogues both the traditional stereotypes and the attempts made to supersede them in the deconstruction and reconstruction of gender. Ann Daly, on the other hand, challenges standard feminist approaches, questioning whether the fashionable notion of the male gaze is really useful in analyzing response to dance. Drawing on Julia Kristeva's idea of chora and taking Isadora Duncan as her model, she insists that kinesthetic expression is a symbolic signifier implying more than it shows. With the body-in-motion as a point of intersection between culture and nature, selfhood is a fluctuant process. This constant flux is ultimately unintelligible to reason but connotes mean-ing on several planes.

Duncan employed the moving body to direct attention to woman's phys-ical integrity and independence; in the 1920s, Mary Wigman arrogated to herself movement techniques that had hitherto been male attributes. Duncan's quest for beauteous harmony was too exclusive for Wigman, who wanted to express human totality with its ugly and stressful aspects. To achieve this totality, as Karl Toepfer's study reveals, she added the voice, seeking to confute the idea that the body is feminine and speech masculine. Sexual differentiation was to be manifested through a tension between the animate (movement) and the inanimate (death). Wigman's postsymbolist fascination with death as the decisive factor in human existence prefigures in striking ways the thanatropic dissolution of gender in Robert Wilson's *Lear.*

The final section of this book allows persons active in performance to speak from their experience. Elaine Savory Fido, who has organized woman's theatre in the Caribbean, provides a contrast with the Balinese, Iranian, and Japanese situations where gender disruptions are played out against a backdrop of comparatively homogeneous tradition. In the black Anglophone Caribbean, a large number of cultural influences struggle for expression, forcing gender's political meaning to the surface. Gender itself can be regarded, in Fido's words, as "a viable and cultural identity," and its most ordinary manifestations become radical by the very act of putting them on stage. For the women she discusses, raising consciousness is the paramount reason to experiment with gender.

A similar rationale lies behind the work of the Omaha Magic Theatre, an old-established firm in the representation of gendered behavior. Megan Terry, Sora Kimberlain, and Jo Anne Schidman take a hands-on approach, regarding the performance of gender as a projection of essences. The possibilities inherent in collective creation offer potential alternatives for both the performers and the audience. Safe consignment to a single gender is taunted and teased by the exuberant transformations undergone by the performers. The teasing of conventional ideas also informs the performance art of Kate Bornstein, whose status as a transsexual lesbian confuses the issue from the start. Her attitude repudiates the kind of surgical transsexualism discussed by Moe Meyer, which emphasizes difference and rejects intermediacy. As her dramaturge Noreen Barnes explains, Bornstein mocks society's desperate urge to define and categorize gender and tries to blur facile attributions.

The concluding essay concerns ritual, in Ronald Grimes's sense of "a transformative performance revealing major classifications, categories and contradictions of cultural processes."[9] John Preston offers a nostalgic retrospect of a rite of passage wherein gender is enacted by voyeur/participant, the scopophilic exhibitionism of all-male sex clubs in the era before AIDS. Public declaration of one's sexual identity through participation in sadomasochistic acts was an initiatory ceremony that, paradoxically, endorsed traditional gender stereotypes. The masculinist approach—"I am man enough to suck cock and don't care who knows it"—vaunts the virility of the so-called deviant as more authentic than that of the average "he-man." Such a ploy calls into question the social markers of manliness while confirming the fundamental value of manliness within the society. If, as Meyer claims, the drag show is gay folk drama, then public sex, in Preston's opinion, is a cultic celebration of tribal folkways and an affirmation of gender choice. Performance once again allows for the trying on and trying out of gender variations not always at one's disposal in narrower walks of life.

Notes

1. Erving Goffman, *The Presentation of Self in Everyday Life* (Garden City, N.Y.: Doubleday, 1959), pp. 208–37.

2. Joan Scott, "Gender: A Useful Category of Historical Analysis," *American Historical Review* 91, no. 5 (December 1986):1067.

3. Marianne Wex, *"Weibliche" und "männliche" Körpersprache als Folge patriarchalischer Machtverhältnisse* (Frankfurt: Frauenliteraturvertrieb Hermine Fees, 1980).

4. Eugenio Barba and Nicola Savarese, *Anatomie de l'acteur. Un dictionnaire d'anthropologie théâtrale,* trans. Eliane Deschamps-Pria (Paris: Bouffonneries Contrastes, 1985), pp. 22–23.

5. Judith Butler, *Gender Trouble: Feminism and the Subversion of Identity* (New York: Routledge, 1990), p. 37.

6. The classic statement is Victor Turner, "Liminal to Liminoid, in Play, Flow, Ritual: An Essay in Comparative Symbology," in *From Ritual to Theatre: The Human Seriousness of Play* (New York: PAJ Publications, 1982), pp. 20–60.

7. Elin Diamond, "(Theoretically) Approaching Megan Terry: Issues of Gender and Identity," *Art & Cinema* 1, no. 3 (Fall 1987):7.

8. Froma I. Zeitlin, "Playing the Other: Theater, Theatricality, and the Feminine in Greek Drama," *Representations* 11 (Summer 1985):79–80.

9. Ronald Grimes, *Beginnings in Ritual Studies* (Washington: University Press of America, 1982), p. 36.

List of Contributors

NOREEN C. BARNES is a freelance director and writer in San Francisco who has served as dramaturge on several productions for Joseph Chaikin, directed Kate Bornstein's *Hidden: A Gender* at Theatre Rhinoceros, and written for a number of periodicals, including the *Medical Tribune, Bay Area Reporter, Performing Arts Resources, Outlook, Callboard,* and *Mother Jones.*

WILLIAM O. BEEMAN is Associate Professor of Anthropology at Brown University and a former Fellow of the Humanities Center at Stanford University. His publications include *Culture, Performance and Communication in Iran*; the entry on the Middle East in the *Cambridge Guide to World Theatre*; and articles in *Journal of American Folklore, Performing Arts Journal,* and other periodicals.

ANN DALY is Assistant Professor of Dance History/Criticism at the University of Texas at Austin. Her writing has appeared in *High Performance, Dance Research Journal, Ballet International, Women & Performance,* and *Theatre Journal.* She edited the winter 1988 issue of *The Drama Review* on movement analysis and is currently writing a book about the significance of Isadora Duncan in early twentieth-century America.

TRACY C. DAVIS, Assistant Professor in Theatre and English, Northwestern University, is North American editor of Routledge's series on Gender and Performance and a former Mellon Faculty Fellow at Harvard University. She has published *Actresses As Working Women: Their Social Identity in Victorian Culture,* as well as articles on nineteenth- and twentieth-century sexual politics, theatrical reception, popular culture, and feminist theatre in a wide variety of journals and collections.

JILL DOLAN is an Assistant Professor of Theatre and Drama and Women's Studies at the University of Wisconsin-Madison. Her book, *The Feminist Spectator as Critic* (UMI, 1988), won the Emily Toth Award of the Women's Caucus of the Popular Cultural Association. Her articles on feminist performance theory have appeared in *Theatre Journal, The Drama Review, Modern Drama, Journal of Popular Culture,* and other periodicals. She is a founding editor of *Women and Performance* and the president of the Women and Theatre Program of the Association for Theatre in Higher Education.

JOSEPH DONOHUE is Professor of English at the University of Massachusetts, Amherst, and general editor of *The London Stage 1800–1900: A Documentary*

Record and Calendar of Performances. His reconstructive critical edition of the first production of *The Importance of Being Earnest* is forthcoming from Southern Illinois University Press. A member of the editorial team now preparing the Oxford English Texts edition of the collected works of Oscar Wilde, he is also at work on a book on Wilde and the theatre of his age.

JOHN EMIGH teaches and directs at Brown University, where he is Professor and Chair of the Department of Theatre. He has served as Chair of the Association for Asian Performance and has adapted Balinese *topeng* techniques in performance. His writing includes several articles on Balinese and Indian performing traditions; a book *Masking and Playing: Studies in Masked Performance* is to be published by University of Pennsylvania Press.

ELAINE SAVORY FIDO has taught at universities in Ghana, Nigeria, and the Caribbean and has worked in theatre there, primarily as a director. She has written articles on various aspects of African and Caribbean theatre and, with Carol Boyce Davies, has co-edited *Out of the Kumbla: Women and Caribbean Literature* (Africa World Press). Her strong interest in gender issues led her to assist in the development of Women's Studies at the University of West Indies, Cave Hill.

ERIKA FISCHER-LICHTE is Professor of Theatre Research at Johannes-Gutenberg-Universität, Mainz, having previously taught at Bayreuth University. Her fields of research include performance theory and analysis, theatre semiotics, and twentieth-century theatre history. Her most important publications are *Bedeutung— Probleme einer semiotischen Hermeneutik und Ästhetik*, the three-volume *Semiotik des Theaters*, the two-volume *Geschichte des Dramas*, and *The Dramatic Touch of Difference*.

SPENCER GOLUB is Associate Professor of Theatre and Comparative Literature at Brown University. He is the author of *Evreinov: The Theatre of Paradox and Transformation* (UMI), the Russian entries in *The Cambridge Guide to World Theatre*, and numerous articles, essays, and reviews. He is presently working on a study of Soviet cultural iconography.

JUDITH LYNNE HANNA (Ph.D. Columbia), an anthropologist, is a Senior Research Scholar at the University of Maryland. Her publications include *To Dance is Human, The Performer-Audience Connection, Dance, Sex and Gender, Dance and Stress*, and *Disruptive School Behavior*, as well as more than three-score scholarly articles and contributions in *The Drama Review, Design for Arts in Education, Washington Post, Stagebill, Dancemagazine, Dance Teacher Now*, and other journals.

JAMER HUNT completed an independent concentration in Performance Studies at Brown University. He has studied *gamelan* music in Bali and is currently a graduate student in the Anthropology Department of Rice University.

ADRIAN KIERNANDER is a theatre director and lecturer in drama at the University of Queensland. In 1985, with the assistance of a scholarship from the French Ministère des Relations Extérieurs, he studied with the Théâtre du Soleil while they were rehearsing their production of *Norodom Sihanouk*. His study of the work of

Ariane Mnouchkine was published by Cambridge University Press in the "Directors in Perspective" series.

SORA KIMBERLAIN is a sculptor, visual arts collaborator, and actor at the Omaha Magic Theatre, designing environments for each play in its repertory. She was co-founder of the arts collective Lovsenko and of the Eclectic Cooperative Artist Gallery, both in Louisville, and from 1980 to 1987, she was co-editor and publisher of *Beef Magazine,* a mobile alternative art gallery. Her works are in private collections from Guam to London, California to Nebraska.

MOE MEYER is a lecturer in the Department of Art History, School of the Art Institute of Chicago. As a performance artist, he has presented his work in the United States, Europe, Asia, and Australia. He has edited *The Politics and Poetics of Camp,* to be published by Routledge in 1993.

JOHN PRESTON is former editor of *The Advocate* and was East Coast editor of *Drummer* during the heyday of the New York sex club. His S&M novels, including *Mr Benson,* the *Master* series, and *The Heir,* have become cult classics. His most recent works are *The Big Gay Book: A Man's Survival to the 90s* (New American Library [NAL]/Plume) and an anthology, *Hometowns: Gay Men Write about Where They Belong* (NAL). His new collection, *Flesh and the Word: An Erotic Anthology,* was published in 1992.

JENNIFER ROBERTSON, who has lived in Japan for nearly eighteen years, is Associate Professor of Anthropology at the University of Michigan, Ann Arbor. Her essays on historical and contemporary Japanese culture appear in *Anthropological Quarterly, Genders, Politics, Culture and Society, Peasant Studies,* and *Monumenta Nipponica.* She has recently published *Native and Newcomer: Making and Remaking a Japanese City* and is writing *Doing "Male" and "Female" in Japan: Learning from the Takarazuka Revue* (both University of California Press).

JO ANN SCHMIDMAN, Artistic Director of the Omaha Magic Theatre, which she founded in 1968, won critical acclaim acting in the Open Theatre's Obie-winning productions *Mutation Show* and *Nightwalk.* She has developed innovative training workshops in all aspects of the theatre and has directed and produced over fifty-seven plays at the Magic Theatre since 1980, writing or co-writing fifteen of them.

VIRGINIA SCOTT is Professor of Theatre at the University of Massachusetts at Amherst. Her Book, *The Commedia dell'Arte in Paris, 1644–87,* won the George Freedley Award of the Theatre Library Association in 1991. She is a former Guggenheim Fellow and edited *Theatre Journal* from 1973 to 1977. She is presently writing a book about the institutionalization of the theatre in France under the *ancien régime.*

LAURENCE SENELICK is Fletcher Professor of Drama at Tufts University and a former Fellow of the Guggenheim Foundation and the Wissenschaftskolleg zu Berlin. His many books include *Russian Dramatic Theory from Pushkin to the Symbolists; Cabaret Performance: Europe 1890–1940;* and *The Age and Stage of George L. Fox.* His recent writing on gender and eroticism in the theatre has appeared in *Journal of the History of Sexuality, Theatre Journal, Theatre History Studies, Russian Review,* and *Teatralnaya Zhizn.*

MEGAN TERRY, author of over sixty plays including *Viet Rock, Approaching Simone, Comings and Going* and *Calm Down, Mother,* is resident playwright at the Omaha Magic Theatre. She has been called "the mother of feminist theatre," and her work has been recognized by grants from the NEA and the Rockefeller and Guggenheim foundations. In her most recent musical, *Body Leaks,* she also appeared as an actress.

KARL TOEPFER teaches dramatic literature and performing arts history in the Department of Theatre Arts at San Jose State University, where he coordinates the graduate program and much of the experimental performance program. He is the author of *Theatre, Aristocracy and Pornocracy* (1991) and *The Voice of Rapture* (1991), as well as articles on drama, dance, and performance theory in *Performing Arts Journal, Scandinavian Studies, Journal of Dramatic Theory and Criticism, Theatre Three,* and *Dictionary of Literary Biography.*

1. Assuming Gender

JILL DOLAN

Gender Impersonation Onstage:
Destroying or Maintaining the Mirror
of Gender Roles?

❦ The title of this paper serves as a way into the more loaded question: Is gender perspective in criticism for women only? Without offering my unequivocal opinion up-front, my hope is to explain my own view of gender perspectives and, by way of specific examples, to evaluate the work men and women, lesbians and gay men, have attempted around the topic.

Theatre scholars have always assumed that the stage is a mirror that reflects cultural and social organization. It seems a fair assumption. Even now, in the era of deconstructionist and postmodern performance, the concern is still with the stage as mirror. Now, however, the avant-garde has shifted its concern from looking into the mirror for an "accurate" representation to questioning the nature of the mirror itself and its ability to reflect what is increasingly seen as an unstable, non-unified self. Attention has shifted from the mirror's image to the mirror's surface and frame. By calling the entire device into question, doubt has been cast on the accuracy of the image it reflects. In retrospect, scholars with a feminist perspective are tracing the mirror's images through theatre history and defining more specifically just what kind of mirror reflected what kind of image.[1]

In Lacanian psychoanalytic theory, the mirror stage—and here the theatrical analogy becomes appropriate—is the scene of sexual differentiation, the entry into a polarized gender structure. Children—although for Lacan, the subject of his analysis is always male children—begin life in the imaginary realm in which they are unable to differentiate themselves from the mother. This is a world without language, based on a kind of sensual unity. In the mirror stage, the child sees himself for the first time—by way of his reflection—as separate from his mother. The child realizes that he has a penis and his mother does not. He sees in the mirror a more perfect self, a kind of ego ideal. Afraid his alliance with the mother will cause him to

[*Editor's Note*: This chapter was first read as a paper at the 1984 American Theatre Association convention in San Francisco on a panel entitled "Gender Perspectives in Criticism: For Women Only?" and then published in *Women & Performance Journal* 2, no. 2 (1985). Jill Dolan has added the "Epilogue" section for this book.]

be castrated, he rejects the mother and proceeds into the symbolic realm of language in which he identifies with the father.

With Lacan's theory in mind, we can extend the analogy between the mirror stage and the social mirror to the stage as mirror of sexual difference. Sexual difference and its concomitant gender identification are embedded in both Western civilization and the stage that has reflected it. Gayle Rubin, in her article "The Traffic of Women: Notes on the 'Political Economy' of Sex," defines this as the "sex/gender system, . . . the set of arrangements by which a society transforms biological sexuality into products of human activity. . . ."[2] While Lacan sees the mirror stage as a universal (male) experience that produces gender differentiation, Rubin and other feminist theorists see gender as an arbitrary construct that has historically become the founding social principle. Women, from kinship systems forward, are use-value in a male economy, objects of trade that relegates them to a biological sphere.[3]

This subjugation can be traced in theatre, which, as an institution of Western society, has historically placed women in a subservient position, as use-value, silenced, fringed, and appropriated by a male model. The male Greek cast playing for a mostly male Greek audience is the seed of Western theatrical tradition. The seeds of gender opposition are already found in the *Oresteia*, where we read that "the parent is he who mounts."[4]

The theatre as a mirror evolved from certain kinds of cultures for very specific reasons. The notions of hubris in Greek drama—the downfall of the powerful, prideful man—and catharsis—collective purging—were techniques used to maintain that particular society's status quo. The theatrical mirror purged Greek society of its bad humors and allowed it to function smoothly. Since the Greek model is still the basis of traditional theatre, it seems reasonable to conclude that theatre continues to reflect a polarized gender system, one in which Western society has a vested interest in leaving undisturbed.

Gender polarization has been a historical fact based on male economic and political necessity. It manifests a particular ideology that in turn reflects a particular hegemonic structure. Gender, it seems to me, isn't the perspective, but the evidence. Once this evidence is clear, it demands a certain kind of critique. I would suggest that feminism is the critique. Feminism exposes and deconstructs these underlying gender assumptions. The theatre, in its peculiar position as the mirrored stage, reflective of "real life" while not *being* real life, is an appropriate place for feminists to continue this ideological investigation. As Herbert Blau recently wrote, "There is an ideology of perception which in turn affects the ideology of performance."[5] The theatrical mirror is really an empty frame. The images reflected in it have been consciously constructed according to political necessity, with a particular, perceiving subject in mind who looks into the mirror for *his* identity.

So far, then, in terms of this panel's primary question, we can safely say that both men and women, lesbians and gay men, are implicated in the polarized gender structure theatre reflects. Men, however, are implicated and involved as the subject of theatrical representation. Women, absent from the system and constituted only as Other, are in the outsider's critical position. In terms of deconstructing gender opposition, then, the feminist perspective edges out the others. Those who look at gender as a crucial issue are those who have the most at stake if the gendered status quo is maintained: women, as historical subjects, who no longer want to be the "woman" constructed as a biological, mythological imperative; and lesbians, who are caught in the netherworld between the polarized genders— as Monique Wittig writes, "not-man, not-woman."[6] I'm not sure that men, heterosexual or, as we will see, gay, have as much at stake.

Let's return, for a moment, to the Greek stage, where male casts performed for predominantly male audiences. Women were effectively made invisible in both the theatre and on the stage, where men appropriated women's roles and their clothing. This cross-dressing is a recurrent theme in theatre history, closely aligned with its foundation on sexual difference. Peter Ackroyd, in *Dressing Up,* points out that in the rituals from which theatre originated, the shamans dressed as women were men appropriating female power, symbolically striving for their own androgynous unity while rejecting the actuality of women.[7] This same schism was reflected onstage. Women were barred from performance while male actors assumed their clothing and their dramatic power.

This tradition presents itself throughout Western theatre history, from Shakespeare's stage to the popular stages of England and America. Roberta Sklar, of the Women's Experimental Theatre, recently suggested that theatre has always been a sanctioned realm for men to play the Other, to appropriate and reject women. Even on the vaudeville stages, female impersonators were usually comics who both belittled women and set standards for their dress and behavior. Here, we find men in control of the mirror, with women looking into it for appropriate reflections. Shining back at them from the male mirror, however, was a socially constructed concept of Woman that served the guiding male ideology.

In gay male drag, women fare no better. Female impersonation here is usually filtered through the camp sensibility, which removes it from the realm of serious gender play and deconstruction. In gay male drag, anthropologist Esther Newton has suggested that the mirror is inverted: "The drag queen looks in the mirror of the audience and sees his female image reflected back approvingly."[8] Still, both spectator and performer conspire to construct a male-identified subject that is left out of the terms of exchange: Women are nonexistent in drag performance, but woman-as-myth, as a cultural, ideological object, is constructed in an agreed upon exchange between the male performer and the usually male spectator. Male drag mirrors women's socially constructed roles.

The camp context of most gay male drag makes it doubtful that the intent is to deconstruct socialized gender. Susan Sontag characterized the camp sensibility as the emphasis of style over content, as the love of artifice, superficiality, and instant character, and as a disengagement with underlying meaning. "Detachment," she writes, "is the prerogative of an elite. . . . Camp is the modern dandyism."[9]

Again, the stakes in the gender game aren't as high for these particular gay men. They can easily assume female roles, knowing that offstage, they wear the clothes of the social elite. The situation for women and lesbians is much more precarious. What might happen if women appropriated gender play onstage, or if lesbians took up male impersonation as their most popular entertainment?

On a stage marked by sexual difference, male impersonation has historically been received much differently than female impersonation. Women in breeches roles on the nineteenth-century stage were described as "Stage Beauties in Male Attire."[10] Women's assumption of male roles was trivialized as an issue, with the suggestion that women playing men were simply "showing off their pretty limbs to an admiring public." In an article on Charlotte Cushman, Yvonne Shafer suggests that nineteenth-century audiences accepted the convention of women playing men, and that the reasons women chose these roles were a "natural inclination toward masculine behavior and appearance, . . . a wish to display ability" and to competitively challenge men, and also because it was a novelty.[11] Shafer at once feels women assumed male roles because there were no "dominating" female roles written at the time, and because these women, Cushman in particular, were playing masculine roles offstage—supporting other women and leading independent lives. She implies Cushman was a lesbian and that playing male roles was more psychologically satisfying than forcing herself into the acceptable female role. The assumption is that Cushman wanted to *be* a man. A parallel assumption was never made, to my knowledge, about boys playing women on the Greek and early English stages. Women taking on gender impersonation were still relegated to the category of their sex—which Wittig writes that women alone cannot be defined outside of.[12] They were either beauties showing off their bodies or women whose "abnormal" psychologies made them feel more comfortable playing men.

Contemporary feminist and lesbian male impersonation is a different story. Sue-Ellen Case writes, "Through the drag role, one can perceive how social constructs are inscribed on the body."[13] This is a politicized view that forces confrontation with gender as a performed role, donned as easily as the male or female clothing that signifies it. While drag is a joke trivialized in the camp context, as a feminist theatrical device meant to point to real-life gender costuming, its effect is quite different. Simone Benmussa's *Albert Nobbs* chronicles a woman's imprisonment in her assumed male role. In Caryl Churchill's *Cloud 9,* cross-dressing is used to foreground the arbitrary construction of gender, suggesting a new vision through the political structure of gender play.

If we can safely say that women are in the forefront of gender experimentation on stage, it seems equally safe to say that male filmmakers are trumpeting gender ambiguity in cinema—but with a very different intent. There are many popular examples of the current fad for gender confusion. But can *Tootsie, Victor/Victoria, The World According to Garp,* and the more experimental *Liquid Sky* truly be considered political explorations of the gender bind? I think not. In *Tootsie,* for example, Dustin Hoffman returns to his male role as Michael Dorsey and gets the girl he's longed for throughout the film. The message is that it's all right to learn a few things about being a woman, as long as you're still a safely heterosexual man.

Gender, then, is a much more serious issue for feminist women and lesbians than for heterosexual or gay men. Heterosexual men, in particular, are still the subjects of theatrical representation. They are invited to identify with the image in the mirror. To complete the identification process, they must perceive women as the objects of their desire. Can men extricate themselves from this process to look clearly at sexual difference? Might they be willing to give up their privileged subjectivity, to consider women's desire, or lesbians, as the subject of representation?

A feminist perspective on gender has to bring to the foreground theatre's representational apparatus. We must make it clear that the hands holding the mirror up to nature have not been our own. Lesbians, in particular, have to debunk the myth that Woman even exists, to reveal instead that she has been created to serve a particular ideological order.[14] In contemporary theatre, women's hands more frequently are those holding up the frame. But even some feminist theatre is disappointing. It wants to create positive images of women, but its goal is often subverted by its means. It might be that sexual difference is too deeply embedded in the mimetic structure of theatrical representation. From what I would ultimately say should be a feminist-only perspective, we might have to question the mirror as an apt analogy for theatre.

Adjusting this analogy would mean adjusting a wealth of expectations. It would no longer be possible to attend theatre hoping for a truthful reflection of oneself. Theatre might become more of a workplace than a showplace. Our socially constructed gender roles are inscribed in our language and in our bodies. The stage, then, is a proper place to explore gender ambiguity, not to expunge it cathartically from society but to play with, confound, and deconstruct gender categories. If we stop considering the stage as a mirror of reality, we can use it as a laboratory in which to reconstruct new, nongenderized identities. And in the process, we can change the nature of theatre itself.

Epilogue

It's a difficult task to return to an article written eight years ago, especially in a field in which research and theory has moved quickly, making quantum leaps into some of the most provocative thinking to grace the current academic scene. "Gender Impersonation Onstage" seems quaint to me now, although I still find it serves an important introductory function and—especially at the time it was first read as a paper at the then-American Theatre Association conference in San Francisco in 1984 and subsequently published in an early issue of *Women & Performance Journal*—carries the polemical force of interdisciplinary feminist methodologies that hadn't yet been brought to bear on theatre studies.

A mere eight years later, much has changed in theatre studies and in feminism. The temptation to rewrite the preceding article is strong but, I think, wrong-headed. It needs to stand as an historical document that can be read alongside the important work that has since been generated in both fields. In 1992, there are several books that offer other historical, critical, and theoretical views on the issues I've essayed here: Helene Keyssar's *Feminist Theatre*; Sue-Ellen Case's *Feminism and Theatre*; my own book, *The Feminist Spectator as Critic*; and several useful and theoretically astute anthologies such as Lynda Hart's *Making a Spectacle: Feminist Essays on Contemporary Women's Theatre* and Case's *Performing Feminisms: Feminist Critical Theory and Theatre*.[15] The field is rife with a variety of feminist viewpoints on the genesis of a misogynist tradition in theatre history, as well as on the potentiality of feminist or women's theatre to make a difference in the world's cultural condition.

My article's emphasis on performance rather than on the realm of dramatic literature is still unique in the field. Several scholars have since chosen to work at nontext-based sites: Jeanie Forte's work on feminist performance art has been influential in documenting how the performance of gender, through impersonation and through foregrounding the actual gender of the performer, has raised issues about theatrical form and its social function. These questions demand revising such fundamental concepts as what defines theatre. Works by lesbian scholars such as Lynda Hart and

Kate Davy, as well as Sue-Ellen Case and myself, have analyzed lesbian performance groups like Split Britches and other denizens of the now-notorious WOW Café in New York, such as Holly Hughes, Lisa Kron, and Reno.[16] These analyses extend the question of the high stakes in lesbian performances' gender impersonations and examine the device as a radical critique of culturally constructed gender meanings. Because many of the texts discussed are not recorded as written scripts, these works also stand as an effort to revise the canon of traditional and contemporary feminist theatre work.

Such work on performance-as-text has focused on the body as representation and has pointed out challenging connections between the performance of gender onstage and the representation of gender in culture. Teresa de Lauretis's work on the technology of gender and Judith Butler's phenomenological analysis of performative acts and gender construction have also been instrumental in arguing for the clear connection between gender impersonation onstage and in social life.[17]

Still, over the course of the intervening years, many of the questions raised in my article still echo through academic discourse, often in even more pressing ways than they did in 1985. The question of whether or not gender perspectives are "for women only," as the participants on the original panel for which this paper was written were asked to ponder, has become a crucial issue in what some perceive as the commodification of feminist theory in the academy. With the ascendance of French poststructuralist and psychoanalytic theories, along with British materialism and cultural studies, the feminist theories of representation outlined by my article have become positioned as part of a "fashionable," some even say "lucrative," academic discourse.

Such a reading of the state of current feminist theory is telling for many reasons and exemplifies the necessity of continuing to ask the original question: Are gender perspectives for women only? From one perspective, I'm heartened by the speed with which radical feminist theories have circulated through the academy and even through certain aspects of the theatre profession. Even the most mainstream theatre conferences I've attended over the last several years seem compelled to address the work of women and persons of color in the field and have been willing to offer forums for overtly feminist and multicultural thinking. Sending feminist perspectives rippling through dominant cultural discourse is crucial to changing the way spectators and cultural consumers think about gender and sexuality, race and class.

But at the same time, the widespread application of feminist theories has promoted an unsettling detachment of this thinking from the political movement by which it was nourished. People writing feminist theory in the

1990s haven't necessarily taken the once requisite step of establishing the connections between their experience and their theory. A certain passion of politics and experience is missing from some of the recent work as a result. In the most extreme examples, the feminist politics of the theory are too comfortably elided.

Likewise, the popularizing of postmodernism's cultural critique requires a rethinking of its political efficacy when looking at gender impersonation onstage. Postmodern theories remain effective in deconstructing the mirror analogy that, as I point out here, has founded traditional theatre criticism. But after several intense years of deconstructive thinking, many feminists are pondering how to achieve a more reconstructive moment. In the face of governmentally sanctioned attacks on the production of images, feminists, lesbians, and gay men, in particular, are calling for the possibility of reinhabiting images that can be circulated in a hostile cultural environment, with an eye toward teaching people about difference and promoting social change. What will images mean in such a context? Will such thinking promote a return to the mirror analogy and the once debunked notion that positive images of difference can be created within it? Considering the debates over the National Endowment for the Arts's censorship of sexual imagery, these questions are vitally relevant.

My emphasis in this article on gender was prompted by my discussion of impersonation and by the notion, just gaining currency at the time, that sexual difference founds the history of representation. Other scholars since have continued to work on this idea, including Sue-Ellen Case, whose *Theatre Journal* article "Classic Drag" continues to cause some consternation. Other feminist writers have taken up other historical and contemporary examples of cross-dressed performances, from Shakespeare to Caryl Churchill to Split Britches' lesbian drag.[18]

But as we enter the 1990s, race, ethnicity, sexuality, and class have become equally important differences under discussion in theories of representation. The mirror analogy—and the genre of psychological realism that continues to give the mirror its most popular embodiment—continues to hold sway in arguments over cross-racial casting, from James Earl Jones playing Big Daddy in Tennessee Williams to Jonathan Pryce playing an Eurasian pimp in *Miss Saigon*. What does impersonation mean, and how does it work when race and ethnicity become variables as well as gender? Why don't the profession and its scholars discuss cross-sexuality casting? What ideologies are at work here?

Given these questions and their important cultural ramifications, the suggestion of the stage as a laboratory, with which my article concludes, still seems apt. The last eight years, in fact, have seen feminist theatre scholars attempt to actualize this proposal by generating articles and conference papers criticizing psychological realism and debating the usefulness of Brecht's epic theatre as a possible replacement. Brecht's theory is certainly more akin to the metaphor of the stage as a laboratory; theorists like Elin Diamond, in particular, have analyzed the potential of interweaving Brechtian technique with methods suggested by materialist feminism,[19] finally to pulverize the already scattered shards of the theatre as social mirror. The work of sweeping up the reflective glass remnants and constructing a perhaps more permeable theatre continues.

Notes

1. For a similar argument in the realm of art and art history, see also *Old Mistresses: Women, Art and Ideology* by Rozsika Parker and Griselda Pollock (New York: Pantheon Books, 1981). The authors argue, "Art is not a mirror. It mediates and re-presents social relations in a schema of signs which require a receptive and preconditioned reader in order to be meaningful" (p. 119). Their argument goes on to suggest that art-as-mirror reflects only the particular ideological visions of those who create it.

2. Gayle Rubin, "The Traffic in Women: Notes on the 'Political Economy' of Sex," in Rayna Reiter, *Toward an Anthropology of Women* (New York: Monthly Review Press, 1978), p. 159. Since the publication of her article, Rubin has substantially altered her views. In her "Thinking Sex: Notes for a Radical Theory of the Politics of Sexuality," in *Pleasure and Danger: Exploring Female Sexuality,* ed. Carole S. Vance (Boston: Routledge and Kegan Paul, 1984), Rubin notes, " 'The Traffic in Women' was inspired by the literature on kin-based systems of social organization. It appeared to me at the time that gender and desire were systemically intertwined in such social formations. This may or may not be an accurate assessment of the relationship between sex and gender in tribal organizations. But it is surely not an adequate formulation for sexuality in Western industrial societies. As Foucault has pointed out, a system of sexuality has emerged out of earlier kinship forms and has acquired significant autonomy. . . . Although sex and gender are related, they are not the same thing, and they form the basis of two distinct arenas of social practice" (pp. 307–8).

3. See Rubin, "The Traffic in Women," for an explication of both Lacanian psychoanalytic theory and for a feminist description of kinship systems. She argues that "since Levi-Strauss sees the essence of kinship systems to lie in an exchange of women between men, he constructs an implicit theory of sex oppression" (p. 171), and that " 'the exchange of women' is a seductive and powerful concept [since] it suggests that we look for the ultimate locus of women's oppression within the traffic of women, rather than within the traffic in merchandise," that is, capitalist social structures (p. 175).

4. I am indebted to Sue-Ellen Case for pointing out this phrase in the context of gender theory and Greek theatre history. See also Linda Walsh Jenkins, "Locating the Language of Gender Experience," *Women & Performance* (1985), 2, no. 1: 5–17. Jenkins writes, "Males created theatre to speak to each other artistically in a public forum. This is simply historically true; there is nothing judgmental about it. Greek women had no access to the public forum and the men were not talking to them in the plays" (p. 14).

5. Herbert Blau, "Ideology and Performance," *Theatre Journal* 35, no. 4 (December 1983):448.

6. See Monique Wittig's writings in *Feminist Issues,* particularly "The Straight Mind" (Summer 1980), "One Is Not Born a Woman" (Winter 1981), and "The Category of Sex" (Fall 1982).

7. Peter Ackroyd, *Dressing Up: The History of an Obsession* (New York: Simon and Schuster, 1979).

8. Esther Newton, *Mother Camp: Female Impersonation in America* (Chicago: University of Chicago Press, 1972), p. 37.

9. Susan Sontag, "Notes on Camp," in *Against Interpretation* (New York: Delta Books, 1966), p. 288.

10. Frank Wilstack, "Stage Beauties in Male Attire," *Washington Post,* Sunday, July 26, 1903.

11. Yvonne Shafer, "Women in Male Roles: Charlotte Cushman and Others," in *Women in American Theatre: Careers, Images, Movements,* ed. Helen Krich Chinoy and Linda Walsh Jenkins (New York: Crown Publishers, 1981), pp. 74–75.

12. Monique Wittig, "The Category of Sex," *Feminist Issues* (Fall 1982).

13. Sue-Ellen Case, "Gender as Play: Simone Benmussa's *The Singular Life of Albert Nobbs,*" *Women & Performance* 1, no. 2 (1984):24.

14. Wittig (see articles cited above) has written that lesbians are not women according to the culture's construction of them.

15. Helene Kayssar, *Feminist Theatre,* rev. ed. (New York: St. Martin's Press, 1990); Sue-Ellen Case, *Feminism and Theatre* (New York: Methuen, 1988); Jill Dolan, *The Feminist Spectator as Critic* (Ann Arbor: UMI Research Press, 1988); Lynda Hart, ed., *Making a Spectacle: Feminist Essays on Contemporary Women's Theatre* (Ann Arbor: University of Michigan Press, 1989); Sue-Ellen Case, ed., *Performing Feminisms: Feminist Critical Theory and Theatre* (Baltimore: Johns Hopkins University Press, 1990).

16. Jeanie Forte, "Women's Performance Art: Feminism and Postmodernism," in *Performing Feminisms,* pp. 251–69; Jeanie Forte, "Realism, Narrative, and the Feminist Playwright: A Problem of Reception," *Modern Drama* 32, no. 1 (March 1989):115–27; Kate Davy, "Constructing the Spectator: Reception, Context and Address in Lesbian Performance," *Performing Arts Journal* 10, no. 2 (1986):74–87; Kate Davy, "Reading Past the Heterosexual Imperative: *Dress Suits to Hire,*" *The Drama Review* 33, no. 1 (Spring 1989):153–70; Sue-Ellen Case, "Toward a Butch/Femme Aesthetic," in *Making a Spectacle*; Jill Dolan, "Desire Cloaked in a Trenchcoat," *The Drama Review* 33, no. 1 (Spring 1989):59–67; Jill Dolan, "'Lesbian' Subjectivity in Realism: Dragging at the Margins of Structure and Ideology," in *Performing Feminisms,* pp. 40–53.

17. Teresa de Lauretis, "Sexual Indifference and Lesbian Representation," in *Performing Feminisms,* pp. 17–39; Judith Butler, "Performative Acts and Gender Constitution: An Essay in Phenomenology and Feminist Theory," in *Performing Feminisms,* pp. 270–82; Peggy Phelan, "Feminist Theory, Poststructuralism, and Performance," *The Drama Review* 32, no. 1 (Spring 1988):107–27.

18. Sue-Ellen Case, "Classic Drag: The Greek Creation of Female Parts," *Theatre Journal* 37, no. 3 (October 1985):317–28; Elin Diamond, "Refusing the Romanticism of Identity: Narrative Interventions in Churchill, Benmussa, Duras," in *Performing Feminisms,* pp. 92–108; Lorraine Helms, "Playing the Woman's Part: Feminist Criticism and Shakespearean Performance," *Theatre Journal* 41, no. 2 (May 1989):190–200; Anne Hermann, "Travesty and Transgression: Transves-

tism in Shakespeare, Brecht, and Churchill," *Theatre Journal* 41, no. 2 (May 1989):133–54.

19. Elin Diamond, "Brechtian Theory/Feminist Theory: Toward a Gestic Feminist Criticism," *The Drama Review* 32, no. 1 (Spring 1988):82–94; Elin Diamond, "Mimesis, Mimicry, and the 'True-Real,'" *Modern Drama* 32, no. 1 (March 1989):58–72.

WILLIAM O. BEEMAN

Mimesis and Travesty in Iranian Traditional Theatre

❧ It is a well-known fact that most forms of traditional theatre in Asia use exclusively male performers even for female roles. Many reasons are cited for this practice, but few researchers have recognized that the depiction of females is carried out in many ways in different theatrical traditions. There have been few if any studies that try to analyze the variety of modes of female representation or the functions these different modes fulfill.

In this discussion, I will examine the practice of travesty in the representation of females in the two traditional Iranian theater forms, *ta'ziyeh* and *ru-hozi,* and attempt to show how this practice fulfills functions on several levels.

In the discussion that follows, I will first provide a general introduction to Iranian popular theater forms. Next I will show how women are represented in these forms. I then explore the cultural and theatrical functions of the different modes of female representation and conclude with a discussion of mimetic functions in theatrical representation.

Forms of Performance in Iran

The two principal dramatic forms in Iran are

1. the passion drama, depicting the martyrdom of the central religious figure in Shi'a Islam, Imam Hosein, called *ta'ziyeh*; and

2. comic improvisatory theater, often called *ru-hozi.*[1]

These two forms have been described at length in a number of publications,[2] but a brief description will aid in our discussion here.

Ta'ziyeh is perhaps the better known of the two forms. It centers on ritual mourning for Imam Hosein, grandson of the prophet Mohammad and contender for the leadership of the Muslim community. The story of Imam Hosein's death is central to the religious beliefs of Shi'a Muslims, occupying roughly the same symbolic importance as the resurrection of Christ occupies for Christians in their religion. Hosein's death at the hands of the Sunni Caliph Yazid after having been trapped with his family and supporters with limited food and water on the plains of Kerbala near present day Baghdad is a story of great tragedy on an epic scale.

Ritual mourning for Hosein developed over many centuries. Perhaps the earliest forms of *ta'ziyeh* were simple recitations of the story of his death accompanied by weeping and self-flagellation. These ceremonies probably included chanting and simple public processionals. By the seventeenth century in the Safavid dynasty, the story of his death was depicted in many ways. Professional panegyrists and eulogizers would recite the events for public and private gatherings.

The clergy, who were dependent on public contribution for their livelihood, made these events the centerpiece of their sermonizing. Eventually, *ta'ziyeh* assumed a major role in the religious calendar of the population throughout the nation, but as a processional rather than a fully dramatic form.

The processions witnessed by foreign spectators during this period consisted of "floats" upon which the figures of Imam Hosein and his family, Yazid and other villains were depicted. The story of Kerbala had already taken on episodic character, and each float depicted an episode of the drama. The elaborateness of the processions clearly shows that there was already a great deal of public expenditure and preparation being lavished on them. Since the charitable contribution of food is thought to confer blessing on the giver, it is likely that community meals sponsored through religious bequest or direct contribution from members of the community was an important feature of the event.

Our first evidence of a fully dramatic form of *ta'ziyeh* performance occurs in the late eighteenth-century *shabih* texts of the Afshar dynasty in southern Iran.[3] (*Shabih,* meaning simulation, is an alternate term for *ta'ziyeh.*) The first European account of *ta'ziyeh* in its full staged dramatic form was rendered by Adrien Dupré, who was part of the French scientific mission to Iran in 1807–1809.

It was a natural development for the episodic floats of processional *ta'ziyeh* to be developed into full-fledged drama during this period. One can easily imagine how community leaders, ever eager to improve the splendor of their rituals, combined the chanting of the story of Imam Hosein by clerics, eulogizers, and panegyrists with the visual spectacle of procession to create episodic tableaux vivants of great elaborateness. Despite the religious purpose, it is hard to believe that these celebrations did not constitute grand entertainment for the general population during Muharram and Safar, the sober months of formal mourning.

The production of *shabih*s became an elaborate cultural industry. Texts were compiled by highly literate individuals, who borrowed heavily from classical poets as well as from sermons and eulogies of the day. The "evil" characters declaimed their lines, but the "good" characters chanted, using classical Persian musical modes. Eventually, distinct modes became associated with particular characters, *shabih*s, and episodes within each *shabih*, indicating a great deal of craft in matching musical expression to literary product. Undoubtedly, during the earliest days of this production there was a great deal of experimentation with these artistic dimensions.

Stage conventions were developed during this period that would allow for the productions to take place within viewing distance of an entire community, no matter how large or small. Hence the development of an arena or *tekiyeh* as the area of performance, often within a special building constructed for the performance, called a *hoseinieh*. Since the rhetorical purpose of the drama was to enhance the mourning experience, much textual material and many visual props were imported from the mundane, everyday life of the audience.

In short, *ta'ziyeh* had moved from being purely a ritual to becoming a community-based art form, contextualized within a mourning celebration and embodying a wide variety of aesthetic dimensions that were elaborated to satisfy a demanding audience.

Ru-hozi may be as ancient as *ta'ziyeh*, but we have very little information about its early origins. It must be very old as a theatrical form, however, since it bears close affinity with many other theatrical forms in South and Southwest Asia, such as Bhavai (from Gujarat), Bhand Pater (from Kashmir), and Alkap (from Bengal). Indeed, many of the theatrical conventions of *ru-hozi* suggest that it may be related to European *commedia dell'arte*.

The principal historical reports of performers in Iran who entertained in a comic mode occur in general accounts of court life down through the centuries. The Sassanian king Khosro Parviz is said to have supported actors. Shah Abbas (A.D. 1585–1628) employed a famous clown, Enayat, whose exploits live in legend. Miniature paintings from the period depict comic performances in court.

During the nineteenth-century reign of the Qajar Shahs, comic performance continued to be a feature of court life. The famous jester to Naser od-Din Shah, Karim Shire'i (from *shireh*, "treacle"), was not only a clown but was in charge of all court entertainment. One of his comedies was recorded, given the generic title: Baqqâl-bâzi[4] dar Hozur (Comedy in the Presence of the King).

In the twentieth century, comic improvisatory theatre suffered a decline. The court no longer supported these artistic endeavors, thus undercutting the financial base for their continuance. Also, Western-style, scripted theatre became popular in urban areas, reducing the support available for the comic improvisatory tradition.

Nevertheless, troupes of entertainers continued to perform in the old improvisatory style in cities and small towns, where they were engaged primarily for weddings and local celebrations. A few of the best clowns and performing troupes continued to be accepted in legitimate theaters throughout the country, particularly in Tehran, Isfahan, and Mashhad.

In villages today, performances take place in a convenient courtyard or open space in the village. Occasionally the only available place is on the village outskirts. Rugs are spread in the center of the playing area for the performers, and the guests at the celebration arrange themselves in a circle around the playing area. Many people sit on the flat roofs of surrounding houses to get a better view.

The central figure in the performance is the clown. He bears the principal burden of comedy performance. He also has the most distinctive makeup. His place within the production is one of studied ambiguity. He addresses the audience and occasionally invades their space. He often articulates thoughts the audience may have about the overall proceedings. He plays off of the other characters, which include Shah, mullah, *hajji* (an elderly merchant so-called because he has made the haj pilgrimage to Mecca incumbent on all Muslims), juvenile male, woman, vizier, and others. Of these stock characters, the *hajji* is the most common.

The stories are generally uncomplicated. They may be loose paraphrases of stories from Iranian folklore or from classic literature already known to the audience. The audience does not need to hear every word to follow the plot or the action.

The humor consists of verbal puns and comebacks and physical slapstick routines that can easily be heard out of context and still retain their humor.

The Representation of Women

The two theatre forms both use male performers in their traditional representation of women; nevertheless, the nature of the representation of women is quite different in each case. In *ru-hozi* theatre, there are two distinct traditions for representing women; in *ta'ziyeh,* there is one. I characterize these three traditions in the following way:

1. Non-mimetic (*ta'ziyeh*)
2. Pretended mimetic (*ru-hozi*)
3. Mimetic (*ru-hozi*)

Non-mimetic representation depicts women by using a conventional semiotic device rather than through the direct imitation of women's overt gender markings: secondary sexual characteristics, voice patterns, characteristic movement, and gesture.

Pretended mimetic representation of women imitates overt gender markings but carries out that imitation in burlesque fashion so that the audience can easily see that the performer is actually a male pretending to be a female.

Mimetic representation depicts women through imitation of overt gender markings with great skill, intending that the audience cannot easily determine whether the performer is really a woman or not.

These three representational conventions have distinct purposes in the two theatrical traditions, which I will deal with later. First, however, I will describe the three forms of representation in more detail.

Semiotization is extremely important in the performance conventions of *ta'ziyeh*. Much of the drama is conveyed through simple representational conventions. Color is one of the most significant. The forces of Imam Hosein are dressed in green, and the forces of Yazid are dressed in red. This convention is observed even in the simplest village performances of *ta'ziyeh* where pieces of red or green cloth with holes cut out for the heads of the actors might be draped on the performers in lieu of costumes. Other conventions are equally simple and straightforward. For example, movement in an arc or circle depicts a long journey; movement in a straight line, actual distance. Good characters chant their lines using traditional Persian musical modes. Evil characters declaim their lines in stentorian tones.

There are very few women named in the traditional accounts of the central events of the death of Imam Hosein. Nevertheless, as I will indicate below, the historical women involved in the tragedy are of great religious importance. They include Fatimeh, the daughter of the Prophet Mohammad, Shahrbanu, wife of Imam Hosein, and Zeinab, his daughter. All have central religious roles. It would be impossible to depict the tragedy without them. There are, incidentally, no women presented on the side of Yazid.[5]

The women are portrayed by males dressed in black cloaks similar to the green and red cloaks worn by the men. In every performance I have seen, they also wear male trousers and shoes. Except for the color of their clothing, the "women" are dressed in virtually the same type of costume as the males, with one exception: They also wear a thin facial veil. Their veil is translucent, allowing anyone to see that the actor is a male and not a female. Moreover, the persons depicting women chant in their normal, identifiably male voices.

Veils are worn by women in some highly conservative sections of Iran, but for the most part, Iranian women cover their hair and arms with a garment known as the *chador* but do not, as a rule, cover their entire faces. Moreover, certain other figures in *ta'ziyeh* also wear veils: the Prophet Mohammad, when appearing in dream sequences, the Angel Gabriel, the King of the Jinn, and all angels. Thus the veil alone does not really indicate female gender. It is the coding of the veil with black dress that indicates that a female figure is onstage.

The females depicted by males in *ta'ziyeh* are thus "labeled" as women by their dress but do not resemble women in their portrayal. The audience knows they are women by semiotic convention rather than through mimesis. This device allows them to be "social" women without being "sexual" women. There is a conventional scene in *ta'ziyeh* performances that depicts the wedding between Qassem, Imam Hosein's nephew, and Zeinab, his daughter. This scene is tremendously moving and evokes tears. Nevertheless, there is no hint of sexual desire between the bride and groom. They are man and wife in a religious sense but not in a physical sense.

There is virtually no semiotic coding of figures in *ru-hozi* except for the clown. The clown is dressed in red, usually in a crazy-quilt costume consisting of jacket and trousers. He is in blackface.[6]

In *ru-hozi,* women portrayed by men are always dressed to resemble women. They wear dresses, wigs, head-coverings, and occasionally false breasts or other "enhancements" to their bodies. Their dress is always contemporary with their audience. Thus in the south of Iran in areas where tribal people have settled, the actor playing a woman will use tribal dress features as part of his costume. In urbanized areas, he will use typical urban dress.

The actors also adopt female gait and vocal characteristics, using traditional female expressions in their speech and a higher pitch to their voices, and imitate feminine arm and hand movements. They use makeup: primarily rouge, lipstick, and occasionally eye liner. The actor playing female roles is known as a *zan-push*: "female dresser."

Since all *ru-hozi* is basically comic in nature, the role of the woman is in comic juxtaposition to the clown and other characters. She is most often the wife of the *hajji,* thus the mistress of the house giving orders to the clown, who is often cast as a servant. Another common role for the woman is as a princess, daughter of the Shah, and a potential love object for the juvenile. In these portrayals, the actor must be able to be humorous, but, most of all, he must be able to "set up" the clown, who gets the big laughs.

There is a distinction between those actors who try to look and act as much like a woman as possible and those who try to achieve "distance"[7] from their female role. The former are actors engaged in mimetic representation of women. The latter are performing what I have termed "pretend mimetic" representation.

The mimetic representers devote a great deal of effort to looking as much like a woman as possible. They acquire elaborate costumes, sometimes sewing these costumes themselves. They have collections of jewelry and wigs that aid in the illusion. Their movements and vocal patterns approximate those of a very feminine woman.

The "pretend mimetic" actors achieve their distancing effect by using exaggerated or ludicrous clothing. If they wear makeup, it is designed to make them look ugly or humorous rather than to evoke a normal female. Their movements are more intense than that of a normal female, and their voice patterns tend to be harsh, ugly, or an exaggerated falsetto.

In *ru-hozi* theater, then, audience members recognize actors playing women as women because of their resemblance to real women, whether that resemblance is calculated to emulate real women or to burlesque them.

Cultural and Dramatic Functions of Female Representation

Ta'ziyeh is as much ritual as theater. Its purpose is to induce weeping and intense mourning in spectators. Its entire purpose as an event is to reinforce the spectators' sense of their moral universe. The bad characters are supremely bad. The good characters are archetypes of good fathers, sons, mothers, daughters, religious and political leaders. Their martyrdom is proof of their goodness.

Nevertheless, the status of *ta'ziyeh* as a religious event is questionable for some religious officials. They oppose it on the grounds that it is a form that depicts human beings, and therefore is a form of idolatry. On this matter there is some difference of opinion.

The practitioners of *ta'ziyeh* have been clever in defining the nature of their performance. The standard defense for their performance is that it does not depict human beings. The performers are rather reciting the story of Imam Hosein in costume in order to enhance the feeling of mourning for the spectators. The distinction is a very fine one, but it is reflected in the stage conventions used in performance.

The women depicted in *ta'ziyeh* are of an especially venerated quality. They are ideal mothers, wives, and daughters. Much of their function in the drama is to show the agony of women in the face of the death of their fathers, husbands, and sons.

Women in orthodox Islam are treated as protected individuals who are always capable of inciting desire in men. It is thought to be unseemly for women to appear in public where they might be the object of lustful desires on the part of men. The depiction of women in a public setting is likewise a sensitive issue. The special nature of the women in Imam Hosein's family depicted in *ta'ziyeh* makes it unthinkable that they be depicted in any way that would identify them as sexual beings or objects of any desire.

In reality, the problem is one of balance between the impossibility of telling the story of Imam Hosein without depicting these women and the difficulty of representing them without presenting them as sexual beings. The compromise that has clearly been reached is to make it eminently clear that they are being depicted by men. Moreover, they are depicted with a respectful facial veil and absolutely no hint of any secondary sexual characteristics. In this way, the depiction of these women is accomplished in a way that is culturally above reproach.

Ru-hozi theater has a very different purpose in Iranian society. As a comic performance undertaken primarily at weddings, its purpose is to call into question all aspects of human social relations. Questions of status, social prerogative, political relations, economic relations, and sexual relations are all fair game for the performers. Weddings are times of special social tension in Iran (as they are almost everywhere on earth). Questions of social status, inheritance, and sexuality are on everyone's mind. Indeed, fights often break out at weddings as old rivalries and community tensions are brought to the fore. Since weddings are also occasions for courting between unmarried members of the community, the atmosphere is often very tense.

Ru-hozi theater serves to confront and dispel much of this tension. The clown fulfills the function of speaking for the everyman in the audience. He says things that audience members are thinking but do not dare say. He gets into situations that reflect the hopes and fears of those watching. The other characters also reflect social archetypes that members of the community easily recognize.

Performers in *ru-hozi* fulfill many artistic roles. They are musicians as well as actors. Most also dance. The *zan-push,* who portrays women, is usually called upon to dance before the comedy actually begins. He thus evokes the sexual nature of his role even before the themes of the comedy are presented.

The women depicted in *ru-hozi* necessarily resemble women, because their role requires that they be sexual beings in the comedies they enact. One episode found in a number of the comedies, for example, has the *hajji* going out for a night on the town and leaving the clown in his place in bed so that his wife will not detect his absence. The clown is uncomfortable with this arrangement, but the *hajji* insists. The *hajji*'s wife immediately figures out what is happening and decides to teach both her husband and the clown a lesson. She flirts with the clown in bed. There is a lot of noise and movement under the blankets, ending with the *hajji* confounded by his wife and the clown getting a beating.

In another comedy, the *hajji* pretends to be dead in order to see what his wife would do as a widow. She immediately goes out, brings her boyfriend to the house, and proceeds to make plans to go abroad with him. With the help of the clown, the *hajji* is "resurrected" and confronts the wife and her boyfriend.

In short, the women depicted in *ru-hozi* are funny *women*. They are not symbolic or revered figures. The situations they are placed in are very human and sometimes very racy. Culturally, the same prohibitions against the display of women in public are applicable in *ru-hozi*. It would be culturally intolerable in many settings to have a real woman on stage in some of the stock *ru-hozi* situations. The fact that a male is playing these roles allows the humorous point of the comedy to be made without offending anyone's sensibilities.

The clear sexuality of the female role is even clearer when it is understood that in a very few instances real women are used by some more urbanized troupes in their presentations. It is very lucrative to do so; the troupe is usually paid more, and the woman herself receives a large fee. In one troupe we witnessed during fieldwork, a real woman played alongside a *zan-push*. There is genuine danger in this arrangement for the woman. The crowd may become unruly at a celebration. In the period before the Islamic revolution of 1978–1979, alcohol was easy to obtain, and men occasionally became inebriated. In these situations, the real women in the troupe would be propositioned or mishandled by the guests on the assumption that they were "available." The female performers had to take elaborate precautions to ensure that their role was not misunderstood. One was married and always had her husband close at hand. Another brought her aged mother and always sat with her when not onstage. A third had a baby that she would nurse conspicuously. All these devices were designed to prevent the men in the audience from approaching the women.

Sexuality is also an important undertone for the "mimetic" female portrayers. These men, who go to elaborate lengths to look like women, really fool a number of men into thinking that they *are* women. The actors, who are often young, may have erotic appeal even for those men who know they are not women, much as has been reported for audience members viewing *ludruk,* the Indonesian performance form extensively treated by James Peacock.[8] Since these actors, with few exceptions, claim to be fully heterosexual males, this situation can be an uncomfortable social position for them.

It is partly for this reason that performers who portray women may distance themselves from their representations of females by making it eminently clear that they are men and neither real women nor men attempting to pass as real women. There is then no way these actors could become erotic objects. In using clearly exaggerated or ludicrous depictions, they are easily able to carry out their comic function without any of the attendant cultural difficulties that might "leak" into their offstage personas. Another reason for choosing the "pretend" mimetic representation may be that the men portraying women's roles are unable, due to age, lack of ability, or to their obvious masculinity, ever to "pass" as a woman on stage. Given this state of affairs, they opt for comic distancing.

Mimesis in Traditional Theatre

Mimesis is often cited as the basis for performance in Aristotle's *Poetics*. Still, mimesis is not adequate as an explanatory principle if it is an unexamined concept. Mimesis occurs on many levels. There are non-mimetic aspects of performance, as in the *ta'ziyeh* treated in this discussion. These non-mimetic aspects are *symbolic* without being *iconic*.[9] In *ta'ziyeh*, color schemes and costume serve to differentiate characters. Masked performances also may partake in this quality. A particular mask may be used to represent a god or goddess without having a specific identification with that deity. The association is conventional rather than mimetic.

Abstract mimesis forms another level of representation for performance. A choreographer might replicate "natural motions" from everyday life, abstract them, and recombine them into a dance. The leg movements might be from bicycle riding, while the arm movements are from throwing a football. In the final dance, the elements might not be clearly recognizable.

Asian dramatic forms such as Noh come closer to direct mimesis. They imitate life, but in a highly stylized form. The drama of the Western spoken stage, as typified by the "Method" in all of its incarnations, is highly mimetic. This imitation can be carried to an extreme in some forms. The actor Spalding Gray performs a number of one-man plays that recount his life as a youth in Rhode Island. His performances are masterful studies in the detail of "real" behavior. While watching him, the audience is led to believe that everything they are seeing is Gray's spontaneous musings. Only after they return the next night and see the same performance nearly exactly as it was performed the night before do they realize that the work is entirely rehearsed. This form is "hyper-real" or "true-real" mimesis—mimesis that cannot easily be distinguished from reality.[10]

Whatever the level of mimetic representation in performance, the content of the performance itself relates directly to human social interaction patterns—a point often made by Clifford Geertz. In performance, we get a display of views on human interaction, human situations, human conditions, human structurings. It is to be expected, then, that the mimetic function undertaken in theatrical representation will reflect the social interactional sensibilities of the communities of performers and spectators.

Added to this outlook, for theatrical purposes, is skill in representation. Performers who carry out their performing functions with greater skill are likely to be able to continue supporting themselves wholly or partially through performance. At the same time, these performers must be cognizant of community standards and norms. If they are offensive to a wide spectrum of the community, they cannot continue their work, even if they are superb in the performance arena.

Mimetic convention takes care of a great number of the problems arising from questions concerning community standards in performance. In Western performing arts, nudity, suggestive or obscene language, and thematic tastes are all issues of controversy. Problems arising from questions regarding these aspects of performance are often settled through legislation or court decisions. Typically, performance that might be offensive to some people is segregated through advance publicity, rating systems, or containment in specific geographic areas.

In Iran, all of these considerations are active in traditional theater. The religious sensibilities that are central to *ta'ziyeh* must be guarded at all costs if the performance is to achieve its desired effect—namely to bring the audience to a heightened sense of their spiritual duty and to express their grief at the central tragedy of their belief system. The highly codified system of representation in *ta'ziyeh* provides a powerful stimulus for the imagination of the audience without offending. The semiotic representation of women allows them to take their proper role in the tragedy, remaining historical and religious figures without becoming erotic or sexual figures.

Since part of the point of *ru-hozi* performance is to extract humor from typical social situations involving relations between the sexes, the direct mimetic representation of women is in some sense necessary. Community standards, however, make it difficult for actual women to participate in the performances. The women of *ru-hozi*, then, are more than just symbolic figures; they imply real human interactions, including sexual interaction, in their mimetic representation.

Those men who portray women, however, must live with the possibility that they might be identified offstage with the female role they portray onstage. It goes without saying that all actors face this problem, not just those in Iran. The option of choosing "pretend" mimesis allows them their comic function without any of the unwelcome offstage implications that arise from cross-dressing.

It is noteworthy that in both *ta'ziyeh* and *ru-hozi*, the normal social interaction patterns of everyday life are replicated and maintained but within different frameworks. *Ta'ziyeh* sees life in its spiritual and religious aspects, and *ru-hozi*, in its secular aspects. Women have a clear place in both, and by varying the representational conventions through which they are portrayed, they are clearly allowed this place.

Notes

1. So-called because it is often performed on a platform set in a courtyard of a house over (*ru*) the courtyard pool (*hoz*). Other common names are *takht-e hozi* ("platform on the pool") and *siah-bazi* ("black play"), after the blackfaced clown

who is central to the performance. For a more complete discussion of Iranian comic theatre, see William O. Beeman, "A Full Arena: The Development and Meaning of Popular Performance Traditions in Iran," in *Modern Iran: The Dialectics of Continuity and Change,* ed. Michael Bonine and Nikki Keddie (Albany: State University of New York Press, 1981); and "Why Do They Laugh? An Interactional Approach to Humor in Traditional Iranian Improvisatory Theater," *Journal of American Folklore* 94, no. 4 (1981):506–26.

2. See William O. Beeman, "Cultural Dimensions of Performance Conventions in Iranian Ta'ziyeh," in *Ta'ziyeh: Ritual and Drama in Iran,* ed. Peter Chelkowski (New York: New York University Press and Sorush Press, 1979); and "Theatre in the Middle East," in *Cambridge Guide to World Theatre,* ed. Martin Banham (Cambridge: Cambridge University Press, 1988); as well as the two works cited in note 1. Also to be consulted are Bahram Beza'i, *Namayesh dar Iran [Performance in Iran]* (Tehran: Chap-e Kavian, 1965); Farrokh Gafary, "Evolution of Rituals and Theater in Iran," *Iranian Studies* 17, no. 4 (1980):361–90; Mohammad Bagher Ghaffari, "The Director Speaks," in *Ta'ziyeh: Ritual and Popular Beliefs in Iran,* ed. Milla Cozart Riggio (Hartford: Trinity College, 1988); Abu al-Qasem Jannati-Ata'i, *Bonyad-e Namayesh dar Iran* (Tehran: Chap-e Mihan, 1955); and the chapter by Peter Chelkowski in P. Avery, G. Hambly and C. Melville, eds., *The Cambridge History of Iran,* vol. 7 (London: Cambridge University Press, 1992).

3. Professor Mayel Bektash of the University of Tehran has one such manuscript from this period in his possession.

4. The term Baqqâl-bâzi literally means "grocer play" but refers generically to improvisatory comedy. The "grocer play" probably was a generic comedy involving the confrontation between a grocer and a clown, ending in a fight. Madjid Rezvani saw a play of this type in 1923 in Gorgon: see Madjid Rezvani, *Le Théâtre et la danse en Iran* (Paris: Maisonneuve, 1962), pp. 112–14.

5. With one exception. This is Hend, a woman depicted in a rarely performed episode in *ta'ziyeh.* She is a woman from Yazid's camp seeking revenge for the death of her son at the hands of a member of Hosein's camp. She is shown eating the raw liver of this man.

6. The clown is dressed virtually exactly as Hajji Firuz, a traditional minstrel who greets the New Year at the vernal equinox with songs and dances. There is also a traditional whitefaced clown little seen today. The blackfaced clown is thought to be quick and lively; the whitefaced clown, slow and lethargic.

7. A usage I borrow from Erving Goffman, who points out that creating ways to demonstrate that one is not playing a role in everyday life "for real" is a very common human performance function.

8. James Peacock, *The Rites of Modernization: Symbolic and Social Aspects of Indonesian Proletarian Drama* (Chicago: University of Chicago Press, 1968).

9. Of course, representation can be both symbolic and iconic. For example, an actor may portray a god, and yet that god may represent the power of the universe.

10. Of course, recounting is itself a performative act, but Gray makes it seem like a spontaneous act.

LAURENCE SENELICK

Lady and the Tramp: Drag Differentials in the Progressive Era

When I was a small act they used to say I was a nance. Now they say, "Dear old Malcolm's so delightfully eccentric!"   MALCOLM SCOTT, English drag comedian (1872–1929)[1]

Women are all female impersonators to some degree.   SUSAN BROWNMILLER, *Femininity*

❦ A new women's magazine full of tips on enhancing one's femininity appeared in New York in 1913. There was nothing unusual in that: "Beauty culture" was booming in the United States as the century turned. Technological advances in the cosmetics industry abetted by sophisticated marketing and advertising techniques promoted a growing interest in the outward appearance of the American woman. Theodore Roosevelt's administration had vigorously endorsed physical fitness; the Gibson girl had offered an image of clean-cut national beauty to be emulated. The average woman was aided in her attempt to meet such standards by beauty parlors, by a growing tolerance of rouge and powder in public, and by a plethora of manuals and periodicals.[2] The unusual aspect of this new magazine, however, was that all the pictures and endorsements in it were of a man.

The Julian Eltinge Magazine and Beauty Hints is perhaps the strangest testament to the unprecedented popularity of a female impersonator, and one that gives unusual insight into the nexus between popular entertainment and the social construction of gender. Eltinge had first come to prominence in 1904 when he appeared at New York's Bijou Theatre in the musical comedy *Mr Wix of Wickham,* whose plot, a variant of the *Charley's Aunt* scenario, required a young collegian to disguise himself as a lovely lady for most of the evening. Eltinge then perfected his illusion in vaudeville and in 1910 attained serious stardom in Otto Hauerbach's *The Fascinating Widow,* another dual role that he was to tour widely for many years. This play would be followed by *The Crinoline Girl* (1914) and *Cousin Lucy* (1915). Eltinge's producer, Al H. Woods, was so pleased with his star's success that he built the Eltinge Theatre on 42d Street and issued the *Julian Eltinge Magazine* as a promotional gimmick, just when the young impersonator was entering films.

Eltinge was obliged for his popularity, it was said, to a female audience that admired his toilettes. The women who filled the seats of downtown variety theatres in the first two decades of the twentieth century were, in modest ways, harbingers of the female emancipation of the "Roaring Twenties"; most of the feminist reforms implemented by the socioeconomic opportunities offered by the Great War and incarnated by the flapper were, in fact, initiated during this earlier period. Although innovation was launched by exceptional figures, the quiet revolutions were carried out by workaday women. As Margaret Deland reported in her description of a "change in the feminist ideal": "Of course there were women a generation ago, as in all generations, who asserted themselves; but they were practically 'sports.' Now the simple, honest woman . . .—the good wife, the good mother—is evolving ideals which are changing her life, and the lives of those people about her."[3] Some of these ideals were propounded by Eltinge's magazine for a readership that sought a *modus operandi* to embody New Womanhood on the home front.

The contents are scrappy but nonetheless revealing. They are prefaced by a 1904 essay by the English novelist Marie Corelli contending that "the British woman remains the prettiest in the world."[4] Such a remark uttered a challenge that a patriotic American woman might meet by availing herself of Julian Eltinge cold cream, liquid whiting, and powder. There follows Eltinge's description of his makeup for *The Fascinating Widow,* his advice that women learn to box, his tales of working the land on his Long Island farm, a clutch of aphorisms, and a statement on "beauty culture." These are interspersed with standard filler, rube jokes, and doggerel verse; and the magazine concludes with several pages of advertisements for cosmetics allegedly prepared from Eltinge's own recipes, lady's footwear bearing his endorsement, photographs of the star, and other shows produced by Woods. The whole is lavishly illustrated with portraits of Eltinge in his extensive female wardrobe, varied by pictures of him in mufti—men's clothes.

From the outset of his career, Eltinge and his press agents had been at pains to demonstrate that his assumed womanliness was a triumph of art over virile nature. Of *Mr Wix of Wixham,* a critic in the *World* observed that "he contrives at intervals to let his masculinity shine through his assumed character, and makes plain that his effort is a part of his acting method, which partly takes the curse off the whole affair."[5] "His success," explained the New York *Mirror,* "is that he gives great attention to the many little details of apparel with which women are very familiar."[6] In the numerous articles Eltinge wrote about how he accomplished his impersonations, he stressed the time-consuming difficulty of it all, particularly the agony of squeezing his bulk into confining corsets that "saw him raw"

to achieve a twenty-four-inch waistline: "I have to go without eating anything or I couldn't have got into them at all!"[7] By 1909, he was lamenting
that his digestive apparatus had been so disordered by tight-lacing that his
Japanese dresser had to massage his back and shoulders with an electric
vibrator between shows.[8] Female readers must have nodded with fellow-
feeling; here was a real he-man who understood what a woman went
through to be attractive.

That women would eagerly take advice on physical self-improvement
from a male cross-dresser is not as grotesque as it may first appear. The
magazine pointed out that men were recognized authorities in the fields of
hairdressing, fashion, and cuisine; no woman would have felt degraded by
seeking counsel from Marcel, Worth, or Escoffier. Eltinge's essay on beauty
culture explains, moreover, that women suffer from a natural disability:
"The greatest drawback to femininity is the fact that the entire sex lacks
stability of character. Most women are apt to run off at tangents. They do
not keep at one thing long enough to master it" (p. 38). Well in tune with
the Progressive agenda, Eltinge was advising women to cultivate the masculine virtues of perseverance and industry. Application and hard work,
long associated with the image of the "industrious apprentice" and with
successful go-getting in business and politics, were being applied to the
achievement of feminine grace. If a man, and a large man at that, was capable of turning himself into an attractive lady, there was hope for all but
the most deformed woman.

Eltinge's example meant not only that women could become more womanly but that they also could become more manly. Carroll Smith-Rosenberg
has argued that the New Woman was perceived as a kind of androgyne,
"a sexually freighted metaphor for social disorder and protest."[9] Products
of higher education, the New Woman seized "men's most central symbolic
constructs [and] invested them with female intent and thus inverting, re-
pudiated them" (p. 265). Smith-Rosenberg tends to conflate a number of
disparate opinions and permutations into a single timeframe, but the androgynous model was certainly an option being offered. Popular fiction of
the period expresses a woman's wish to be, if not a man, then like a man;
the dilemma was encapsulated in a syndicated comic strip by Nell Brinkley,
who has one of her young woman characters ask in 1913, "Am I Not a
Boy? Yes, I Am—Not."[10] This desexualization or resexualization was
adopted most readily by those female professionals or reformers who were
at the forefront of the changes. Eltinge's audiences were composed primarily of American-born, middle-class housewives who might read long-
ingly about the daring breakthroughs of their more advanced sisters but
who personally displayed the traditional "feminine" interest in adornment
and fashion. Their daring might best be expressed sartorially.

The physical ideal of American femininity had changed since the turn of the century, when advertisements in popular magazines displayed a "well rounded" type with "gentle, motherly expressions, soft billowy hair, and delicate hands" in immobile positions. "After 1910, they are depicted as more active figures with more activity taking place outside their homes."[11] The Gibson girl, an energized version of the Edwardian professional beauty, served as prototype—golfing on the links or cycling down the road like any of her male admirers. But the offered ideal was remote from reality, her hourglass figure, abundant chignon, and porcelain complexion too expensive, constraining, and time-consuming for the average homemaker to replicate. Moreover, the Gibson girl was disdained by female emancipationists as a blazon of traditional allurement whose ultimate aim was to appeal to men. Unfortunately, the "1914 girl" who supplanted her, with her "slim hips and boy-carriage," was equally daunting as a model for housewives, who might read in their morning papers that the "new figure is Amazonian, rather than Miloan. It is boyish rather than womanly. It is strong rather than soft."[12] Women's fashions began to discount hips and bust and to tolerate a large waist. Age boundaries between matrons and young women were to be eliminated: "The face alone, no matter how pretty, counts for nothing unless the body is straight and yielding as every young girl's."[13] The emphasis on youth may have been as discouraging to the American wife and mother as had been the Gibson girl's carefully kempt beauty.

Eltinge's gender intermediacy qualified him to serve as a middleman between traditional standards of curried comeliness and the newer ideal of "masculinized" femininity. The genteel woman of ripe charms whom he impersonated was licensed by his status as a biological male to engage in adventures and to show off an ostentatious wardrobe without provoking complaints that such behavior was respectively unladylike and unwomanly. This ambisextrous (coined by the critic Percy Hammond to describe Eltinge) empowerment is typified by a song in his vaudeville repertoire, "The Modern Sandow Girl." Clad in a chic gymslip, Eltinge performed the calisthenic muscle-building exercises promoted by the strong-man Eugen Sandow as he sang:

> In the days gone by all the girls were shy
> And domestic in their way,
> They would never roam they would stay at home
> And they'd sew and they'd cook all day. . . .
> But the girl of to-day is a wonder they say
> She goes in for athletics and sport. . . .
> Years ago the man saved the drowning maid
> Now-a-days the maid will save him,
> Woe to him who thinks on the court or links

He can win with ease, no doubt,
It is an even bet that the lady will get
Ev'ry game if he doesn't watch out.[14]

The chorus, however, makes it clear that the Sandow girl is not a genuine threat to established order since her new outfit and "statuesque poses" have girlish charms of their own. The edge of any threat would also be blunted by the fact that the "muscular Venus" was not in fact a strapping Amazon but a man.

To achieve both the illusion of femininity and the authority of masculinity, Eltinge's own sexual nature had to remain in the shadows. Despite the constant harping that he was just an average fellow, he seems to have had no love life. After he had become a screen star, a species advertised as possessing an overactive libido, Eltinge made vague hints about furnishing his Italianate Hollywood castle with a wife; but he explained his bachelor state by saying that career and matrimony didn't mix, that audiences cooled when their favorites wed. Recently, information has surfaced to suggest that he had an intimate and enduring relationship with a male sportswriter that almost erupted into scandal.[15] But during his lifetime, he jealously guarded his privacy and nothing marred the image of pristine wo/manhood.

The emphasis on virility in Eltinge's publicity went beyond an appeal to the would-be New Woman; it was also a ploy to deflect any suspicion of "abnormal" tendencies on his part and to clear him of the average female impersonator's unsavory personal reputation. When Eltinge first appeared in *Mr Wix of Wixham*, most New York critics deplored the advent of a female impersonator as the lead in a musical comedy, diagnosing it as a symptom of advanced degeneracy in the theatre. The middle-brow magazine *Current Literature* even felt called upon to cite German sexologist Magnus Hirschfeld's recent clinical study *Transvestismus*.[16] Critical shock was aggravated by the simultaneous arrival of Bothwell Browne, whose vaudeville impersonations included a suffragette in bloomers and a dancing Cleopatra. Hoping to emulate Eltinge's success, he starred in a musical comedy, *Miss Jack,* playing a college boy forced to masquerade as the inmate of a ladies' seminary. The critics were unforgiving. Finding Browne "as insipid as he is disgusting," *Leslie's Weekly* (21 September 1911) hoped that "it will be a long time before we will see anything more of this kind on the stage of New York or anywhere else." The rest of Browne's long career was played out on the variety stage, held to be the proper venue for female impersonation, where its "bad taste" was less glaring.[17]

The distinction drawn between musical comedy and vaudeville is revelatory. Musical comedy had been, since *The Black Crook* of 1866, a showcase for feminine pulchritude, shapely legs displayed in tights and opulent bosoms festooned with jewelry. Lillian Russell, the paragon of the type, offered a cynosure for male desire, while the Florodora Sextet and its widely publicized marriages to wealth provided women with a model of upward mobility through stage glamour. For a male to compete with these voluptuous icons suggested that he was angling for stage-door Johnnies himself.

In early variety, on the other hand, female impersonators had been either knockabout comic dames or "male sopranos" singing sentimental ballads in a reasonably *salonfähig* manner. Although glamour drag was introduced to variety from minstrelsy and from the homosexual subculture[18] in the 1870s, by 1900 refined vaudeville had leached it of any overt sexuality. As a solo act emphasizing technical expertise and quick change and sandwiched between other displays of virtuosity, it remained safely within the theatrical frame. The audacity of Browne and Eltinge lay in elevating the glamour drag impersonation from its more anodyne vaudeville ambience into the erotic aura that imbued the heroine of a musical comedy plot. The fixation of the male spectator on an actress who served both as character in a romance and as available courtesan was displaced to a man in convincing disguise. The consequences were unnerving. Critical outrage cast Browne back into the outer darkness of vaudeville circuits; yet Eltinge survived and thrived in his chosen genre. How and why he did so is instructive.

"A quiet, sturdy young American dressed in neat tweeds,"[19] "Eltinge is a typical college man, big, brawny, polished, vigorous and forcible."[20] These are typical journalistic descriptions. Eltinge's "collegiate" beginnings were a point in his favor. Amateur drag was respectable, given imprimatur by such venerable institutions as the Hasty Pudding Club at Harvard and the Mask and Wig Club at the University of Pennsylvania, and by long-standing academic tradition in preparatory schools. Eltinge had, in fact, first worn women's clothes under his real name, William Dalton, at the age of fourteen in the all-male revues of the First Corps Boston Cadets; he moved up to the soubrette role in a Boston Bank Officer's Association production of *Miss Simplicity* in 1899 and to Mignonette in an amateur staging of *Miladi* at the Tremont Theatre the next year. Working as a bank clerk and detesting his work, he accepted offers to go professional against the advice of his friends.[21] Later he was to claim that he turned down the vaudeville offers because "until I went on the professional stage, I could not stand this sort of act myself, and I am doing it merely for the money there is in it."[22] Most of his pre-war interviews ended with the statement that he hated his profession and would keep at it "only another two years" before taking up another specialty. If Eltinge could simply be regarded as a red-blooded varsity type working his way through college by masquerade, his transvestism might be rendered harmless.

Even after Eltinge had become a screen star, a reviewer remarked that "nearly every right-minded person resents the entrance of a man into the realm of the weaker sex. Women are undoubtedly people, but female impersonators seldom are."[23] To be a "drag artist" carried its own opprobrium, since the choice of profession was seen as legitimizing and advertising a perversion. A report of the Chicago Vice Commission in 1911 noted that female impersonators teemed on the small stages found in disorderly saloons, and that these " 'supposed' women solicited for drinks, and afterwards invited the men to rooms over the saloon for pervert practices."[24] One of Eltinge's lesser competitors, "The Famous Edward Russell," a headliner of 1913, told a later interviewer that common features of the life were hustling the audience in clubs, dating millionaires, police raids, and arrests for wearing their own hair long instead of donning wigs.[25] Eltinge was obliged to divorce himself from his disreputable colleagues in order to maintain his personal reputation and hence his preeminence. "The trouble is," he complained,

that many of the impersonators have given the outsider good cause to believe all he hears of a man who wears women's clothes on stage. . . . It is not pleasant to be classed with others who have brought the impersonation into disrepute, . . . to go to a house on a Monday morning and be regarded with suspicion by my fellow players, but I find that they soon learn that I am a real man, and by Wednesday I have gained their respect. For the casual comment of the outsider there is no redress. I try not to be any more like a woman than I have to be. Off the stage I do not have to try to be a man.[26]

Despite that last disclaimer, Eltinge's press-cuttings constantly allege that he affirmed his manhood with his fists. One report has it that, at the onset of his professional career, he and his managers staged a rough-and-tumble fight in a saloon at 42d Street and 9th Avenue, where Eltinge tossed the troublemakers into the street.[27] His beauty magazine balanced a photograph of "Julian Eltinge Telling His Mother the Good Qualities of the Julian Eltinge Cold Cream, Whiting and Powder" with one of him sparring with James J. Corbett. Although he admitted to one reporter, "I take pride in saying that in all my experience I have never had trouble anywhere,"[28] the papers regularly ran stories on how he knocked down a stagehand or playgoer who had dared to question his manliness. The bare-knuckle virtues of the frontier were used to certify the testosterone of a man who was showing the New Woman the road to fulfilment.

While Eltinge was busy demonstrating his brute force offstage, another female impersonator was winning fame by unabashed camping. In 1916, while American women were being exhorted to refine themselves in Eltinge's image, the New York *Dramatic Mirror* reported on the popular double-act of Bert Savoy and Jay Brennan: "The turn is built on the assumption that a man, in comic feminine garb, can be as coarse as he pleases."[29]

Eltinge had come out of what might be called the genteel tradition of female impersonation: amateur and student performances, polite vaudeville, and minstrelsy. Savoy had trained in a rougher school. As a boy named Everett Mackenzie, he had made his debut as a chair dancer in a Boston dime museum, had sung in bowery bars, and had slept in hallways. Taking a cattle boat to London, he walked on as a pantomime super in girl's clothes. Back in New york and frequenting Steve Brodie's Bowery bar in a red wig and a riding outfit stolen from a show, he was nicknamed "Maude" in honor of a racehorse. "Maude" first came onstage in a concert hall in Deadwood, South Dakota, after the fit-up company in which Mackenzie served as chorus boy was stranded. He exploited the role in honky-tonks and winerooms in the Dakotas, Montana, and the Yukon, passing as a woman.

The Far West had long been a congenial breeding ground for gender switching, not simply because of a paucity of women. The stag audience in mining camps and frontier outposts seemed to prefer the simulation of gender to the genuine article. In San Francisco theatres of the 1860s and 1870s, male sopranos and minstrel "wenches" did as good a business as the peroxide blondes, whose popularity improved when they donned trousers. Ella Wesner, a lesbian who played fast young men, "bewitched the town" in 1871: "It's a pity that ladies can't go to the Bella Union, they would all fall in love with Ella Wesner."[30] She made such a hit that the city's leading burlesque actress, who had been displaying her abundant curves to great applause, switched to male impersonation.

Mackenzie tried working his way back east as a fortuneteller, Mme. Veen, but was arrested in Baltimore, tried, and sentenced to sixty days, all the while wearing his Sarah Bernhardt makeup ("It's an eccentricity," he told the judge).[31] Obviously, female impersonation was a way of life for him. After taking the name Bert Savoy, he contracted a *mariage blanc* with a chorus girl, and they came to New York as Savoy & Savoy. The act and the marriage collapsed at about the same time; she was running a theatrical boarding house when their divorce was made final.

Savoy's break came around 1912 when he replaced one of the Russell Brothers in their servant-girl act, slapstick dame comedy that raised the ire of Irish-American antidefamation leagues. It was in that act that he developed his characteristic big-mouthed laugh. After John Russell retired, Savoy met another out-of-work chorus boy, Jay Brennan. Brennan had begun in show business in 1905 as a singing juvenile in *The Bachelor Club* in Baltimore, had toured variety in a four-man act, and had sold tickets for major circuses.[32] They teamed up, Brennan writing the material for a song-and-dance act with Savoy in drag. When they discovered that their interjected jokes were better received than the musical component, they worked the jokes up into a thirty-minute comedy routine, first performed in Rockaway. They were then booked on the Sullivan-Considine circuit and played the small time until they were featured in *The Passing Show of 1915*. Savoy's character, nattering on about her girlfriend Margie, had developed a chic that allowed it to fit into the sophisticated atmosphere of the Winter Garden.[33] There followed *Miss 1917, The Ziegfeld Follies of 1918, Hitchy-Koo, Cinderella on Broadway,* and several seasons of *The Greenwich Village Follies* (1920–1923). At the height of his fame, Savoy, walking on the sands of Long Beach, Long Island, was killed by a bolt of lightning that struck the locker key around his neck. Broadway's most successful farceur, Avery Hopwood, had been writing a play to feature him, a move that would have made a racy female impersonator the star of a Broadway comedy. The Great White Way had to wait some sixty-five years for *Torch Song Trilogy* for that to occur.

Variety, an expert at taxonomy, regarded the "overdressed and exceedingly gabby female" presented by Savoy to be "the evolution of the type first popularized in variety by the Russell Brothers";[34] in other words, the ungainly comic dame rejuvenated and tarted up in a mockery of the latest fashions. But the comic dame was an elderly spinster or widow whose frustrated and postmenopausal sexuality surfaced only in ridiculous longings. Edmund Wilson's description of Savoy's stage persona is more acute: "a gigantic red-haired harlot . . . reeking with the corrosive cocktails of the West Fifties, . . . the vast vulgarity of New York incarnate and made heroic."[35] If voyagers to Manhattan first encountered Miss Liberty as a symbol of the American ideal, they might later behold Savoy's outsized and blowsy dame standing for its realities—the urban underbelly exposed with a Rabelaisian lack of shame.

Savoy insisted on the realism of his character with the doggedness of a transvestite Zola; in reply to accusations of vulgarity, he explained, "Our sketches and jokes get over with the public [because] they are the natural things people say and do. . . . The more risqué the joke, the harder they laugh."[36] If his Titian-haired tart seemed to take an inordinate interest in hanky-panky, it was because all women did. "It's the women that lead me on to say the awful things I say on the stage. Out in front they lead me on with their knowing laughter, and from home they write and telephone me little feminine things which they have done and which they think will betray womankind in our act."[37] It was betrayal in a double sense: Savoy's act both unpacked and foreswore women. It revealed them as more sensual and knowing than they seemed and suggested that, stripped to their essence, they were like the garish man-in-woman's-clothing onstage—aggressive and dangerously promiscuous. Savoy resembled the doxies and slatterns portrayed by George Luks, Reginald Marsh, and the "Ash-Can School" of painting; those hussies are themselves back-alley reductions of the Messalinas and *belles dames sans merci* who people the drawings of Félicien Rops, Aubrey Beardsley, and other image-makers of the *fin de siècle*.[38] This amalgam of earthy naturalism and epic proportions launched Savoy as a thrusting figurehead for the good ship Venus.

It was a time of middle-class leisure and affluence, when forward-looking women freed of economic constraints were calling for "fulfillment in life in general and in marriage in particular."[39] To achieve the sexual fulfilment this goal entailed, greater candor was needed; but, as is invariably the case, the trend towards equality was countered by a reactive and reactionary "purity" movement that tried to suppress open discussion of birth control, venereal disease, and the societal causes of prostitution, while it spread hysteria about "white slavery" and "suggestive" literature. A tug-of-war between these two countervailing impulses, the need for sexual liberation and the need to maintain traditional values of domestic femininity, was played out in the minds of many educated Americans.

Female sexuality comprised a serious problem for even those Progressive factions that did forcefully attack prostitution, an abuse they believed could be eliminated by reformed working conditions, slum clearance, sex education, and wholesome recreation. The reform attitude held that prostitution resulted from economic injustice, but this belief co-existed with the traditional attitude that it was inimical to women's basic nature. A common assumption maintained that men were sexually overdeveloped because their "unbridled instincts" had been allowed full play, whereas women, spiritualized by their enforced chastity, preferred abstinence.[40] In the profusion of plays about white slavery that occupied the stage at this time, "fallen women" were portrayed as hapless victims of want or brute force; no prostitute was shown to be plying or enjoying a freely chosen trade.

As a man, Savoy could get away with playing a brazen hussy who reveled in her libidinousness in a way no woman could. But he was careful to describe his stage persona as the sort "that wants to make you believe how bad she is and never gives herself the chance to be bad—laughs herself out of it."[41] Everything was ersatz. Some commentators assert that Mae West borrowed much of her risqué character and intonation from Savoy; but since she was biologically a woman, the caricature she presented could actually indulge the appetite she flaunted. West was thus dangerous, especially in the live theatre; her insouciant sexuality offended the traditional image of feminine purity and led, on various occasions, to her arrest or muzzling by the censors. Savoy was never even threatened with a summons, because his gender belied his sex.

Overt sexuality was the badge of not only the prostitute; it could taint the New Woman as well. It constituted the dark side of her new-found liberation, which could be construed as subversion of masculine prerogatives. One historian has posited the emergence of a "virility impulse" in the Progressive period, "an exaggerated concern with manliness and its conventional concomitants—power and activity—. . . the Big Stick and the Bull Moose . . . strenuous, dedicated efforts to alter America and the world."[42] The eagerness of women to plunge into movements of social reconstruction was, another historian states, "in perfect accord with the utilitarian and activist notions of a blustering, masculine society which credited activity above thought, visible accomplishment above ideas."[43] Although the women Julian Eltinge impersonated were freed to engage in more active spheres, entering the professions, playing tough outdoor sports, and asserting dominance according to the best models of their age, this disruption of traditional roles had a disturbing effect on men.

Breadwinning was the standard test of manhood, but this measure was undermined by both competition from women in the workplace and the shrinking of the workplace itself. The entrepreneurial and self-employment boom of the late nineteenth century had ended. In 1907, at the time of a serious financial panic, a speaker at the University of Chicago convocation, noting the "considerable anxiety by reason of the disappearance of traditional landmarks," counseled the importance of "a manhood of discipline, capacity and power."[44] This ideal was difficult to achieve when the growth of leisure, it was feared, was diverting many men from aggressive activity to receptive passivity.

Consequently, an antifeminine (though not antifeminist) strain runs through the writings of many reformers and "muckrakers," a touchy distrust of anything that could be construed as affected, languid, or "aristocratic" behavior,[45] whether it be the parasitic indolence of the well-to-do housewife or the submissive dependency of her husband. With too much time on their hands, commentators complained, women employed sex as a trap into which such men willingly stumbled. The traditional admonition was heard that overmuch concern with sex led to "effeminacy," a particularly dangerous trait when women were vying with men in the arena of progress.

The success of Savoy and Brennan came just when attacks on effeminacy in all aspects of life were increasing. In the theatrical sphere, these attacks were aimed not at the Eltinge school of female impersonators, who blazoned their offstage virility. Even when critics found the spate of Eltinge epigones in vaudeville obnoxious in their sameness, they still certified the acts as "clean." Rather, indignation was directed at "the offensive, disgusting, effeminate male or 'fairy' impersonator."[46] The fairy himself was being introduced to the American public through gossipy periodicals and comic postcards: In 1923–1924, for instance, *Broadway Brevities* ran a series on his haunts, and the Midwestern men's magazine *Hot Dog* regularly pilloried the maidenly male in anecdotes and cartoons. Even Eddie Cantor's first successes relied on an original type, a bespectacled blackface sissy euphemistically denigrated by Robert Benchley as a "neurotic Negro."[47] The roster of effeminate males included the chorus boy, now classified as a distinct species, as well as the "tango pirate" or "lounge lizard"—"too dependent on women, overly concerned with their grooming and feminine in their attention to clothing."[48] The swelling ranks of effeminates were a bogie used to alarm the common reader and ordinary spectator.

Even so, Savoy and Brennan got away with outrageous camping. One critic explained,

There was no need for "cuts" in their dialogue, and yet it could not be called innocent by the broadest minded. . . . [Savoy] walked a verbal high wire and kept a sure footing, made doubly hard by his vesture and manner of feminism, which in itself challenges so many theatre-goers to a very virulent antagonism. . . . [Yet] the few not enthusiastic . . . were not hostile.[49]

In addition, Savoy was the most quoted comedian of his time. Uttered with a distinct lisp, his catch phrases, "You must come over," "You don't know the half of it, dearie," "You should have been with us," "I'm *glad* you ast me," "My nerves is all unstrung," and "You slay me," were avidly taken up and entered the language. George and Ira Gershwin featured the "You Don't Know the Half of It, Dearie, Blues" in their hit musical *Lady Be Good*.

In contrast with Eltinge, Savoy maintained his fey outrageousness offstage, employing feminine pronouns to refer to himself and a circle of like-minded friends. Rumor ran that he had exclaimed, "Mercy, ain't Miss God cutting up something awful!" just before he was struck by lightning.[50] The show business world evidently acknowledged his inclinations with a tolerant shrug. The comic Lou Holtz, referring to Savoy and Brennan as "a great, great act," recalled, "Sure, I know they were supposed to be fags. But who cared? They didn't bother me."[51]

Despite Savoy's claim that his character was based on a loud and vulgar woman overheard one night at Rector's restaurant,[52] it is manifest that his patter about Margie was a somewhat laundered version of the *patois* of the homosexual subculture. Compare these two samples. The first is from "The Mutterings of Margie" by Savoy and Brennan (Brennan, the brains of the act, was writing a book of that title but gave it up after Savoy's death); published in *Variety* in 1917, the monologue purports to be Margie's own reflections.

But listen, dearie, I have been flitting my tin hips around this country for seven long years with this act and I never had a chanct to talk. They say there's a change in every one's life in every seven years. I suppose this is the change in mine, and, believe muh, I am going to take the opportunity to make a camp of this an' tell the past, present and future, an' I don't care if I die for it the very next minute, so help me I don't.[53]

It ends, "And ain't this the grand place for a camp, a camp—just grand! Goo-bi, dearie! Come up and dish the dirt again."

"Dishing the dirt" was tagged as "fag parlance" by *Broadway Brevities* six years later, "a form of lewd gossip." In its series on Manhattan's fairyland, it printed an alleged transcript of a colloquy overheard in Child's restaurant between 58th and 59th streets:

Flo, why to you I tell it dearie, Flo doesn't know when she's well off. Cro-s-s-s-s my heart an' hopetodie when she took up with that lieutenant person she gave up one of the fine-s-s-st stronge-s-s-s-st men alive. And—say, don't turn around now—but later, look at the miserable weakling she's traps-sing around with now.[54]

Although it is likely that the phrases and inflections of a performer as popular as Savoy would be picked up by demotic speech, he and Brennan were clearly mining a colorful seam from a minority lode that held the advantage of novelty for the general public. George Ade had already accomplished the same thing in his *Fables in Slang,* using the argot of the commercial traveler; and in vaudeville, Junie McCree had popularized the jargon of dope addicts and gangsters. The Chicago Vice Commission of 1911, describing the homosexual community as a cult, had reported on "a much applauded act" in a large music hall performed by a man

who by facial expression and bodily contortion represented sex perversion, a most disgusting performance. It was evidently not at all understood by many of the audience, but others wildly applauded. . . . One of the songs recently ruled off the stage by the police department was inoffensive to innocent ears, but was really written by a member of the cult, and replete with suggestiveness to those who understood the language of the group."[55]

Savoy and Brennan were taking advantage of this *double entendre,* employing a code easily cracked by the initiate but that could also be appreciated on a superficial level. Some of the material, like that performed in the Chicago music hall censured by the Vice Commission, was aimed at a minority audience that could be expected to catch the nuances, while the majority laughed at the more obvious gags.

The question recurs, How was Savoy able to get away with such material at a time when effeminacy was under increasing attack? Here the locale and ambience of his performance have some bearing on his immunity from prosecution. When Savoy moved out of vaudeville, it was not into the lush, romantic sphere of musical comedy or into the respectable realm of legitimate drama, but into the *louche* world of revue and speakeasy. Their habitués hoped to be taken for jaded cosmopolites unfazed by what their more ingenuous compatriots might call decadence; they dropped the names of Freud, Krafft-Ebing, and Havelock Ellis with aplomb. When critics objected to the frequency of "queer doings" in *The Ritz Revue* and *Artists and Models,* a letter to *Broadway Brevities* (December 1924) queried why the audience seemed to enjoy them so much if they were as disgusting as journalists claimed.[56] Moreover, the stage homosexual who behaved like a stereotypical fairy obtained a kind of licence: His limp wrist, lisp, mincing gait, and fluttering eyelashes constituted a kind of clown costume that warded off serious opprobrium by raising mirth. It divorced him from everyday behavior, but his difference was so extreme and blatant that it neutralized any danger his otherness might pose.

Savoy, of course, did not portray a fairy; indeed, his partner Brennan, in the opinion of Ashton Stevens, "would make the more ladylike impersonator of the two."[57] A photograph of them in costume that appeared in *Theatre Magazine* (25 March 1917) was captioned "The Show Girl and the Johnnie," firmly establishing their types as a recognizable and admissible, albeit reversed, couple from theatrical bohemia. This pairing was an important ingredient in their success. Unlike Eltinge, a large man with a mild tenor voice who went through ordeals of depilation and constriction to disguise his bulk as feminine daintiness, Savoy was a large, bald man with a hoarse baritone voice who went to extremes to magnify his enormity. Burlesquing the fashion of the moment, his plumed Merry Widow hats and flaming ginger wig made him tower over his more delicate partner. A flamboyant variant of the free-spirited chorus girl, wielding a foot-long, jade cigarette holder, Savoy was Progressive Womanhood carried *ad absurdum,* her assertiveness turned to aggression, her outspokenness to raucousness, her sexual forthrightness to licentious innuendo. The traces of his own large-boned masculinity bloated the androgynous ideal into hermaphroditic freakishness. By contrast, the predatory male, invested in Brennan, dwindled into the compliant "feed," effeminized and "swish," donning the characteristics his better half had doffed. However much a spectator might fear such gender inversions in his or her own life, none would be likely to identify with either monstrosity.

In interpreting the traditional American minstrel show, Berndt Ostendorf defined the popular stage as a social ritual whose function is to promote acculturation. The threat of alien or "different" cultures is mitigated by exaggeration and stereotyping. He quotes Mark Twain's introduction to Bret Harte's sketch of the "heathen Chinee": "The Chinaman is getting to be a pretty frequent figure in the U.S., and is going to be a great political problem and we thought it well for you to see him on the stage before you had to deal with that problem."[58] Like the corked-up white man portraying a black man, the stage Chinaman, however inaccurate a portrait, presented a facsimile of the Chinese that was acceptable to the public because it ascribed to the outsider a lower social and emotive status. The role concept of the dominant group was thus stabilized and re-endorsed, and the outsider was put in his place.

An analogous process may be observed in the drag performances of Eltinge and Savoy. The threatening aspects of the New Woman, her self-fulfilment in the workplace, the playing field, and the bedroom, could be diminished if she were depicted by a man. When, as in Eltinge's case, the male performer preserved normal gender boundaries by asserting, even overasserting, his masculinity offstage, the spectators were reassured. Eltinge's stage persona as well as his magazine seemed to paint a sympathetic picture of the physical and possibly emotional costs of femininity. He allowed the women in his audience a frisson of daring at the same time that he validated the potential of their own less fashionable charms. These were the women, in search of wish fulfilment, who were to become the most faithful of filmgoers—the "matinee crowd"—thus enabling Eltinge's easy and successful transfer from stage to screen.

Savoy's case seems, at first sight, more conventional, coming as it did out of a tradition as old as the Wife of Bath—the mockery of female desire. The male anxieties and fantasies he tapped into are obvious, but apparently he also appealed to the female playgoer who wanted to show off her sophistication and insouciance in matters of sex. These habituées of revue would appear to have been younger, more moneyed, and less tied to domestic routine than was the audience for refined vaudeville. On the other hand, Savoy's approach was more subversively complex than Eltinge's: He took those highly sexed beings whom the general public found unsettling in real life—the New Woman and the fairy—and made them acceptable by conflating them just as they were caricatured in the popular imagination. A biological woman or an effeminate man indulging in such racy dialogue would invite censure, but Savoy's transvestism effected an intricate transmutation that absorbed the effeminacy into a larger-than-life, make-believe woman. No wonder that Mae West's image, constructed along the lines of Savoy's female impersonation, added a new element of lighthearted sauciness ("camp") to feminine sexuality.

Ostendorf's analysis of minstrelsy provides another insight: While maintaining the cultural integrity of the dominant group, such an entertainment form gets so close to the oppressed group, even as it idealizes it, that it ends up integrating genuine elements from it. By blackening their faces, the minstrels moved into culturally taboo territory, and, identified with or contaminated by the object of their mimesis, they were able to accommodate new desires. The various denials and sublimations of self required by the dominant culture could be discarded under the aegis of this licensed disguise.

The drag performer has always exercised this function. Even as Eltinge showed housewives a paradigm of female emancipation, inviting them into an active male world, he was also suggesting that the heftiest, most virile man had the capacity for traditional womanly grace and charm. Savoy enabled his mixed audience to enjoy the wit and angle of vision of a private, proscribed coterie while providing the coterie a public, licit forum. The different traditions from which the two performers sprang converge in the licensing of both to celebrate difference; but the legacies they have left are distinct.

Savoy is remembered primarily by historians of entertainment and chroniclers of camp; but the subculture from which his mannerisms and style were drawn preserves these. His example is followed by those impersonators who reinvent women through caricature and who use the grotesque mask they have assumed to sanction outrageous commentary and assaults on the bastions of right-thinking. Divine was Bert Savoy writ large.

If Savoy remains the tutelary genius of Aristophanic camp, Eltinge is the patron saint of cross-dressing that bears the Good Housekeeping Seal of Approval. Those (usually heterosexual) transvestites who wish to pass as women still worship his memory. Even today, specialized magazines for cross-dressers pay tribute to him and advise their readers to take his tips on beautification (such tips, followed to the letter, would create an anachronistic look, but an Edwardian opulence might be suitable for heavy-set men in female attire).[59] His clean-cut image lends an aura of respectability to suburban sorties into women's wardrobes. Eltinge's folkloric status has even won him an apotheosis, for in the novel *What's Bred in the Bone*, Robertson Davies vaunts him as the inspiration of his hero's inner utopia: "the Mystical Marriage, the unity of the masculine and feminine in himself, without which he would have been useless in his future life as an artist and as a man who understood art."[60] This glorification is to turn into an epicurean symposium what began as a skillfully prepared serving of Hasty Pudding.

Notes

I would like to thank Prof. Martha Vicinus of the University of Michigan for her perceptive and generous comments on an earlier draft of this essay.

1. Quoted in *Variety* obituary of Malcolm Scott (25 September 1929).

2. See Lois W. Banner, *American Beauty* (Chicago: University of Chicago Press, 1983), pp. 202–34.

3. Margaret Deland, "The Change in the Feminine Ideal," *Atlantic Monthly* 105 (March 1910):291. See also James R. McGovern, "The American Woman's Pre-World War I Freedom in Manners and Morals," *Journal of American History* 65 (September 1968):315–33; his views are questioned by Howard I. Kushner, "Nineteenth-Century Sexuality and the 'Sexual Revolution' of the Progressive Era," *Canadian Review of American Studies* 9, no. 1 (Spring 1978):34–49. The roots of the Roaring Twenties in the previous decade are also traced in Paula S. Fass, *The Damned and the Beautiful: American Youth in the 1920's* (New York: Oxford University Press, 1977).

4. *Julian Eltinge Magazine and Beauty Hints* (New York: A. H. Woods, 1913), p. 1. Martha Banta, *Imaging American Women. Idea and Ideals in Cultural History* (New York: Columbia University Press, 1987), takes the copyright date of the Corelli essay to be that of the magazine and thus mistakes the era.

5. Quoted in "The Advent of the Male Prima Donna," *Current Literature* (November 1911):550–51.

6. Undated clipping, Eltinge file, Harvard Theatre Collection. Typical reportage includes "Interview with Julian Eltinge," New York *Standard* (25 May 1906):4; P. R. Kellar, "Making a Woman of Himself," *Green Book Magazine* (December 1909); Julian Eltinge, "How I Portray a Woman on the Stage," *Theatre Magazine* (August 1913):57–58, ix; and his "The Troubles of a Man Who Wears Skirts," *Green Book Magazine* (May 1915):813–17. No full-scale studies have been devoted to either Eltinge or Bert Savoy, although they are touched on in standard works on vaudeville and popular accounts of drag performance. These latter include E. Carlton Winford, *Femme Mimics* (Dallas: Winford Co., 1954), pp. 13–15, 58–61; Roger Baker, *Drag. A History of Female Impersonation on the Stage* (London: Triton, 1968), pp. 211–14; and Anthony Slide, *Great Pretenders. A History of Female and Male Impersonation in the Performing Arts* (Lombard, Ill.: Wallace-Homestead, 1986), pp. 20–29, 32–34.

7. *Julian Eltinge Magazine*, p. 13.

8. "A Dressing Room Marvel," *Variety* (11 December 1909):153. There were even martyrs to the profession: Joseph Hennella collapsed offstage during a performance in St. Louis in 1912 and died of what was diagnosed as apoplexy and kidney trouble caused by tight-lacing. "Tight Lacing Kills Actor," New York *Times* (5 November 1912).

9. Carroll Smith-Rosenberg, *Disorderly Conduct. Visions of Gender in Victorian America* (New York: Oxford University Press, 1985), p. 246. The research of the contemporary scientist Helen Thompson concluded that men and women were similar in "the strength of the emotional nature, the form of its expression and the degree of impulsiveness in action," but that the New Woman was, by her inherent feminine nature, too inhibited to act on her principles of frankness and daring. See Rosalind Rosenberg, *Beyond Separate Spheres. Intellectual Roots of Modern Feminism* (New Haven: Yale University Press, 1982), pp. 76–77.

10. Quoted in McGovern, "Pre-World War I Freedom," p. 322.

11. Ibid., p. 321.

12. Boston *American* (20 March 1914, 11 June 1916), quoted in McGovern, "Pre-World War I Freedom," p. 324.

13. Eleanor Chalmers, "Facts and Figures," *Delineator* 84 (April 1914):38. The

ticket prices at the Broadway theatres at which Eltinge appeard would bar admission to most immigrant and working-class women, who usually frequented cheap neighborhood theatres; see Kathy Peiss, *Cheap Amusements. Working Women and Leisure in Turn-of-the-Century New York* (Philadelphia: Temple University Press, 1986), esp. pp. 144–45. Albert F. McLean, Jr., characterizes the vaudeville audience of this time as primarily "the rising army of white-collar workers" (*American Vaudeville as Ritual* [Lexington: University of Kentucky Press, 1965], p. 98).

14. Harry B. Smith and Gus Edwards, *The Modern Sandow Girl* (New York: Gus Edward Music Pub. Co., 1907). In fact, the propaganda for female athleticism starts earlier, with such programs as "the Vassar model for health"; see Sheila M. Rothman, *Woman's Proper Place. A History of Changing Ideals and Practices, 1870 to the Present* (New York: Basic Books, 1978), esp. chap. 1.

15. Information from filmmaker Mark Berger.

16. "The Advent of the Male Prima Donna."

17. Browne was one of those performers who revealed his true sex to the audience at the act's conclusion. He occasionally partnered Kathleen Clifford, a male impersonator. See clippings file, Lincoln Center Library of the Performing Arts.

18. Laurence Senelick, "Boys and Girls Together: Subcultural Origins of Glamour Drag and Male Impersonation on the 19th-century Stage," in *Crossing the Stage*, ed. Leslie K. Ferris (London: Routledge, 1992).

19. "A Dressing Room Marvel," p. 28.

20. *Julian Eltinge Magazine,* p. 40.

21. Paul Waitt, "Here's a 'Woman' Who's Going to Marry a Woman," Boston *Traveler* (16 January 1918).

22. "Eltinge Says He Didn't," *Variety* (6 January 1906):12.

23. H. U., "On the Screen," undated unidentified clipping in Eltinge file, Harvard Theatre Collection.

24. *The Social Evil in Chicago. A Study of Existing Conditions with Recommendations by the Vice Commission of Chicago* . . . (Chicago: Gunthorp-Warren, 1911), p. 297.

25. Bebe Scarpie, "Famous E. Russell," *Drag* 3, no. 12 (1973):22–25.

26. "Eltinge Says He Didn't," p. 20.

27. Joe Laurie, Jr., *Vaudeville: From the Honky-Tonks to the Palace* (New York: Henry Holt, 1953), pp. 92–93; Abel Green and Joe Laurie, Jr., *Show Biz from Vaude to Video* (New York: Henry Holt, 1951), p. 32. The female impersonator Frances Renault ran a photo in *Variety* showing himself knocking out featherweight champion Harry Bregin with the caption, "Nothing ladylike about this," and distributed postcards of himself in the ring, but Laurie remarks it had no effect in camouflaging Renault's offstage effeminacy.

28. Waitt, "Here's a 'Woman.'" The dichotomy is clearly expressed in a notice of Eltinge's vaudeville act in the New York *Star* (3 September 1910): After describing him as "gorgeous" in "The Bride," the reviewer notes that, upon leaving the theatre, Eltinge "is quite the manly man again. If you don't believe it, go and say something he doesn't like and see how he takes it" (p. 9).

29. New York *Dramatic Mirror* (22 February 1916), quoted in Slide, *Great Pretenders,* p. 33.

30. San Francisco *Figaro* (6 July 1871, 9 August 1871). For more on male impersonation in the Far West, see L. Senelick, "The Evolution of the Male Impersonator on the Nineteenth Century Popular Stage," *Essays in Theatre* 1, no. 1 (November 1983):31–44.

31. For details on Savoy's early career, see his obituary in *Variety* (28 June 1923); and Jay Brennan, "Christmas with Klondike Kate and Bert Savoy," *Variety* (4 January 1950). "Eccentricity" as a euphemism for "swish" behavior has a long-lived history. When Kenneth Williams and Hugh Paddick created the outrageously "camp" interior decorators Julian and Sandy on the British radio show *Round the Horne* [sic] in 1965, the troubled BBC censors asked Williams if the characters were meant to be homosexuals. "Oh no," he lied, "just eccentric." (Private information; see also Kenneth Williams, *Just Williams. An Autobiography* [London: Collins, 1987], pp. 153–54.)

32. "Twenty Years of Stage Life," New York *Sun* (7 October 1925).

33. "Who's Who on Stage," New York *Times* (21 February 1926).

34. Bert Savoy and Jay Brennan, "The Mutterings of Margie," *Variety* (28 December 1917):13.

35. Edmund Wilson, "The Theatre," *The Dial* (August 1923):205.

36. B. F. Wilson, "'You Should Have Been with Us!'" *Theatre Magazine* (February 1923):26.

37. Ashton Stevens, *Actorviews* (Chicago: Covici-McGee, 1923), p. 115.

38. The work currently cited on the subject is Bram Dijkstra, *Idols of Perversity. Fantasies of Feminine Evil in Fin-de-siècle Culture* (New York: Oxford University Press, 1986); but much of its contents was prefigured in Mario Praz, *The Romantic Agony,* trans. A. Davidson (New York: Meridian Books, 1956), esp. chap. 4; and in Philippe Jullian, *Dreamers of Decadence. Symbolist Painters of the 1890s,* trans. R. Baldick (London: Pall Mall, 1971).

39. John C. Burnham, "The Progressive Era Revolution in American Attitudes toward Sex," *Journal of American History* 59 (November 1973):885–908.

40. Robert E. Riegel, "Changing Attitudes toward Prostitution (1800–1920)," *Journal of the History of Ideas* 29 (1968):449. See also Mark Thomas Connelly, *The Response to Prostitution in the Progressive Era* (Chapel Hill: University of North Carolina Press, 1980); and Ray Lubove, "The Progressives and the Prostitute," *Historian* 24 (1961–1962):308–30. Judith L. Stephens in her article "Gender Ideology and Dramatic Convention in Progressive Era Plays, 1890–1920" claims that the stage at this time "reinforced such gender ideology" as the image of the "morally superior woman"; but her conclusions derive solely from the "legitimate" drama in New York, and she completely ignores the widely toured white slavery plays and the popular theatre (*Performing Feminisms. Feminist Critical Theory and Theatre,* ed. Sue-Ellen Case [Baltimore: Johns Hopkins University Press, 1990], p. 292–93).

41. Stevens, "Gender Ideology," p. 117.

42. James R. McGovern, "David Graham Phillips and the Virility Impulse of Progressives," *New England Quarterly* 29 (September 1966):335–36.

43. Egal Feldman, "Prostitution, the Alien Woman and the Progressive Imagination, 1910–1915," *American Quarterly* 19 (1967):205.

44. Albert Shaw, *The Outlook for the Average Man* (New York, 1907), pp. 12, 17; quoted in McGovern, "David Graham Phillips," p. 352.

45. McGovern, "David Graham Phillips," p. 343. The Swiss psychologist Auguste Forel in *The Sexual Question* (1905) advanced the idea that what he called "Americanism" led to degenerative neurasthenia; in his formulation, "the American woman has an increasing aversion to pregnancy, childbirth, suckling and the rearing of large families" and a concern only "to preserve her delicate skin and graceful figure." Like Theodore Roosevelt, he recommended prolific procreation

to cure this problem, but, unlike most American commentators, also advised heavy manual labor. See Sander L. Gilman, "Sexology, Psychoanalysis, and Degeneration," in *Difference and Pathology: Stereotypes of Sexuality, Race, and Madness* (Ithaca: Cornell University Press, 1985), pp. 202–4.

46. F. M. McCloy in *Variety* (1 October 1915); a similar slur directed at "pansies" in nightclub acts can be found in Jack Kofoed's foreword to Jimmy Durante, *Night Clubs* (New York: Alfred A. Knopf, 1931), p. 35; "It is not the Urning as a class that can be objected to, for he has suffered an unkind quirk of nature. It is only those who flaunt and accent their mannerisms for pay that arouse the disgust of normal men."

47. Robert Benchley in *Life* (26 July 1923).

48. Lewis A. Ehrenberg, *Steppin' Out. New York Nightlife and the Transformation of American Culture 1890–1930* (Westport, Conn.: Greenwood Press, 1981), p. 84; Harold Benjamin, "The Chorus Man," *Green Book Magazine* (March 1912):547–53. When the United States entered the Great War, this hostility was compounded with animosity towards draft-aged men who remained civilians; producer Charles Dillingham refused to engage chorus boys for a new musical comedy in order to discourage slackers. "No Slackers to Be in Fred Stone Show: Only Girls in Chorus," *New York Star* (8 August 1917):9.

49. Walter J. Kingsley, "Bert Savoy," New York *Times* (1 July 1923).

50. Marian Spitzer, *The Palace* (New York: Athenaeum, 1969), p. 51.

51. Bill Smith, *The Vaudevillians* (New York: Macmillan, 1976), p. 124.

52. Kingsley, "Bert Savoy."

53. Savoy and Brennan, "Mutterings of Margie," p. 13.

54. "Night No. 10 in Fairy-land," *Broadway Brevities and Society Gossip* 3, no. 24 (October 1924):53.

55. *Social Evil in Chicago*, p. 297.

56. Quoted in George Chauncey, Jr., "The Policers and the Policed. Stratagems of Survival on Times Square, 1920–1950," in *Inventing Times Square: Commerce and Culture at the Crossroads of the World, 1880–1939*, ed. W. Taylor (New York: Russell Sage Foundation, 1911), note 9.

57. Stevens, "Gender Ideology," p. 11.

58. Quoted in Berndt Ostendorf, *Black Literature in White America* (Sussex: Harvester Press, 1982), p. 75.

59. "Cover Girl Sylvia Meets Julian Eltinge," *Transvestia* 3 (1986):4–13; Rona, "Julian Eltinge," *Transvestia* 33 (1965):45–52. Successful female impersonators of this period appear to have inspired and focused inchoate longings in many of their audience members. In the William Seymour Theatre Collection of Princeton University Library, there is a fan letter ca. 1910 from an Australian amateur transvestite to the American impersonator Vardaman; the correspondent masquerades as a woman until halfway through and then reveals his ordinary gender identity.

60. Robertson Davies, *What's Bred in the Bone* (Harmondsworth: Penguin Books, 1985), p. 124.

JENNIFER ROBERTSON

The "Magic If": Conflicting Performances of Gender in the Takarazuka Revue of Japan

Spectators come to the theater to hear the subtext. They can read the text at home.
STANISLAVSKY[1]

❦ The all-female Takarazuka Revue was founded in 1913 in the hot springs resort of Takarazuka by Kobayashi Ichizô (1873–1957), the Hankyû railroad and department store tycoon. The Revue has maintained two huge theatres in Takarazuka and Tokyo since the 1930s, where productions are staged year-round, and it regularly schedules regional and international tours. These, along with frequent radio and television broadcasts, have made the Revue one of the most widely recognized and watched of the so-called "theatres for the masses" (*taishû engeki*) created in the early twentieth century.[2] Takarazuka productions range from Japanese historical dramas, such as the *Tale of Genji*, to Western musicals, such as *Madama Butterfly* and *Oklahoma*, although the latter far outnumber the former.[3]

The Revue's actors are called "Takarasiennes," after Parisiennes, in recognition of the early influence of the French revue. They include *otokoyaku*, the "male"-gender specialists, and *musumeyaku*, the "female"-gender specialists. Upon their successful application to the Takarazuka Music Academy, founded in 1919 as a part of the Revue complex, the student actors[4] are assigned (what I call) their "secondary" genders. Unlike "primary" gender, which is assigned at birth on the basis of an infant's genitalia,[5] secondary gender is based on both physical (but not genital) and sociopsychological criteria; namely, height, physique, facial shape, voice, personality, and to a certain extent, personal preference. Secondary gender attributes or markers are premised on contrastive gender stereotypes themselves; for example, men ideally should be taller than women, have a more rectangular face, a higher bridged nose, darker skin, straighter shoulders, narrower hips, and a lower voice than women, and should exude *kosei* (charisma), which is disparaged in women. The assignment of gender involves the selection and cosmetic exaggeration of purported physical differences between females and males and reinforces socially prescribed and culturally inscribed behavioral differences between women and men. The apparent irony, of course, is that in the Takarazuka Revue, gender (and gendered) differences that are popularly perceived as residing "naturally" in female and male bodies are embodied by females alone.

In the pages that follow, I will explore some of the competing and conflicting ways in which gender is constructed and performed, or deployed, in the Takarazuka Revue. My exploration of gender constructs includes consideration of the effect of the Stanislavsky System of acting, employed by the Revue, on the representation and performance of "female" and "male" gender. Konstantin Stanislavsky (1863–1938) developed a system of training and rehearsal at the Moscow Art Theatre for actors that, generally speaking, bases a performance upon inner emotional experience rather than upon the transmission of technical expertise *per se*. Takarazuka directors, notably Kishida Tatsuya and Shirai Tetsuzô, probably learned firsthand of the Stanislavsky System during their travels throughout western Europe in the latter half of the 1920s. Their contemporary, the playwright Mori Iwao, toured the Soviet Union in 1926. By the mid-1930s, knowledge of the System was widespread in Japanese modern theatre circles and Stanislavskian principles were incorporated into treatises on acting and acting manuals.[6] Stanislavsky's writings (in Russian and English) were available in the Revue's own library where they could be perused and adapted by the directors and instructors. I am unable to determine, either through interviews or from historical texts, the actual extent to which Takarazuka Music Academy instructors in the 1920s and 1930s employed Stanislavskian principles in preparing their students for the revue stage. Since the postwar period, however, the System has been adapted for use in training Takarasiennes.

The tension animating gender discourse cannot be accounted for in terms of simple oppositions—an all-male management versus female actors, for example, in the case of the Takarazuka Revue. Directors and actors are only two of the many agents in this ongoing, tensely charged, and sexually divided discourse, which also includes (mostly female) fans and (mostly male) critics. My general emphasis here is on a dialogical process whereby these interlocutors engage—indeed coexist—on several overlapping levels or thresholds (textual, performative, allegorical, political) of significance. Moreover, as Stanislavsky recognized, it is important to see drama itself as dialogical, for it includes "inner dialogues": "The character's 'I' is also a 'you' with whom he [or she] is in dialogue."[7] What are the implications of a female actor in dialogue with her "male" character, or her "female" character for that matter?

One of the modes in which competing discourses on gender are manifested is in the dissonance and disjunction between text and subtext.[8] It has been said of the Stanislavsky System that the priority given to training actors "led to the deconstruction of performance texts."[9] Restated in the context of the Takarazuka Revue, the emphasis on training actors in their secondary genders has, at the same time—prominently, at various historical junctures—undermined Kobayashi's patriarchal text and underscored a lesbian ("butch"–"femme") subtext. To elaborate on this observation, I must first situate the Takarazuka Revue in its sociohistorical and theatrical context.

Embodying and Choreographing Gender

The Takarazuka Revue was among the modern theatres that marked the return of females to a major public stage after being banned from public (Kabuki) performances in 1629 by the Confucian-oriented Tokugawa Shogunate.[10] At the time the Revue was founded, actresses (*joyû*) were still publicly denounced as "defiled women" who led profligate lives. For example, Mori Ritsuko (1890–1961), one of the best known Shinpa (New School) actresses, was erased from the graduation register of the girls' school she had attended when the administrators discovered she had pursued a career in the theatre.[11] Theatre critics proclaimed the newly coined term *joyû*, with its connotations of superiority and excellence (*yû*), preferable to the older term *onnayakusha*, with its historical connotations of itinerant actress associated with unlicensed prostitution.[12] As I will explain, Kobayashi used the word *yaku* in a different sense to underscore the duty-like role of the "male" and "female" gender specialists (*otokoyaku* and *musumeyaku*). It seems that Kobayashi founded the Takarazuka Music Academy not only to train students in the Western and Japanese theatrical arts but also to reassure parents that their daughters were under the constant supervision of academy officials whose responsibility it was to prevent the young women from falling into a decadent lifestyle.[13]

Kobayashi chose to name the "female"-gender specialist *musumeyaku* (daughter-role player) instead of *onnayaku* (woman-role player) in keeping with the dominant representation of femininity codified in the Meiji Civil Code, which was operative from 1898 to 1947.[14] Whereas *onnayaku*, like *joyû* (in the context of the modern theatre), alluded to a wayward woman, *musumeyaku* connoted filial piety, youthfulness, pedigree, virginity, and an unmarried status. These characteristics were precisely those Kobayashi sought in the Takarazuka actors as a whole and marked the makings of the "good wife, wise mother" extolled in the Civil Code. The *otokoyaku*, on the other hand, were to glorify masculinity and ultimately to enhance the "good wife, wise mother" gender role for women. Kobayashi theorized that by studying males and performing as men, the *otokoyaku* would learn to understand and appreciate the masculine psyche. Consequently, when they eventually retired from the stage and married—which he urged them to do—they would be better able to perform as "good wives, wise mothers," knowing exactly what their husbands expected of them.[15]

Kobayashi's patriarchal agenda for the Revue was extended by the Stanislavsky System, which is premised on the principle that the

quality of an actor's performance depends not only upon the creation of the inner life of a role but also upon the physical embodiment of it. . . . An actor must . . . answer the question, "What would I do *if* I were in . . . [X's] position?" This "magic *if*," . . . transforms the character's aim into the actor's.[16]

The "magic if" techniques for the inner construction of male-authored characters led the Takarazuka actors to reproduce the dominant gender ideology and attendant hierarchical gender typologies codified in the Civil Code. The femininity performed by the *musumeyaku* served as a foil for highlighting, by contrast, the masculinity of the *otokoyaku*. Despite a history of protest from Takarasiennes and their fans, the (male) directors continue to use *musumeyaku* to define the contours of the "male"-gender specialist. That an all-female cast should enact a system of male superiority and female subordination illustrates how differential definitions of both "female" and "male" gender are projected onto female bodies and internalized by females, while male bodies in effect remain neutral.[17] Significantly, with the exception of patriotic youths in wartime productions, the Revue has never staged a play featuring contemporary Japanese characters. Plays with Japanese characters are limited to stories set in the Heian through Edo periods, roughly the ninth through midnineteenth centuries. Plays set in the twentieth century present non-Japanese "male" and "female" characters exclusively. Consequently, the repertoire of an *otokoyaku* does not include contemporary Japanese men, although the Takarasienne learns about masculinity by watching, among others, Japanese males. Not only are male bodies unavailable for gender experiments but contemporary Japanese "male" gender appears to be off limits to representation by Takarazuka *otokoyaku*. Moreover, in this connection, the "good husband, wise father" was never invented as a trope for social order, nor was social disorder ever linked to a "man problem."

Kobayashi conceived of the Takarazuka *otokoyaku* or "male"-role player as the complement of the Kabuki *onnagata* or "female"-role player (literally, "female" model); however, whereas *onnagata* were exemplary models (*kata*) of "female" (*onna*) gender for females offstage to approximate, the *otokoyaku* were regarded as performing a duty not for males but for females on- and offstage to internalize. The gender(ed) difference between the Kabuki and Takarazuka performers is also evident in the discourse of the body.

In Kabuki, the theory linking the body and (secondary) gender of the "female"-gender specialist was formulated by onnagata Yoshizawa Ayame in the early Edo period (1603–1868). It is a twist on the Buddhist concept of henshin, or bodily transformation or metamorphosis. Hen is the term for change, in both a transitive and intransitive sense. Shin (also pronounced mi) is the term for body in the most comprehensive sense; that is, a physical, mental, social, historical, and spiritual entity.[18] The term henshin originally referred to the process whereby deities assumed a human form the better to promulgate Buddhist teachings among the masses of sentient beings.

The process of henshin is also central to the Kabuki theatre, and refers specifically to the process by which an onnagata becomes Woman, as opposed to impersonates a given female/woman. Ayame's theory resembles the Buddhist concept of henshin with the exception that gender (and not sex) is involved in an onnagata's transformation from a man into Woman. He did not perceive of the onnagata as "a male acting in a role in which he becomes a woman," but rather as "a male who is a woman acting a role."[19] In other words, the transformation is not part of the role but precedes the particular role. Henshin, as defined by Ayame, appears to be quite close to Stanislavsky's notion of "emotional memory," whereby an actor, through what might be called "active empathy," makes the transformation from a witness who shares feelings to the principal who actually feels them.[20] An onnagata, however, does not put himself in the place of another person (that is, a female) but rather becomes Woman; his past emotions may be deployed as creative material, but the onnagata is obliged to refrain from both studying real females and from getting close to them emotionally lest sympathy for them be transformed into feelings of his own.[21] One Japanese theatre critic has even declared that Kabuki and the Stanislavsky System are "diametrically opposed to each other": Unlike the System, "Kabuki is not motivated by the what-how-why questions" that accompany an empathic sensibility.[22]

Ayame insisted that an onnagata embody femininity in his daily life.[23] Simply impersonating a given female/woman was neither adequate nor appropriate. To clinch his point, Ayame insisted that the construction of Woman could not be left up to the idiosyncratic notions of a particular actor. Instead, he introduced ideal-type categories of Woman, each with predetermined characteristics. The role of a "chaste woman" (teijo), for example, was to be based on Onnadaigaku (Greater Learning for Females), a primer written in the early eighteenth century by a Confucian scholar.[24] Given the Kabuki theatre's ambivalent reception by the Tokugawa Shogunate and the low, outsider status of actors during the Edo period, the construction and performance of femininity on the basis of a leading sa-murai-class (male) intellectual's influential treatise on "female" gender likely added a modicum of legitimacy to the urban theatre.[25]

Henshin is not a process either (officially) prescribed or recommended for Takarazuka *otokoyaku*. Kobayashi, the Revue's founder, was no Ayame, and was keen on limiting an *otokoyaku*'s appropriation of masculinity to the Takarazuka stage. A masculine female outside the context of the Revue was censured by him, as well as by early twentieth-century sexologists, as abnormal and perverted.[26] Kobayashi proclaimed that "the [Takarazuka] *otokoyaku* is not male but is more suave, more affectionate, more coura-geous, more charming, more handsome, and more fascinating than a real male."[27] But, although her body was appropriated as the main vehicle for the representation of masculinity, an *otokoyaku* was not to become un-equivocally Man, much less a model for males offstage to emulate. Whereas the *kata* in *onnagata* means model or archetype, the *yaku* in *otokoyaku* connotes serviceability and dutifulness. Revue directors have thus referred to the actor's achievement of "male" gender not in terms of transformation or metamorphosis (*henshin*) but in terms of "putting something on the body" (*mi ni tsukeru*), in this case, markers of masculinity. As they see it, a Takarasienne who plays a man is but performing a duty.

A major part of the training of the academy students and Revue actors includes learning a repertoire of gestures, movements, intonations, speech patterns, and the like, through which they extend their bodily defined sec-ondary genders. An *otokoyaku*, for example, must stride forthrightly across the stage, her arms held stiffly away from her body and her fingers curled around her thumbs. A *musumeyaku*, on the other hand, pivots her fore-arms from the elbows, which are kept pinned against her side, constraining her freedom of movement and consequently making her appear more "fem-inine."[28] In keeping with the patriarchal values informing the Takarazuka Revue, and similar to the Kabuki *onnagata*, the *musumeyaku* have repre-sented and performed the male-identified fictional Woman with little if any connection to the historical experiences and feelings of actual females. The *otokoyaku*, however, have been actively encouraged to study the behavior and actions of real males offstage, as well as those of theatre and film char-acters, to idealize men on stage more effectively, be they samurai or cow-boys.

Commercial reasons notwithstanding, Kobayashi conceived of the Taka-razuka theatre as an appropriate site for the resocialization of ("bour-geois") girls and women whose unconventional aspirations had led them to the Revue stage. Once onstage, however, the System-trained Takara-sienne was placed "within the range of systems that . . . oppressed her very representation on stage."[29]

Kobayashi, like Stanislavsky, perceived of the theatre as "a pulpit which is the most powerful means of influence,"[30] and he maintained that the Takarazuka Revue served a didactic purpose. The female actors were trained to perform gender roles that would facilitate their postretirement reentry into a more conventional lifestyle. Significantly, Kobayashi referred to the actors as "students" (seitô), for he believed that a wedding ceremony marked the start of a woman's real career, whereupon she became a full-fledged actor—the conjugal household her stage and her husband and children her audience. Their stage duty as members of the Takarazuka Revue was deemed analogous to their eventual duty as "good wives, wise mothers" in a patriarchal household.[31] But, as I have hinted and will discuss in the next section, many Takarazuka actors used the Revue stage as a site for resisting and redressing conventional and oppressive gender roles.

Redressing Gender, Rehearsing New Gender Roles

The public vocation of the Takarasiennes reversed the usual association of females with the private domain. Kobayashi was keen on bringing the interpersonal sphere of women in the conjugal household into the light of public scrutiny and edification.[32] But despite his early efforts to represent the otokoyaku in particular as performing a patriotic, civil duty, the "male" role players eventually were singled out and denounced in the daily press as the "acme of offensiveness." In August 1939, the Osaka prefectural government banned otokoyaku from public performances in that prefecture, signaling the beginning of a generalized castigation of the Revue. All Takarasiennes were chastised in the mass media for their "abnormal and ostentatious" lifestyle, and government censors ordered the uniforms of academy students changed from the original hakama, or formal Japanese-style outfit, to the military-like uniform worn today. They were not permitted to answer fan mail, much less to socialize with their fans.[33] Kobayashi, who from July 1940 to April 1941 served (in the second Konoe cabinet) as minister of commerce and industry, colluded with government censors to produce patriotic musicals that exalted the image of the "good wife, wise mother," an image further reified at that time as Nippon fujin, or "Japanese Woman."[34] Typical of the musicals staged during the late 1930s and early 1940s, a period of militarization and state censorship, was Illustrious Women of Japan (Nippon meifu den, 1941), a nationalistic extravaganza dedicated to heroines, mothers of heroes, and "women of chastity."

What provoked these charges of an "abnormal lifestyle"? The belief that female actors performing men's roles were behaving in an "unnatural" and "perverse" manner grew out of the "psychiatric style of reasoning" imported from Europe and the United States in the late nineteenth and early twentieth centuries. The theories of Sigmund Freud, Havelock Ellis, Richard von Krafft-Ebing, and Otto Weininger[35]—the latter three in particular—were employed by Japanese sexologists and forensic medicine specialists to define "normal" and "natural" against "abnormal" and "unnatural" gender identity, sexuality, and sexual desire. Women such as the *moga*,[36] the Japanese "flapper," and the Takarasiennes, many of whom openly rejected the state-sanctioned "good wife, wise mother" model of "female" gender, were severely criticized in newspaper, journal, and magazine articles as "masculinized" (*danseika*) females who "had forgotten how to be feminine."[37]

"Same-sex love" (*dôseiai*) relationships, between females especially, attracted much popular and medical attention in the early twentieth century. Girls' schools, including the Takarazuka Music Academy, and their (unmarried) female instructors and students were singled out by (mostly male) sexologists and social critics as the sites and agents of homosexuality among females. By the same token, not a few claimed that the phenomenon of "masculinized" females could be attributed to the detrimental influence of the revue theatre and foreign films.[38]

In 1910, four years before the first performance of the Takarazuka Revue, one of the first articles on the subject of lesbianism was published in a leading women's newspaper, the *Fujo Shinbun*. Distinctions were drawn between two types of homosexual relationships between females: *dôseiai* (same-sex love) and *ome no kankei* ("male"-"female" relations).[39] It is clear from the article that what the editorial staff meant by "same *sex*" was actually "same *gender*," and that *ome* referred to a "butch-femme"-like couple (that is, same sex, different gender). A *dôseiai* relationship was characterized as a passionate but supposedly platonic friendship and was regarded as typical among girls and women from all walks of life, but especially among girls' school students and graduates, female educators, female civil servants, and thespians.[40] Such relationships were also referred to as "S" or "Class S" (*kurasu esu*)—the "S" refers to sister, *shôjo*, or sex, or all three combined. Class S continues to conjure up the image of two schoolgirls, often a junior-senior pair, with a crush on each other.

Ome relationships, on the other hand, were described as

a strange phenomenon difficult to diagnose on the basis of modern psychology and physiology.[41] . . . One of the couple has male-like (*danseiteki*) characteristics and dominates the [female-like] other. . . . Unlike the [*dôseiai* couple], friends whose spiritual bond took a passionate turn, the latter have developed a strange, carnal relationship (*niku no sesshoku*) . . . stemming from their carnal depravity (*nikuteki daraku*). . . . The masculine female is technically proficient at manipulating women. . . . Doctors have yet to put their hoes to this uncultivated land (*mikaikonchi*).[42]

This article and others like it[43] make it clear that even an overheated *dôseiai* (i.e., homogender) relationship was not pathological in the way that an *ome* (i.e., heterogender) relationship was, the latter being not only acknowledgedly sexual but also an heretical refraction of the heterosexual norm codified in the Meiji Civil Code. The most objective writers, not surprisingly, referred to an *ome* couple as *fufu* (husband and wife), a marital metaphor that safely contained (and conveniently camouflaged) the difference embodied by the two women and denied the alterity of females as subjects of their own desire.

The *Fujo Shinbun* article introduced recent "medical" findings in surmising that females were more prone than males to homosexuality. It was postulated that the "natural" passivity (*muteikôshugi*) of females made them susceptible to neurasthenia (*shinkeishitsu*), which, in turn, occasioned a pessimism expressed in the form of homosexuality.[44] *Ome* ("butch-femme") relationships, however, seemed to stymie the sexologists and worry the social critics of the day, since unmarried women in particular were stereotyped as blissfully unaware of sexual desire and females in general were certainly not supposed to play an active role in sexual relations of any kind. "Moral depravity" fostered by modernization (westernization) seemed to be the only viable explanation the "experts" could forward to rationalize *ome* relationships among urban women—at least until the appearance of Takarazuka *otokoyaku* prompted critics to come up with new ideas to account for the increasingly visible "masculinized" female. The author of a 1930 newspaper article on the Takarazuka Revue went so far as to assert that the emergence of *ome*-type relationships was the "direct result of females playing men's roles" and to suggest that the Revue was the medium through which Class S couples were transformed into *ome* ("butch-femme") couples, an evolutionary thesis absent from the *Fujo Shinbun* article published twenty years earlier.[45]

The erotic potential of the Takarazuka *otokoyaku* was recognized within a decade of the Revue's founding. In his 1921 book on the lifestyle of the Takarasiennes, Kawahara included a chapter on love letters from female fans, which he regarded as examples of "abnormal psychology" (*hentai seiri*).[46] Eight years later, in 1929, the mass media began to sensationalize the link between the Takarazuka Revue and lesbian practices. A leading daily newspaper ran a series on Takarazuka called "Abnormal Sensations" (*hentaiteki kankaku*). The (male) author was alarmed that the *otokoyaku* might begin to feel natural assuming "male" gender. Their private lives, he fretted, would soon "become an extension of the stage."[47]

His worst fears came true when, less than a year later, the leading dailies exposed the "same-sex love" affair between Nara Miyako, a leading *otokoyaku*, and Mizutani Yaeko, a leading woman of the Shinpa theatre. What this critic and others found most alarming was nothing short of a revolutionary change of context; namely, the transformation of the *otokoyaku* from the showcase of masculinity to the stereotype of the masculine female.

What had been presented and perceived as artifice onstage had revealed itself as daily practice offstage. Inasmuch as many Takarasiennes had applied to the academy because they were avid fans and wanted to be closer to their idols, or because they wanted to do "male" and in some cases "female" roles, the stage was an extension of their private lives, and not the reverse. For Takarasiennes and their fans, resistance to prescribed sex and gender roles was possible precisely through a change of context.[48]

The critics seemed particularly disturbed by the realization that the Takarazuka *otokoyaku*, like the "modern girl" (*moga*), could effectively undermine a gender role (the "good wife, wise mother") that was premised on the conflation of sex, gender, and sexuality and on women's dependence upon and subordination to men. Consequently, Nara, the man, was pushed into the limelight of damnation. For an anatomical female to assume "male" gender was for her to rise in the gender hierarchy, a subversive act from a patriarchal point of view. Therefore, Kobayashi, along with media critics, sought to limit the scope of the *otokoyaku*'s masculine behavior to the Takarazuka stage. Mizutani was treated more leniently for the likely reason that, as the woman, she did not appear different enough to be perceived as a heretic.[49]

Offstage, a masculine female is dangerous to the social order not because she may be homosexual but because, in appropriating "male" gender, she, like the *moga* who eschewed conventional femininity, embodies the rejection of wifehood and, most importantly, motherhood. Moreover, regarding onstage *otokoyaku*, female fans across age, class, and educational lines perceive not an ideal man but rather a female body performing in a capacity that the majority of women cannot.[50]

The brouhaha that erupted over the Nara-Mizutani affair was part of the larger sociocultural discourse on the problematic relationship between eros and modernism in the early twentieth century. The revue *Parisette*, staged in 1930, ushered in Takarazuka's overtly modern and erotic phase.[51] From this production onward, Takarasiennes ceased to apply the traditional stage makeup, *oshiroi* (whiteface). Modernism warranted a transition from denaturalized flesh to its naturalization. The Takarasienne's whiteface mask, as it turned out, had not so much hidden as revealed her "masculine" nature—her gender role and sexuality.

The appropriation of masculinity continued with *otokoyaku* Kadota Ashiko's sudden decision to cut off her hair in the spring of 1932. As reported in the press, Kadota was irked by the unnaturalness of having to stuff her regulation-long hair under every type of headgear except wigs, for the all-male management had deemed that wigs would give *otokoyaku* an overly natural appearance. Takarazuka fans and *moga*, on the other hand, had sported short hair at least a decade ahead of their idols.[52]

Hair has been a symbolic element throughout Japanese history. Prior to the *moga,* short hair announced a woman's withdrawal from secular and sexual affairs. The "modern girl" turned hair symbolism on its head, and short hair became the hallmark of the extroverted, maverick, and in the eyes of critics, dangerous woman. *Otokoyaku* gave short hair yet another layer of symbolic meaning: "butch" sexuality. The Takarazuka management eventually sought to divest short hair of its radical symbolism by assuming authority over haircuts. At least since the postwar period and probably before, a student assigned the "male" gender is required to cut her hair short by the end of her first semester at the academy. Until ordered to do otherwise, all junior students are required to wear their hair in shoulder-length braids.

In the prewar period, *otokoyaku* sought to appropriate and naturalize masculinity and were, along with the Revue as a whole, castigated severely. One aspect of the postwar revival of Takarazuka has been the efforts of *musumeyaku* to make femininity more than just a foil for masculine privilege. Significantly, in a fan magazine (*Takarazuka Fuan*) published independently, and occasionally in those published by the Revue, Takarasiennes and their female fans refer to the actor not as *musumeyaku* (daughter-role player) but as *onnayaku* (woman-role player), thereby claiming a nomenclatorial parity with the *otokoyaku.* This act of re-naming is a reminder that the "sex-gender system . . . is both a sociocultural construct and a semiotic apparatus, a system of representation which assigns meaning (identity, value, prestige, . . . status in the social hierarchy, etc.) to individuals within the society."[53] The actors began to stress their female being over their status as daughters and, accordingly, to demand more definitive roles.

The all-male directorship responded to these demands by creating highly visible, dynamic, and often overtly sensuous woman characters, such as Scarlett O'Hara in *Gone With the Wind* and Jacqueline Carstone in *Me and My Girl.* However, in a move which undercut *musumeyaku* intentions, the directors assigned these new roles to *otokoyaku.* In this way, the construction and performance of femininity remained the privilege of both males and "male" gender specialists. *Musumeyaku,* on the contrary, almost never have been re-assigned to men's roles: The transposition of gender is not a reciprocal operation. As several *musumeyaku* have remarked, "Japanese society is a male's world, and Takarazuka is an *otokoyaku*'s world."[54]

It is also important to note that those plays whose charismatic women characters have been performed by *otokoyaku* are Euro-American plays. Earlier I noted how, in the early twentieth century, the Paris-inspired revue and Western films were deemed accountable for the "masculinization" of Japanese females. In this case, however, the directors felt that the requisite innocence and naiveté of the *musumeyaku* would be irreparably compromised by roles that called for (hetero)sexually literate characters. Although all Takarasiennes by definition are unmarried and ostensibly (hetero)-sexually inexperienced, *otokoyaku*, by virtue of their "male" gender, were perceived as less likely to be corrupted by assuming the roles of charismatic women—an ironic twist on the rationale for the emergence of the Kabuki *onnagata* in the 1600s.

Many *otokoyaku*, along with disfranchised *musumeyaku*, protested the directors' gender-switching antics, and many *otokoyaku* claimed to have experienced, as a result of playing women's roles, a sense of conflict or resistance (*teikô*) and a loss of confidence. Gô Chigusa, an *otokoyaku* who retired in 1972, also remarked that on the rare occasion when she was assigned a woman's role, her fans complained bitterly of their resultant dis-ease (*kimochi warui*)—that eerie feeling when the familiar suddenly is defamiliarized.[55]

Some actors such as Minakaze Mai who had enrolled in the academy specifically to do "male" gender were assigned instead to do "female" gender. Minakaze was assigned to women's roles because of her short (160-cm) stature. To resolve the conflict between her offstage desires and her onstage role—or, in Stanislavskian terms, in order to dialogue with her character's "I"—she has "stopped wearing blue-jeans" and "always exerts [herself] to the fullest to be a *musumeyaku*, even in [her] private life."[56] Minakaze is not alone in originally believing that females encountered less resistance when performing women's roles. She now agrees with several of her colleagues that locating "the woman within the female poses a perplexing problem."[57] Similarly, after ten years of performing only men's roles, *otokoyaku* Matsu Akira, who retired in 1982, was unable to perform a woman's role: "Even though I am a female, the thing called woman just won't emerge at all."[58] Whether in terms of "resistance" or "emergence," the Takarasiennes have drawn attention to the incompatibility between their experiences as females and the dominant construction of "female" gender. In keeping with Schechner's earlier remarks on the Stanislavsky System, the actors' training in their secondary genders has led to the deconstruction of femininity, which, as a gender role, can be understood as a performative text.

Kobayashi's assertion that "Takarazuka involves studying the male" is only partially correct.[59] "Female" gender is also taught and studied; this, in fact, is the ultimate objective of the academy. Takarasiennes who are assigned a (secondary) gender contrary to their personal preference represent all Japanese females who are socialized into gender roles not of their own making. And like the *musumeyaku* in particular, girls and women are suspended between the depiction and definition of femininity and the achievement or approximation of such—ironically, a limbo many young women have sought to avoid by enrolling in the academy.[60]

Nevertheless, the Revue offers Takarasiennes an alternative to, or at least a respite from, the gender role of "good wife, wise mother." One actor declared that for her, to become an *otokoyaku* was tantamount to "realizing her personal ideals."[61] Another enrolled in the Takarazuka Music Academy specifically because, "despite her female body, she could assume a masculine persona." She made a point of referring to herself as *boku*, a self-referent that signifies masculinity.[62] As *otokoyaku*, the actors have access to, and can provide fans with vicarious access to, a wide range of occupations limited to males, from general to matador to gangster. Many "male"-gender specialists have noted that, had they not joined Takarazuka, they would have pursued—as if employment opportunities were equal—careers such as import-export trader, airplane pilot, train engineer, and lumberyard manager, among others; occupations essentially limited to males.

Leading *otokoyaku* have been provided the opportunity to realize their forfeited careers in one fan magazine's "magic if" series titled, "What if you had not joined Takarazuka?" Asami Rei and Haruna Yuri, for example, would have been a train engineer and airplane pilot, respectively. For the series, the two *otokoyaku* dressed in the appropriate uniforms and assumed their foregone careers for a day. Haruna toured but did not pilot a jet, and Asami was given lessons and actually drove a Hankyû train.[63] Theoretically, they subverted the male-dominant occupational hierarchy, but in actuality, as well-known *otokoyaku*, their act was neither presented nor perceived as a redressing of conventional "female" gender roles.

In recent decades, Takarasiennes and their fans have often referred to the *otokoyaku* as females who have metamorphosed (*henshin shita*), indicating a recontextualization of this hitherto androcentric term to fit their stage experience.[64] Their use of the term outside the Buddhist and Kabuki (*onnagata*) contexts may have been prompted by the tremendous, continuing popularity of the "*henshin* dramas" (*dorama*) that were first aired in the late 1960s. These television dramas, some of them animated, feature mostly "ordinary" boys and young men who have the ability to change (*henshin*) suddenly into another, more powerful form. The brainy Pa-man, for example, in another incarnation is Mitsuo-*kun*, an average elementary school student. His inventors suggest that what audiences find intriguing is the possibility of "one person living in two worlds."[65]

To digress for a moment, the Takarazuka Revue was and is attractive to audiences for much the same reason. The Paris-flavored Revue in the 1920s and 1930s, for example, provided Japanese viewers with a glimpse of another (i.e., Western) world. And for female fans in particular, the tuxedo-and-gown outfitted actors allowed for the vicarious experience of an alternative to the state-prescribed kimono, along with an alternative to the "good wife, wise mother" gender role. Of great significance in this connection, the public vocation of the Takarazuka actor reverses the conventional association of females with the private domain; consequently, distinctions between "private" ("women's work") and "public" ("men's work") are neither incumbent upon nor possible for Takarasiennes.[66]

One result of this is that although [the actor] is aware of the dominant rules governing the society of which her small dramatic world is a part, her experience permits her to fuse the value-systems, and to bring the naturally secluded private interpersonal sphere of women in the home into the light of public scrutiny.[67]

It is in this light that the unabated postwar popularity of Takarazuka among girls and women is partly explained. Voting rights (1947) and nominal equal employment opportunity laws (1986) notwithstanding, sexist discrimination against girls and women—from the boys-first order of school roll calls to short-term "mommy track" jobs—is the prevailing state of affairs. "Women inside, men outside" remains the dominant gender ideology, reinforced by "public opinion" polls commissioned by the prime minster's office and others, despite the fact that over 60 percent of all adult females work for wages outside their homes, 80 percent of whom are married and mothers.[68] Since the postwar period, from roughly the 1950s onward, girls and women have constituted the overwhelming majority of the Takarazuka audience and fan population. Throughout the pre- and interwar years, about half of the audience was made up of boys and men, although the most zealous (and problematic) fans were female. The management, playwrights, and directors, however, continue to be exclusively male.

One of the reasons the newly revived musical *The Rose of Versailles,* first staged in the mid-1970s, has been such a colossal success among female fans of all ages is that it dwells on the adventures of Oscar, a female raised as a "male" in order to succeed her father in a patrilineage of generals.[69] The Oscar character represents the slippage between sex and gender and, significantly, has been acted by *otokoyaku* exclusively, whose own acting careers in the Revue have followed a similar trajectory. The subtextual meaning of this play about the French Revolution is that clothing as performance threatens to undercut the ideological fixity of gender differences.[70]

By the same token, *The Rose of Versailles* is also one of the Revue's most reflexive productions in that the relationship between Oscar and her/his father is analogous to that between the *otokoyaku* and the Revue's all-male administration. Note, when reading the following dialogue between Oscar and the General, that Kobayashi had insisted that Takarasiennes call him "Father."

OSCAR: Father, please answer me!

GENERAL: Oscar?!

O: If . . . if I had been raised as an ordinary female, would I have been forced to marry at age fifteen like my sisters? I could be playing the [clavichord], singing arias, dressing up every night in fine clothes and laughing away the time in high society. . . .

G: Oscar!!

O: Please answer me! I could be wearing velvet beauty marks and rose perfume; I would fill my arabesque compact with cosmetics; I could bear children—and raise them.

G: Oscar!!

O: Answer me, please!

G: [Pensively.] Yes, it's as you say—had you been raised as an ordinary female.

O: Father, thank you.

G: [Is taken aback.]

O: Thank you for giving me a chance to live the kind of life I have, in as broad a world as I have, even though I am a female. Even while struggling to deal with the stupidity of pathetic people. . . .

G: Oscar.

O: I am no longer remorseful. I . . . I'll live as the child of Mars, god of war. I'll devote this body of mine to the sword; I'll devote it to the cannon. My livelihood is the military and I'll serve as the child of Mars, god of war. . . .[71]

Oscar (and by the same token, the Takarazuka *otokoyaku*) is able to transcend the fixed, narrow life course of "ordinary females" because of Father's pragmatically patriarchal decision to name her "son." Recognizing that masculinity affords access to a wider world, Oscar is effusively grateful for the opportunity to be the household's *otokoyaku*. Oscar's military uniform not only accentuates the difference between "male" and "female" gender—the former identified with swords and cannons, the latter with flowers and children—but magnifies the tension between masculinity and the female body it camouflages. The overall effect exaggerates the slippage between sex and gender even as it cloaks it. Both the General and the audience know that Oscar, like the actor, is a "masculinized" female. The notion that gender is a property of attribution, instruction, and convention and not of anatomy is made doubly obvious by the synonymy between Oscar and the *otokoyaku* performing Oscar. At the same time, both demonstrate the sexist irony that access to a more supposedly "liberating" gender identity is granted only by privileged father figures.[72]

Concluding Concatenations

"Performance at its most general and most basic level is a carrying out, a putting into action or into shape." Takarazuka performances "carry out" at least several competing actions in several different forms, because a theatrical performance always exceeds the elements—such as the "master" text—from which it is composed and extends into many spheres of action.[73] More specifically, the meeting of performers, who include actors as well as directors, fans, critics, "I," and "you," may be a cooperative and/ or contested interaction or dialogue.

The significance of Takarazuka Revue to the discourse on gender and sexuality was its impact on Japanese society at different historical junctures in several, often contradictory ways, as I have shown. For example, whereas Kobayashi argued that the *otokoyaku* participates not in the construction of alternative gender roles for females but in the glorification of masculinity, both government censors and female fans viewed the actor as doing just the opposite. The former interpreted the *otokoyaku* as "abnormal" and offensive enough to be banned from the stage in 1939. Female fans, on the other hand, continue to view the *otokoyaku* in a number of affirmative ways, including as a lesbian "role model" and as an exemplary female who can negotiate successfully both genders and their attendant roles and domains without (theoretically) being constrained by either. Watching the "male"-gender specialists on stage, (female) fans enjoy vicariously what they too might be able to do if—magically—they were, not male, but *otokoyaku*. Takarasiennes, and particularly the *otokoyaku*, like the character of Oscar, provoke the recognition of gender as, in part, a costume drama in which clothing—in addition to gesture and voice—undercuts the ideological fixity and essentialism of conventional femininity and masculinity.[74] The technologies of gender construction utilized in the Takarazuka Revue have both drawn from and informed—and redressed—a socio-historically situated discourse of gender and sexuality. Enactment, in short, entails interaction, and vice versa.

Notes

1. Konstantin Stanislavsky, in Sonia Moore, *The Stanislavski System* (New York: Penguin, 1988 [1960]), p. 28.

2. See Jennifer Robertson, "Gender-bending in Paradise: Doing 'Male' and 'Female' in Japan," *Genders* 5 (1989):50–59, for an exploration of the various interlocutors in the discourse of sex, gender, and sexuality on and off the Takarazuka stage.

Another all-female revue, the Shôchiku Revue, founded in Tokyo (Asakusa) in 1928 and formally disbanded in early 1990, quickly became Takarazuka's main

rival—or "other"—in every respect. Whereas Takarazuka productions were stereotyped as naive and romantic, the Shôchiku actors performed more allegedly mature and erotic revues. Fans partial to one or the other revue rarely attended
performances staged by the rival troupe.

3. For pertinent research on the production of *Madama Butterfly* in Japan, including by the Takarazuka Revue, see Arthur Groos (Cornell University), "Return
of the Native: Japan in *Madama Butterfly/Madama Butterfly* in Japan" (typescript).

4. From the beginning, the academy has solicited applications from females between fifteen and twenty-four years of age. Today, most of the applicants are nineteen years old and, as required, are either junior high or high school graduates.
Academy officials continue to claim that the young women are from "good families," and although detailed information about their socioeconomic status is kept
confidential, it is widely understood that those families are affluent. The Revue
itself, however, attracts (mostly female) fans who represent a wide variety of age,
educational, economic, and class groups.

5. I am not here unconsciously conflating genital sex with gender but rather
taking note of the conventional practice in Japan. Regardless of their popular conflation, there is a major difference between "sex roles" and "gender roles." The
former term refers to the various capabilities of female and male genitalia, such as
menstruation, seminal ejaculation, and orgasm. Gender roles refer to sociocultural
and historical conventions of deportment and costume attributed to females and
males. "Sexuality" may overlap with sex and gender but remains a separate domain
of desire and erotic pleasure. See Suzanne Kessler and Wendy McKenna, *Gender:
An Ethnomethodological Approach* (Chicago: University of Chicago Press, 1985
[1978]), pp. 1–12; and Carol Vance, "Pleasure and Danger: Toward a Politics of
Sexuality," in *Pleasure and Danger: Exploring Female Sexuality*, ed. Carol Vance
(Boston: Routledge and Kegan Paul, 1985), p. 9. Sex, gender, and sexuality may
be related, but they are not the same thing. The degree of their relationship or the
lack thereof is negotiable and negotiated constantly. Although the three may be
popularly perceived as irreducibly joined, this condition remains situational and
not permanently fixed.

6. Ôzasa Y., *Nihon gendai engekishi: Taishô, Shôwa shoki hen* (Tokyo: Shi-
romizusha, 1986), p. 264; for example, Hiroo M., "Gendai engekisaku haiyûron,"
Chûô Kôron 3 (1936):140–51; and Hachida M., *Enshutsuron* (Tokyo: Takada
Shoin, 1940 [1937]).

7. Moore, *The Stanislavski System*, p. 71.

8. Pribram's explication of "text" offers a useful clarification of the term as I
employ it here in the sense of dominant discourse or master narrative.

  The function of a text is to position the spectator to receive certain flavoured—
  and restricted—meaning which the text "manages" for the viewing subject in
  keeping with dominant ideology. In this model the spectator is not an active
  part of the production of textual meaning but the passive side of a unidirectional
  relationship in which the text disperses meanings while the spectator . . . receives them. The spectator can only interpret (be interpreted by) a text in terms
  preformulated by gender difference. There is no possibility of a mutually informing relationship between spectator and text, and therefore no accumulative
  building of textual meaning. . . . The intention of the text and the reception of
  textual meaning are defined as one and the same (E. Deidre Pribram, "Introduction," in *Female Spectators: Looking at Film and Television*, edited by E.
  Deidre Pribram [New York: Verso, 1988], p. 4).

A text then, as a technology of gender, is invested with "power to control the field of social meaning and thus produce, promote, and 'implant' representations of gender" (Teresa de Lauretis, *Technologies of Gender* [Bloomington: Indiana University Press, 1987], p. 18). But, as de Lauretis argues, "the terms of a different construction of gender also exist, in the margins of hegemonic discourses" and texts (ibid.). I use the term "subtext" in reference to marginalized, alternative discourses—which are marginalized and alternative only in relation to a dominant ideology and its attendent practices.

9. Richard Schechner, *Performance Theory* (New York: Routledge, 1988), p. 210.

10. Although a female—the legendary dancer Okuni from Izumo—is credited with having initiated Kabuki at the start of the seventeenth century, females have been banned from that stage since 1629. Apparently, the newly installed Shogunate was disturbed by the general disorder, including unlicensed prostitution, following the performances, when patrons quarreled with each other for access to their favorite dancers. Replacing the females with boys did not solve the problem, for the male patrons were equally attracted to their own sex. Eventually, the prohibition of females, and later boys, prompted the emergence of the *onnagata*, adult males who specialize in "female" gender. See Donald Shively, "*Bakufu* versus *Kabuki*," in *Studies in the Institutional History of Early Modern Japan,* ed. John Hall and Marius Hall (Princeton: Princeton University Press, 1970 [1955]), pp. 231–61.

11. The Shinpa theatre movement arose around the 1890s in Osaka through the efforts of amateurs who, with a smattering of knowledge of the Euro-American theatre world, staged "Western" dramas in colloquial Japanese. The word *shinpa* continues to be used to describe plays with a contemporary setting. On Mori, see Ozaki H., "*San-nin no joyû o chûshin ni,*" in *Meiji no joyûten,* ed. Hakubutsukan, Meiji-mura (Nagoya: Nagoya-tetsudô, 1986), pp. 14–15.

12. Asagawa Y., "*Joyû to onnayakusha,*" *Josei Nihonjin* 4 (1921):112.

13. Much like Stanislavsky System-based acting schools and theatres in the United States, such as the American Laboratory Theatre and the Goodman School, the Takarazuka Music Academy provides a two-year curriculum designed to teach the students ensemble playing and to equip them with the skills necessary to play a variety of roles. Presently, forty hours a week during the first year are devoted to lessons in voice (ten hours), musical instruments (two), music history (one), Japanese dance (seven), Western dance (seven), modern dance (six), acting and theatre theory (three), and cultural history, performing arts theory, and etiquette (three). The second-year curriculum is essentially the same. Like pupils at the Goodman School, the first-year students are responsible for doing the "dirty work": washing the floors and windows, cleaning the toilets, dusting the furniture, and so on. In the 1960s, the Goodman School posted a 50 percent attrition rate; although students do drop out of the spartan Takarazuka Music Academy, the actual rate of attrition is not made publicly available. See Richard Schechner, "Stanislavski at School," *Tulane Drama Review* 9, no. 2 (1964):203; Ueda Y., *Takarazuka ongaku gakkô* (Tokyo: Yomiuri Raifu, 1986), p. 48; and Ronald Willis, "The American Lab Theatre," *Tulane Drama Review* 9, no. 1 (1964):113.

14. The Meiji period (1868–1912) was marked by both the restoration of the emperor to a ruling position and the promulgation of a European-informed constitution and attendant government offices. Strict distinctions between female and male divisions of labor and deportment were codified in the Civil Code. Generally speaking, the industrialization, militarization, and imperialism of the Meiji period

escalated during the succeeding Taishô (1912–1926) and Shôwa (1926–1989) periods, particularly during the 1930s and 1940s.

15. Kobayashi I., *Takarazuka manpitsu* (Tokyo: Jitsugyô no Nihonsha, 1960), pp. 38, 91.

16. Moore, *The Stanislavski System*, pp. 52, 25.

17. See Rosalind Coward, *Female Desires: How They Are Sought, Bought, and Packaged* (New York: Grove Press, 1985), p. 229.

18. Gunji M., "Kabuki to nô no henshin, henge," *Shizen to Bunka* 19 (1988):4–9; Hattori Y., *Hengeron: Kabuki no seishinshi* (Tokyo: Heibonsha, 1975), pp. 31–35; Ichikawa H., "Mi" no kôzô: Shintairon o koete (Tokyo: Aonisha, 1985), pp. 38–47; Imao T., *Henshin to shisô* (Tokyo: Hôsei Daigaku, 1982), p. 29.

19. *Otoko ga onna ni nari yaku o enjiru. Onna de aru otoko ga yaku o enjiru.*

20. [Konstantin] Stanislavsky, *An Actor Prepares*, trans. Elizabeth Hapgood (New York: Theatre Arts, Inc., 1936), p. 178.

21. Ibid., p. 179.

22. Tobe K., "Sutanisurafusukii shisutemu to kabuki no engi," *Makuai* 5 (1954):47.

23. *Onnagata wa nichijoteki ni onna de aru koto.* Such an *onnagata* is more specifically referred to as *ma no onnagata*, or "true" onnagata, in contradistinction to some present-day Kabuki actors who perform as *onnagata* in addition to a plethora of men's roles.

24. Imao, *Henshin to shisô*, pp. 147–153.

25. Political leadership during the Edo period was monopolized by the Tokugawa clan under the leadership of the shogun, who ruled from the capital city of Edo. The Confucian orientation of the shogunate is reflected in the four-part social status hierarchy, according to which samurai occupied the top rank, followed by farmers, artisans, and merchants. Actors, along with outcastes and criminals, were lumped into a fifth "non-people" category below the merchants. Although individuals of higher status could fall into the lowest category, the inverse was not possible. Kabuki was among the literary, fine, and performing arts whose development accompanied the consolidation of a mercantilistic urban culture during this period.

26. See Jennifer Robertson, "The Politics of Androgyny in Japan: Sexuality and Subversion in the Theatre and Beyond," *American Ethnologist* 19, no. 3 (August 1992):1–24.

27. Kobayashi, *Takarazuka manpitsu*, p. 38.

28. See also Ueda Y., *Takarazuka sutâ: sono engi to bigaku* (Tokyo: Yomiuri Shinbunsha, 1974), pp. 99–100.

29. Sue-Ellen Case, *Feminism and Theatre* (New York: Methuen, 1988), p. 122.

30. Moore, *The Stanislavski System*, p. 3.

31. Kobayashi's interest in girl's and women's education followed the precedent set by Mori Arinori (1847–1889), the leading architect of modern education, who, speaking for the Meiji state, proclaimed that "the foundations of national prosperity rest upon education; the foundations of education upon women's education"; and that the household was the "ultimate school" (Sharon Nolte, "Women, the State, and Repression in Imperial Japan," Women in International Development Working Paper, no. 33. [Lansing: Michigan State University, 1983], p. 5).

32. See Juliet Blair, "Private Parts in Public Places: The Case of Actresses," in

Women and Space: Ground Rules and Social Maps, ed. Shirley Ardener (New York: St. Martin's Press, 1981), p. 205.

33. *Osaka Asahi* (15 May 1939); *Osaka Nichinichi* (20 August 1939); *Kokumin* (6 September 1940); *Osaka Asahi* (20 August 1939); *Osaka Nichinichi* (19 August 1940).

34. *Osaka Chôhô* (7 September 1940); Kamura K., *Itoshi no Takarazuka e* (Kobe: Kobe Shinbun Shuppan Sentâ, 1984), pp. 96–98.

35. Briefly, the works of these sexologists marked the emergence of a "new metaphoric system . . . in which physical disease . . . bespoke social disorder" (Carroll Smith-Rosenberg, *Disorderly Conduct: Visions of Gender in Victorian America* [New York: Oxford University Press, 1985], p. 272). Females were negatively defined in contrast to males as diseased "others" and dismissed as creatures of passion and emotion, immature, small-minded, and prone to sexual deviance. Similar descriptions of females are found in the Confucian literature of the Edo period (1603–1868). For more information on the application of Freud, Ellis, Krafft-Ebing, and Weininger in a strikingly similar context, see Smith-Rosenberg, *Disorderly Conduct*; and her "Discourses of Sexuality and Subjectivity: The New Woman, 1870–1926," in *Hidden from History: Reclaiming the Gay and Lesbian Past,* ed. Martin Duberman, Martha Vicinus, and George Chauncey, Jr. (New York: New American Library, 1989); and George Mosse, *Nationalism and Sexuality: Middle Class Morality and Sexual Norms in Modern Europe* (Madison: University of Wisconsin Press, 1985).

36. *Moga* is an abbreviation of *modan gâru,* or "modern girl."

37. For example, *Osaka Mainichi* (10 February 1932, and 31 January 1935); Sugita M., "*Seihonnô ni hisomu sangyakusei,*" *Kaizô* 4 (1929):70–80, and "*Shôjo kageki netsu no shinden,*" *Fujin Kôron* 4 (1935):274–78; Ushijima Y., *Joshi no shinri* (Tokyo: Ganshodo, 1943); and Yasuda T., "*Dôseiai no rekishikan,*" *Chûô Kôron* 3 (1935):146–52.

38. Sugita, "*Seihonnô ni hisomu sangyakusei*" and "*Shôjo kageki netsu no shinden*"; Tamura T., "*Dôsei no koi,*" *Chûô Kôron* 1 (1913):165–68; Ushijima, *Joshi no shinri*; and *Osaka Mainichi* (31 January 1935).

39. Although *dôseiai* is a generic term for "same-sex love" or homosexual relationships, it is defined more specifically in the *Fujo Shinbun* article as an essentially platonic if passionate relationship.

40. In Fukushima S., *Fujinkai sanjûgonen* (Tokyo: Fuji Shuppansha, 1984 [1935]), p. 561. See also Tamura, "*Dôsei no koi*"; and Yasuda T., "*Dôseiai no rekishikan.*"

41. This is in reference to the fact that the masculinized female was not intersexed but had a "normal" female body.

42. Fukushima, *Fujinkai sanjûgonen,* p. 562.

43. For example, Tamura, "*Dôsei no koi*"; and Yasuda T., "*Dôseiai no rekishikan.*"

44. *Shinkeishitsu* originated around the turn of the century as a category of socio-sexual dis-ease, with special relevance to urban middle-class women (who represented about 30 percent of the female population).

45. *Osaka Nichinichi* (21 July 1930). See also Yoshiwara R., "*Gekkyû shôchôki ni aru musume o motsu okasama e,*" *Fujin Kôron* 3 (1935):187, for essentially the same argument.

46. Kawahara Y., *Takarazuka kageki shôjo no seikatsu* (Osaka: Ikubunkan, 1921), p. 113.

47. *Shin Nippô* (16 March 1929).

48. Kawahara, *Takarazuka kageki shôjo no seikatsu,* p. 16; Nestle, "The Fem Question," in Vance, *Pleasure and Danger: Exploring Female Sexuality,* p. 236.

49. Nestle, "The Fem Question," p. 234.

50. See Maruo C., *Takarazuka sutâ monogatari* (Tokyo: Jitsugyô no Nihonsha, 1950), pp. 252–78; *Osaka Jiji* (12 December 1934); "*Shôjokageki o kataru—musume to haha no kai,*" *Fujin Kôron* 4 (1935):288–97; Tanabe S. and Sasaki K., *Yume no kashi o tabete: waga itoshi no Takarazuka* (Tokyo: Kodansha, 1983), pp. 135–36.

51. *Kyoto* (20 November 1930).

52. *Osaka Asahi* (17 July 1923).

53. De Lauretis, *Technologies of Gender,* p. 5.

54. Kamura, *Itoshi no Takarazuka e,* p. 185; *Takarazuka Gurafu* 1 (1967):54.

55. *Takarazuka Gurafu* 1 (1967):71; 5 (1968):70–71; 4 (1971):49; 7 (1974):68; 7 (1977):38.

56. *Watakushi seikatsu de mo musumeyaku ni narikirô to kyôryoku shite iru.* *Nihonkai* (18 April 1987).

57. *Onna no naka no onna'tte muzukashii no yo. Hankyû* 6 (1987).

58. *Onna de arinagara, zenzen onna to iu mon ga denai. Takarazuka Gurafu* 7 (1974):68.

59. *Takarazuka ga dansei no kyôiku shite-iru.* Kobayashi I., "*Omoitsuki,*" *Kageki* 271 (1948):29.

60. The number of applicants in the postwar period ranges from 579 (57 admitted) in 1946 to 734 (42 admitted) in 1985, with a low of 175 (70 admitted) in 1959 to a high of 1,052 (49 admitted) in 1978 (Ueda, *Takarazuka ongaku gakkô,* p. 25). The 1978 peak reflects the tremendous popularity of the musical, *The Rose of Versailles* (1974–1976), attended by more than 1.4 million persons (Hashimoto M., *Takarazuka kageki no 70 nen* [Takarazuka: Takarazuka Kagekidan, 1984], p. 89).

61. *Jibun no risô o takuseru mono desu. Takarazuka Gurafu* 7 (1986):45.

62. *Takarazuka de wa onna no hito demo otoko no kakkô ga dekiru to iu no de haitta. Takarazuka Gurafu* 12 (1969):39; and 6 (1966):42.

63. *Takarazuka Gurafu* 11 (1976):50–51; and 7 (1977):57–58.

64. For example, *Takarazuka Gurafu* 7 (1986):48–49.

65. *Asahi Shinbun,* Osaka ed. (13 January 1968).

66. Paraphrase of Blair, "Private Parts in Public Places," p. 205.

67. Ibid. I appreciate Blair's perceptive analysis of the social ramifications of "the actress" but am puzzled by her use of "natural" to describe what she otherwise seems to acknowledge is an ideological construction, namely the "private interpersonal sphere of women."

68. See *Asahi Shinbun,* Osaka ed. (29 March 1990); Reiko Atsumi, "Dilemmas and Accommodations of Married Japanese Women in White-Collar Employment," *Bulletin of Concerned Asian Scholars* 20, no. 3 (1988):54–62; and *Japan Times* (10 April 1990).

69. In 1989, the play was revived, ostensibly to satisfy nostalgic "old fans" and attract new fans.

70. Annette Kuhn, *The Power of the Image: Essays on Representation and Sexuality* (London: Routledge and Kegan Paul, 1985), p. 53. See also Komashaku K., *Onna o yosou* (Tokyo: Keiso Shobo, 1989); and Tsuji M., *Niji no fuantajia* (Tokyo: Shinromansha, 1976), pp. 107–30.

71. In Tsuji, *Niji no fuantajia*, pp. 165–66.

72. Kuhn observes that if "clothing can be costume, capable of being modified at the wearer's will, it follows that the gender identity conventionally signified by dress may be just as easily changeable" (*The Power of the Image*, p. 53). What is most problematic with this theoretical statement with respect to the Takarazuka *otokoyaku* is the matter of the "wearer's will." "Will" neither figures in one's initial gender assignment (based on genitalia), nor is a Takarasienne's secondary gender assignment necessarily confluent in every respect with her will.

73. Marie Maclean, *Narrative as Performance: The Baudelairean Experiment* (New York: Routledge, 1988), pp. xi, xii.

74. Kuhn, *The Power of the Image*, p. 53.

Acknowledgments

My fieldwork and archival research in Japan (Tokyo, Kyoto, Takarazuka) were funded by the following fellowships and grants: Japan Foundation Professional Fellowship (June–September 1987); Northeast Asia Council of the Association for Asian Studies Grant (June–September 1987); Social Science Research Council Research Grant (June–September 1987); University of California, San Diego, Japanese Studies Program Travel Grant (Summer 1987); University of California, San Diego, Affirmative Action Faculty Career Development Grant (July–September, November–June 1989–1990); Fulbright Research Grant (January–August 1990 and September–October 1991). Earlier and different versions of this chapter and related articles include: "Gender-Bending in Paradise: Doing 'Female' and 'Male' in Japan," *Genders* 5 (1989):188–207; "Theatrical Resistance, Theaters of Restraint: The Takarazuka Revue and the 'State Theater' Movement," *Anthropological Quarterly* 64, no. 4 (1991):165–177; "The Politics of Androgyny in Japan: Sexuality and Subversion in the Theater and Beyond," *American Ethnologist* 19, no. 3 (1992):1–24. Special thanks to Maria Teresa Koreck for her insightful reading.

All translations from Japanese to English are my own unless otherwise indicated. For Japanese individuals, the family name precedes the given name.

MOE MEYER

Unveiling the Word: Science and Narrative in Transsexual Striptease

❦ It was Sunday night at Club La Cage, and the Holly Brown Show was under way.[1] Just after seeing an obese transvestite on roller skates do an impression of Shirley Temple, I was waiting for the tenth act to begin. The audience appeared to be in various states of intoxication, the smoke-filled lounge loud with chatter that sometimes continued even while the actors were performing. The crowd was in a holiday mood.

The lights dimmed slowly to black, signaling the start of another act. Out of the darkness came the sound of the theme song from the television sitcom "I Dream of Jeannie," an appropriation from pop culture that sent a clear message—we would be experiencing "High Camp," the grandest manifestation of the gay subcultural aesthetic.[2]

The only set piece on the now visible stage was a four-foot-high genie bottle. That, and the cloud of smoke that issued from offstage, marked the entrance of what could only be an impression of Barbara Eden in her role as Jeannie from the television series. No sooner were the signals received than a beautiful impersonator emerged from the cloud, giving a very believable impression of the bosomy blonde star.

Covered by a floor-length, gold lamé cape, the impersonator strutted the length of the stage while the audience responded to the comedy with enthusiastic laughter, screams, and applause. It was still too early to know where Jeannie would go with this act. The television theme song would be over shortly, and the performer would have to surpass the quality of the entrance.

As the song came to a close, Jeannie executed a few spins on her spiked heels, sending yards of gold lamé into the air after the style of Loïe Fuller. As the cape came to rest, she opened it with outstretched arms, displaying a very female figure. A gold lamé halter supported the ample breasts, while scant gold panties barely covered the crotch. Over this was a body harness made up of numerous strands of rhinestones positioned to accent the narrow waist and long legs. We got a good look before the cape closed again.

The crowd became uncommonly silent for a moment. We had been misled. This wasn't a female impersonator; this was a transsexual.[3] A female nude in this venue would be inappropriate and would hold no interest for the predominantly gay male audience. This incongruity was the clue to the transsexual identity of the dancer. The realization complete, the music and attitude onstage changed radically. A soft disco tune, ironically entitled "Jeannie's Got to Go," charged the space with a relentless, pulsing beat. The original impression of Barbara Eden was surrendered, seriousness replaced camp humor, and Jeannie turned her efforts to the dance.

In the remaining four minutes, Jeannie removed her costume piece by piece. Sensuous yet strong walks carried her from one side of the stage to the other; her arms, hands, and wrists moved fluidly while her hips swayed with a suggestive undulation—all meant to signify femininity. Spins and turns created oversized, abstract shapes as the cape billowed about her. Several times in the dance she moved downstage to accept money from approving spectators, enveloping one of them in the folds of her cape as it closed over his face, which was buried in her crotch; her eyes glazed with a studied aura of syrupy desire.

Between these movements, her clothing slowly disappeared. The massive cape would close briefly to obscure the motions of her hands as they undid various fastenings. First, the rhinestone harness was discarded, revealing the smooth skin and hairless body. This was followed by the halter, uncovering large, perfectly formed breasts whose nipples were graced with pasties. The panties were next, leaving Jeannie with nothing but a g-string. As a finale, she pulled down the g-string and executed two full turns to display her artificially created vagina. With the cheesecake completed, she darted offstage as the house went silent and dark. Pause. Applause.

The Transsexual Narrative

I first saw Jeannie's performance in 1988 while carrying out an ethnographic study of female impersonators. The subjects of the fieldwork were the transvestite performers of the Holly Brown Show, an ongoing drag revue staged weekly at La Cage nightclub in Milwaukee, Wisconsin. Several times a year, Jeannie performs as a solo guest artist in the revue, making a colorful addition to the work of the resident company.

I was immediately drawn to her biological realism. It contrasted sharply with the performances of the transvestites whose gender illusions depended on the manipulation of costume and makeup. Jeannie's art, on the other hand, was marked by a process of costume reduction that terminated in a theatrical display of her nude body, something the other performers could not duplicate.

Further comparison, primarily of characterization technique, provided additional distinctions between Jeannie's striptease act and the work of the impersonators. The other drag show performers I have seen achieve success through sustained portrayals of mass culture media stars, which serve as binding referents. Though Jeannie began her dance in character, ostensibly a representation of Barbara Eden, she terminated the impersonation after only one minute into the act. By discarding this convention in mid-performance, Jeannie produced an uncommon and unsettling effect. At first viewing, it seemed that an impersonation was irrelevant to the main body of the performance. Why, then, was a character painstakingly constructed only to be discarded like an article of her clothing?

Paul Bouissac, in his structural analysis of circus acts, has identified key features in the pattern of successive transformations characterizing many of the performances, from acrobats to clowns. He defined the principal divisions as:

1. Identification of the hero, who incidentally is often introduced as a non-autochthon.

2. Qualifying test, which the artist considers a warm-up exercise.

3. Main test, which can consist of several tests presented in a variety of sequences.

4. Glorifying test, which is usually preceded by a special announcement and accompanied by a drum roll.

5. Public acknowledgment of the fulfillment of the task.[4]

He illustrates this sequence in a diagram (fig. 1).

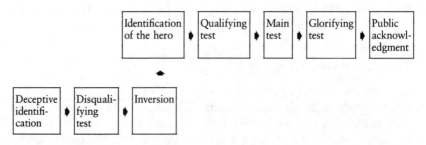

Fig. 1. Progressive stages of acts. Based on Paul Bouissac, *Circus and Culture* (Bloomington: Indiana University Press, 1976), p. 26.

Citing V. Propp's work on the morphology of folk tales, Bouissac observes that this same structure is common to many forms of Western folk theater, of which circus is one.[5] The plots involve the entrance of the hero, who arrives purposefully disguised and therefore unrecognized.[6] After being misidentified by the other characters and/or audience, the hero calls attention to his deception and makes a claim to an alternate and supposedly true identity.

The hero is then required to submit to a series of tests to verify his claim. The tests consist of any series of actions appropriate for validation of the social role claimed by the hero, and their administration forms the basis of the plot. The testing process involves the accomplishment of increasingly difficult tasks, culminating in a finale whose outcome supports, beyond a doubt, the hero's claimed identity.

In my opinion, the drag show falls into this category as the basic folk performance form for the gay male subculture. Jeannie's initial deception as a Barbara Eden impressionist, then, is a necessary precondition for administering the tests. In her exotic dance, the hero—in this case a man who has undergone a sex change—is tested through a progressive disrobing, each article of clothing removed constituting a single test whose revelations lead us on a journey that culminates in a view of the genitals, the ultimate test of the dancer in support of her claim to a transsexual identity. Incidentally, Propp states that the final identification is often made by recognition of a wound or other idiosyncratic mark that the hero alone is known to possess.[7] In Jeannie's act, this identifying mark would be the surgical alteration whose display is both the purpose and culmination of the performance.

Using Bouissac's diagram and divisions of the process of heroic identification, I outline Jeannie's dance as follows:

1. She arrives, a heroine disguised as Barbara Eden. This disguise sets the scene so that the dancer can claim an alternative and true identity, making it necessary to submit herself to the tests of proof.

2. The first opening of the cape to display her body in tableau serves both to disqualify her as Barbara Eden and to make an initial claim to a transsexual identity. At this moment, a liminal moment when the performer is between representations, the character is inverted, neither one character nor the other.

3. The main test, consisting of several subtests, is the removal of individual costume pieces. In sequence, she removes the rhinestone body harness to reveal the female silhouette; the halter to display the breasts; the panties, which only partially expose the crotch.

4. The glorifying test, the finale, is the removal of the g-string, forcing the audience to inspect her genitals, the proof final of the hero's—or heroine's—sociosexual status.

5. The objective being met, the public offers acknowledgment in the form of applause.

Why is Jeannie's deceptive impression of Barbara Eden necessary to the performance? What function does this theatrical structure play in the interpretation of transsexual striptease?

Miss Bobbi St. Charles, who worked as a professional female impersonator in Chicago from 1972 to 1979, says he has seen the device of the
introductory deceptive impression used by many performing transsexuals.
This practice, he told me in an interview on 8 April 1989, was "to freak
out the audience, of course." In other words, the realization of the transsexual identity of the performer was most effective when the cueing mechanism contained the element of surprise.

In terms of the drag show revue, the revelatory shock accompanying
recognition of the transsexual's status was necessary for the dance's inclu-
sion. Complete clothing removal by a female would not occur in a drag
show. To clarify the intention of the performance, Jeannie first had to create
a link to the conventions of female impersonators. Through the Barbara
Eden impression executed in a camp aesthetic, she fulfilled audience expectations of the genre's style of sexual representation while simultaneously aligning herself to the subcultural values of the audience. Without
her doing so, there could be confusion or possible resentment in the presence of female eroticism on a stage presumably dominated by same-gender
male sexuality. The shock or "freak-out" induced by Jeannie is, then, a
justification.

Just in case a few audience members have not made a successful identification, Holly Brown—the show's director—comes out after Jeannie's
dance and tells them, "Don't get yourself too worked up over her. It's all
man-made." On all levels of production, the goal of the performance is
proper identification of the transsexual body.

Jeannie also does striptease in Las Vegas nightclubs for a nongay audience and with co-performers who are biological females. The fact that
she is a transsexual is never revealed and is irrelevant under these circumstances. But when the act is performed as part of the drag show, it is the
transsexual body, not the female body, that becomes the object of the gaze.
It is the introductory deceptive impression that is responsible for the subtle
shift from female to transsexual subject. Simultaneously, the transfer engages a plot borrowed from the narrative of the mythic hero.

Teresa de Lauretis has explained that the mythic narrative can be reduced to a transaction between a hero and an obstacle. The story defines
"two positions of a sexual difference thus conceived: male-hero-human . . .
and female-object-boundary-space."[8] This marking of sexual difference in
the mythic narrative—its very goal according to Lauretis[9]—explains why
Jeannie's introductory deceptive impression can produce a transsexual
subject.

When Jeannie wishes to appear as a biological female in a nongay nightclub, there is no attempt to work through a mythic narrative. She thus
dances a straightforward striptease with a single female image. But by en-

gaging the mythic narrative in the drag show, she introduces the hero who, appearing as a female impersonator, functions as a male signifier overlaying and containing the female dancing image. Her clothing removal then reads as a series of tests or female obstacles that, by spatializing the feminine body through segmentation, sexually differentiates it from the male hero in the abrupt transition from Barbara Eden impression to striptease dance. Simultaneously acting as male-hero and female-obstacle, the transsexual becomes both subject *and* object of the performance, a double identification with both gaze and image.

The two versions of Jeannie's dance—gay and nongay, transsexual and female subject—suggest that it is the narrative collapse of gaze and image that produces the transsexual. To support this contention, I have noted the deployment of this narrative sequence in the sex-change surgery itself. Both the transsexual identity and physical body are brought into existence through an identical narrative, in an example of what Lauretis describes as "a subject engendered precisely by the process of its engagement in narrative genres."[10] The structure of Jeannie's performance becomes a quotation of the surgical theory and procedure of the sex-change operation.

Before I argue this point I want to look first at the particular character chosen by the performer in the deceptive impression. Not just an impersonation of a media star—Barbara Eden—but the particular role played by that actress is my point of departure for deconstructing Jeannie's exotic dance. Exposing the identity of the narrative's hero is a necessary "test" that, if passed, will reveal an ideological framework that supports the hidden seams joining scientific knowledge and narrative.

The Fallen Woman

Jeannie's introductory double impression of Barbara Eden in her role as a sitcom character—also named Jeannie—fulfills a dual presentational aesthetic that is a particular responsibility of a transsexual stripper in a drag show. This responsibility is manifested in the need to present simultaneously two images of women. The drag show performer utilizes a convention of impersonating larger-than-life women whose images are appropriated from pop and mass culture; while, as Roland Barthes has noted, the stripper adopts representations of the Exotic Other.[11]

Jeannie cleverly responded to the situation by creating an impression of a pop star in her television role as an exotic, oriental female. The sitcom "I Dream of Jeannie" portrays the title character as an oriental genie possessing unlimited magical powers together with the alluring sexual attributes of a voluptuous woman, magnified by a vulnerable naïveté. Dressed in the garb of a harem girl, Barbara Eden's character is a peculiar interface of the dynamic, erotic woman and Daddy's little girl.

This double-edged femininity, the erotic and the domestic, forms the core of that type of television comedy called "battle of the sexes." The plots revolve around a domestic woman, usually a housewife, forced into a strait-jacketed, superficial existence whose efforts toward independence are continually thwarted by the husband. She attempts to liberate herself by becoming the erotic and exotic, often with an arsenal of cruel and practical jokes. The husband's efforts to restrain the naughty girl and the game of mental chess that follows result in comedy.

The representation of exoticism teamed with naughtiness is, perhaps, most extreme with Barbara Eden's Jeannie. Yet it is echoed to varying degrees in numerous other sitcoms: for example, the character of Lisa Douglas in "Green Acres" and Samantha Stevens in "Bewitched." Even that seminal entertainment "I Love Lucy" achieves its status through Lucy's continual conflict between wife/mother and show girl.

Barbara Eden's oriental exotic, Jeannie, is a simplistic character seen as humorous in a contemporary sitcom; yet the motivation behind her disruptive antics is a clearly articulated erotic impulse. This all-powerful harem girl will stop at nothing to win the heart of the show's male protagonist, even if it requires placing him in uncomfortable if not actually life-threatening situations. Take away the canned laughter from her enactments of violence, and Jeannie emerges not as the naughty girl but as the evil woman. As such, Jeannie is clearly a recent representation of the *femme fatale,* the image of feminine evil inherited from the nineteenth century during which it achieved a spectacular prominence.

The *fin-de-siècle femme fatale* was a woman of independence, seducing and then leading men to their doom as sacrifices to her self-indulgent sexual desires. Far from being comic, this free-thinking woman was seen as a deadly threat to upstanding men and society in general. This concept of Woman was symbolized by the oriental female, often portrayed as a dancing girl. The oriental female as a symbol for the erotic and independent woman, the antithesis of the domestic wife, evolved from a nineteenth-century representation of a sexualized Orient, an erotic landscape on which were projected the sexual fantasies of repressed Victorian culture.[12]

It is not difficult to understand the public furor and charges of indecency that surrounded the appearance of a generation of oriental, exotic, Salome, hootchy-kootchy, and Little Egypt dancers at the end of the century. It wasn't that the dances themselves were obscene but that the connection between the oriental female and erotic sex was firmly fixed in the American mind. In the public's eye, the oriental female was a metaphor for the sexual act.[13]

Having been yoked to notions of sex, the image of the oriental dancing girl became a convenient repository for erotic characterization in general, a site wherein multiple concepts of Victorian sexuality could converge to find expression through a single representation. The image of the oriental female as a sexual metaphor thus found an additional application as an image of the prostitute.[14]

The *femme fatale*/prostitute image established itself as the visual representation of one side of the binary concept of Woman, wherein she was defined either as asexual and domestic or erotic and independent. Like Barbara Eden's Jeannie, she was both "the virgin and the whore, the saint and the vampire—two designates for a single dualistic opposition: that of woman as man's exclusive and forever pliable private property, on the one hand, into a polyandrous predator indiscriminately lusting after man's seminal essence, on the other."[15]

The implicit evil within the image of the *femme fatale* was not simply fantasy. The paintings and posed photographs of Arab harem girls, Indian nautch girls and maharanis and the perennial dancing nymphs provided a concrete visual articulation and an aesthetic imagery for the women of commerce whose proliferation pressed itself ever more noticeably upon the public landscape; for while the *femme fatale* flourished in art, prostitution was flourishing in nineteenth-century America.[16] Outside of marriage and domesticity, women had few options for achieving economic independence other than factory labor or prostitution. In such a situation, it was not surprising that so many women chose the more viable economics of the streets. This choice between extremes only reinforced the concept of women as virgins or whores. It was there to see, enacted in daily life.

The fear and sexual evil that permeated the image of the oriental dancing girl was a projection of the hostility expressed toward the prostitute. Her independence was blamed as the cause of all social ills: violent crime, disease epidemics, social anarchy, economic ruin, atheism, and the spiritual rot of American culture.[17]

But help was on its way. Victorian medical theory joined the concepts of the *femme fatale* and the prostitute to create the cultural paradigm of the Fallen Woman, a female pathology of erotic sex in which all sexual practice outside marriage and reproduction was treated as a disease symptom.[18] This belief in a biological source of morality, with its roots in social Darwinism and developed by medical thought on prostitution, had far-reaching social effects. "It presumed a . . . female deviance based on sexual inclination rather than specific acts of misconduct"[19] and shifted the basis of diagnosis from the body to the psyche and, finally, to lifestyle. The prostitute was diseased because she had the *potential* to engage in some types of sexuality. Michel Foucault has discussed how this ideology, freed from specifically physical symptomology, was extended to encompass diagnosis based solely on the *object* of sexual desire.[20]

The Fallen Man

The pathologizing of the prostitute opened the door for extending this diagnosis to homosexuals.[21] Because of their potential or desire to engage in some types of sexuality, homosexuals joined prostitutes in the medical line-up. The newly arrived medical science of sexual aberrations described the homosexual as "a personage, a past, a case history, and a childhood, in addition to being a type of life, a life form, and a morphology." In fact, the term "homosexual" was invented only in 1869 as part of the developing vocabulary in the field of sexology.[22]

"The majority of researchers believe that self-identified gay people are strictly a phenomenon of the last 75–100 years,"[23] one factor in the development of a public sexual identity that "was part of the contemporaneous debate over an ideological definition of housewife and mother,"[24] on the one hand, and the erotic and independent woman on the other; a debate that resulted in the invention of the homosexual. Homosexuality, though previously considered a sin that could be committed by any man, was fixed by medical literature into a "type" of personality that exists independent of specific sexual activity.[25]

The number and visibility of prostitutes had provided the impetus for pathologizing sexual misconduct, the diagnoses being based on the application of visual criteria to public deportment; but which features of the nineteenth-century homosexual subculture were making it noticeable to the medical community? The sexual act itself was practiced behind closed doors, so what exactly were scientists seeing? Which behaviors and activities, if not explicitly sexual, were being used as the criteria for classification?

The clear separation of males and females while socializing in the nineteenth century meant that men, when not at home, spent their time in the company of other men. Two men together, as opposed to contemporary social interpretation, would not have indicated homosexuality. In fact Peter Gay believes that gay men were safe from discovery in a Victorian culture precisely because same-sex socializing and companionship was the norm.[26] As is known today, most gay men are unrecognizable from their nongay counterparts. Who were the medical researchers observing?

I assert that, because of their extreme visibility and because homosexuality was automatically associated with them, the new classification was derived from observations of effeminate men and transvestites. In the early stages of concept formation about homosexuals, acts of cross-dressing became, at times, the only distinguishing feature with which to identify homosexuals; consequently, many scientists believed that transvestites constituted the entire social subgroup.

"The earliest descriptions of homosexuals do not coincide exactly with the modern conception. There is much more stress on effeminacy and in particular on transvestism, to such an extent that there seems to be no distinction at first between homosexuality and transvestism."[27] The equation of transvestism with homosexuality was firmly established in the foundational medical studies.[28] As late as 1934, scientific writers such as Wilhelm Stekel vehemently disagreed with Havelock Ellis's initial conceptual separation of the two terms, stating that he was confusing the issues and was erroneous in attempting to separate cross-dressing from homosexuality.[29]

Among the invert population itself, the association of homosexuality with transvestism was no less marked. Effeminate and cross-dressing men defined themselves as homosexual. Their partners, if not exhibiting such outward behavior, were classified as heterosexual by both the gay and non-gay publics regardless of their participation in same-gender sexual activity.[30] George Chauncey, in his analysis of courtroom and other public documents of the era, concluded that it was not sexual activity that labeled a man homosexual but his choice and use of particular signifying gestures of social gender role enactment.[31]

The specific disease these transvestite-homosexuals suffered from was "gender inversion." The term and accompanying discourse developed from the writing of Karl Ulrichs, an activist lawyer for homosexual rights in Germany, who saw the homosexual as a "third sex" in whom the soul of a woman is trapped in the body of a man.[32] The invert was seen as a type of hermaphrodite whose condition was manifested in a mind/body split. The body was male, but the mind was female. The supposed characteristics of homosexuality, "passion, emotional ill-discipline, and sexual looseness,"[33] were those associated with the Fallen Woman. It was the feminine evil of the homosexual psyche that formed the link to Victorian medical theory and brought about its conception as a form of female sexual pathology.

Returning to the striptease dance, Jeannie's oriental dancing girl also reads as an image of the nineteenth-century gender invert whose transvestism links him to the paradigm of the Fallen Woman/prostitute through specific representation of the erotic. Both historically and in this stage act, the transsexual body is prefigured in a display of the sexualized Exotic Other.

Inventing the Transsexual

The study on male sexuality issued by Alfred Kinsey in 1948 was a major factor in the social redefinition of homosexuality. Kinsey's report indicated that the number of homosexuals was far greater than had been imagined. His figures suggested that as many as 37 percent of all men had engaged in homosexual activity and that 10 percent were actively homosexual at the time. Prior to this report, it was believed, by some authorities, that homosexuals constituted only .1 percent of the population.[34]

The Kinsey report not only brought about a new understanding of the prevalence of homosexuality but reconceptualized the gay personality and social role. Gay men, it was found, could and usually did look and act like heterosexual men. This discovery was a radical development, breaking with past models that saw homosexuals as effeminate. The study was as surprising a revelation to the gay community as it was to nongay Americans.[35] The minority status of transvestites within this group was finally established. The transvestite-homosexual link had been broken.

Though the classification of "invert" had faded from usage, now replaced by the "homosexual" of Kinsey's report, the particular pathology indicated by the former term found a new application under another name. In the 1960s, a condition known as "transsexualism" took the place of the older "gender inversion."[36] One of the leading medical authorities, Erwin K. Koranyi, defines the transsexual as one who is "anatomically a man by current available biological measurements, but with a distinct core identity of a woman, the male transsexual feels, grows up, acts and behaves as closely to the female as he can."[37] But lest we forget what is really being discussed here, Koranyi adds that "their identity is often described as 'females, locked in a male's body.'" He goes on to state that transsexuals like to spend their time engaging in female social behavior. Specific activities leading to diagnosis are suggested, such as "girltalk and shopping."[38]

These beliefs clearly have their source in the discourse on the "third sex" of Karl Ulrichs, while the definition of the transsexual remains identical to nineteenth-century writings on "gender inversion." What is different are the demographics. No longer confusing transvestites and homosexuals, as before, the medical community prefers to see transsexualism as an extremely rare psychic disturbance, by no means to be confused with homosexuality.[39]

The sex-change operation, or conversion therapy, is now an accepted cure for the transsexual condition, eliminating the psychological self-perception that one is a woman trapped in a man's body.[40] There is one flaw, though, in this medical narrative of mega-cure: that is, the term "transsexual" was not invented until the early 1960s and was not in medical usage until the late sixties and early seventies. When Christine Jorgenson submitted to her sex-change operation in 1953, there had been twenty-eight prior surgeries performed between 1932 and 1952.[41] Conversion therapy predates the condition it is supposed to cure by almost three decades!

The implications of this surgical dating are, first, that the sex-change surgery was to have been a cure for "gender inversion," a hi-tech surgical intervention that would harmonize the mind/body split of the invert; and, second, that the concept of transsexualism was based on outdated theories discontinued in the academy in order to provide the new technology with a justification after the demise of "gender inversion" as a legitimate area of research. I do not think it beyond coincidence that Christine Jorgenson became a celebrated techno-body immediately following the release of the Kinsey report, with its attendant reconceptualization of homosexuality.

The pathological condition known as transsexualism did not achieve recognition as a distinct condition until the late sixties and early seventies. I suggest that this differentiation was connected with the rise of the Gay Liberation Movement. Beginning in the late sixties, militant gay activists mounted an intensive attack on medical authority, which forced the American Psychiatric Association to remove homosexuality from its index of mental disorders in 1973. The loss of control over the issue of homosexuality—the medical community's great bastion of nineteenth-century sexual pathology—was an attack against the cultural legitimacy of the profession, calling into question its privileged position regarding social morality. John D'Emilio has argued that the last century's discourse on sexology formed the basis for a professional narrative on social and cultural legitimation, a major tool in the acquisition of political power.[42] The 1973 victory of gay activists thus represented not only an assault on the discourse of a specific pathology but an attack against one of the profession's metanarratives.

Rather than humbly relinquishing theories of "gender inversion," the community recognized transsexualism as a symbolic pathology where antiquated beliefs in a biological source of morality could be played out. This realignment resulted in a curious, but perhaps not uncommon, phenomenon in American medicine—the cure predating the disease. The discrepancy did not escape attention. In *Hartin v. Director of Bureau of Records,* New York State (1973), the court described the sex-change operation as "an experimental form of psychotherapy in which mutilating surgery is conducted on a person with the intent of setting his mind at ease."[43] Though the American Medical Association has successfully appealed this law that refused to grant female gender status to their sexually reassigned clients, the surgery is still perceived by many as having no therapeutic value. The question I ask is, What exactly is being performed by the surgeons during the conversion therapy? When attention is directed away from the transsexual body and directed toward the physician, an interesting hypothesis emerges.

Letting the Genie Out of the Bottle

According to descriptions by Harry Benjamin, Deborah Feinbloom, and Erwin Koranyi,[44] conversion therapy is performed in phases over the course of several years. The procedure is initiated by ordering the patient to assume a female social role in full female attire. Next are the external alterations, including electrolysis, estrogen therapy to create a female silhouette, addition of breast prostheses, and cosmetic surgery to feminize facial features. This step is followed by surgery consisting of castration, amputation of the penis, and creation of the vagina. After surgery, the patient receives a new set of legal documents such as birth certificate, passport, and so on, which confer a female social status.

The sex-change surgery and conversion therapy follow the folk performance plot based on the mythic narrative identified by Bouissac, which is also operative in Jeannie's striptease act. The familiar process of testing and heroic identification manifested in transsexual stage performance are again detected in the therapy. I outline the five stages of the folk plot as follows:

1. The patient arrives with the false identity of a biological male. He makes a claim to an alternate and true identity—a woman. This claim sets the scene, making it necessary to submit the patient to tests of proof.

2. The disqualifying test is given by the physician. The hero, still possessing the physical attributes of a male, is ordered to live, work, dress, and pass as a woman in daily life for a period of exactly one year. During this phase, the character is inverted, a liminal moment when the performer is between representations, neither one character nor the other.

3. The main test, consisting of several subtests, is the removal or alteration of individual body parts. In sequence, the transsexual, through the agency of the physician, removes body hair, removes Adam's apple, takes female hormones to begin breast development, hip enlargement, and shrinking of the penis, receives breast prostheses and cosmetic alterations of the face, removes testicles, and amputates the penis.

4. The glorifying test, the finale, is the creation of the vagina, the proof positive of the hero's—or heroine's—sociosexual status.

5. The objective being met, the public offers acknowledgment in the form of a recognized legal status and a new set of public documents.

Evidenced by its repetition, the main theme of this performance is inversion. There are the obvious examples of this theme—the theories of gender inversion that inform the surgery—as well as more interesting manifestations. Notable among these is Bouissac's use of the term theatrical "inversion" in his diagram. In this surgical example, Bouissac's character inversion occurs precisely at the moment the patient assumes a social role that is identical to nineteenth century descriptions of gender inverts. In addition, the creation of the vagina is described by surgeons as "genital inversion," a literal and physical inverting of the male organs to create female ones.

The concept of genital inversion has its origins in a medical discourse that predates nineteenth-century theory by more than one thousand years. The fourth-century physiologist, Nemesius of Syria, put forth that "women have the same genitals as men, except theirs are inside the body and not outside it."[45] This belief dominated medical education from Galen to the seventeenth century, when anatomical textbooks could be found depicting the vagina as an inverted penis.[46]

The discovery of the theme of inversion in conversion therapy indicates that medical practice is not the linear evolutionary advance of scientific knowledge that is professed by physicians. To follow a line of thought initiated by Michel Foucault and Susan Sontag, medical science is, in any given procedure, a conglomeration of images, theories, beliefs, and technologies drawn from a variety of sources and assembled into what I call a "therapeutic score."[47] There may be more than a suggestion that medical science is itself a narrative genre, a complex tradition of folk theatre whose performers are known as physicians.

At first, it would appear that the active figure in Jeannie's striptease dance is Jeannie herself. I maintain that her dance is the *surgeon's* performance. Both the transsexual identity and the physical body of the dancer are creations of medical science. The striptease could not have been presented without the surgeon's prior labor. His presence, even on the stage of the drag show, is implicit at all times.

Transsexuals are classified as preoperative before surgery and postoperative afterward. This vocabulary defines the transsexual by her relationship to the surgeon's activities, establishing the centrality of the medical practitioner. Transsexuals also use the appellations of "Pre-op" and "Post-op" in self-description to clarify the relationship.

The active role played by the physician is often resented by the patients, who sometimes feel the practitioner's demands are unreasonable and that they are being forced, against their better judgment, into compliance with a therapeutic score that is not always rational. A TV broadcast of "The Sally Jessy Raphael Show" on 15 May 1989 presented a panel of preoperative transsexuals. One of them, speaking about the tests administered by the physician, stated that the demand that they live and pass for women in daily life for one year in order to qualify as "true" transsexuals was an alogical directive that put them in a vulnerable position and subject to possible public attack. Many of them must perform this task before physical alteration occurs, while still bearing recognizable characteristics of biological men and before they can achieve an ideal social gender image. Statements like these amount to textual criticism and locate the transsexuals as an outsider to the surgeon's performance.

The comments made by some transsexuals concerning the difficulties of the required year spent as a transvestite prior to surgery answer a major question regarding transsexual origins. If transsexualism is a medical model originating in outdated nineteenth-century discourse, then where do physicians find men who still identify themselves as gender inverts in a society that has renounced homosexuality as a pathology?

I assert that the transsexual is created during the first-year test in which he is ordered to become a transvestite in daily life. The surgeon demands that this task be fulfilled in order to confirm a transsexual identity. Yet, in reality, the process forces the patient into conformation with the pre-established medical model and its mythic narrative. The first-year therapy amounts to an educational program in which the subject is trained to look and act like a nineteenth-century gender invert. This being accomplished, the surgeon has created his transsexual—a homosexual golem—who can now be put through conversion therapy.

The mythic narrative used by Jeannie in her dance is a representation of the surgical procedure itself, while conversion therapy dictates the striptease aesthetic. As performed by Jeannie, the unveiling of her body is accomplished utilizing the same pattern of successive transformations that unfolds in the sex-change surgery. Beginning with the mistaken identity of the performer, followed by the process of identification, and then in the exposure of body parts that are viewed in a temporal progression identical to the surgeon's handiwork sequence—all this amounts to scientific display, a showcase for medical technology.

The duplication by the striptease of the surgical plot gives evidence that each is bound to the other through a folk narrative that has been engaged both to define and justify its object. In this regard, Jean-François Lyotard has discussed at length the reliance of scientific knowledge upon narrative.[48] He argues that scientific knowledge can only claim its status by positing narrative as an Other against which to define itself, and that efforts toward legitimation and validation of scientific knowledge must necessarily invoke narrative in the process. Further, "knowledge is only worthy of that name to the extent that it reduplicates itself by citing its own statements in a second-level discourse that functions to legitimate itself."[49]

Jeannie has only one narrative to express, and that is the one that gave her birth and in which she experiences existence—the Victorian myth of the gender invert. The transsexual striptease, then, is an integral part of the surgery, functioning as a second-level discourse that legitimates the statements of scientific knowledge through citation on the stage. Her dance is a reduplication of the folk narrative which serves as the Logos of the transsexual body while providing the repetition of discourse needed to elevate its first utterance to the status of scientific knowledge.

Without a way to reduplicate itself, the ideology and legitimacy of the sex-change surgery would dissolve, and the striptease would vanish. Without cultural legitimacy, Jeannie would be trapped in a bottle, a no-exit techno-body stripped of meaning. Like her stage character's prototype— Salome—she celebrates the body while flirting with death; for as long as she dances, both the transsexual body and its creative narrative can feed off each other, prolonging life and knowledge.

Notes

1. Holly Brown, director, *The Easter Re-Run Show*, Club La Cage, Milwaukee, Wisconsin, 3 April 1988.

2. For definitions of camp, see Michael Bronski, *Culture Clash: The Making of Gay Sensibility* (Boston: South End Press, 1984), pp. 43–44, 97, 126–27; Joseph P. Goodwin, *More Man Than You'll Ever Be: Gay Folklore and Acculturation in Middle America* (Bloomington: Indiana University Press, 1989), pp. 38–40; Morris Meyer, "Glamour as Environmental Art," *High Performance* 26 (Spring 1984):34–35, 82, 86; and Esther Newton, *Mother Camp: Female Impersonators in America* (Chicago: University of Chicago Press, 1972), pp. 104–11.

3. For reasons that I will argue in this essay, I define the "transsexual" as one who has a direct relationship with medical authority through engagement in conversion therapy, that is, the sex-change surgery. This definition includes those preparing for, are in the process of, or have completed therapy. I have also limited the study to male-to-female transsexuals, since the female-to-male may be expressing a different narrative that is not within the scope of this paper to explicate adequately.

4. Paul Bouissac, *Circus and Culture: A Semiotic Approach* (Bloomington: Indiana University Press, 1976), p. 25.

5. Ibid.

6. V. Propp, *Morphology of the Folktale* (Austin: University of Texas Press, 1968), p. 60.

7. Ibid.

8. Teresa de Lauretis, *Alice Doesn't: Feminism, Semiotics, Cinema* (Bloomington: Indiana University Press, 1984), p. 121.

9. Ibid.

10. de Lauretis, *Alice Doesn't*, p. 108.

11. Roland Barthes, "Striptease," in *What Is Dance?*, ed. Roger Copeland and Marshall Cohen (Oxford: Oxford University Press, 1983), p. 512.

12. Edward Said, *Orientalism* (New York: Vintage Books, 1978), pp. 184–90.

13. In this regard, it is of interest to note the difficulties Ruth St. Denis had in attracting an audience. So strongly was oriental dancing linked to sex that it took more than a decade for her to establish and reeducate an audience to experience more than sexual titillation from her art. See David Dressler, "Burlesque as a Cultural Phenomenon" (Ph.D. diss., New York University, 1937), p. 54; Olga Maynard, *American Modern Dance* (Boston: Little Brown, 1965), p. 83; Joseph H. Mazo, *Prime Moves* (New York: Morrow, 1977), pp. 94–96; Walter Terry, *The*

Dance in America (New York: Harper and Row, 1956), p. 49; and Irving Zeidman, *The American Burlesque Show* (New York: Hawthorn Books, 1967), p. 13.

14. John D'Emilio and Estelle B. Freedman, *Intimate Matters: A History of Sexuality in America* (New York: Harper and Row, 1988), pp. 132–34.

15. Bram Dijkstra, *Idols of Perversity: Fantasies of Feminine Evil in Fin-de-Siecle Culture* (Oxford: Oxford University Press, 1986), p. 334.

16. D'Emilio and Freedman, *Intimate Matters*, pp. 130–38.

17. Barbara Meil Hobson, *Uneasy Virtue: The Politics of Prostitution and the American Reform Tradition* (New York: Basic Books, 1987), pp. 111–14.

18. Charles Baudelaire, *The Painter of Modern Life and Other Essays* [1863], trans. Jonathan Mayne (New York: Garland, 1978), pp. 36–37; Vern L. Bullough, "Homosexuality and the Medical Model," *Journal of Homosexuality* 1 (1974):103; Estelle B. Freedman, "Sexuality in Nineteenth-Century America: Behavior, Ideology, and Politics," *Reviews in American History* 10 (December 1982):203–5; John S. Haller and Robin M. Haller, *The Physician and Sexuality in Victorian America* (Urbana: University of Illinois Press, 1974):91; and J. K. Huysmans, *Against Nature* [1884], trans. Robert Baldick (New York: Penguin Books, 1959), pp. 65–66.

19. Hobson, p. 114.

20. Michel Foucault, *The History of Sexuality,* vol. 1, *An Introduction,* trans. Robert Hurley (New York: Vintage Books, 1980), pp. 19–22, 40–41.

21. Jeffrey Weeks, "Movements of Affirmation: Sexual Meanings and Homosexual Identities," *Radical History Review* 20 (Spring/Summer 1979):168.

22. Foucault, *History of Sexuality*; Peter Gay, *The Tender Passion,* vol. 2, *The Bourgeois Experience: Victoria to Freud* (Oxford: Oxford University Press, 1986), p. 224.

23. Martin Bauml Duberman, "Reclaiming the Gay Past," *Reviews in American History* 4 (December 1988):519.

24. Weeks, "Movements of Affirmation."

25. Bullough, "Homosexuality and the Medical Model," p. 1983; George Chauncey, Jr., "From Sexual Inversion to Homosexuality: Medicine and the Changing Conceptualization of Female Deviance," *Salmagundi* 58–59 (Fall-Winter 1983):114–46; D'Emilio and Freedman, *Intimate Matters*, pp. 109–38; Foucault, *History of Sexuality*; Gay, *The Tender Passion,* pp. 222–35; Weeks, "Movements of Affirmation."

26. Gay, *The Tender Passion,* p. 202.

27. Mary McIntosh, "The Homosexual Role," in *The Making of the Modern Homosexual,* ed. Kenneth Plummer (London: Hutchinson, 1981), p. 37.

28. Peter Ackroyd, *Dressing Up: Transvestism and Drag. The History of an Obsession* (New York: Simon and Schuster, 1979), pp. 25, 62; Harry Brierly, *Transvestism: A Handbook with Case Studies for Psychologists, Psychiatrists, and Counselors* (Oxford: Pergamon Press, 1979), pp. x, 10; Havelock Ellis, *Studies in the Psychology of Sex* (New York: Random House, 1936), pp. 1–110; Jonathan Katz, *Gay American History* (New York: Thomas Y. Crowell, 1976), pp. 39–52; John Marshall, "Pansies, Perverts, and Macho Men: Changing Conceptions of Male Homosexuality," in *The Making of the Modern Homosexual,* ed. Kenneth Plummer (London: Hutchinson, 1981), p. 146; Richard von Krafft-Ebing, *Psychopathia Sexualis: A Medico-Forensic Study* [1886] (New York: Putnam Brothers, 1969), pp. 61–383.

29. Dave King, "Gender Confusions," in *The Making of the Modern Homosexual,* ed. Kenneth Plummer (London: Hutchinson, 1981), pp. 163–64.

30. Quentin Crisp, *The Naked Civil Servant* (New York: Holt, Rinehart and Winston, 1977).

31. George Chauncey, Jr., "Christian Brotherhood or Sexual Perversion? Homosexual Identities and the Construction of Sexual Boundaries in the World War One Era," *Journal of Social History* (Winter 1985):189–211.

32. James D. Steakley, *The Homosexual Emancipation Movement in Germany* (New York: Arno, 1975), pp. 6–8.

33. Simon Sheperd, "Gay Sex Spy Orgy: The State's Need for Queers," in *Coming on Strong: Gay Politics and Culture,* ed. Simon Sheperd and Mick Wallis (London: Unwin Hyman, 1989), p. 214.

34. Erwin K. Koranyi, *Transsexuality in the Male: The Spectrum of Gender Dysphoria* (Springfield, Ill.: Charles Thomas, 1980), p. 21.

35. John D'Emilio, *Sexual Politics, Sexual Communities: The Making of a Homosexual Minority in the United States, 1940–1970* (Chicago: University of Chicago Press, 1983), p. 37.

36. Harry Benjamin, *The Transsexual Phenomenon* (New York: Julian Press, 1966), p. 14; King, "Gender Confusions," pp. 171–72.

37. Koranyi, *Transsexuality in the Male,* p. 27.

38. Ibid.

39. Ibid., pp. 25–28.

40. Ibid., pp. 111, 127.

41. King, "Gender Confusions," pp. 171–72.

42. D'Emilio and Freedman, *Intimate Matters,* pp. 146–47.

43. Koranyi, *Transsexuality in the Male,* p. 111.

44. Benjamin, *The Transsexual Phenomenon*; Deborah Heller Feinbloom, *Transvestites and Transsexuals: Mixed Views* (New York: Delta, 1976); Koranyi, *Transsexuality in the Male.*

45. Emily Martin, *The Woman in the Body: A Cultural Analysis of Reproduction* (Boston: Beacon Press, 1987), p. 27.

46. Ibid., pp. 28–29.

47. Michel Foucault, *The Birth of the Clinic: An Archaeology of Medical Perception,* trans. A. M. Sheridan Smith (New York: Vintage Books, 1975), p. 199; Susan Sontag, *AIDS and Its Metaphors* (New York: Farrar, Straus and Giroux, 1988), p. 8.

48. Jean-François Lyotard, *The Postmodern Condition: A Report on Knowledge,* trans. Geoff Bennington and Brian Massumi (Minneapolis: University of Minnesota Press, 1984).

49. Ibid., p. 38.

ERIKA FISCHER-LICHTE

Between Difference and Indifference: Marianne Hoppe in Robert Wilson's *Lear*

❦ The beginning reads like a fairy tale. After producing a string of operas such as *Einstein on the Beach* (1976), *Death, Destruction & Detroit* (1979), and *the CIVIL warS* (1983/4), and prior to moving on to direct plays, Robert Wilson had long nursed the idea of doing Shakespeare's *King Lear*. Each serious attempt to convert the somewhat vague idea into a concrete project had foundered when it came to casting. No one fitted his concept of Lear. Then, by chance, in 1988 he met Marianne Hoppe in the theatre in Frankfurt and promptly spoke of nothing but "Marianne." Wilson seemed to have found the ideal lead in the then 77-year-old actress:

Marianne Hoppe is King Lear. She is the right age, she has the right face, the right image. And she has the strength to speak Shakespeare's language without interpreting it, simply, full of emotion. And I believe this comes closest to the work itself.[1]

The production premiered in Frankfurt in late May 1990. Among critics, it provoked a somewhat mixed if not negative reaction. Helmut Schödel from *Die Zeit* pronounced it "frankly a flop" and proclaimed that Wilson was a failure in directing Shakespeare.[2] Peter Iden from the *Frankfurter Rundschau* came to the conclusion "that despite all his talent for the artificial, Robert Wilson has not come close to the play itself."[3]

A similarly mixed response dominated the appraisal of Marianne Hoppe's Lear. For all their admiration for her great artistic effort, the critics felt obliged to criticize her for the very same reason that Wilson cast her as Lear. Peter Iden continues:

[Marianne Hoppe] is the most disciplined speaker in the performance, although even she is only rarely permitted in Robert Wilson's plan to transform the accurate declamation of text . . . into a theatrical quality. Ms. Hoppe's voice is ageless— emphatically present and incisive. The actress's readiness to offer herself up to Wilson's experiment and to explore it earns her the greatest respect. But one must be familiar with Lear's fall, keep the play vividly in mind, because fate as *interpretation,* as theatrical experience, is not the key to this production. Insofar as choreography and rhetoric are not fundamentally bound to one another, it is possible to cast a woman as King Lear. But the real reason for such a device . . . is not evident in this production.[4]

Gerhard Stadelmaier from the *Frankfurter Allgemeine Zeitung* writes:

[Lear] is no king. Neither his sex nor his soul are the issue here. Lear is Marianne Hoppe. She comes from a realm in which every sentence clashes, every emotion freezes, every phrase is a sparkling coloratura. A piercing voice, formidable posture: a tough old lady. She transforms her life experience and pain into such absolute directness and clarity that one seems to trust the surface at once wholly and completely. There simply cannot be anything underneath or within. She is every inch anti-sentimental. A cold, noble machine. Despite the occasional stumble and falter, Ms. Hoppe remains virtuoso throughout. She gives Lear all that Robert Wilson demands from Lear: Lear pure, Lear's mechanics, Lear's choreography, Lear's formula, Lear's text. But she only offers these things to him, she does not transform herself into him. We observe the skill of the magician, not the magic. Bob Wilson's "Lear" is "Lear" for no reason at all.[5]

Verena Auffermann from the *Süddeutsche Zeitung,* on the other hand, unreservedly rates the presentation of Lear through Marianne Hoppe in positive terms:

Marianne Hoppe plays the last days of the king and whisks the art world from the stage. It is a great solo act for her near 80 years, that we fear not the fragility of an aged woman but the dynamic of a person who experiences Shakespeare's genius. Marianne Hoppe's Lear is not a tragic character. The king disempowered by his own choosing is a wise person, neither man nor woman, simply a person, independent, a person who can experience rage but who is not afraid of anything any more. . . . Marianne Hoppe has played with Wilson and gone beyond him. She has invented a character that moves between heaven and earth and knows both levels. Sly as a fox, colossal, powerful, without the ambition of the victor yet nimble as only one who has discovered laughter as the ultimate can be.[6]

While the male critics seem unable to decide why a woman should be the ideal casting of Lear ("in any case, wicked old men are plentiful in Germany at the moment: Lear's shadow lurks around every corner, but not in this production"[7]), the female critic views Ms. Hoppe as the ideal interpreter of Lear—but *outside* a Wilson production. She praises Marianne Hoppe's Lear for exploding the framework of Wilson's theatre aesthetic. Confusion seems complete.

To untangle this confusion, we must first deal with two issues that arise both in Wilson's own commentary and in the praise and censure of the reviews:

1. Who or what does Marianne Hoppe represent in her performance of Lear? and,

2. How does this representation relate to the principles of Wilson's theatre aesthetics?

As all the critics aptly point out, Marianne Hoppe does not disguise herself as a man. The costume code chosen by the production is indifferent to sex: All the characters wear a suit of one color, with either a T-shirt of the same color or nothing underneath. Regan alone wears a skirt instead of trousers and high-heeled instead of flat shoes. Relations between the characters are in part established through the color of these suits: Lear's suit is yellow (mustard), Goneril and Albany green (petrol), Regan and Cornwall red (aubergine), Cordelia and the Fool white, Gloucester and Edmund black, Edgar dark blue, Kent brown, and the King of France beige. In part, additional articles of clothing differentiate the characters: Lear and Gloucester wear coats over their suits. While Gloucester's is black like his suit, Lear's red coat stands out in contrast to his suit. Indeed, Lear is the only character to wear more than one color. He is further distinguished from the other characters, moreover, in prologue B (the division of the kingdom, I,i) by a large, gold, cardboard crown.

Clearly, Lear's character is not identified as masculine through costume; rather, one is unavoidably faced with an old woman who does not make even the slightest attempt on the stage to disguise her own hair under a wig or to transform her impressive face and almost childlike round blue eyes into that of a man's by makeup.

Marianne Hoppe makes just as little attempt to reproduce in posture, movement, or gesture any characteristics or behavior patterns that might be classified as typically male. Nothing in her outward appearance suggests that she is acting a man: She looks like an old woman, and she behaves like an old woman. This effect was clearly so overwhelming that all the critics remarked on it, describing Marianne Hoppe's Lear as "Queen Lear,"[8] as a "tough old lady,"[9] as "the visit of the old lady to a blue castle," or with the words "grandmother tells us the tale of Lear."[10]

This latter impression is pre-programmed to a certain extent by the superimposed prologue A. The performance opens with a scintillating whirring sound and a dull drum roll (music by Hans Peter Kuhn). A narrow, vertical rod of light passes from left to right in the frame of the proscenium arch, dazzling the audience. As the glare subsides, the audience perceives twelve figures spaced across the whole stage wearing floor-length, royal blue coats—the "*dramatis personae*" of the play, with the exception of the servants. One of the lights focuses on Marianne Hoppe's face at the back and right of the group. While the light on the stage grows alternately brighter and dimmer and as the music and sounds swell and subside, she recites, immobile, William Carlos Williams's poem, "The Last Words of My English Grandmother." The poem, which is also printed in the program,[11] contains a multitude of motifs that are picked up on again in the course of the performance.

The "cry for food"—"gimme something to eat" (line 9)—corresponds to Lear's call for food, "Dinner, ho! dinner!" (I.iv.42, in Wilson's version scene 2B). The triple "no, no, no" (l.12) with which the grandmother objects to being carried off to the hospital is taken up again in scene 12 (IV.vi) when Hoppe as Lear turns toward the blind Gloucester (l.179). The words, "Let me take you to the hospital, I said" (l.14–15), are a pre-echo of the many moments in the performance when a younger character guides or gives an arm to an older character (scene 6B, Kent to Lear [III.iv], scene 8 [IV.i], scene 12 [IV.vi], scene 14 [V.ii], Edgar to Gloucester, scene 13 [IV.vii], and scene 15 [V.iii], Cordelia to Lear). The "stretcher" (l.23) is picked up again on both visual and textual levels: the shape of Lear's bed in scene 13 (IV.vii) or Kent's words upon Lear's death, "O! let him pass! He hates him / That would upon the rack of this tough world / Stretch him out longer" (V.iii.313–15). The line, "Is this what you call / making me comfortable?" (l.24–25), resounds in Lear's words to Regan in scene 5 (II.iv)—"thy tender-hefted nature shall not give / Thee o'er harshness. Her eyes are fierce, but thine / Do comfort and not burn" (l.170–72)—as he offers himself to Regan's care. The accusation, "Oh you think you're smart / you young people, she said, but I'll tell you / you don't know anything" (l.27–30), is taken up in Edgar's last words: "The oldest hath borne most; we that are young / Shall never see so much nor live so long" (V.iii.325–26). The last elements of reality that the grandmother can relate to, the "fuzzy-looking things out there," the "trees" (l.38/39), find visual echo in the tree that stands on stage in scene 14 (V.ii) under which Gloucester dies.

The "Last Words of My English Grandmother" is thus constantly picked up and drawn into the course of the performance, and the theme of grandmother is upheld throughout.

On the other hand, prologue A, which bears the title "Unbutton the button. Knöpf mich auf. Die letzten Worte meiner englischen Grossmutter," refers directly to two passages of the *Lear* text that are thereby highlighted quite specifically. Before Marianne Hoppe begins to recite the poem, the other characters slowly mime different, stylized actions of unbuttoning with their fingers. In III.iv, Lear encounters Edgar (as Tom) and comes to the recognition that man "is no more but such a poor, bare, forked animal," continuing with the request, "Off, off, you lendings! Come unbutton here" (III.iv.105–8). In V.iii, as Lear comprehends that Cordelia is indeed dead ("Thou'lt come no more, / Never, never, never, never, never" [l.307–8]), he begs those around him, "Pray you undo this button," and dies. The unbuttoning mime in prologue A thus calls up the two moments in the text when Lear crosses the boundaries into madness and death.

Thus, prologue A also proposes a relation between Lear's death and that of the grandmother in Williams's poem. In doing so, a very specific way of directing reception is undertaken right from the very start that enables a preliminary, trial semantification of the material in hand: the theme of "death" is struck—the same theme to which Wilson alluded in his productions of *Death, Destruction & Detroit I* (1979) and *II* (1987) and that he extended in the parallel Stuttgart productions of Gluck's *Alceste* and Euripides's *Alcestis* (1986). In *Lear,* however, prologue A leads to a characteristic variant: the death of an old person at the end of a long life—the death of the old woman in the poem and the death of the old man in the tragedy.

Our first question might thus be answered in a trial way with a hypothesis: Marianne Hoppe represents the death of an old person. To support and exemplify this thesis, the fundamental aspects of the course of events in which death is presented must be analyzed.

Clearly, the division of the kingdom (I.i) does not at first belong to this process. As prologue B, the scene is distinctly separate from the scenes that follow. Here, Lear realizes absolute dominance. Ms. Hoppe stands erect at center stage front with chin lifted—first facing the audience, then turning her back to it. As she curses Cordelia, she raises her left arm straight out, threateningly. When Kent contradicts Lear (I.i.144ff.), she snatches the scepter fixed in the floor to her left and holds it with raised arm towards Kent as a sign of royal authority.

The excessively dominant behavior Lear employs corresponds exactly to the submissive behavior of Regan and Goneril. Both declaim their declarations of love (l.54–60, l.68–74) from a prostrate position. Cordelia, on the contrary, rises immediately after prostrating herself briefly on the ground and speaks from a standing position (l.94–103).

The behavioral model characterized by dominance and submission realized here is not picked up again in this form or to this extent in the later course of the play. It is bound to the crown, to Lear's position of power in the world. The moment Lear relinquishes his power, further demarcation is brought into the theme—the stage suddenly becomes as bright as day. Goneril, Regan, Albany, and Cornwall step forward and, with splayed fingers, raise their hands behind the crown. They take it, and, opening it out flat, place it on the floor at center stage. It reappears there in scenes 2A (I.iii) and 2B (I.iv), highlighted in a beam of light, before disappearing entirely from the world of the play.

The process of Lear's death commences at the close of prologue B. At this point, the old behavioral model oriented on Lear's dominance and the submissiveness of others no longer serves a function. Instead, it is superseded by new models: Lear is the last to exit at the end of prologue B. Holding the scepter horizontally at waist height in both hands stretched out in front of her, Ms. Hoppe walks erect with chin in the air upstage right, turns slightly and moves across the back of the stage, parallel to a large white screen (which blocks off the back of the stage), to stage left, where she turns a small half circle as an about face and, passing parallel to the screen again, exits stage right. Halfway along the last part of this walk, she suddenly throws the scepter up in a playful way, catching it again in the right hand. At the same time, she lifts her left leg testingly in a kind of skip or dance step, before exiting quietly stage right.

The moment of transition to a new state is thus marked by a new movement model—a movement the audience will be able to interpret to the full in the following scenes as typical of the Fool—the dance. The dissolution of the old status (king—in the sense of holder of political power) makes the function of the behavioral model, valid till now, redundant. The onset of death opens the possibility of new experiences, the trial or trying out of new movements and behavioral patterns that, in their turn, will provoke new behavioral models in the other characters.

In scenes 2B (I.iv) and 5 (II.iv), Lear tests new patterns of behavior, first on his daughters and sons-in-law and then on the Fool and Kent.

In scene 2B, Lear sits at the head of a long, narrow table that stands at right angles to the front edge of the stage, almost dividing the stage into two halves. The back of Lear's chair almost suggests the form of a guillotine, set against the white background. The crown lies on the floor at front stage before the table in a beam of light. At Lear's words: "Does any here know me? This is not Lear. / Does Lear walk thus? speak thus? Where are his eyes? / . . . Who is it that can tell me who I am?" (l.225–26/229), Marianne Hoppe stands up and walks to the front with one hand feeling along the surface of the table. She then bends graciously over the table, lifts one crooked leg, and waves her arm through the air. There follow Lear's words to Goneril: "Your name, fair gentlewoman?" (l.235). A similarly playful movement that also serves the function of ironic commentary is executed by Ms. Hoppe in scene 5. Regan refuses to accommodate Lear and suggests he return to Goneril and beg her forgiveness. At this, Ms. Hoppe, who is sitting behind a low black screen that divides the stage into two parts, front and back, in this scene, dangles both arms over the edge and rolls her head back and forth and, drawing single locks of hair in her fingers, speaks the lines: "Ask her forgiveness? / . . . Dear daughter, I confess that I am old; / Age is unnecessary; on my knees I beg / That you'll vouchsafe me raiment, bed, and food" (l.150, 152–54).

Lear's ironically intended, playfully pretend-submissive behavior provokes a reaction from the daughters and sons-in-law representing force and dominance: Kent is tortured on the wheel in Lear's place. In scene 5 (II.iv), Cornwall stands with his back to the audience before the wheel at front stage right and aims his lance from above at Kent's face. He freezes in this pose for a few seconds so that the image has a lasting effect on the audience. Lear's new pattern of behavior in relation to his daughters provokes acts of violence from them that, in turn, provide Lear with wholly new experiences.

Such experiences contrast entirely, however, to those Lear undergoes in relation to the Fool and Kent. In scene 2B (I.iv), the Fool lays his head on the table before Lear, who places his hand over it. In scene 5 (II.iv), they sit back to back behind the screen, with their heads leaning back against each other. Lear then stands, walks around to the Fool, who still sits, holds his face close to that of the Fool, and says: "O fool, I shall go mad!" (l.285). He then grasps the Fool by the hair, and they make an exit together locked in this position. In scene 6A (III.ii), the Fool kneels behind Lear, leaning his head against him, while Lear puts his hand round his shoulder. This new theme of caring and tenderness provokes corresponding behavioral patterns: Kent walks behind Lear and the Fool with wide, outstretched arms as if to protect them from the storm. He slowly lowers his arms until they are at right angles to the floor, stretched forward towards Lear to guide him into the hut. As he slowly retreats in this position, all three move across the stage from left to right in a kind of group or tableau of protection, caring, and tenderness. A similarly lasting moment is the frozen image that concludes Lear's trial scene (scene 6C/III.vi): Lear leans his head on Edgar's shoulder and holds his hand. Before them, Kent crouches on the floor, his right hand raised. As the light on stage gradually dims, one light remains focused on Kent's hand, which is the last object to remain visible.

The first stage of death is thus characterized by a probationary taking on of new behavior patterns, as well as by the new experiences of caring and violence that these new patterns have provoked. In the next phase ("Lear's madness," scene 12/IV.vi), these new patterns of behavior are activated to the full.

Marianne Hoppe enters with skipping steps and swaying movements. In a relaxed pose, she sits on the "tree stump" with legs slightly bent and her hands on her knees. After calling "no, no, no" (in place of "now, now, now, now!" l.172), which Ms. Hoppe speaks with the same intonation as in the prologue, she stretches her legs out in front of her, draws her coat around her knees, and lifts her toes so that only her heels lightly graze the ground. At the words "And when I have stol'n upon these son-in-laws, / Then kill, kill, kill, kill, kill, kill!" (l.187–88), she marks the rhythm of the words "kill . . ." by beating both arms vertically through the air down between her knees. Finally, at "I will be jovial" (l.201), she makes dancing movements with her feet, puts her hands on Edgar and Gloucester's heads, and rises with the words: "I am a king" (l.201). Then, standing, she lifts her right foot high with bent knee, then repeats the same with the left.

With both arms stretched out to the front (as at the end of prologue B where she holds the scepter), she exits with a hopping, skipping step stage left.

In this scene, playful gestures and dance steps are realized naturally alongside gestures of caring and tenderness. All the behavioral models Lear has tested since the onset of his death are at his fingertips, without being explicitly substantiated or negated by the reactions of others (in this case, Edgar and Gloucester).

In scene 13 (IV.vii), the process of dying seems to have entered a new stage. Lear lies on a long, narrow bed ("stretcher"), and Cordelia kneels by his side. Slowly, and with obvious effort, Marianne Hoppe sits up. With a smiling face, she says, "Pray you now, forget and forgive; I am old and foolish" (l.85). Once she is sitting, Cordelia moves behind her and holds her left arm up as if it were a stick—as if she were Charon at the rudder carrying the dead across the river Lethe in his bark to the underworld.[12] She guides Lear with her right hand slowly forwards. Now, the babble and clatter, only barely perceived in the background up to now, grow increasingly louder. It might be emanating from a canteen or, equally, from the entrance hall of a hospital. The intertextual association with the poem of prologue A just evoked by the presence of the bed thus receives further amplification.

A similar blocking pattern is repeated in a special way in scene 15 (V.iii). Cordelia holds Lear in her arms. Slowly they walk backwards towards the screen, moving parallel to it, before exiting (entering prison), when the group dissolves. The image appears one last time at the end of the performance in characteristic reversal: Lear enters from upstage left holding the (dead) Cordelia in his arms in front of him. The upper part of Cordelia's body leans back against Lear, her arms dangle behind her over those of Ms. Hoppe. The pair move slowly towards center stage, where they turn slightly and walk in a straight line to the front. Slowly, Cordelia slides to her knees against Ms. Hoppe; both are facing the audience. Lear is in this position when he dies—a moment marked only by an increase of light, when Ms. Hoppe simply ceases to speak, to laugh, or to move.

Marianne Hoppe thus portrays dying as a *rite de passage*:[13] Death commences with the phase of dissolution where the old status and the former behavioral patterns bound to it are relinquished. In the following transitional or liminal phase, new models of movement and behavior, which the new experiences release and create, are tried out before being adopted and fully activated. The person undergoing such a transformation now enters the last stage of the transition rite—the phase of incorporation. Guided by a leader of souls or the dead, he or she is admitted into the fellowship of shadows in the kingdom of the dead. This last phase is given additional signification in the production: After Edgar's concluding words declaring the tragedy, Cordelia rises and slowly and quietly stands behind Lear. The (dead) Edmund also rises; the other characters enter the stage, and together the dead and the living create a single tableau. Downstage center stands Lear, behind him, Cordelia. Cornwall, Goneril, Edmund, Regan, and Albany are spread out on the right half of the stage, while on the left stand Edgar, Gloucester, the Fool, and far upstage left, the King of France. The tableau thus highlights specific changes to that of prologue A. The light grows ever dimmer, and just before it fades entirely, the characters appear once more contrasted as silhouettes against the screen. When it is completely dark, the music also ceases—incorporation in the fellowship of shadows is complete.

As a rite of transition, death is wholly indifferent to sex: It commences with the dissolution of the old identity to which sexual identity also belongs. Though Ms. Hoppe's outward appearance and voice identify her death as the death of an old lady, the accompanying text qualifies it as the death of a man—Lear. Marianne Hoppe does not represent the death of a specific individual in a specific, sociohistorical situation but rather death as a rite of transition, at the end of a long life, into a new condition, a new reality.

Now we can address the question of how Ms. Hoppe's representation might relate to the principles of Wilson's aesthetic.[14] Critics and theatre scholars alike agree that there are two significant aspects of performance typical and characteristic of a Wilson production: on the one hand, heavily formalized, abstract, stylized gestures and physical movements, and, on the other, a consequent detachment of physical movement from the simultaneously spoken text. Gesture and word stand side by side in no apparent relation to one another; language is wholly separate from the body of the speaker. Wilson employs both techniques in *Lear,* though he does not take this uncoupling of word and physical movement as far as in other productions, where the text is also communicated simultaneously via loud speakers.

As the examples of Marianne Hoppe's performance detailed above show, neither technique is used by her. Her gestures are only barely stylized, if at all: When Lear expresses his demand for food, she thumps her fist on the table; in answer to Goneril's presumptuousness, she vigorously shakes her head (scene 2B/I.iv); and she holds hands with the Fool or rests her head on Edgar's shoulder (end of Scene 6C/III.vi). All these gestures are directly comprehensible to a member of our culture because they can be recognized in everyday life. They can be identified as gesture signs that give expression to specific volitional and emotional circumstances—independent of their specific marking by an individual subject. Ms. Hoppe's gestures are thus in this sense "natural," that is, nonstylized, yet not colored in the slightest way by individual psychology.

Like the rare use of stylized gestures, the uncoupling of gesture and language is also seldom seen in Marianne Hoppe's performance. Rather, she presents, as illustrated in the examples above, a very tight relationship between word and gesture in completion, affirmation, ironic commentary, illustration, and so on.

Since Marianne Hoppe does not employ either of the techniques generally held to be typical and characteristic of Wilson's actors, the conclusion might be drawn that she wholly undermines Robert Wilson's theatre aesthetic with her performance, that she whisks his "art world from the stage."[15] Such an obvious deduction appears somewhat rash, however, when one considers the specific function of this technique within Wilson's aesthetic. The uncoupling of word and gesture presents both as equal and indifferent to each other. In this process, the difference between them (which laid the foundations of the Western theatre tradition in the dominance of word over gesture) is thoroughly eradicated. The absolute equivalence of gesture and word is given additional signification through formalization and stylization. Both techniques can therefore be explained as functioning in the context of the *postmodern discourse on the Other*. In this respect, the techniques serve a similar function to Wilson's frequent adoption of elements of Far Eastern (predominantly Japanese) theatre in his productions.[16] Just as the process of uncoupling denies the dominance of language over the body and directs the relationship between them towards absolute mutual indifference, so the adoption of elements of different cultures annuls the hierarchy of difference derived from and postulated by Western culture; the elements of different cultures are presented in Wilson's productions as wholly equivalent and stand indifferently, side by side.

From these findings, we can draw the conclusion that one of the fundamental principles of Wilson's aesthetic is to describe the passage of difference into indifference and that this movement is defined and executed on many varied levels. Since members of the Western culture are inclined to orient themselves according to difference and the hierarchies inherent in difference, Wilson's theatre offers the key to wholly new experiences.

It is beyond question that the same principle is equally important to Marianne Hoppe and underpins her performance. It is not a question here of the difference between language and body—even less the difference between cultures—nor is it realized in the process of uncoupling word and gesture; rather, it is modeled on the difference between the sexes. While Ms. Hoppe's outward appearance clearly defines the character she portrays as a woman, the text she speaks proves irrefutably to be that spoken by a man. The difference between text and physical appearance, between man and woman, does not indicate the dominance of either one or the other but actually leads to absolute indifference: Each is realized as wholly equivalent to the other, side by side. Marianne Hoppe does not shake the very foundations of Wilson's aesthetic, therefore, but actually provides the very incarnation of Robert Wilson's Lear.

The denial of the differences between the sexes in Marianne Hoppe's Lear is accorded an even greater semanticization within the production than is usual in Wilson's work. Ms. Hoppe portrays death as a *rite de passage,* as the process of transition into a new condition, a new reality. As Edward Gordon Craig, one of the forefathers of Wilsonian theatre, earlier proposed in his programmatic article, "The Actor and the Übermarionette" (1908), death is the metaphor of an "imaginary world" for a new, not yet visible or describable reality that he referred to as "ideal life":

that mysterious, joyous and superbly complete life which is called Death, . . . the life of shadows and of unknown shapes, where all cannot be blackness and fog as supposed, but vivid colour, vivid light, sharp cut form, and which one finds peopled with strange, fierce and solemn figures, and those figures impelled to some wondrous harmony of movement. . . ."[17]

To make the transition into this world—whose aesthetic "pre-image"[18] can be seen in Wilson's production—it is first necessary to dissolve the old status that is derived out of difference. The cancellation of the differences between the sexes in Marianne Hoppe's Lear thus appears as the precondition for crossing into the new state, the new world, which is only to be found outside the patriarchy and a patriarchal society oriented around difference. In this sense, Marianne Hoppe's Lear qualifies as nothing short of a subversive reference to the future as is nowhere to be found in contemporary German theatre other than perhaps in Heiner Müller's work.

In Müller's play *Leben Grundlings Friedrich von Preussen Lessings Schlaf Traum Schrei* (1976), the theatrical change of sex gives birth to an almost Dionysian, world-creating force: Emilia Galotti and Nathan the Wise recite key moments from their roles ("Gewalt! Gewalt! Wer kann der Gewalt nicht trotzen? [Power! Power! Anyone can knock it down!]" *Emilia Galotti* V.7; the end of the parable of the ring in *Nathan der Weise,* III.7).

Police siren. Emilia and Nathan exchange heads, undress, embrace, kill each other. White light. Death of the machine in the electric chair. Stage grows black. Voice (and projection):WHITE HOT HOUR DEAD BUFFALO IN THE CANYON SQUADRON OF SHARK TEETH IN THE BLACK LIGHT THE ALLIGATORS MY FRIENDS GRAMMAR OF EARTH-QUAKE MARRIAGE OF FIRE AND WATER PEOPLE OF NEW FLESH LAUTREAMONTMALDOROR DUKE OF ATLANTIS SON OF THE DEAD[19]

The sex change, copulation, and killing of Emilia/Nathan is identified in the projected images as a cosmic marriage ("marriage of fire and water") that will produce "people of new flesh." Accomplished in the "white hot hour" and after the "grammar of earthquake"—the traditional symbol of theophany—the act is accorded a utopian dimension that gains additional authentication through the "Duke of Atlantis." The cancellation of difference in Emilia/Nathan's sex change (laceration), copulation, and death releases a tremendous utopian potential.

Marianne Hoppe's Lear also unlocks a similarly utopian dimension. Here, no child or young person is the bearer of hope but rather a character steeped in age-old wisdom who is as much woman as man, as much grandmother as King Lear. Set in a Wilsonian space of light and sound and moved by him into groups and tableaux,[20] she effortlessly succeeds in abolishing difference—with ease, with enormous facility, and with naturalness. The realm of light and shadow that the character she portrays must finally enter thus becomes the *promesse de bonheur,* the pre-image of a better, new world.

Notes

1. Statements from an interview cited in *Vorwort,* Schauspiel Frankfurt, 23 (1990):22. All translations are by the author.
2. Helmut Schödel, "König Licht," in *Die Zeit,* 23 (1 June 1990):68.
3. Peter Iden, "Queen Lear—mehr 'Vogue' als Wahrheit," in *Frankfurter Rundschau* 122 (28 May 1990):8.
4. Ibid.
5. Gerhard Stadelmaier, "Königingroßmutter der Nacht. Marianne Hoppe spielt, Bob Wilson inszeniert Shakespeares 'Lear' in Frankfurt," in *Frankfurter Allgemeine Zeitung* 122 (28 May 1990):33.
6. Verena Auffermann, "Die Kunst der Künstlichkeit. Triumph für Marianne Hoppe: Ihr König Lear in Robert Wilsons Frankfurter Inszenierung," in *Süddeutsche Zeitung* 121 (28 May 1990):15.
7. Schödel, "König Licht."
8. Iden, "Queen Lear."
9. Stadelmaier, "Königingroßmutter der Nacht."
10. Schödel, "König Licht."
11. König Lear, Schauspiel Frankfurt, Spielzeit 1989/90 (n.p.). The poem is taken from William Carlos Williams, *Collected Earlier Poems* (New York, 1938).
12. This association is suggested and confirmed in the preceding scene (IV.vi) where Edgar leads the blind Gloucester with a long rod. He holds the rod out in front, pointing towards the floor, thereby igniting a zigzag strip of light on the floor. Their walk is accompanied by bell-like music that becomes quieter with every change in direction they take, swelling again until the next change of direction. When Edgar and Gloucester halt at the point where Gloucester intends to end his life by leaping over the edge of the cliff, Edgar jams the rod under his arm so that he stands erect on the stage, towering above him. His pose is reminiscent of the Japanese god of death in Suzuki Tadashi's production of Euripides' *Trojan Women,* or again, Charon at the rudder. Cordelia's outstretched arm, like Edgar's rod, transmits the association.

13. See Arnold van Gennep, *The Rites of Passage* (Chicago: University of Chicago Press, 1960).

14. On Wilson's aesthetic, compare, among others, Stefan Brecht, *The Theatre of Visions: Robert Wilson* (Frankfurt am Main, 1979); Erika Fischer-Lichte, "Postmodernism: Extension or End of Modernism?" in *The Zeitgeist of Babel,* ed. Ingeborg Holstery (Bloomington: Indiana University Press, 1990); Wolfgang Max Faust, "Tagtraum und Theater. Anmerkungen zu Robert Wilsons 'Death, Destruction & Detroit,'" *Sprache im technischen Zeitalter* 1 (1979):30–58; Hans Thies Lehmann, "Robert Wilson, Szenograph," *Merkur. Zeitschrift für europäisches Denken* 7, no. 39 (July 1985):554–63; Bonnie Marranca, *The Theatre of Images* (New York: Drama Book Specialists, 1977); Otto Riewoldt, "Herrscher über Raum und Zeit. Das Theater Robert Wilsons," feature in *Südfunk* (3 June 1987); John Rockwell, ed., *Robert Wilson. The Theatre of Images* (New York: Harper and Row, 1984); Peer de Smit/Wolfgang Veit, "Die Theatervisionen des Robert Wilson," *Bühnenkunst* 4 (1987):4–22; Ralph Willett, "The Old and the New: Robert Wilson's Traditions," in *Studien zur Ästhetik des Gegenwartstheaters,* ed. Christian W. Thomsen (Heidelberg: Quelle und Meier, 1985):91–98.

15. Auffermann, "Die Kunst der Kunstlichkeit."

16. On Wilson's productive reception of elements of Japanese theatre in the *Knee Plays,* compare Erika Fischer-Lichte, "Zum kulturellen Transfer theatralischer Konventionen," in *Literatur und Theater. Traditionen und Konventionen als Problem der Dramenübersetzung,* ed. Brigitte Schultze, Erika Fischer-Lichte, Fritz Paul, and Horst Turk (Tübingen: Gunter Narr, 1990):35–62; Erika Fischer-Lichte, Josephine Riley, Michael Gissenwehrer, eds., *The Dramatic Touch of Difference. Theatre, Own and Foreign* (Tübingen: Gunter Narr, 1990).

17. *The Mask* 2 (1908):3–15.

18. On the concept of "pre-image," see Ernst Block, *Ästhetik des Vor-Scheins* (Frankfurt am Main: Suhrkamp, 1974).

19. Heiner Müller, *Herzstück* (Berlin, 1983), p. 36.

20. On the structure of the performance, see Erika Fischer-Lichte, "Passage to the Kingdom of Shadows. Robert Wilson's production of *King Lear* in Frankfurt," in *Handbook of Performance Analysis,* ed. William Sauter, Jacqueline Martin (London: Routledge, 1991).

2. Revising Women

VIRGINIA SCOTT

Les Filles Errantes: Emancipated Women at the Comédie-Italienne, 1683-1691

❦ In 1682, Louis XIV, the king of France, moved his court to Versailles from Paris, a city he disliked and feared. He himself paid rare visits to his capital, and he insisted that his courtiers refrain from going to Paris or from talking about events taking place in Paris.[1] As a result, the city and its culture were increasingly dominated by the tastes and values of the bourgeoisie.

The three Paris theatres, the Comédie-Française, the Comédie-Italienne, and the Opéra, unlike the troupes irregularly supported by royal patronage before 1680, became established institutions of the state, expected to travel to Versailles or Fontainebleau to entertain the court in addition to maintaining daily performances in Paris. The Comédie-Française and the Opéra played the same repertory for courtiers and citizens, but the Comédie-Italienne, a *commedia dell'arte* troupe brought from Italy in 1662, developed a double repertory. In the city, the Italians began to present plays with scenes in French devised by French playwrights to appeal to the bourgeoisie; at court, they were required to play their standard improvised entertainments in Italian. In the latter venue, the troupe soon fell out of favor. The king gradually ceased to attend any theatrical performances, and the courtiers had little interest in antique diversions conducted in a language no one understood. Thus, the Comédie-Italienne, although still subsidized by the monarchy, became a commercial theatre catering to the tastes of its middle-class, urban audience.

One attempt to appeal to these tastes was the introduction of female characters unlike any seen earlier on either the French or the Italian stages. The French playwrights who collaborated with the troupe after 1683 developed, in partnership with two young actresses, a duo of emancipated, worldly, clever, and none too virtuous *fin de siècle* bourgeoises. Françoise Biancolelli's Isabelle and Catherine Biancolelli's Colombine pursued their economic and sexual intrigues to the delight of the Parisian audience, and Catherine Biancolelli became the first great female star of the Italian troupe.

The Biancolelli sisters were the daughters of Domenico Biancolelli, Arlequin, and his wife Orsola Cortesi, Eularia. Françoise was born in Paris in December 1664, Catherine, ten months later in October 1665. They entered the Comédie-Italienne on half-shares in April 1683 and made "official" debuts in *Arlequin Protée* the following October. Donneau de Visé welcomed them in the October *Mercure galant* with high praise: "Never has been seen such intelligence for theatre combined with such youth. There is no point of character into which they do not enter, and they acquit themselves with such good grace that whenever they appear in whatever scene, they seem uniquely born for the characters they play." What Donneau de Visé neglected to mention was that, French born, they were perfectly suited to dominate the new repertory being introduced in French.

Françoise played Isabelle, an *amoureuse,* while Catherine played Colombine, sometimes a *servante* or *suivante,* heir to the Italian *serva,* but equally often a bourgeois wife or daughter. Their characters are not yet developed in *Arlequin Protée.* The surviving text provides little information about Isabelle, and Colombine, although the daughter of one of the *vieillards,* shows few signs of the worldly Parisian she is to become. A scene between the Arlequin and Colombine—although in French—demonstrates a typical *commedia dell'arte* relationship. Arlequin-Proteus is a French actor named La Comète who wants to enlist Colombine in his troupe.

ARLEQUIN: . . . If you'll join my troupe, I'll give you a good role.

COLOMBINE: Oh, yes, Signor, I have a great genius for the theatre. So, as you say, I want a good role. For instance, the role of the doorkeeper who takes the money. That's a good role.

ARLEQUIN: Depends on the weather and the play.

COLOMBINE: So what play are you doing first?

ARLEQUIN: We'll begin with *The Burning of Troy.*

COLOMBINE: Oh, yes, I like that, that's a good scenario. And what character will you play?

ARLEQUIN: The principal character. The Trojan horse.

COLOMBINE: Could you please tell me the story?

ARLEQUIN: Of course. It's . . . It's . . . But everybody knows it.

COLOMBINE: I don't, and I really like to.

ARLEQUIN: It's . . . It's awfully long.

COLOMBINE: Doesn't matter.

ARLEQUIN: Well, here it is, then. The Fire has a bone to pick with Troy, and one day he decides to attack. But at the same time there's a very hard rain which comes to the aid of Troy and dampens the Fire considerably, so he goes away in a rage, and the story ends in a lot of smoke.

COLOMBINE: No, no, I don't like it. It'll give everyone sore eyes. We need to find something more elevated. . . . For instance, the loves of Pyramus and Thisbe, or Angelica and Medora. No! We need something even more elevated.

ARLEQUIN: We could play the loves of the Pyrenees. That's a very elevated
  subject.[2]

This Colombine is smarter than Arlequin, which is not unusual, and leads
him on to make a fool of himself. In a later scene, she plays Bérénice in a
parody of Racine's tragedy and exhibits a sophisticated self-consciousness
of the contrast between herself and the tradition of French tragic acting
that she burlesques. However, she is Italian rather than French, she is not
involved in any romantic intrigue, and she does not have the opportunity
to define an attitude toward women and society that she will have in so
many later plays.

In less than two years, however, Isabelle and Colombine had developed
into title characters, young women who could lead the action, devise intrigues, and survive by their wits, most unusual in French seventeenth-
century comedy. In February 1685, Françoise Biancolelli starred in *Isabelle
médecin,* too fragmentary in Gherardi's version to permit a reconstruction,
but with some interesting features. Isabelle has been jilted by Cinthio,
whose father has sent him to Paris to court Colombine, daughter of the
Docteur, a bourgeoise with a dowry of twenty thousand *écus.* Isabelle follows, disguised as her own brother, a physician.

The play revolves around two issues typical of the decade: the luxurious
lifestyle of rich Parisians and marriage for love versus marriage for property.
Cinthio suspects that twenty thousand *écus* do not go far, once you have
outfitted your "Paris girl" with furniture, clothes, and jewels. "Should a
young man enslave himself for life," he asks, "for the sake of a little property? If you balance the aggravations of marrying a rich wife against the
money you get, my word, a wise man would do better to marry out of
inclination than self-interest."[3] He concludes that, if his father forces him
into the marriage, he will betray Colombine with the first woman who pays
attention to him.

That woman is Isabelle, whom he conveniently fails to recognize. When
she tells him that she is an orphan, tyrannized by a brother who mistreats
her and wants to steal her fortune, he advises her to find a "decent, rich,
and complaisant husband" and volunteers himself. Cinthio, in this play and
in others, is offensively self-absorbed.

The most interesting aspect of *Isabelle médecin,* however, is the relationship between the two women. Isabelle, disguised as her physician
brother, makes a house call on Colombine, who is pretending to be ill. After
a rather conventional medical burlesque, Colombine begins to seduce the
"doctor." When he tries to take her pulse, she suggests he could learn more
by gazing into her eyes. When that stratagem fails, she moans with pain,
and when Isabelle feels up and down her body trying to find the source of
it, Colombine purrs with satisfaction. When Isabelle's hand reaches her
breast, she says, "Oh, Monsieur, you return me to life. Your hand has

stopped my pain. . . . If your hand produces such good effects, you will have to hurry to my side whenever I ask for you."[4] The scene continues with more sexual equivocations, until Colombine declares herself and asks Isabelle to marry her. When Isabelle declines, Colombine announces that she will abide by her father's wishes and marry Cinthio. This declaration forces Isabelle to accept her patient's proposal and swear to love her forever.

Young women deserted by their lovers, disguised as men, even pretending to be their own brothers are scarcely novelties of comic plotting. These behaviors are staples of the Italian and Spanish plays used as plot sources by *commedia dell'arte* troupes. Where *Isabelle médecin* differs is in the way the female characters dominate circumstances. Isabelle demonstrates a degree of cunning and assertiveness not common in the conventional young leading lady. Although she is accompanied by a *zanni,* she makes all the choices that control the plot, maintaining her deception until she is forced to reveal her identity in the last seconds of the play. The sexual ambiguity of the action is also unusual, and the denouement, unsatisfying. Isabelle tries to evade her marriage to Colombine by claiming that her brother will marry Colombine's cousin Lenore instead. Colombine's frenzied neurasthenic response forces Isabelle to pretend that she was merely testing the depth of Colombine's love, and the two embrace in a parodistic facsimile of a typical romantic climax. Only when the Docteur threatens to throw his daughter's seducer out of the window does Isabelle confess. Colombine is more upset by the fact that Isabelle is not a doctor than that she is a woman and agrees to marry Octave. Cinthio then claims Isabelle, who forgives both his original betrayal and his interest in marrying the doctor's "sister." The play's ending is a cursory acknowledgment of the traditional wedding that ends Renaissance comedy. It conveys no sense that the relationships will be either gratifying or lasting. Isabelle wins the game, to be sure, but Cinthio is a paltry prize. Satisfaction is in the game itself.

Colombine avocat pour et contre, produced three and a half months later, rests on similar circumstances. Colombine is looking for Arlequin, the lover who has deserted her and come to Paris in the guise of a marquis to woo Isabelle. The plotting is less conventional but also less intricate. Colombine adopts various disguises, a tour de force for the young actress whose father was famous for his *travesties.* In each disguise, she plays a scene with Arlequin, then reveals herself, saying "perfidious traitor, you will have me in your eyes if not in your heart." At the end, she appears at Arlequin's trial both as the accuser and as a lawyer for the defense.

In this final scene, she reveals herself emotionally and morally as well as physically. She wants to base her life on the "satisfaction of her heart," and she is willing to adopt whatever wiles and subterfuges necessary to have the contemptible Arlequin. She says to him, "Isn't it true that Colombine, without property, without a fortune, has the resources to provide you with an easy life? You know, rascal, that I'm acquainted with all the big financiers. How can a husband be unemployed when a young wife has such useful acquaintances? Or, if you don't want a job, can't you play cards and live honorably in Paris, like hordes of men as poor as you?"⁵

Parisian marriage was the subject of a series of comedies of manners presented by the Italians beginning in 1687. The first of these was *Le banqueroutier,* in which Colombine joins Arlequin to rescue their master, Persillet, whose wife has forced him into shady dealings to support her life as a fashionable lady. The next play in the series, *La cause des femmes,* produced in December 1687, features Isabelle and Colombine and introduces the issue of marrying young women to old men. The rich bourgeois Bassemine, newly widowed, has a daughter who loves to gamble and who is courted by poets, wits, and impoverished aristocrats. Unlike his predecessor Persillet, who dislikes being called a bourgeois and looks forward to the ennoblement of his grandsons, Bassemine fears having an aristocrat for a son-in-law, someone he will see only when creditors are pressing. He plans to marry his daughter, Isabelle, to a physician, Monsieur Tuëtout, a man of barely seventy with whom he can play bowls on Sundays and holidays. Colombine, again an intriguing servant, believes that a young woman who likes to gamble should be married as soon as possible to someone rich and complaisant, but Isabelle tears up the marriage contract. Colombine arranges for a Commissaire to arbitrate between father and daughter, and Isabelle delivers a tirade in her own defense that ends: "I can only say, with the inflexibility of a rock, that I will never give up the hatred I have conceived for this old man who dares to threaten my freedom."⁶ Monsieur Tuëtout has the grace to withdraw.

Another kind of incompatible marriage is the subject of *Le divorce,* the first play that the well-known French playwright Jean-François Regnard devised for the Italians. Isabelle is the unhappy young and noble wife of Sotinet, an old tax farmer, who jealously tries to keep her in isolation. Colombine is her *servante* who devises the scheme to procure a separation. The divorce proceedings are judged by the god Hymen; Colombine as Maître Braillardet speaks for Isabelle and wins her case. She retrieves her dowry of sixty thousand *livres* (a dowry that had, in fact, never been paid) and is granted an annual income besides. Sotinet is certified as a lunatic and sent to St-Lazare for having married a young girl.

In all of these plays, a bourgeois husband or father attempts to cling to traditional values of male dominance and the domestic isolation of women. In none of the plays does he have the force of character necessary for success, and, in the *Cause des femmes* and the *Divorce,* the young women triumph. One might imagine that a bourgeois audience would side with

Bassemine and Sotinet, especially the latter, whose complaints about the irregular lifestyle of his wife are well grounded from a traditional point of view. She has, after all, introduced the pernicious custom of separate beds, "the mortal enemy of reconciliation and the fatal knife that cuts the throat of posterity," and few bourgeois men—or women—would approve of anything so remote from the patriarchal marriage model. On the other hand, Sotinet is a tax farmer, one of those hated financial swindlers who enriches himself at the expense of merchants and artisans. He is also guilty of having participated in a social ritual that brought misery to many young women.

Poor young noblewomen were sometimes sold by their families to bourgeois men who wanted an aristocratic connection as well as a young wife. A *bon bourgeois,* however, was likely to have little sympathy for anyone who expected such a bargain to lead to a happy life. Although arranged marriages took place among the upper bourgeoisie, the petty bourgeois merchants and artisans who filled the *parterre* at the Comédie-Italienne would have agreed that Sotinet got what he deserved and would have cheered old Monsieur Tuëtout, who refused Bassemine's offer of his daughter.

Two of the most interesting and most cynical comedies of Parisian life played by the Italians were introduced after the death of Domenico Biancolelli in August 1688. They featured Angelo Costantini, Mezzetin, along with the Biancolelli sisters. The first, *Le marchand dupé,* introduces Isabelle and Colombine as fully emancipated young women, under no tutelage, living alone and at the expense of their suitors. A father, the cloth merchant Friquet, and his son, played by Mezzetin, both hope to enjoy the favors of Isabelle, who collaborates with the son to trick the father. Friquet *fils* is stealing his father blind, Friquet *père* is spending whatever his son leaves him on the young lady, and the neighbors are predicting ruin.

Colombine is a fully developed intriguer with a clear vision of men and society. She knows exactly how Isabelle must behave if she wants to get married. "Man is a species of animal who wants to be ruled; he is attracted to whoever rejects him. The minute you appear sweet and complaisant, this fop of a suitor thinks to himself that you are smitten and that his perfections have taken hold of your heart. But when you treat him with indifference, . . . you will see the clown . . . spare no cares nor expense to please you."[7] To this conventional advice, Colombine adds: "With the men of today, a girl must be crafty, deceitful, on her guard, even ready to ignore the law if the chase demands it." Isabelle insists that a girl should be sincere and marry for love. Colombine tells her to go back to Lyon. "We have no more money, you refuse to learn how to pluck the pigeons."[8]

Isabelle agrees to play the game. She allows Friquet *fils* to court her, thinking he is rich. He proposes, thinking she is. Friquet *père,* although avaricious by nature, loosens the purse strings when Colombine forces him to recognize that "no one loves old men for nothing." As Isabelle is entertaining the father, the son—disguised as a masquer—interrupts, kicks and beats his father, and threatens to throw him out of the window.

By act 3, Isabelle is completely converted to Colombine's point of view. "With a little resolution," she says, "and a little wit, men can be led. As long as a girl has nothing to reproach herself for on the matter of honor, all the rest is a trifle." And although she is found out by the Friquets and makes the sad discovery that her rich pigeon is the penniless son of the besotted bourgeois, she does not suffer for her sins. Friquet wants his money back but is forced to make a hasty exit out the back door when Madame Friquet arrives downstairs, ready to scratch her husband's face off. Then Isabelle's former lover Aurelio enters to announce that he will die of grief if Isabelle marries another and that her father has forgiven her. Isabelle, once again a proper bourgeois daughter, donates Friquet's money to Colombine for a dowry.

Le marchand dupé is an unpleasant play. The men are duped by the women and yet are punished—Friquet when Isabelle "drops a little note" to his wife and Friquet *fils* when his father has him incarcerated. The women, both Isabelle the pupil and Colombine the teacher, are not punished, not even with the social isolation experienced by Molière's Célimène when found out in similar circumstances. Isabelle, reinstated in society, gets the husband she has wanted from the beginning. Colombine gets the cash.

Once again we might ask why this play appealed to a bourgeois audience, and especially to the *parterre.* The answer may be that, within the scheme of bourgeois values, the men are guilty of behavior that deserves to be punished. Both allow themselves to be deceived by women. The father foolishly wastes his substance and ignores the son's thievery; the son violates the traditional respect a son owes a father. The women are also guilty of rapacious and fraudulent dealings, and they are "rewarded" by being restored to their conventional roles in society. What they lose is their emancipation, a status that is not secure but that offers more freedom than most women of the period ever experienced.

Mezzetin plays another offensive character in *Colombine femme vengée.* A self-described "man of the sword," he returns from his travels accompanied by Olivette (Isabelle), a young woman he has seduced and promised to marry. His wife Colombine, a fashionable Parisienne devoted to a life of pleasure, is less than overjoyed when she discovers that Olivette is not the innocent new *servante* she has taken her to be. The two women tell each other all, make common cause, and surprise Mezzetin with a beating. They then have him arrested for gambling and taken before a magistrate. The judge divides Mezzetin's property between the two women and gives Colombine the right to "correct him with the same stick she used before in order to be, like all the other wives, absolute mistress in her house." In this play, the man loses everything. The women, although Colombine's behavior is equivocal, win everything. Mezzetin is, of course, clearly in the wrong, seducing Olivette and planning to establish a bigamous household. Not only are his actions iniquitous, his social status is indistinct. He describes himself as a man of war, thus an aristocrat, while Colombine describes herself as a bourgeoise married to a man of the sword "who never dares use it" and who has dissipated her property. To the bourgeois in the *parterre*, Mezzetin represents a disreputable element in society, a cowardly professional soldier who spends his time gambling in his garrison or, in Paris, spending his wife's hard-earned bourgeois dowry.

In August 1690, Regnard's *Les filles errantes* reintroduced the theme of young women abandoned by their families, separated from their lovers, and on their own in Paris. Colombine is not, however, the cynical sophisticate of the earlier plays but a seemingly artless victim. This characterization is an effective irony that relies on audience expectations developed over several years of experience with the character. Her ingenuous tale presents both Colombine seduced and Colombine seductress. The daughter of an innkeeper, she tells how she was approached by a polite young cavalier wanting a room. She showed him several rooms but, unwilling to seem less polite than he, deemed none of them to be suitable. Finally, still out of politeness, she showed him to her own room, which he found delightful. Unwilling to inconvenience her in any way, however, he insisted that she continue to occupy it with him, and she felt obliged to agree—out of politeness.

While Colombine plays the *naïve*, Isabelle finds herself in an ambiguous situation. She has taken a job in an inn and is treated like the servant she pretends to be. Mezzetin solicits her, and she is rescued by Cinthio, the man who originally deserted her and who now refuses to recognize her, certain that "Isabelle is not capable . . . of throwing herself at all comers, as I myself saw you do." When Arlequin, the innkeeper, comes to see what the argument is about, Cinthio complains that Isabelle has "served to the first comer what she should have served to him alone." Isabelle responds:

ISABELLE: I presented him with a young chicken, tender, plump to the fingertips, like me. The gentleman was not happy, he wanted another.

CINTHIO: Ah, don't believe her. I would have been very happy with the chicken, I'm not such a big eater; but I know that it was offered to all comers. It had already been served on twenty different tables, and I am not a man to accommodate myself to the rest of the whole earth.

ARLEQUIN: Good heavens, Monsieur, watch what you say. I won't listen to this nonsense. Nothing is served in my inn but fresh meat; tell me, have you ever eaten the same chicken here twice?

ISABELLE: The man simply doesn't know what he's talking about? No one had touched it; it was a delicate fowl, that I took great care to raise and that I fed by hand, with as much pleasure as if it were myself. Everyone who saw her wanted to eat her, but I kept her only for Monsieur.[9]

The men in the play are anything but admirable. Cinthio holds Isabelle responsible for having attracted Mezzetin, while Mezzetin plays two objectionable characters: the ex-soldier who offers Isabelle money for a little rest and relaxation, and the brother of Colombine whose attitude towards his "fallen" sister is excessively punitive. Male hypocrisy in sexual matters is summed up by Colombine, no longer naïve, when she says, "I only know one secret of how not to be betrayed by men, and that's to betray them first. . . . The most necessary virtue of a woman in our century is a little inconstancy seasoned occasionally with perfidy."

The war of the sexes was succeeded by a return to the bourgeois family in *La fille sçavante,* produced in November 1690. The plot centers around a legacy of 150,000 *livres* left to Angélique (Colombine) if she marries, or to Isabelle if her sister refuses to do so.[10] The issue is the conflict between generations. Their father, the merchant Tortillon, is bewildered by his daughters. "The more I look at myself, the less I find that my daughters resemble me. Angélique speaks of nothing but books, Isabelle likes only officers. What the devil does all that have to do with me . . . whose business is to live a good bourgeois life in Paris." He is especially out of countenance with his learned daughter who, "in the heart of the city, by God, on the rue St-Denis, has turned my house into a school of philosophy."[11]

Angélique is pedantic in the extreme, forbidding her father to "give her good day" since a gift "according to jurisprudence is the transmission of property," and he is not the owner of "good day." She refuses marriage, because men are brutal, drunken, jealous, and debauched gamblers. Isabelle is apparently as compliant as her sister is unyielding, a sheep according to her father, who is about to marry her off to the son of a fellow merchant. But Isabelle suddenly arrives in captain's uniform, scolding her sergeant-recruiter. To the astonishment of her father, she is off to join the army. Disgusted by the softness and indolence of her sex, she has decided to disguise it if she cannot change it. Nor is she interested in marriage: "Should I pass, like other women, two-thirds of my life before a mirror? Should I be always busy with children, nurses, furnishings, skirts, laces, collars, perfumes, and all the rubbish that makes up the happiness, or more justly, the misery of our sex?"[12]

The denouement of the play has not survived, although Angélique is apparently converted to marriage by a "professor of love" who teaches her how to be womanly. She gives up her books and gloats over Isabelle, who is going to lose out on the legacy. Angélique's apparent conversion is not necessarily to be trusted, however, since its outcome is a large income and the freedom implied by having money of one's own. Isabelle's fate is unrevealed.

A final comedy of manners in this sequence, Regnard's *La coquette,* was first seen in January 1691, and, once again, marriage of daughters is the subject. Colombine is a coquette, a veritable mantrap; her cousin Isabelle is distinctly *bien élevée.* Men are seen as "clever fish who come and trifle with the bait but rarely bite the hook"—a more conventional view of the war of the sexes. Isabelle, who wants a husband, is unable to find one. Colombine, who enjoys her life as a coquette, is besieged by potential husbands.

Colombine is once again witty and self-confident, essentially misanthropic, cynical, and sophisticated. She takes enormous pleasure in conquests and constructs elaborate schemes to forestall a marriage arranged by her father to a country bailiff.

Unlike her suitors, the bailiff, played by Arlequin, is not especially eager to marry Colombine. "You have a daughter," he says to her father, "*ergo* you have some rubbish you want to be rid of; because a daughter is a flower that fades if it's not picked in time."[13] The bailiff is belligerent, bad tempered, a drunkard, and a gambler, although he thinks of himself as the best of all possible sons-in-law. When he finally meets Colombine, however, he admits that, although he has seen some pretty women in his day, he has never seen one of her caliber before. Colombine describes Parisian marriage to him; he is appalled. Nonetheless, he has gone to the expense of the trip, and he will keep his promise to marry her, provided she will immediately return with him to the country and "rule over the capons in my barnyard." Colombine's schemes to escape this unendurable fate occupy the rest of the play until, thoroughly humiliated, the bailiff is sent packing back to his poultry. The veil of comic civility he has briefly worn falls away, and his original brutality returns: "Go to the devil, you and your daughter, you mean, miserly little shrimp! Goodbye, my beauty, I don't think there is in the world a more vicious creature than you."[14]

Early in the last decade of the century, the Comédie-Italienne produced two comedies with an unexpected turn of plot. In both *Les deux Arlequins* (September 1691) and *La fille de bon sens* (November 1692), Isabelle agrees to marry an old man. In the former, she chooses Géronte over the young Octave, because Octave is parsimonious while Géronte is "free and liberal." In the latter, she goes even farther and marries her old lover not for money or freedom but because she loves him. He loves her as well.[15]

These old men, generous and loving, are preferable to the young men who appear in the plays I described previously. Throughout the comedies of manners that feature Isabelle and Colombine, the young men—the *amoureux*—as well as Mezzetin and Arlequin are obnoxious fortune hunters and unsavory deceivers. They are contemptuous of women, calling them "rubbish" and "vicious creatures." The women, while hardly models of chastity and probity, are witty and charming and far more intelligent and attractive than the men they choose to remain faithful to and often to marry. Their fidelity may seem unreasonable, but it reflects the ambiguous legal and social position of adult, unmarried women—*les filles majeures*—in seventeenth-century France. Marriage could result in domestic isolation and enslavement, but it also offered the possibility of social emancipation, depending on the complaisance of the husband. It also offered the possibility of widowhood, the state of greatest freedom for women. Very few women chose to remain unmarried; although single women could be legally as well as socially emancipated, their status was not as high and their virtue questioned. Thus, although we may not find appealing a marriage between Isabelle and her censorious Cinthio or between Colombine and her affected Arlequin, the seventeenth-century bourgeois audience—less tainted by romantic ideas of marriage—would have concluded that these young women were making the best choices and would probably continue to outwit the men in the game of marriage.

After 1691, a number of changes prompted a different repertory at the Comédie-Italienne. The theatre was reconstructed to permit the production of elaborate machine plays based on classical romances.[16] Colombine played Circé and Galatea rather than a Parisian bourgeoise or *suivante*. Then, in June 1692, Charles Dufresny wrote his first play for the Italians, *L'opéra de campagne*, which began a new genre of successful musical afterpieces, most of them featuring Catherine Biancolelli. Françoise Biancolelli was seen less frequently as her personal life began to interfere seriously with her professional life.[17] Later in the decade, several plays featured Parisian life, but they lack the concentration on the plight of young women in French society seen in the plays offered between 1683 and 1691. Angélique, who replaces Isabelle, is a more conventional *amoureuse*. Colombine is older, more worldly, sometimes even a demimondaine. Scenes are set at the fair, in the Tuileries, in the Bois de Boulogne, and at the swimming baths at the Porte St-Bernard, all places of assignation. The fictional world reflects the degenerate Paris society of the war years and not the internal world of the bourgeois family.

The last years of the century saw an effort to reaffirm traditional family values and roles, especially in the upper classes. Throughout the seventeenth century, some women had gradually achieved a kind of freedom, at least compared with the way of life specified by the feminine model promoted during the Middle Ages and the Renaissance. Perhaps the best-known example of the liberated woman of the Baroque is Célimène, the aristocratic young widow of Molière's *Le misanthrope*. Free of tutelage by father, husband, brother, or son, in control of her fortune and her life, Célimène entertains her poets and *petits marquis*, substitutes *bon esprit* for *bon sens*, and refuses to give up the delights of Paris salon society for domestic isolation with Alceste.

In the 1680s, however, a new model for women emerged. This model was "Sainte Françoise," Madame de Maintenon, Louis XIV's plain, pious, and prudish morganatic wife. She joined with Bishop Fénelon to promote a movement "designed to produce hard-working, frugal, and simple mothers of noble families."[18] With the publication of Fénelon's *De l'éducation des filles* (1687) and the foundation by Madame de Maintenon of the school for girls at St-Cyr (1687), theory and practice joined to promote domesticity. Fénelon believed that girls should eschew humanistic study and learn the domestic arts and the principles of household management. Maintenon carried out his intentions at St-Cyr. This was a reactionary movement, an attempt to reimpose the traditional Christian model on upper-class women who had begun to taste a modest degree of freedom. It was also allied to a general movement led by Bishop Bossuet, the conscience of the court, against the pleasures and frivolities of Baroque society.

The Italians did not become moralists as a result. The plays they produced in the 1690s were no more high-minded and respectable than their earlier works; indeed, the reverse was often true, and the police began to observe performances, looking for indecencies and obscenities. What characterizes these later plays, however, is a shift from satire and the depiction of bourgeois society to exotica, fantasy, and spectacle. The later plays are entertainments, largely unconnected to issues relevant to the bourgeois audience and certainly no longer focused on the status of bourgeois women. Although it is difficult to determine exactly why this change took place, chances are it reflects a substantial modification in audience composition and/or taste.

Between 1683 and 1691, the characters of Isabelle and Colombine, although constructed by playwrights and actresses to feature the talents of Françoise and Catherine Biancolelli, were designed to appeal to an audience that had also played an important role in their genesis. In the traditional *commedia dell'arte*, a nomadic enterprise, troupes rarely played for more than a few months at a time in any one city. Actors' assumptions about audience response were based not on knowledge of a specific audience but on overall experience and generalized inferences about audience behavior. The characters, originally specific to Venice or Bologna or Bergamo, also became generalized, at home throughout Italy and beyond its borders. In Paris, however, the situation was quite different. The Comédie-Italienne had been established there for thirty-five years, and the audience was made up in large part of habitual playgoers. The relationship between theatre and audience was one in which audience approval was openly solicited and audience expectations regularly fulfilled. Although the traditional *commedia* characters underwent mutations to conform to French tastes, the Biancolelli sisters were among the first members of the troupe to develop new characters specifically for the Parisian audience, which responded by making them favorites.

Many references in the Gherardi repertory support the assertion that the audience that stood in the *parterre* was extremely influential and that the troupe flattered, even toadied to, this group of bourgeois men, often characterized as the Parterre. When, for example, in *La coquette* the bailiff complains that the actors have gone so far as to refer to the Parterre as "Monseigneur," Colombine leaps to the defense. "The Parterre benefits everyone; he reforms the writers, he keeps the actors going; no fop can sit down on the stage benches with impunity in front of him."[19] Not only were spectators in the *parterre* usually the most numerous, they were also the most openly critical and, armed with whistles, were capable of suspending any performance they disliked.

It is understandable that this fraction of the audience would appreciate the burlesque of the minor nobility implicit in Arlequin's many appearances as a *petit marquis* and would enjoy watching Colombine or Isabelle expose his absurdity. Their favorable response to the humiliation of financiers and tax farmers and the punishment of bullies, spendthrifts, and old goats is also easy to comprehend. But why they should be expected to approve of the freedom, even license, experienced by the young women is more difficult to construe.

Although we assume the bourgeoisie to be a conservative element in any society, Elinor Barber points out in *The Bourgeoisie in 18th Century France* that middle-class conservatism there was based on secular rather than religious assumptions. The bourgeoisie had no place in the "traditional religious and aristocratic conception of man and society."[20] The female model promoted by the Church from the time of St. Paul was, then, somewhat remote from the French bourgeoisie, whose ethical standards—unlike those of their Calvinist counterparts in England and Germany—included the pursuit of happiness, meaning wealth and the pleasures of the flesh. Those bourgeois men who went to the theatre were probably less conservative than the bourgeoisie at large, more worldly. They were also the husbands and fathers of bourgeois women who patronized the theatre. Another probable proposition can be inferred from Jean-Nicolas de Tralage's remark that the audience at the Comédie-Italienne was full of tired businessmen: "Cléante or Jourdain only amuses himself at the Italian plays where every act ends with somersaults or a beating. This is some ignorant partisan or wholesale merchant who, after having heard nothing but accounts, disputes, lawsuits, is happy, at least one day a week, to hear comic things which violate reason and verisimilitude."[21] Perhaps these merchants and money men were titillated by the young women's rakish conversation and immodest behavior. On the other hand, though the *parterre* was full of unaccompanied bourgeois men, the *amphithéâtre* and second *loges* welcomed their wives and daughters, who may have taken pleasure in a feminine model that was self-reliant and self-serving, hard-headed and hedonistic.

The Italians were not alone in reflecting changes in women and their lives. In the 1680s, comedy became the leading genre at the Comédie-Française, and the view of Paris life is similar at the two theatres, although the plays written for the French are far more likely to treat bourgeois women as objects of satire.[22] The young female characters of the *comédie italienne* are rarely satirized, although the bluestocking Angélique in *La fille sçavante* is mocked in the tradition of Molière. In general, the young women are given the opportunity to speak for themselves and to defend their behavior, and usually they get what they want and see their opponents defeated and even humiliated. They are also far more active in the intrigue than are the young women in plays written for the French company, probably the result of the youth and popularity of the Biancolelli sisters. If the Italian actresses owed anything to the French, it was probably to Mlle Beauval, the actress for whom Molière wrote such roles as Dorine and Toinette, characters who are clever and assertive although never as cunning, as worldly, as ethically ambiguous as Colombine.

In the clash of values that characterized the 1690s—pious court versus corrupt city—the Comédie-Italienne chose to appeal to its urban audience and fell into disrepute with the authorities. As early as 1688, the Italians were told to clean up their act, and throughout the 1690s, various complaints and official memorandums single out the Italians for their indecent postures and equivocal language. In 1697, the Italians were dismissed, ostensibly for performing a play that burlesqued Madame de Maintenon but more probably because they had not conformed to restrictions being imposed by the now publicly devout Louis XIV. What influence the liberated (or libertine) female characters may have had on official attitudes cannot be specifically determined, but Bishop Bossuet's attack on the theatre, *Maximes et réflexions sur la comédie*, reserves some special venom for actresses.

In spite of continuing efforts to regulate and censor, in spite of the reactionary ideology promulgated by Gallican churchmen and supported by the king and his functionaries, the social emancipation of women continued to grow during the disordered last decade of the century. Perhaps the war, which lasted from 1688 to 1697, promoted social changes favorable to women, as wars often do. Numerous indications also support the assertion that women began to experience a greater degree of legal emancipation, especially after 1700.[23] The women who astonished d'Argenson, the lieutenant-general of the police, by refusing arranged marriages or by deserting the conjugal domicile "to live alone and free" in the early eighteenth century may have been the beneficiaries of the young women who held the stage at the Comédie-Italienne a decade or two before, whose images and voices survived time and official censure.

Notes

1. Orest Ranum, "The Court and Capital of Louis XIV. Some Definitions," in *Louis XIV and the Craft of Kingship*, ed. John C. Rule (Columbus: Ohio State University Press, 1969), p. 274.

2. Evaristo Gherardi, *Le théâtre italien* (Paris: Cusson et Witte, 1700, vol. 1):108–10. All translations from the Gherardi repertory are my own. Most of the early plays of the Gherardi repertory are attributed to Monsieur D***, usually identified as Anne Mauduit de Fatouville. The possibility exists, however, that Monsieur D*** is a pseudonym invented by Gherardi, who did not know who had written the French materials performed before he joined the troupe. Material from this collection, especially from plays first performed in the 1680s, must be used with a certain caution, since the printed versions may represent reprises. For a fuller discussion of these possibilities, see Virginia Scott, *The Commedia dell'Arte in Paris, 1644–1697* (Charlottesville: University Press of Virginia, 1990), pp. 276–83.

3. Gherardi, *Le théâtre italien*, vol. 1:279–80.

4. Ibid., 1:293–94.

5. Ibid., 1:432.

6. Ibid., 2:76.

7. Ibid., 2:221.

8. Ibid., 2:223.

9. Ibid., 3:23–24.

10. Scott, *The Commédia dell'Arte*, 362. Although the character is named Angélique in the 1700 text, in 1690 she was probably Colombine. There is a third female character in the play, the maid Toinon, probably played by Angela Toscana who entered the company ca. 1690 as a *servante*, Marinette, and who played Angélique after the retirement of Françoise Biancolelli.

11. Gherardi, *Le théâtre italien*, vol. 3:54–55. Part of the joke here may rest on the fact that an audience would expect a very different sort of "school" on the rue St-Denis—then, as now, the resort of Parisian prostitutes.

12. Ibid., 3:90–91.

13. Ibid., 3:145.

14. Ibid., 3:224.

15. Although "Angélique" is indicated in the text, the frontispiece shows Isabelle.

16. Scott, The Commedia dell'Arte, 314–17.

17. Françoise Biancolelli was married, although irregularly, to a young guards officer in 1691. His parents accused her of abduction and disinherited him. Her character last appears in the Gherardi repertory in La fontaine de sapience (July 1694). For a full accounting of the marriage and its attendant difficulties, see Scott, The Commedia dell'Arte, 257–58.

19. Carolyn C. Lougee, Le Paradis des femmes: Women, Salons, and Social Stratification in Seventeenth-Century France (Princeton: Princeton University Press, 1976), p. 175.

19. Gherardi, Le théâtre italien, vol. 3:312–13.

20. (Princeton: Princeton University Press, 1955), pp. 36–37.

21. Jean-Nicolas de Tralage, Recueil, Bibliothèque de l'Arsenal Ms. 6544, fol. 205v.

22. See H. C. Lancaster, A History of French Dramatic Literature in the Seventeenth Century. Part IV. The Period of Racine (Baltimore: The Johns Hopkins Press, 1940), vol. 2:530–90.

23. Jacques Saint-Germain, La vie quotidienne en France à la fin du grand siècle (Paris: Hachette, 1965), p. 76.

JOSEPH DONOHUE

Women in the Victorian Theatre: Images, Illusions, Realities

Given the complex circumstances of gender studies at the present time, a male author setting out to write about women in the Victorian theatre—on the stage, in the drama, in the audience, or behind the scenes—may well doubt how much insight he can bring to the subject; or he may sense that his readers will harbor such doubts no matter how confident he himself may be. One way or the other, the enterprise seems to retain that tenuous validity that John Stuart Mill once suggested clings to any male efforts in that direction. "We may safely assert," Mill said in his now famous essay *The Subjection of Women* (1869), "that the knowledge which men can acquire of women, even as they have been and are, without reference to what they might be, is wretchedly imperfect and superficial, and always will be so, until women themselves have told all that they have to tell." As if this difficulty were not sufficiently daunting, Mill raises an additional complexity. "The greater part of what women write about women," he observes, "is mere sycophancy to men."[1]

One begins to wonder how men will ever be able to distinguish truth from falsehood, even after women "have told all that they have to tell." Yet, for all his professed skepticism, Mill himself managed to write a profoundly revealing book. In its wake have followed numerous books and essays by male and female authors alike, a still rapidly expanding shelf of studies of mothers and daughters, sweethearts and wives, relative creatures and complex cinderellas, madwomen in attics, sane women at writing desks, determined women at barricades, stern suffragettes and devoted sisters of mercy, fancy kept women in St. John's Wood and despairing Magdalenes on London Bridge. Among this wealth of literary, historical, and sociological criticism and commentary, the theatre historian might find it curious that relatively little attention has been given to a subject, in fact to an entire institution, that bears so broadly on this question—the Victorian English theatre.[2] The nineteenth century is one of the great ages of the theatre, and its activity over this long period is characterized by an extraordinary proliferation of theatre buildings, unprecedented developments in dramaturgy and dramatic genres, extensive changes in acting style, and remarkable advances in the technique and technology of *mise en scène*. These phenomena are closely bound up with pervasive changes in the society itself and, consequently, in theatrical audiences. It is inevitable that, during this gradual but thorough transformation over the course of a century, women played crucially important parts, both onstage and off. Yet we do not understand as much as we should about the nature of women's presence nor about the contributions they made in the theatre during the age of Victoria and during the span of nearly fifty years before Victoria ascended the throne, when the revolution in France and contemporaneous social and demographic changes in Britain were already diverting the theatre and the drama toward new and unforeseen directions.

It seems appropriate, then, to pose questions that may frame the wider artistic and social contours of the subject. Given the great wealth of theatrically oriented images that survive from the period, an iconographic approach seems especially useful. Employing a method derived partly from rhetorical systems of gesture and attitude reflected in eighteenth- and nineteenth-century acting manuals but incorporating more broadly based analytical strategies of recent historians,[3] I propose to investigate what images of women were on view to audiences assembled in the burgeoning theatres of the time and to ask how those images related to the realities of contemporary life. Were they apt? Did they represent, epitomize, or distort? Another question, even more fundamental, seems important: What, after all, is the relationship in any age, and in this age in particular, between theatrical and dramatic art and common life?

The strategy of this essay is to concentrate on a familiar image, or cluster of images, of women and, through scrutiny of their essential features and the variations in them that emerge over the century, to identify a recurrent, indeed pervasive and revealing, pattern—one that might tell us, simultaneously, important things about nineteenth-century society and about the theatre itself. This pattern, instantly recognizable to any student of nineteenth-century culture, underlies, perhaps more than any other, our sense of the problematic relationship—the predicament—between men and women in the society of that time and, indeed, of our own.

The pattern is that of the distressed female in apparent need of rescue by a resourceful male. Early and late, wherever one goes in the drama of the nineteenth century, one encounters damsels in distress. The alliteration in the all-too-familiar phrase emphasizes the strong connection in nineteenth-century cultural attitudes (a connection frequently exemplified in traditional and contemporary romance and fairy tale as well as in drama) between maiden innocence and the likelihood that its possessor is in difficulty, and further suggests a prime value placed on the importance of rescue. The rescuer is, of course, the male.

A print in the Folger Shakespeare Library dating from the beginning of the century establishes the ideal type of heroic deliverer, presented in the context of an appreciative public. The play is Richard Brinsley Sheridan's spectacular historical melodrama of 1799, *Pizarro*. The scene depicts a wild expanse of Peruvian country: Upstage, a crude bridge spans a torrential waterfall; downstage right, a group of menacing Spanish soldiers has entered, while at left is Rolla, the selfless Peruvian hero. In his downstage hand, he effortlessly holds high the infant son of his beloved Cora, while with the sword in his other hand he defies Pizarro's threatening band. Only moments later, as Rolla retreats upstage and crosses the practicable bridge, a Spanish bullet will find its mark. In a subsequent scene, the heroic rescuer, now dying but valiant and resourceful to the last, will deposit the child in Cora's arms and expire on the spot.[4] The occasion commemorated by the print is a command performance attended by King George III and his retinue, in evidence in the royal box, complemented by a swelling crowd of loyal subjects who instinctively might sense an analogy between the solicitous exertions of Sheridan's idealized stage hero and the presence of a monarch who tacitly endorses the hero's efforts.[5]

With images as complex and full of information as this one, it is important to gloss the significance of concrete theatrical qualities by placing them in larger social, even mythical, contexts. The myth clearly in evidence here is that of male sufficiency, which is very deep in the culture of the age and inevitably engages questions of power and control (among other values). To rescue a woman from danger, to save her from disaster, requires the male's assertion of his physical strength, his bodily power, his ability to outmaneuver or outwit accident, chance, or evil in the world at large. The contrary force may be as impersonal as a Spanish soldier's bullet or as personally threatening as an arch-villain. Images of the early nineteenth-century actor George Frederick Cooke and his younger contemporary Edmund Kean in one of their most frequently performed roles, that of Shakespeare's (to be more precise, Colley Cibber's) Richard the Third, capture a prevailing sense of intense malice, sometimes almost to the point of caricature.[6] James H. Hackett's recollection of Kean's first entrance and soliloquy ("Now is the winter of our discontent . . .") underscores the impression one derives from prints of Kean in the role of an ambivalent combination of nonchalant attitude and underlying body tension. "Gloster enters hastily," Hackett reports, "head low—arms folded"; on the line, "In the deep bosom of the ocean buried," he "unfolds his arms and walks the stage," "grins and frets." As Richard explains that he is "not shap'd for sportive tricks," Kean "stands and pulls on his gauntlets tighter and keeps the centre writhing his body R & L and using his right hand."[7] Altogether, Kean's performance carries an aggressive, threatening message, one whose concentrated force Anne, the hapless widow of the dead king, will feel in the next scene as the strong-willed Richard bends her to his purpose. The colored engraving in the Folger Shakespeare Library depicts the moment: Kean's Richard kneels in seeming submission to Anne but in actuality offers her a painful choice: "Take up thy sword—or take up me." "Choose," he insists, in effect, "between the male power represented by this sword— if you dare—or submit to me by bidding me rise." Anne, not surprisingly, bids him rise. The intense power conveyed by these images of male dominance is a familiar iconographic phenomenon, evident again, for example, in Thomas Hicks's memorable oil of the American actor Edwin Booth as Iago, whose evil eyes stare the onlooker into complacency.[8] Through numberless variations, the myth states and restates itself: power, strength, resourcefulness, commanding presence. A highly idealized drawing of Kean as the morose Byronic hero of Charles Robert Maturin's Gothic tragedy *Bertram; or, the Castle of St. Aldobrand* (1816) offers a striking image of the type, departing from any sort of accurate rendering of Kean's diminutive form and frenetic style of acting in order to transform himself into the graphic epitome of colossal power.[9] The drawing highlights the preoccupation of the age with images of male sufficiency while, in this case, blithely ignoring Kean's modest physical stature and, by implication, the tragic demise of his character.

Throughout the century, the archetypal male heroic character stands for the embodiment and assertion of authority and strength, as in a poster advertising one of the most popular melodramas of the mid-Victorian stage, *East Lynne*. In this drama, a woman is tempted into infidelity by what she has concluded is a loveless marriage. In the poster, the forsaken husband is stricken with the impact of loss but ever righteous in his assumption of strict moral virtue; hanging upon him and begging forgiveness, but to no avail, is the fallen heroine Isabel.[10] Another image depicts Isabel departing for a life of sinful pleasure, as the audience is persuaded to suppose, with her seducer Captain Levison pointing out the straight and narrow path to perdition (Fig. 1). A composite of scenes from the play intended as a stock advertisement elucidates the wages of sexual sin with simple clarity. In the top scene, Isabel flees the affluent but cheerless home; in the bottom scene, she lies dying, much lamented but obviously a terminal case, her adultery having made her unfit for rescue or for anything, ultimately, except the free gift of pathetic response that her death seemed able to elicit from audiences.[11]

Still later in the period, one finds the same assertiveness of virtue, authority, and power in a sketch by Bernard Partridge illustrating the exposure scene in act 3 of Henry Arthur Jones's problem play of 1900, *Mrs. Dane's Defence*.[12] A supremely confident, contemptuous Sir Daniel Carteret, portrayed by Charles Wyndham, acting as a combined prosecuting

Fig. 1. Poster advertisement of *East Lynne*. Reproduced in *Scenes from the 19th-Century Stage in Advertising Woodcuts,* ed. Stanley Applebaum (New York: Dover, 1977) Plate 128, p. 74.

attorney and judge, levels a finger of accusation at the supposed Mrs. Dane, played with carefully restrained anxiety by Lena Ashwell. He reveals her as a woman with a shameful past who has presumptuously tried to "get back" into polite society and even be chosen in marriage by the Wyndham character's unsuspecting son. Sir Daniel asserts the undeniable truth: "You are Felicia Hindemarsh!" The artist has rendered the character so that the body's weight falls securely back on a well-braced rear leg, with just enough tension in the accusing arm and hand to prevent it from falling by his side— the last word, graphically speaking, in olympian confidence and haughty righteousness.

Pursuing these images of male sufficiency and authority through the century, we must conclude that the need to assert power of this kind is a deeply compelling and enduring one. Perhaps it is the desire for control that leads to this need for power, for access to force—physical, moral, or spiritual— sufficient to countermand the otherwise inevitable march of society and the world (and of one's own self) toward chaos, toward disintegration.

In any case, we can follow this line of analysis a crucial step further and observe that, in the arena of relationships between men and women, the male need for access to power exerts itself through response to a correlative need to construe the female as helpless, as powerless. To put the same idea

obversely, a woman must demonstrate her helplessness in order to be rescued by a man or, more precisely, to merit rescue. A strong-willed, self-
sufficient woman, Harriet Martineau believed, is fit for living alone and,
by the age of thirty, is "certainly qualified to take care of herself"; as the
independent-minded Martineau indicated in her autobiography, such a
woman does not need rescue.[13] Another sort of woman, who may need
rescue no more than Martineau, would nevertheless be careful to give every
sign of requiring it, as the poet Coventry Patmore artlessly explained in his
midcentury narrative poem about domestic bliss, *The Angel in the House*
(written 1854–1856), a Victorian best seller exceeded in popularity only
by Tennyson's *Idylls of the King*. Patmore's description of this domestic
angel is, despite our impulse to read it otherwise, entirely free of irony:

> A rapture of submission lifts
>   Her life into celestial rest;
> There's nothing left of what she was;
>   Back to the babe the woman dies,
> And all the wisdom that she has
>   Is to love him [the husband] for being wise.
>   . . . .
> And evermore, for either's sake,
>   To the sweet folly of the dove,
> She joins the cunning of the snake,
>   To rivet and exalt his love;
> Her mode of candour is deceit;
>   And what she thinks from what she'll say,
> (Although I'll never call her cheat,)
>   Lies far as Scotland from Cathay.
> Without his knowledge he was won;
>   Against his nature kept devout;
> She'll never tell him how 'twas done,
>   And he will never find it out.[14]

It is evident that a strong woman, a woman who does not "die," as
Patmore puts it, "back to the babe"—who does not appear to regress to
an innocent, childlike state and become the necessarily frail, defenseless
female—is therefore not a candidate for the institution invented by society
for such rescue: marriage. Generally, all unmarried females were presumed
to be candidates for Patmore's submissive connubial rapture, unless age,
disposition, or attitude disqualified them, at which point they became, as
William Rathbone Greg characterized them in 1862, "redundant." Among
the numerous single women encompassed in Greg's ruthlessly comprehensive term are those "whose brains are so analogous to those of men that
they run nearly in the same channels, are capable nearly of the same toil,
and reach nearly to the same heights; women . . . of hard, sustained, effective *power*; women who live in and by their intelligence alone, and who

are objects of admiration, but never of tenderness, to the other sex. Such are rightly and naturally single; but they are abnormal and not perfect natures."[15] For Greg, the combination of the qualities of powerfulness and tenderness is a quintessentially male characteristic;[16] where women do not submit to domination and so become the objects of tender solicitation, abnormality exists.

The notion of Harriet Martineau as somehow "redundant" is surely repellent to us now; we must nevertheless conclude that, throughout the period, the exclusion of the ostensibly self-sufficient woman as a suitable object of a strong man's interest and solicitude remained a consistent intention of society. Whether marital relationships were entered into naïvely or with the angelic cunning and deceitfulness of the selfless, devoted wife described in Patmore's poem, the resultant drama of the century is crowded to overflowing with images of yielding, often helpless, feminine women. Examination of a series of portraits and scenes will illustrate the prevailing features.

There seems no better place to begin than with Sarah Siddons, the greatest actress of her age and, of all actresses, one of the most extensively represented in contemporary (and later) illustration.[17] The oil portrait by Thomas Gainsborough dating from 1785, frequently reproduced, presents a woman serenely independent of the tragic roles in which she made her reputation as a player. Gainsborough portrays a lady of high fashion, cool, elegant, reserved, almost regal in her black ostrich feather hat, fur muff, silk dress, and ribbon choker. Not by any means the submissive type, one gathers; nor was Siddons afraid to project a masterful dominance and control when portraying strong-minded, assertive characters such as Shakespeare's Lady Macbeth. The contemporary water colorist Mary Hamilton recorded a remarkable series of characters of Siddons's such as Lady Macbeth, Elvira—Pizarro's fiery mistress in Sheridan's play—and Zara in Edward Young's *The Revenge,* among other roles from the traditional seventeenth- and eighteenth-century repertory.[18] Yet, there is evidence that Mrs. Siddons herself conceived of the role of Lady Macbeth as in some sense "a fair, feminine, nay, perhaps, even fragile woman."[19] Another frequently performed Siddons character, the long-suffering wife of Beverly, the eponymous character in Edward Moore's domestic tragedy *The Gamester,* follows this same ideal of frail femininity (Fig. 2). Imprisoned for debt, a remorseful Beverly tells his devoted spouse that his heart bleeds for her. The graceful arch of her body, the comforting arm, the bent head, the hair in disarray, and the requisite white dress of the heroine all proclaim Mrs. Beverly the distressed but ever-faithful wife, all the more an object of pathos because her husband is no longer in fact her protector.

Some additional examples of the yielding, defenseless woman may add

Fig. 2. Mrs. Siddons as Mrs. Beverly in *The Gamester.* From the Art Collection of the Folger Shakespeare Library.

further substance to the outline. One of Sarah Bernhardt's most popular roles was that of the self-effacing courtesan Marguerite Gautier in the Alexandre Dumas *fils* drama *La Dame aux camélias* (1852) (Fig. 3). The look in her eyes as she gazes into her mirror tells us that Marguerite sees herself for what she is, and that she finds the portrait a sobering one. The photographer's careful adjustment of shadow on the near side of the face creates a visual contrast that helps convey a lucid pathos. Bernhardt's younger contemporary Evelyn Millard, who as a young actress in the 1890s specialized in romantic heroines at George Alexander's St. James's Theatre, appears in a luminous photograph published in *The Theatre* in 1892.[20] The pose conveys a seriousness in the face, character in the straight line of the

Fig. 3. Sarah Bernhardt as Marguerite Gautier in *La Dame aux camélias*. From the collections of the Theatre Museum. By courtesy of the Board of Trustees of the Victoria & Albert Museum.

nose, a limpid soulfulness in the eyes, and, in contrast, a nice, careful de-mureness in the angle of the fan, interposed between subject and viewer and ready, it would appear, for immediate extension at any hint of impropriety or embarrassment. Ultimately, the impression is one of elegant yet subtly calculated modesty.

The differences in emotional coloring among various images are important to observe. In contrast to the relatively calm images of Bernhardt and Millard, others reveal the extreme responses of women under the duress of violent feeling. Three examples, early, middle, and late, of the distressed heroine subjected to great, threatening adversity exemplify an important iconographic tradition. One of Mary Hamilton's subjects in her series of

Fig. 4. Mrs. Siddons as Calista in *The Fair Penitent.* Watercolor by Mary Hamilton in the Print Room, British Library. By courtesy of the Trustees of the British Museum.

Siddons's characters is Calista, the greatly tried heroine of Nicholas Rowe's early pathetic tragedy *The Fair Penitent* (1703) (Fig. 4). Hamilton records Mrs. Siddons's line spoken at that moment: "Scorned by the women and pitied by the men! Oh! insupportable!" Prominent features of the composition are the arm thrown up to the forehead and the angle of the arched back, giving an essential emotional tenor to the moment. These details appear again, strikingly intact—this time with both arms thrown up—in the attitude and gesture of the unnamed heroine in Honoré Daumier's starkly black and white painting *Le Drame,* dating from the late 1850s.[21] Showing us a view of the stage from the midst of a crowded and eagerly attentive audience, Daumier floods his subject with seemingly authentic-looking limelight from offstage right, showing us that the cause of the heroine's calamity is the dead body on the stage floor, a corpse that in life may have been husband, lover, or, possibly, father. The burden of painful emotion is carried in the attitude of the woman, the arms thrown up to the side of the head and the head itself thrown up, the back deeply arched. This particularly complex attitude projected a vulnerability signified by the completely open, unprotected stance, on the one hand, and, on the other, an impulsiveness to catch the head and the body itself to prevent collapse onto the floor. Daumier uses the arms of the actor standing at the heroine's left, set like a clock precisely to a quarter to five, in a compositional way to call attention simultaneously to distressed heroine and dead body; the actor's dramatic function itself seems quite secondary. In this predicament, seemingly no one can save the heroine, and the situation is clearly desperate. Daumier's painting suggests an archetypal situation, with suitably conventional attitudes and gestures. An implication of archetypal importance occurs again in a third example of the distressed heroine, a photograph of the actress Eva Moore and others in a highly embarrassed discovery scene from Alfred Sutro's drama of 1907, *John Glayde's Honour* (Fig. 5). The attitude of the heroine in this photograph is obviously conventionally identical to those of the two earlier examples by Hamilton and Daumier. The late date of this last image underscores the remarkable persistence of this icon of a female in distress.

Distress may be rendered in the highly stylized and simplified attitudes of Siddons, by Daumier's anonymous melodramatic heroine, or by Moore in Sutro's heated drama of adultery discovered; or it may be depicted in the more realistic reflections of an accusatory scene from the St. James's 1893 premiere of Arthur Wing Pinero's *The Second Mrs. Tanqueray,* the drama of an ill-fated attempt to rescue a fallen woman through marriage (Fig. 6). The futility of Aubrey Tanqueray's misguided efforts to reclaim Paula, played by Mrs. Patrick Campbell, from her disreputable life is clearly on display in her self-accusing eyes as she gazes out of the fictional frame toward the engaged viewer. A remarkable aspect of the photograph is the extent to which it replicates the emotional content and the pose itself of the stricken young woman in Holman Hunt's well-known painting *The Awakening Conscience.*[22] In the latter, the subject is captured in the moment of a sudden realization of her compromised circumstances. Moreover, in both instances the female character seems to be looking out—in the case of Hunt's subject, literally out of a window—at a world outside, in-

Fig. 5. Matheson Lang, George Alexander, and Eva Moore in *John Glayde's Honour* (1907). From the collections of the Theatre Museum. By courtesy of the Board of Trustees of the Victoria & Albert Museum.

habited by us as onlookers, as judges, or perhaps even as intruders.[23] In the Hunt painting, the male figure is oblivious to what is happening, whereas in the Pinero photograph, the Aubrey Tanqueray character (played by a sober-faced George Alexander) is aware of the crisis and gravely concerned about it. The two images nonetheless comprise an important continuity in the iconographical representation of social and ethical values regarding the fallen woman. Again and again, early and late in the period, in a variety of pictorial media, the language of gesture, attitude, and facial expression speaks with great consistency and eloquence of the plight of the female in a hostile, menacing world.

In these ways, the language of gesture and mime offers notable insights into women's feelings and situations. In employing this visual language as a critical tool, however, we may feel some of the discomfort Mill admitted to, suspecting that the conventionalities of pictorial form and expression disguise or distort at least as much as they convey. For example, it seems evident that Hamilton the female water colorist and Daumier the male painter in oils rely upon the same cultural palette, so to speak, undiffer-

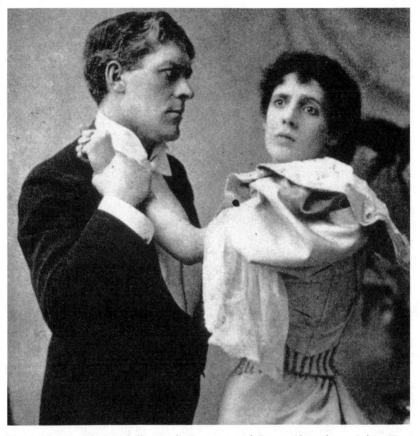

Fig. 6. Mrs. Patrick Campbell as Paula Tanqueray and George Alexander as Aubrey Tanqueray in *The Second Mrs. Tanqueray* (1893). Photograph in the author's collection.

entiated by any conscious sense on the part of the artist of her or his own gender. Certainly the difference in medium is trivial (in an intellectual or critical context), and even the historical distance of nearly half a century between the artists' works appears negligible. What connects them is a homogeneous artistic approach toward rendering women in the grip of strong emotion, an approach conditioned to an important extent by a long-standing, traditional language of gesture and attitude employed in theatrical performance since well before the Restoration and still thriving on the Edwardian stage.[24] The fact that one can detect in these images a separate set of conventions regarding an artist's rendering of a three-dimensional subject on a two-dimensional plane—conventions that, for example, reflect

assumptions about what constitutes good composition—does not cloud
the perspicuous representation in them of authentic human emotion. All
the same, we must finally acknowledge that such a representation, no matter how clear in outline and substance, is culturally overdetermined. A good
example of this overdeterminacy lies in the images of upturned eyes in the
faces of women (and men as well) in uncounted portraits and scenes from
the theatre of the period. It seems only natural for us to interpret the rolling,
upturned gaze, with much of the white of the eye showing underneath, as
an expression of real emotional duress, perhaps even desperation. If so,
however, how are we to evaluate August Strindberg's explanation of the
phenomenon in his preface to *Miss Julie*? Strindberg advocates there the
removal of the footlights from the stage on the grounds that "the lights
hurt the performers' eyes, so that the full play of their expression is lost.
The foot-lights strike part of the retina usually protected . . . and therefore
one seldom sees anything other than a crude rolling of the eyes, either side-
ways or up towards the gallery, showing their whites."[25] Strindberg seems
to be saying that the glare of the footlights promotes a crudeness of emotional expression that might be more convincingly rendered if freed from
the distorting influence of strong light emanating from below the subject;
but he does not examine the nature of the expression itself. We are left to
wonder whether the actress who rolls her eyes markedly upward is, at least
partly, engaged in an instinctive effort to protect her eyesight instead of an
attempt (which better technology might allow her to refine) to vent the
overflow of violent emotion. Mill's anxiety about the possibly permanent
inscrutability of the subject may be justified in ways he did not even have
in mind: We may never be able to go far enough beyond the conventional
languages of the stage, of painting, of the arts in general to find the un-
trammeled truth. In fact, does such truth exist apart from these culturally
overdetermined representations themselves?

An unsettling question, perhaps; yet, we may be able to make some progress by bearding this cultural lion in its den—by looking for images that
indisputably reflect distortion of some kind and that can be evaluated by
comparison with apparently unaffected related images. Thus scrutinizing
the polarities of female roles in the nineteenth-century theatre, we may gain
an understanding of how the projection of male needs and expectations
can, in fact, mask or distort the true realities of male-female relationships.

One of the most poignant examples of this kind of grave miscommun-
ication in the history of the Victorian theatre occurs in the case of Ellen
Terry and her early, disastrous marriage to the painter George Frederick
Watts. Most frequently associated with Henry Irving's Lyceum Theatre in
the last years of the period, Terry performed the Shakespearean and other
roles through which she became almost an institution in her day as Irving's

leading lady. "Of pretty faces there are plenty," Percy Fitzgerald commented, "but how few of expression or intelligence!"[26] Instantly recognizable, Terry's characteristic, clear-eyed face shines out from the innumerable portraits and other images made of her during her very long life on the stage.[27] As a very young actress, however, she moved in and out of the arena of the professional theatre more than once. George Frederick Watts, one of the most talented painters of the day but also one of its strangest, most self-centered personalities, was almost forty-seven years of age when he married Ellen Terry, then hardly sixteen—"a raw girl," as the actress described herself in her memoirs, "undeveloped in all except my training as an actress."[28] Brought together by friends, they made one of the most colossal mismatches of the day; the marriage lasted ten months and ended as quickly as it began. It seems likely that each of the principals had been seriously misrepresented to the other by the well-meaning friends who arranged the match. "Pray God one be not a well-meaning friend one's self!" Terry exclaimed in her memoir of the episode.[29] She met Watts on a visit with her older sister Kate to Holland House, where the painter, maintained by a wealthy patroness, lived and worked—"a paradise," as it seemed to the impressionable girl, "where only beautiful things were allowed to come," where "all the women were graceful, and all the men were gifted." Watts instantly spotted her as the perfect model for his purposes. "My face was the type which the great artist who had married me loved to paint," Terry recalled; "I remember sitting to him in armour for hours, and never realising that it was heavy until I fainted!"[30] Those sittings are memorialized in such paintings as Watts's *Watchman, what of the night?* (earlier entitled *Joan of Arc*).

There is some evidence that, in marrying an actress thirty years his junior, Watts had persuaded himself he was rescuing her. In a letter to his friend Lady Constance Leslie, Watts declared himself "determined to remove the youngest [Miss Terry] from the temptations and abominations of the stage, give her an education and if she continues to have the affection she now feels for me, marry her."[31] Significantly, Watts failed to record his own feelings of affection, whatever they may have been, for his intended spouse. In his famous painting of 1862, *Sir Galahad*, the knight is Watts himself, but idealized as a hero of Tennysonian chivalry, as the art historian David Loshak points out in a perceptive, illustrated essay on Watts and Terry. To Loshak's eye, the paintings by Watts in this period have a certain air of enchantment about them not discoverable earlier or later. Nowhere is this mood clearer than in a small painting of this period called *Knight and Maiden*. Loshak's description of it is much to the point:

. . . The hero is unmistakably Watts himself. No less certain is the identification of the frail young girl who delicately embraces him as Ellen Terry, the inclination of her head the very embodiment of yielding tenderness. The middle-aged knight leans on his lance and gently looks down at her, protectively, with a kind of sad satisfaction; satisfied perhaps at being able to shield her from what he conceived to be the dangers and temptations of her previous life, yet sad precisely because age and long habits of abstinence obliged him to be protector rather than lover.[32]

These same qualities are a salient feature of Watts's testimony in his petition, some years later, for divorce. After their formal separation, Terry had returned to the stage. She had then fallen in love with the architect Edward William Godwin and had left the theatre a second time to live with him. During those years, the separation of Terry and Watts remained a constant, and still later, Watts divorced her, perhaps at Terry's own request since she promptly married the actor Charles Wardell. In his testimony, Watts declared "that although considerably older than his intended wife he admired her very much and hoped to influence, guide and cultivate a very artistic and peculiar nature and to remove an impulsive young girl from the dangers and temptations of the stage." Those temptations were perhaps obvious enough to remain unspecified, but Watts's testimony links his perception of Terry's nature with her theatrical upbringing—"a most restless and impetuous nature," as he described it, "accustomed from the very earliest childhood to the Stage and forming her ideas of life from the exaggerated romance of sensational plays. . . ."[33]

Regrettably, in Watts's declaration there is no consciousness at all that he may have been in the grip of exaggerated fantasies of his own, Tennysonian chivalric ideals of father-rescuers. In his book The Subjection of Women, Mill offers an apposite definition of the "spirit of chivalry," whose peculiarity, he says, is "to aim at combining the highest standard of the warlike qualities with the cultivation of a totally different class of virtues— those of gentleness, generosity, and self-abnegation, towards the non-military and defenseless classes generally, and a special submission and worship directed towards women." Chivalry, Mill explains, represents "the acme of the influence of women's sentiments on the moral cultivation of mankind," and, as such, it substantially mitigates the bad effects of the subordination of women by men; but, he adds, it is an anachronism in a later age (the age of Victoria, he means) when true equality is the only basis for social relationships. "The main foundations of the moral life of modern times," Mill concludes, "must be justice and prudence; the respect of each for the rights of every other, and the ability of each to take care of himself."[34] One may discern glimmerings of a more personalized, or individualized, quality underlying the older, more familiar chivalric forms in the well-known painting in the Tate Gallery by John Singer Sargent of Ellen Terry as a statuesque but still quite human Lady Macbeth.[35]

Victorian chivalry has some complicated psychological aspects that cannot be scrutinized here. It should be evident, nonetheless, that the male act of rescue in this age bears a heavy freight of meaning, despite its seemingly simple outlines in the morally uplifting, often spectacular rescue scenes that serve as climax to the melodramas, comedies, and other kinds of dramatic art—from burletta to problem play—that achieved popular currency on the stage of the day. Rescue from danger and distress took many forms, some of them embodying a reversal of expectations, as in the rescue scene in act 2 of Augustin Daly's sensation play *Under the Gaslight*. In an advertising poster for this play, we see the heroine, Laura Cortland, breaking out of the shed in which she has been imprisoned just in time to rescue the low comedy character, Joe Snorkey, who has been tied up and left on the rails directly in the path of an onrushing locomotive.[36] Deliverances such as these may seem all too predictable and easy, accomplished as they so often were with the formidable technology for producing illusion developed in the theatre in the course of the century.

Another example is provided in the act 2 climax of Boucicault's Irish comedy-drama *The Shaughraun* (1874), in which the eponymous character, Conn, an irrepressible ne'er-do-well, appears to have been mortally wounded in the ruins of St. Bridget's Abbey where, masquerading as the patriot Robert Ffolliott, he has hidden from the British soldiers.[37] Boucicault gives us not one, but two distressed females in the scene—Arte O'Neal and Claire Ffolliott. Conn, however (played in the early productions by Boucicault himself), is only pretending to be wounded by the villain's henchman, and he survives to rescue both the hero and heroine by the end of the play. By turning the low comedy character, the stage Irishman, into the heroic rescuer and by adding a second distressed female, Boucicault manages to introduce some noteworthy innovation into an already familiar pattern.

In contrast, in some cases rescue is exceedingly difficult or tragically impossible, as for Shakespeare's Macbeth and his guilty lady. "Canst thou not minister to a mind diseas'd," Macbeth asks the doctor toward the end of the tragedy, "Pluck from the memory a rooted sorrow, Raze out the written troubles of the brain . . . ?" The doctor's answer proclaims him an early prototype of the modern mental physician: "Therein the patient Must minister to himself" (V.iii.40–46). Sargent's sketch of Ellen Terry in the role, showing her evidently in anxious flight, does not appear to represent a specific dramatic moment but suggests, all the same, the frenzied mentality of the sort Macbeth describes, a diseased mind harboring a secret sorrow manifested in compulsive movement.[38] Looking at the details of gesture and attitude in the representation of madness here and comparing them with other examples, one might note a conspicuous continuity over the length of the century. An early example, Mrs. Siddons's sleep-walking

Lady Macbeth, as depicted in a painting by the Regency artist George Henry Harlow,[39] sets a precedent for a series of visual representations of Lady Macbeth culminating in Ellen Terry's portrayal three quarters of a century later.

In all these images, the staring eyes—transparent signs of spiritual crisis—are the surest indicators of the mental instability produced in female dramatic characters when they find themselves beyond rescue or redemption. We see those eyes everywhere, it seems. We see them in Holman Hunt's *The Awakening Conscience,* highly praised by John Ruskin for its iconographic fidelity to the details of middle-class life and their underlying moral significance.[40] We see them in the face of the forlorn Nelly Armroyd, standing in the window of a fashionable London house, in a scene (act 2, scene 3) from Watts Phillips's melodrama *Lost in London* (1867).[41] An earlier scene (act 2, scene 1) of Phillips's play appears to reenact the very moment of awakening captured in Hunt's middle-class allegory of stricken conscience.[42] Here, in the act 2, scene 3 discovery scene, Nelly, the fallen heroine, is recognized by her long-suffering, persistent husband Job, who has followed her and her seducer Gilbert Featherstone from the simple miner's house Job and Nelly once shared to the wintry, decadent London of the middle and end of the play.

Again we see the eyes, this time cast down, in Watts's rendering of Ophelia (1878/79).[43] Watts's model is unmistakably Ellen Terry, and the expression of the face seems consistent with the sense of a "restless and impetuous" nature that Watts described in his divorce testimony and actually went so far as to characterize there as "an insane excitability."[44] This painting, completed around the time of their marriage but retouched in 1878–1880 when Terry and Irving were reviving *Macbeth* at the Lyceum, anticipates Watts's later painting *The Madness of Ophelia,* dating from about 1880. In the later work, the eyes speak unmistakably of a personality whose forts of reason have been entirely broken down.[45] The contrast between this case of evident madness and a photograph of Ellen Terry as Ophelia is instructive. One senses immediately the predominant quality of quizzical sanity in the eyes. Equally instructive is the pencil sketch Watts made from the photograph. As before, the eyes tell that tale. "Through his paintings," Nina Auerbach comments, "Watts played the Victorian husband's role: he created a wife who shaped herself into submission, and he did so with a sympathy he had never known and would never know again."[46] All the same, Loshak is surely right in suggesting that Watts tended to identify his former wife with that side of Shakespeare's heroine "that was to lead to alienation"[47]—a natural enough tendency, perhaps, given the character. Nonetheless, from the long perspective of the theatrical and graphic art and the values and preoccupations of the century, Watts's paintings of his child bride hold a larger, really emblematic, significance.

Fig. 7. Leaving the Lyceum Theatre in 1881. Print in the Victor Glasstone Collection.

We shall probably never be able to discover in much depth and detail just how these highly dramatic images affected the audiences that thronged to London's numerous theatres over the course of the century. The problematic relationship between the art of the theatre and common life is pertinent to whole archives of materials, whose meanings may be further clarified by our broadening theoretical understanding of performance and audience reception; yet the relationship is never quite satisfactorily explained. An enigma emerges here, I believe, that forms part of the essential fascination of the theatrical subject itself, and its seemingly endless social and cultural ramifications. The enigma is on view in an engraving showing a fashionable audience leaving the Lyceum Theatre, some waiting amidst the hustle and bustle for their cabs (Fig. 7). Allowing one's eye to wander over the illustration, one soon finds the true center of interest—not in the physical center of the print but, rather, in the dynamic interaction of the two groupings at either side. On the viewer's right, two couples, presumably husbands and wives, are chatting. One of the men is distracted, however, and quite nonplussed as he looks across to his right at another couple, at the viewer's left. This couple is obviously caught up in themselves, the woman noticeably younger than the well-dressed man carrying her shawl and to whose arm she clings, a man who bends solicitously toward her and whose attentions are focused entirely on her as they walk briskly away. Is this woman possibly the gentleman's mistress? Is there some combination of indignation and jealousy or is it simple envy reflected in the face of the gentleman on our right, the man who follows their departure with his eye. Does he know the inside story of the departing couple, giving us no more than an inkling? We shall never know. We may only surmise that life's drama is sometimes every bit as heated as the impassioned encounters enacted on the stages of actual theatres by the Ellen Terrys and Henry Irvings of the day.

Be that as it may, what becomes ever more remarkable as one looks into the characteristics of female dramatic characters from this period is the extent to which, in their essence, they reflect the general life of the age. This realism strikes me as remarkable, at any rate, because so many critics and historians have assumed that the drama of this age has a high component of fantasy, that it consequently makes things come out "right" at the end in blithe, uncomprehending defiance of probability and the facts of ordinary life, not to mention the dictates of common sense. But fantasy in dramatic art exists because fantasy is there in life itself, there on the stage as a projection of the needs and desires, not always conscious ones, that pervade life and so characterize and qualify it in fundamental ways. Dramatic art has a seemingly limitless capacity to act out, to reify, to realize needs that may be forbidden in the culture, to represent behavior that involves prohibitively high risk, to play out actions that result in dire consequences most people strive to avoid. Consequently, the plots often do seem implausible, and the endings, inconsistent with what we like to believe is true to life. Yet the characterizations are often shrewdly apt; despite the broad style necessary for communication with an unsophisticated audience in a cavernous theatre—and despite the seemingly more "natural" style of sophisticated performance in the later period, which may also strike us now as distinctly formalized—sometimes they are profoundly convincing. The verbal codes of this complex kind of communication, the explicit dialogue and stage directions from the scripts of these plays, seldom identify the rich concentration of deeply plausible cultural signals conveyed to an audience in actual performance. These factors, these facts, about the theatre of the age of Victoria and the century she dominated suggest that the art form has much to tell us not only about the women of the period but about the men as well, and about ourselves—much of which we may have yet to learn.

Notes

1. John Stuart Mill, *The Subjection of Women*, intro. by Wendell Robert Carr (Cambridge: M.I.T. Press, 1970), p. 26.
2. This statement, of course, is not to slight a number of important contribu-

tions. Some recent studies of women in the Victorian theatre include, among others, Nina Auerbach, *Ellen Terry: Player in Her Time* (New York: W. W. Norton, 1987); Kathy Fletcher, "Planché, Vestris, and the Transvestite Role: Sexuality and Gender in Victorian Popular Theatre," *Nineteenth Century Theatre* 15 (Summer 1987):9–33; John Stokes, Michael R. Booth, and Susan Bassnett, *Bernhardt, Terry, Duse: The Actress in Her Time* (Cambridge: Cambridge University Press, 1988); Tracy C. Davis, "The Spectacle of Absent Costume: Nudity on the Victorian Stage," *New Theatre Quarterly* 5 (November 1989):321–33; Gail Finney, *Women in Modern Drama: Freud, Feminism, and European Theater at the Turn of the Century* (Ithaca: Cornell University Press, 1989); two doctoral dissertations: Mary T. Heath, "A Crisis in the Life of the Actress: Ibsen in England" (University of Massachusetts at Amherst, 1986) and Joanne Elizabeth Gates, "Sometimes Suppressed and Sometimes Embroidered: The Life and Writing of Elizabeth Robins, 1862–1952" (University of Massachusetts at Amherst, 1987); and Tracy C. Davis, *Actresses as Working Women: Their Social Identity in Victorian Culture* (New York: Routledge, 1991).

3. See especially Martin Meisel, *Realizations: Narrative, Pictorial, and Theatrical Arts in Nineteenth-Century England* (Princeton: Princeton University Press, 1983); and Joseph R. Roach, *The Player's Passion: Studies in the Science of Acting* (Newark: University of Delaware Press, 1985). Representative examples of the earlier symbology of gesture and attitude are Gilbert Austin's *Chironomia; or a Treatise on Rhetorical Delivery* (London, 1806)—see the edition by Mary Margaret Robb and Lester Thonssen (Carbondale and Edwardsville: Southern Illinois University Press, 1966)—and Henry Siddons, *Practical Illustrations of Rhetorical Gesture and Action, Adapted to the English Drama* (London, 1807). See also note 24 below. Because the number of illustrations included in the present essay must necessarily be limited, I have had some recourse to extended verbal description, for which I ask the reader's patience.

4. The print is reproduced in Joseph Donohue, *Dramatic Character in the English Romantic Age* (Princeton: Princeton University Press, 1970), Plate 21, after p. 130.

5. For a discussion of the political and cultural contexts of Sheridan's play, see Donohue, *Dramatic Character,* chap. 6; and John Loftis, *Sheridan and the Drama of Georgian England* (Cambridge: Harvard University Press, 1977), chap. 6.

6. See, for example, Plate 41, George Frederick Cooke as Richard III, opp. 275, and Plate 46, Kean as Richard III, opp. 306, in Donohue, *Dramatic Character.*

7. *Oxberry's 1822 Edition of King Richard III with the Descriptive Notes Recording Edmund Kean's Performance Made by James H. Hackett,* ed. Alan S. Downer (London: Society for Theatre Research, 1959), p. 19.

8. Hicks's painting is reproduced on the cover and as Plate 99 in Charles H. Shattuck, *Shakespeare on the American Stage: From the Hallams to Edwin Booth* (Washington, D.C.: Folger Shakespeare Library, 1976), opp. 140.

9. In the Folger Shakespeare Library, reproduced in Donohue, *Dramatic Character,* Plate 14, after p. 82.

10. Reproduced as the frontispiece in Gilbert B. Cross, *Next Week—East Lynne: Domestic Drama in Performance 1820–1874* (Lewisburg: Bucknell University Press, 1977).

11. The advertisement is reproduced in *Scenes from the 19th-Century Stage in Advertising Woodcuts,* ed. Stanley Appelbaum (New York: Dover, 1977), Plate 128, p. 74.

12. Reproduced as Plate 9 in *English Plays of the Nineteenth Century*, vol. 2: *Dramas 1850–1900*, ed. Michael R. Booth (Oxford: Clarendon Press, 1969), opp. 408.

13. *Harriet Martineau's Autobiography and Memorials of Harriet Martineau*, ed. Maria Weston Chapman (1877), excerpt in *Victorian Women: A Documentary Account of Women's Lives in Nineteenth-Century England, France, and the United States*, ed. Erna Olafson Hellerstein, Leslie Parker Hume, and Karen M. Offen (Stanford: Stanford University Press, 1981), pp. 153–55.

14. Coventry Patmore, *Poems*, 4th ed. (1890), excerpt in *Victorian Women*, 138–39.

15. William Rathbone Greg, "Why Are Women Redundant?" *National Review* (April 1862), excerpt in *Strong-Minded Women and Other Lost Voices from Nineteenth-Century England*, ed. Janet Murray (New York: Pantheon, 1982), p. 51. The italics are Greg's.

16. I have heard the music of Brahms described in exactly these terms.

17. See the iconography appended to the entry on Siddons in Philip H. Highfill, Kalman A. Burnim, and Edward A. Langhans, *A Biographical Dictionary of Actors, Actresses, Musicians, Dancers, Managers and Other Stage Personnel in London, 1660–1800*, 14 vols. to date (Carbondale: Southern Illinois University Press, 1973–   ), vol. 13.

18. The series now resides in the Print Room of the British Museum.

19. Sarah Siddons, "Remarks on the Character of Lady Macbeth," reprinted in Thomas Campbell, *The Life of Mrs. Siddons* (1834), 2:11. See the discussions of Mrs. Siddons's ostensibly contradictory approach to Shakespeare's character in Joseph Donohue, "Kemble and Mrs. Siddons in *Macbeth*: The Romantic Approach to Tragic Character," *Theatre Notebook* 22 (Winter 1967–1968):65–86; and in Donohue, *Dramatic Character*, 254–56.

20. *The Theatre* 20 (1892) opp. 160, reproduced in *Oscar Wilde's* The Importance of Being Earnest: *A Reconstructive Critical Edition of the Text of the First Production, St. James's Theatre, London, 1895*, ed. Joseph Donohue with Ruth Berggren (Carbondale: Southern Illinois University Press [forthcoming]), Plate 42.

21. A familiar image, often reproduced; see, for example, Meisel, *Realizations*, Plate 1, p. 9, and Meisel's discussion, p. 8.

22. Now in the Tate Gallery, London. Reproduced in Meisel, *Realizations*, Plate 166, p. 366.

23. See Austin E. Quigley's discussion of *The Second Mrs. Tanqueray* in *The Modern Stage and Other Worlds* (New York: Methuen, 1985), pp. 69–90.

24. B. L. Joseph explored the influence of rhetorical gesture and action on the Elizabethan stage in *Elizabethan Acting*, 2d ed. (Oxford: Oxford University Press, 1964). For the later period, see also Roach, *The Player's Passion*, and the discussion of Henry Siddons's *Practical Illustrations of Rhetorical Gesture and Action* (1807) in Donohue, *Dramatic Character*, p. 344ff. The persistence of the tradition is on view in the early film, peopled in many cases by actors from the legitimate theatre; see Nicholas A. Vardac, *Stage to Screen: Theatrical Method from Garrick to Griffith* (Cambridge: Harvard University Press, 1949); and David Mayer, "The Victorian Stage on Film: A Description and a Selective List of Holdings in the Library of Congress Paper Print Collection," *Nineteenth Century Theatre* 16 (Winter 1988):111–22.

25. *Six Plays of Strindberg,* trans. Elizabeth Sprigge (Garden City: Doubleday, 1955), p. 72.

26. Percy Fitzgerald, *The World Behind the Scenes* (1881; reprint, New York: Arno, 1977), p. 122.

27. See, for example, the illustrations accompanying Michael R. Booth's study of Terry in Stokes, Booth, and Bassnett, *Bernhardt, Terry, Duse;* the illustrations in Auerbach, *Ellen Terry;* and, in particular, the nearly one hundred images, mostly of Terry, published in the limited edition of Terry's *The Story of My Life* (1908) and included also in the reprint by Benjamin Blom of *Ellen Terry's Memoirs,* ed. Edith Craig and Christopher St. John (1932; New York, 1969). One of the most striking is the photograph of a reflective, spiritualized seventeen-year-old Ellen Terry after her marriage to Watts, taken by Julia Margaret Cameron in 1865; see Auerbach's discussion of this photograph in *Ellen Terry,* 96–99.

28. *Ellen Terry's Memoirs,* ed. Edith Craig and Christopher St. John (New York: G. P. Putnam, 1932), p. 46. See also the accounts in Roger Manvell, *Ellen Terry* (London: Heinemann, 1968), pp. 35–57; and in Auerbach, *Ellen Terry,* 82–120.

29. *Ellen Terry's Memoirs,* 46.

30. Ibid., 42, 43.

31. Quoted in David Loshak, "G. F. Watts and Ellen Terry," *Burlington Magazine* 105 (November 1963):476.

32. Ibid., 484.

33. Ibid., 483.

34. Mill, *Subjection of Women,* 85–86.

35. The painting is reproduced in Auerbach, *Ellen Terry,* 262; Manvell, *Ellen Terry,* Plate 26, after p. 230; and *Ellen Terry's Memoirs* (reprint edition by Blom), n.p.

36. *Scenes from the 19th-Century Stage,* Plate 115, p. 66.

37. A contemporary engraving capturing the moment is reproduced in *Plays by Dion Boucicault,* ed. Peter Thomson, British and American Playwrights (Cambridge: Cambridge University Press, 1984), p. 206; for another example, see *The Dolmen Boucicault,* ed. David Krause (Dublin: Dolmen, 1964), p. 173. The scene is reminiscent of the fatal shooting of Rolla in Sheridan's earlier play, still on the boards in Boucicault's time.

38. Reproduced in Manvell, *Ellen Terry,* Plate 24, after p. 230.

39. A print in the Folger Shakespeare Library based on the painting is reproduced in Donohue, *Dramatic Character,* Plate 39, opp. 243.

40. "I suppose that no one possessing the slightest knowledge of expression could remain untouched by the countenance of the lost girl, rent from its beauty into sudden horror; the lips half open, indistinct in their purple quivering, the teeth set hard, the eyes filled with the fearful light of futurity, and with tears of ancient days." Ruskin, letter to the *Times* (25 May 1854):7, signed "The Author of 'Modern Painters.'"

41. Reproduced in *Scenes from the 19th-Century Stage,* Plate 77, p. 44.

42. See the stage directions describing the moment in the edition of the play in *Hiss the Villain: Six English and American Melodramas,* ed. Michael Booth (London: Eyre and Spottiswoode, 1964), p. 233; and Meisel's discussion of Phillips and Hunt in *Realizations,* 368–69.

43. Reproduced in Loshak, "Watts and Terry," Plate 21; and in Auerbach, *Ellen Terry,* 112.

44. Quoted in Loshak, "Watts and Terry," 483.

45. Reproduced in Loshak, "Watts and Terry," Plate 22; and in Auerbach, *Ellen Terry*, 112.

46. Auerbach, *Ellen Terry*, 100.

47. Loshak, "Watts and Terry," 485.

TRACY C. DAVIS

Shotgun Wedlock: Annie Oakley's Power Politics in the Wild West

❦ Amidst the basic formats of variety and circus, "Buffalo" Bill Cody's Wild West show combined the performance traditions of diorama, parades, melodrama, minstrelsy, dressage, and what would ultimately be termed rodeo with the conventions of nineteenth-century ethnographic museums and zoological gardens.[1] Generous measures of national chauvinism and the ethnocentrism arising from westward expansion and the frontier wars molded these ingredients into a meal, fulfilling Don Handelman's rule that "all public events began sometime and somewhere, regardless of whether their existence is attributed to 'tradition' or to invention."[2] From a political and cultural standpoint, the Wild West genre was a realization of its historical moment and, in a sense, a prototype of living history museums, complete with the ideology of rightful white dominion of the American West.[3] For her part, Annie Oakley (a staple of Cody's show for seventeen years) also synthesized entertainment traditions and subsumed cultural codes to transform old ingredients into something new. She drew on numerous circus and variety turns—including equestrianism, equilibrism, acrobatics, and animal acts—and played on the contemporaneity of female athleticism in formatting a scientific demonstration of up-to-the-minute discoveries.

From a technical and scientific viewpoint, Oakley's act could not have developed any earlier. It had performance antecedents in circus and variety, but it depended on newly manufactured weaponry with unprecedented accuracy; its appeal rested in the practical demonstration of these ballistic inventions.[4] Accurate long-range target rifles by Remington and Sharps, which became available in the mid-1870s, were proven at the Creedmore and Sea Girt Range Schuetzenfests, sponsored by the National Rifle Association (NRA; established 1871). However, these long-range competitions were far eclipsed in popularity by traps and short-range target shooting, sports that became enormously popular in the last decades of the century, both among participants and spectators.[5] Like the NRA events—which were instigated to humiliate the New York militia into raising competence to the level of Canadian, Irish, and English teams—Cody's performance occurred in the context of chauvinistic exploits with patriotic obligations. In addition, Cody corroborated the gun's phallic surrogacy with the power invested in masculinized chivalric characteristics such as strength, honor, and violence in a "moral" cause. Instead of appropriating this tradition, Oakley combined the taste for novel mechanical entertainments with an exhibition of female athleticism in the context of the growing middle-class recreations of short-range target and pigeon shooting.

Oakley's personally designed costumes visually proclaimed her allegiance to feminized social norms but, at the same time, distinguished her from the female performance traditions of equestrian dance, ballet (such as *Catarina, ou la Fille du Bandit*),[6] burlesque leg shows (including the "Female Sharpshooters" of 1870), and knockabout "rough soubrettes" who engaged in gymnastics.[7] Unlike their counterparts in European-style entertainments, all the women in Cody's shows eschewed flimsy costumes; their ersatz western costuming had an exoticism of its own, but it was definitely not aided by anatomical display. Oakley's costumes proclaimed that she was feminine yet serious, a disciple of western pragmatism and pioneer work ethics, while perpetuating show business traditions with particularly roisterous pretences.

Performance antecedents are part of the interpretive context surrounding Annie Oakley, augmented by less obvious precedents involving intersections between her public presentations and other cultural tropes, including signals of gender allegiance and conventional interactions between the sexes. In his analysis of circus performance, Paul Bouissac endorses the consideration of "not only material objects but also systems of relations between these objects, i.e., what some ethnologists call cultural units, units of world view, or folk ideas, such as the compatibility or incompatibility of certain situations and certain behavior."[8] In an expansive study of public events, Handelman describes the "kind of relationship where certain components exist elsewhere, but are brought into some sort of connectivity with others that are present," rendering the event "a symbolic structure." While this action makes the performance a world unto itself, it also brings the lived-in world into the performance.[9]

Mary Poovey extends this idea in her study of gender in the Victorian era, usefully describing coherent institutions and practices that are "actually fissured by competing emphases and interests." Historical evidence may break down into groups or clusters symbolically associated by metonymy or metaphor, but it is important to realize "that the middle-class ideology we most often associate with the Victorian period was both untested and always under construction; because it was always in the making, it was open to revision, dispute, and the emergence of oppositional formulations."[10] This problem-solving approach, employing evidence from theatrical tradition and everyday life, suits Annie Oakley ideally—particularly when inconsistencies and contradictions of gender are respected. It is also helpful in unraveling the late nineteenth-century interpretive context of her duo act, for it is crucial to remember that Oakley always performed with her husband and that much of the act's excitement depended upon her regularly imperiling him.

Annie Oakley's childhood was spent remote from the arena and every other venue of popular entertainment. Unlike the belles of European circuses, she did not apprentice in contortionism, stilt walking, the slack rope, high wire, trapeze, and equestrianism.[11] Her only formal apprenticeship occurred in a county workhouse, from which she graduated to become a domestic servant and child minder for a tyrannical farmer. She was a precocious rifle shot but entirely self-taught. In 1876, she married an actor, Frank Butler, who gave a duo precision shooting exhibition in the entr'actes of melodramas. Oakley's stage debut occurred in 1882, when she allegedly stood in for Butler's ailing male partner. No one ever told Annie to get a gun, but she probably was instructed in riding since, the next year, she signed up with the Sells Brothers Circus as an equestrienne. Biographers ignore the illogic of this engagement and do not attempt to account for Oakley's sudden equestrian prowess. It is likely that she developed these skills in the first six years of her marriage (1876–1882), a period about which nothing specific is known; it is just as plausible that she stayed at home with her mother, followed Butler's show, attempted to bear children, or took up trick riding in preparation for a performing career. There is the most circumstantial evidence for the last scenario.

In the first years of Oakley's career, neither she nor Butler seemed to favor shooting over either acting or riding. In their second season with the Sells Circus (1884), Oakley and Butler were billed together as "The Great Far West Rifle Shots"[12]—she being from western Ohio and he from Ireland—a novel permutation of the pseudo-ethnic male/female double acts popular in variety houses.[13] Shooting acts were often configured with a male in control of the firearms and a family member (frequently a daughter or wife) being the facilitator of effects. Oakley's and Butler's poodle participated in the classic William Tell stunt, but, as an exhibition at the Leicester Skating Rink in 1884 demonstrates, the more typical casting had quite different implications.

Captain Austin, who is a noted shot, fired at a potato on his wife's forehead in the ordinary position with success. He next attempted to shoot a potato while lying on his back. As soon as the rifle was fired the woman uttered a scream and fell on the stage, the blood streaming from her forehead.[14]

When they joined Cody in 1885, Butler was dropped from the billing and Oakley was featured as a lady-shot (though he continued to assist her in performance, unbilled and unpaid) in a synthesis of equestrianism and precision shooting, with a complete overturning of the gender norms of shooting acts. Some of Oakley's riding feats were utterly conventional circus turns, such as "sliding head-down from her saddle and untying a handkerchief from the pastern joint of her horse while going at full speed. And in the same position, picking up handkerchiefs and her whip."[15] Other parts of the performance consisted of Oakley destroying glass balls hurled by Butler as their horses galloped around the arena; Oakley varied conventional equestriennes' balancing feats by shooting from a standing position atop a moving horse. In 1887, she added a variation from acrobats' repertoire by performing similar moves on a bicycle.

According to one source, at least sixteen other women were publicly exhibiting rifle shooting when Oakley first went onstage.[16] During Oakley's first season with Cody, a second female sharpshooter joined the company. In the jaundiced words of one of Oakley's biographers, the Californian Huntress, Lillian Smith, "was a rawboned girl without a trace of grace or magnetism,"[17] a succinct way of saying that, unlike Oakley, Smith had no time for horticulture, needlework, or baking and was completely devoid of feminine finesse. Oakley admitted in 1917, years into her retirement, that "it was up-hill work for when I begun [sic] there was a prejudice to live down,"[18] but she overcame the difficulties and eclipsed Lillian Smith as the model for later female sharpshooters.

Managers and publicists seemed to prefer women who combined sharpshooting expertise with conventional femininity offstage. One of the most successful was May Lillie. Her skill with the lariat and rifle was tempered by reports of her Quaker upbringing (like Oakley) and education at Smith College, an equation of civility with eastern institutions. This model was typical of the liberated Gibson girl formula, combining independence, intelligence, beauty, and social eminence.[19] J. F. Muirhead's delineation of the compound Miss Undereast is a variation of the young American achiever type to which Lillie relates:

She could ride almost before she could walk, and soon became an expert shot. . . . When, at last, she went to graduate at the State University of Colorado, she paid for her last year's tuition with the proceeds of her own herd of cattle. . . . Miss Undereast carried on her musical studies far enough to be offered a position in an operatic company, while her linguistic studies qualified her for the post of United States Custom House Inspector [in New York].[20]

Another study of western types affirms the vitality and adaptability of western women who went East. In her native territory, Hurricane Nell "lighted cigars while riding at full speed, drank whiskey, shot guns, [and] swore like men," but she was capable of transformation:

Before long, she was tamed and tidied and introduced into Eastern Society where she retained the sexual effect but lost the habits of the Amazon. Provided with skirts instead of buckskin pants, a cart rather than a saddle, she was removed from the usual arena of wild Western fiction and settled in the cities. There she achieved a lustrousness with which Eastern girls, who combined magnetism and prudery, could hardly compete. For the wild women who entered our main literature were healthy, not depraved; they imbibed from the mountain air its purity and its pungency.[21]

The Western Girl (another variant of Howard Chandler Christy's New Woman) was also popular in European fiction—H. J. Boyesen remarked that "her pistol-firing and her amusing rowdyism relieve the monotony of many a dull novel"[22]—and Oakley personally contributed to the fad while touring. Oakley was an exotic without gaucherie whose personal etiquette demanded that she greet the Princess of Wales before recognizing the Heir Apparent. This gentility comes from the sharpshooter, not republicanism.

In an article of 1900, another female shooter, Louise Mulhall (who grew up in a Wild West outfit), was described in the following terms: "Little Miss Mulhall, who weighs only 90 pounds, can break a bronco, lasso and brand a steer and shoot a coyote at 500 yards. She can also play Chopin, quote Browning, construe Vergil, and make mayonnaise dressing."[23] Carazo, a female crack shot in Adam Forepaugh's Wild West, defied the type but did so consistently with other foreign-born heroines: her exoticism was heightened through "lineage of the Aztec race," and she was explicitly likened to a "skillful metaphysician."[24] She appeared on the bills with the all-male Bogardus team, whose place in Cody's Wild West was filled by Oakley.

Famous female sharpshooters antedated Oakley, many others performed in Wild Wests, and most who were American followed Oakley's model; yet none but Oakley made a livelihood out of directing bullets toward her husband in public. Sarah Blackstone, a recent historian of Cody's Wild West, contends that "it did not matter if the performer was male or female, big or small, old or young, as long as he or she could shoot with great accuracy," for casting in Cody's outfit was strictly by merit: "When they could do a job, they were assigned it."[25] This point is debatable, for life on the ranches could be as elaborately gender and race coded as in the eastern American and European cities and towns where the Wild West played. In nineteenth-century America, very few (if any) institutions completely disregarded a person's sex or race,[26] and popular entertainments thrived on the commercial exploitation of Caucasian femininity. This point is crucial to remember with respect to Oakley and Butler, for as Joan Wal-

lach Scott argues in *Gender and the Politics of History,* "gender is a constitutive element of social relationships based on perceived differences
between the sexes, and gender is a primary way of signifying relationships
of power."[27] Oakley and Butler were the only members of the troupe widely
known as spouses (almost inherently a power imbalance), and though Butler was not billed, audiences knew him to be the star's husband (a reversal
of gender role expectations). Unlike the male western hero of verse and
folklore, Oakley did not shoot to kill, but what she aimed with was un-
deniably deadly. The engagement with risk and demonstration of conjugal
trust was reciprocal—he prepared all the shells and guns for her to handle,
and she, in turn, shot at objects in close proximity to his body—but in
performance his presence barely registered. Both the ballistic and the drawing power were in her hands; few descriptions of their act acknowledge
Butler, but visual sources reveal that his presence was constant and dynam-
ically very important.

Oakley was a trick rider in the traditions of the circus but not a trick
shooter. Despite the overtones of alchemy in her constant experimentation
with the chemical formulations of casings, shot, and gunpowder,[28] her
skill—not illusionism—prevailed. Her aim and ammunition (with openly
acknowledged concessions to the audience's safety) were authentic, and
neither contemporaries nor later biographers have doubted that she was a
bona fide shot.[29] She did not use "theatrical" firearms, invent ballistic gim-
micks like the quadruple-barrelled Scurrimobile, or perpetrate illusions.
Nevertheless, there were important resemblances to standard turns of performance magic that lent vital cultural information to her acts. Without
resorting to illusion, she utilized the latest ballistic inventions while quoting
some classic moves in performance magic, translating them back into the
language of conjurors' tricks that, by definition, combine natural magic
(that is, science) with feats of dexterity.

The typical components of the act are included in Annie Swartout's
(Oakley's niece) description of the order of events in the 1887 command
performance before Queen Victoria. (Seventeen years of performing are
allowed to collapse into one description to highlight the typical, routine
patterning of the performances, in contrast to protean variations.) Following the initial equestrian segment, "From one side of the arena two cowboys
entered carrying a kitchen table on which were placed a number of guns.
They also carried in two trunks in which were mounted clay pigeon
traps."[30] Publicity photos from various points in Oakley's career employ
a table decorated with the insignia and tools of her success. In performance,
a more rugged version of the table supported the properties needed in her
act. Though probably unintentional, the table's and trunks' appearance and
function were strikingly similar to the tables and cabinet apparatuses that

were invariably used by magicians and that became symbolic of that performance specialty. At the same time, Swartout's description of the aid as a *kitchen* table suggests a female realm shared by pioneers and eastern housekeepers alike. Swartout's report continues:

Now came the remainder of the act: Frank [Oakley's husband] stood about fifty feet from Annie and held a small, two by five inch card. . . . With a twenty-two rifle Annie shot through the small red heart as many as fifty times in succession. Next Frank held the cards with the edge toward her, and she, using a pistol, would cut the cards in two. Sometimes they used a common playing-card, usually the five of hearts, and she would shoot through the card many times.

Here they use the very instruments, though not the techniques, of legerdemain.

Although female exponents of card, pocket, and small apparatus tricks emerged as early as 1863,[31] performance magic remained such a predominantly male specialty that in 1983 the *International Conjurors' Magazine* pondered the dearth of female magicians.[32] In Oakley's time, women were far more likely to do spirit rapping or perform on the musical glasses than rigorously practice the techniques of prestidigitation. Oakley was the antithesis of the genteel mentalist, for, like John Nevil Maskelyne (who presided at the Egyptian Hall), she was an antispiritualist demonstrating physical skill and scientific technology, not mysteries and chance. Her version of the Matter Through Matter Effect—whether cards or clay pigeons—was real.

The next part of her act was a variation on a feat dating from antiquity. In the ancient Roman theatre it was performed by knife throwers known as *ventilatores*. "Frank would swing a cord around his body, at the end of which was a glass ball; Annie would lie backwards over a chair, and with the gun upside down, would break the ball." This act combines ventilation with a version of an equilibrist's stunt traceable to the Regency period.[33] A more orthodox version, with a stationary target, was performed by her lesser Wild West colleage Johnny Baker and by Europeans in the music halls. Oakley also varied the stunt in the manner of *ventilatores* by using a polished knife or mirror to reflect the image of Butler and the moving ball (or stationary card) while shooting backwards over her shoulder. Nineteenth-century *ventilatores* often used trick knives, but, in defiance of this hoax, Oakley next performed an even closer imperilment of her partner.

According to her niece, Oakley "said by this time [in the performance] she was in good practice, and would prove it by shooting the ashes from a cigarette which Frank held in his mouth." This trick is usually gimmickry, for as critics of fake shooting warn:

When you happen to see one man standing, cigar in mouth, and another pretending to shoot off the ash without cutting the weed or hurting his pal, you should recollect that the cigar in question is a property affair, and that it contains a wire running through its centre, which, when pushed by the tongue of the smoker, causes the ash to drop off, even though no bullet should have passed near it.[34]

Oakley's distinction is demonstrated by the often cited story of Crown Prince Wilhelm, who invited Oakley to prove the authenticity of the trick, stuffing his own cigar in his mouth. Other popular performers masked their lack of ballistic precision by demonstrating bulletproof shields; in such acts, the chief performers, and in one case a horse, took the personal risks rather than the assistants. The French progenitor of the feat, Monsieur Dowie,

used to explain all about this shield, and would then fasten it on to a horse, and, picking up a carbine, fire at the bullet-proof target. The horse would give a kick, but the shield certainly stopped the bullet. The inventor would then don the cuirass, and invite any marksman to step forward and shoot at him. Soldiers used to take up this challenge, but, beyond a slight stagger, Dowie suffered no ill effects.[35]

Demonstration of Oakley's precision and reliability at the peril of her unprotected husband occurred again in the next segment, when he "held a dime between his first and second fingers, with the edge toward her, and with a twenty-two rifle she hit it, sending it whizzing through the air."[36] This act, like much that preceded it, is a genuine version of the usually bogus "gun trick." Philip Astley claimed to invent the gun trick in 1762 as a way to prevent a fatal duel between two of his fellow regiment members, but a printed source from 1631 claims Coulew of Lorraine caught bullets in his hand, a deception later taught to Ojibway shamans. *The Annals of Conjuring* record: "So long ago as 1723 they [the shamans] allowed themselves to be shot at with marked bullets, using balls made of earth and rubbed over with lead, which were broken in the barrel of the gun by the ramrod."[37] This eliminated the danger by demolishing the projectile or, alternately, by excising it from the barrel with a hollow ramrod and secreting the marked bullet for later presentation. A variation appears in 1787 bills of an itinerant card magician who claimed to catch bullets on a knife point. In the 1840s and 1850s, the magicians Adam Epstein, Robert-Houdin, and Eugene Bosco popularized the gun trick, and it remained in vogue for decades.[38] It was not foolproof: in 1820, the German conjuror Linsky killed his wife while performing the gun trick; six years later, Edmond de Grisy, a French aristocrat, killed his son when a real bullet was substituted; and in 1918, the magician Chung Ling Soo perished as the "living target."[39]

The gun trick is not a precision act and, in this respect, differs from Oakley's exacting attack on the dimes between Butler's fingers, but the two are alike in that the performative effect of the magic illusion "No Harm" is enacted. The magicians relied on deception to "catch" or "survive" the bullets, but Butler merely needed a steady hand and stout gloves. There was no miracle such as in the "No Harm" trick of substituting quicksilver for shot, firing at flying swallows, and reviving the felled birds a few moments later.[40] This sleight-of-hand deception was extremely lucrative in Oakley's time, despite rampant positivism, scientific medicine, and the popularization of ballistics.

In seventeen years of Wild West performances, Butler and Oakley never had an accident. He never misloaded; she never misfired. Skill, practice, precision, and timing—the credo of good performance magicians, whether illusionists or escapologists—preserved their lives. Imminent and inherent danger contributed to the excitement, as it did for the magic acts of disappearance, living pincushion, and dismemberment utilizing large cabinet apparatuses (all based on the illusionist principle of "False Harm"). But what boldly sets Oakley and Butler apart from the magic performative traditions is the gender dynamic of the act.

For an actor, Butler had a remarkably inactive ego. There may have been some glory in merely standing up and facing the barrage, but apart from duo trapezists, it is unusual for male manager-husbands to share in the danger. He retired from the trigger end of performance sharpshooting when they joined Cody's outfit and concentrated on devising the components of the act that would regularly imperil him. He designed the act in direct contravention of the gender roles both in magic and marriage, yet it is instructive to examine what the act borrowed from their traditional performative and cultural tropes.

Apart from the spiritualists, few nineteenth-century female performance magicians headlined an act until after their husbands' deaths; what they learned as "magicians' wives" they turned to their sole benefit as widows. Performance magic is still a stunningly sexist pursuit, as the very names of some of the standard effects belie: "Crushed Girl," "Sawing a Woman in Half," and "Shooting Through a Woman." These are performance traditions as well as marketing nomenclature, functioning as ideological documentation.[41] They continue to provide an expression for social processes usually veiled in privacy, linking what is seen in public to what is unseen in individual households. Robin Morgan cites contemporary northern Ireland as just one local instance of the link between public and domestic violence. In Belfast women's shelters, the words of Patrick Pearse, an Irish hero executed in 1916, are bitterly recalled:

"Bloodshed is a cleansing and a sanctifying thing, and the nation which regards it as the final horror has lost its manhood." And these women further observed that for the street violence to end, the domestic violence at its root must end, "the nation must lose its manhood."[42]

The equation of violence with masculinity—personified individually or as national patriotism—explains feminists' early choice of chauvinism as the favored epithet of blame. As a trope, chauvinism was succeeded by the concept of patriarchy: Isolated oppressors came to be seen as merely agents of an all-encompassing system of oppression, degradation, and sanctified violence institutionalized globally.

In these terms, magic acts are cultural evidence of institutionalized patriarchy. The "Disappearing Woman," for example, is traceable to cabinet magicians throughout recorded history. As an enactment of misogynist wish fulfillment, the concept ranges from the comic ("Take my wife—please!") to gruesome domestic horror. Colonel Stodare (Jack English) performed the Disappearing Woman trick in 1865 as the "Indian Basket Feat." In his version, a reluctant woman was blindfolded and imprisoned in a basket; enraged at her unruliness, he repeatedly stabbed the basket. The woman's screams gave way to a death moan as the magician triumphantly brandished the bloody sword. The violence and enactment of harm are what captivates spectators, yet the pretence of make believe is what qualifies the act as magic and stage illusion. The woman (in this case protesting) succumbs to the rite, terror and death are enacted, yet the magician's prerogative to create illusion is underlined when the woman reenters—smiling and intact—from the wings.[43] A narrative of "False Harm" organizes the event's conclusion.

Invention of a related maneuver, the basic decapitation trick, is credited to a Babylonian Jew in antiquity. It reappears in a Dutch record of 1272, occurred at fairs throughout the medieval and Renaissance periods, and was still in vogue in the eighteenth century.[44] John Nevil Maskelyne performed it as a comic sketch between two men (reminiscent of the rustic and mock doctor in mummings), but Charles de Vere made it sinister in the 1870s by ostentatiously wielding a machete before decapitating a young woman.[45] The eradication of comedy and the substitution of a woman are significant. P. T. Selbit introduced the "Sawing a Woman in Half" variation in 1921, bisecting his victim's body from various angles with plate glass, steel blades, and finally a two-handled saw.[46] It was a great crowd pleaser, as *The Magic Circular* explained:

Congratulations to Selbit on his clever idea and his still more clever handling of the publicity side of the production. To advertise for victims at £5 a night was an inspiration—to offer Christabel Pankhurst £20 a week as a permanent sawing block, that was genius.[47]

Of course, Pankhurst, one of a notorious family of British suffragists, did not take up the offer. Selbit's imitators were legion. Servais Le Roy varied the sawing specialty with a device to bayonet his wife, Mercedes Talma, repeatedly, combining new and old versions of the theme.[49] After setting down his buzz saw, Richiardi, Jr., had nurses dab antiseptic on the severed body of his female assistant, while spectators came up to inspect the wound. The additional props may seem performatively gratuitous, but their narrative continuity with comparable reports in the popular press makes the aesthetics of violence done to compliant women's bodies ideologically piquant. Goldin tried using a man as his sawing victim but, not surprisingly, found that "False Harm" against women (who, at the time, were winning suffrage in most Western countries) was more successful, especially when morticians, nurses, and interns were conspicuously posted around the theatre. Dorothy Dietrich was the first magician to reverse the gender casting fully: In the 1980s, she sawed through Garry Moore (former host of "I've Got a Secret") on national television and is quoted as saying, "the producers think it one of the funniest shows of the series."[49]

The specifics of casting greatly affect what is presented for interpretation: With female victims, dismemberment acts are mysterious, tension invoking, and apparently surgical, but with reversed casting they are merely comic. Dismemberment routines mirror public rituals of symbolic sacrifice as well as common domestic imbalances of power. If the routine is plotted into a play rather than a magic act, *grand guignol* results. Carol Clover astutely recognizes these elements in the horrible murders of women by demonic men in the slasher films, recent cinematic progeny of *grand guignol:*

The preferred weapons of the killers are knives, hammers, axes, icepicks, hypodermic needles, red hot pokers, pitchforks, and the like. Such implements serve well a plot predicated on stealth. . . . But the use of noisy chainsaws and power drills and the nonuse of such relatively silent means as bow and arrow, spear, catapult, and even swords, would seem to suggest that closeness and tactility are also at issue.[50]

Stealth and proximity are thus essential to the horror of female victims' deaths, just as in the Indian basket feat and the classic sawing routine. Clover continues, "It is no surprise that the rise of the slasher film is concomitant with the development of special effects that let us see with our own eyes the 'opened' body."[51] Oakley's and Butler's act is remarkable for its ability to reverse the simulacrum without suggesting either hostility or comedy; this achievement may be partly due to the physical distance put between them as an essential part of conveying skill at firearms.

Oakley used firearms rather than sabres and saws, but the gender lesson from dismemberment routines is salient. The noise and smell of exploding gunpowder was integral to the act, emphasizing the reality and imminence of danger, but the purpose was resolutely not to "open up" Frank Butler's body. Oakley's and Butler's act is inherently dangerous, yet there is no pretence of enacting harm or wishing to do so. Neither is there comedy, or Amazonian revolution. Like the most gruesome renderings of the decapitation and sawing illusions, they surround the performance with much contextualizing material to encourage an appearance of authenticity, utilizing deadly props; but by eschewing mystery and illusion, they are closer to the spirit and traditions of scientific and mechanical entertainments, including Dowie's bullet deflector, than to *grand guignol*. Although the emphasis is still on the chief performer's skill, the contextualization is not violent, and the authenticity belongs to a scientist/athlete rather than to a magician/executioner. Contemporary audiences knew of Butler's comparable skill,[52] yet with this particular casting—"wife puts husband at gunpoint"—it was possible to draw attention to Oakley's skill without any invocation of gender hatred or exploitation of power inequities.

Magic, like *Grand Guignol*, often enacts the submission or death of an assistant or victim. In the nineteenth and twentieth centuries, the wielding of power within this fiction was elaborately gendered (and often ethnically exoticized).[53] The Wild West show pretended meritocracy, where skill (not gender or ethnicity) determined the distribution of work, but it is arguable that in its melodramatic scenarios and the emphasis on honorable rivalry, combat, and competition, power was a distinctly masculinized, white concept. As Nancy Hartsock points out, our legacy from Platonic philosophy is a political economy wherein the powerful protect privilege through violence in an ongoing struggle for dominance.[54] These politics are fully played out in the melodramatic scenarios of racial supremacy and continental conquest in Cody's Wild West. The elaborate fiction of western life in the acts surrounding Oakley's and Butler's performance included what was presented as the "victimization" of Caucasian women and the slaughter of natives in scenarios such as "The Attack on the Settlers' Cabin." Like Oakley, other leading women in the company also demonstrated skills, but it was up to the men to carry out the prerogatives of Manifest Destiny—including explicit "historicized" acts of genocide and chivalry amid the smoke and noise of exploding gunpowder. This gender differentiation helps explain why Oakley did not appear in dime novels of the sort that brought Cody his original and lingering fame.[55] Women had a place in the Wild West milieu but no agency upon the course of history. The gender *mentalité* of late nineteenth-century American culture of the western high literary tradition allowed Oakley to be an iconoclast and prodigy,[56] but other cultural and social traditions prevented her from embodying violence or from playing out a script of domination.

Nineteenth-century reporters stressed the liveliness of Oakley's movements, her amazing stamina, and her unequaled technique and accuracy;[57] such praise matches Hartsock's equations of men's power with women's energy, capacity, and potential.[58] Yet it must not be forgotten that Oakley performed her gun act (a typically masculinized means to violence) with a male partner who was, even more to the point, her husband. In addition to contradicting economic norms, therefore, Oakley and Butler also represent the feminization of power wherein no "ruling" or "inequality" is implied. Unlike the natives in Wild West scenarios, Butler was not scripted to receive wounds or die. Nor was he, like Cody and his allies, ideologically inviolable or, perhaps, even immortal. Hartsock points out "the denial of the importance of the body and of mortality" through "risking of physical death in favor of legendary immortality" as a central characteristic of male economies;[59] Butler acts out this destiny, but with none of the combative elements of the classic masculine heroic destiny. Throughout, it is his partner's skill rather than his own that seems to determine his fate. Oakley's shooting has implications for her domestic future rather than for history.

In many ways, Oakley breaks the "rules" of frontier literature and history as well as the Wild West show: She, not her husband, determined the family's peregrinations, and he, not she, followed out of affection.[60] This role reversal is not symbolic of phallic power appropriation; after all, she fetched her guns from the magic/kitchen table, not from her hip, avoiding metonymic phallic appropriations and the prerogatives of western gunslingers. Her remarkable skills would have been an asset at the frontier— she was a considerably better shot than Cody—but she chose an image of conspicuous femininity. In some respects, she is a representative of the New Womanhood, displaying athleticism (but not in Amazonian proportions) and dress reform (but not mannishness), always in the realm of the physical rather than the intellectual. Her strength and endurance were widely recognized, and, because of the popularity of shooting sports, audiences readily conceded the authenticity of her feats. Unlike the strongman Samson, who retained his reputation despite bolting down the barbell that he then invited hapless volunteers to try to lift,[61] Oakley's act did not require deception to convey the female's prerogative to wield strength and to display unparalleled expertise. There is an implicit questioning of order in this design, but not a radical agenda for reordering. Handelman explains the outcome of such power inversions as inherently conservative:

My own view is that inversion keeps to the mold of the phenomenon, the foundation for inversion, that actually is inverted. Therefore, inversion maintains the relevance of its foundation, and is a discourse about its validity. For instance, the inversion of a stratified order is still a discourse about that very order of stratification that is inverted. The inversion of gender remains a discourse on gender, and so forth.[62]

Thus, Oakley did not harbor a veiled agenda designed to counter male traditions or plan to usurp power by creating an oppositional sexuality, performance mode, or political order, and she was not perceived as threatening by either perspicacious or naïve spectators.

Nevertheless, Oakley's choice to depart from the traditions of circus costuming and accessories gave a strong visual iconoclasm to her act and is indicative of her agency, resistance, and public feminism (something enacted, not verbally espoused) within the arena. She adopted a feminized persona but specifically eschewed an appearance that was strongly sexualized, rejecting the vixen and the virago. In her act, differentiation of gender typologies was open ended, not absolutely binary. In private life, she gardened, embroidered, kept her tent tidy, cooked, hunted game, rode astride, won shooting competitions, and advocated women's armed self-defence in a highly individual combination of gender contradictions.

Oakley valued her feminine public persona and singularity: When syndicated Hearst newspapers reported in 1903 that she was a thief, a drug addict, a cross-dresser, and Bill Cody's daughter-in-law, she sued for libel. The insult of the imposture was compound: It suggested that Oakley was not lawful or pure, that she was artificially lively, that she rose to fame by nepotism rather than through skill, and that she was unfeminine. She won the case, in city after city.[63] It was an important public correction, not only for her pride and dignity or the reputation of her marriage but also for the personification she gave to feminized power.

Notes

1. For the best descriptions, see William Brasmer, "The Wild West Exhibitions and the Drama of Civilization," in *Western Popular Theatre,* ed. David Mayer and Kenneth Richards (London: Methuen, 1977), pp. 133–56; and Don Russell, *The Wild West: or, a History of the Wild West Shows* (Fort Worth: Amon Carter Museum of Art, 1970).

2. Don Handelman, *Models and Mirrors: Towards an Anthropology of Public Events* (Cambridge: Cambridge University Press, 1990), p. 17.

3. For comparative material, see Warren Leon and Margaret Piatt, "Living-History Museums," in *History Museums in the United States: A Critical Assessment,* ed. Warren Leon and Roy Rosenzweig (Urbana and Chicago: University of Illinois Press, 1989), pp. 64–97; and Tracy C. Davis, "Annie Oakley and her Ideal Husband of No Importance," in *Critical Theory and Performance,* ed. Joseph Roach and Janelle Reinelt (Ann Arbor: University of Michigan Press, 1991).

4. James Cranbrook, "The Guns of Annie Oakley," *Guns* (2 May 1956):5–17; correspondence from Paul Fees, curator of the Buffalo Bill Museum, to Shirl Kaspar (18 March 1985) and Tracy C. Davis (6 November 1989) is also relevant.

5. David F. Butler, *United States Firearms. The First Century 1776–1895* (New York: Winchester Press, 1971), pp. 168–73; and James B. Trefethen, comp., *Americans and Their Guns: The National Rifle Association Story through Nearly a Cen-*

tury of Service to the Nation, ed. James E. Serven (Harrisburg, PA: Stockpole Books, 1967), pp. 104–5.

6. In a portrait ca. 1846, Lucille Grahn is depicted as this Spanish heroine, with a pair of pistols at her waist and a rifle in her hand. The female chorus also carries rifles.

7. Shirley Staples, *Male-Female Comedy Teams in American Vaudeville 1865–1932* (Ann Arbor: UMI Press, 1984), pp. 22, 58–59.

8. Paul Bouissac, *Circus and Culture: A Semiotic Approach* (Bloomington: Indiana University Press, 1976), p. 7.

9. Handelman, *Models and Mirrors,* 13.

10. Mary Poovey, *Uneven Developments: The Ideological Work of Gender in Mid-Victorian England* (Chicago: University of Chicago Press, 1988), p. 3.

11. This is the classic progression for women from Miss Woolford to Zaeo. *The Town* (London) (17 October 1840):1.

12. Isabelle S. Sayers, *Annie Oakley and Buffalo Bill's Wild West* (New York: Dover, 1981), p. 12.

13. Staples, *Male-Female Comedy Teams,* 27.

14. *St. James's Gazette* (1 February 1884), reprinted in the introduction to [Ellen Barlee], *Pantomime Waifs; Or, a Plea for City Children* (London: S. W. Partridge, 1884).

15. Annie Fern Swartout, *Missie; An Historical Biography of Annie Oakley* (Blanchester, OH: Brown, 1947), pp. 115–16.

16. Courtney Ryley Cooper, *Annie Oakley. Woman at Arms* (New York: Duffield, 1920), pp. 128–29.

17. Walter Havinghurst, *Annie Oakley of the Wild West* (New York: Macmillan, 1954), p. 71.

18. Typescript letter to the *Tribune* (2 February 1917), Oakley scrapbooks, Buffalo Bill Historical Center, Cody, WY.

19. Harvard Theatre Collection, programme for Pawnee Bill's Historic Wild West, ca. 1890. See also William Wasserstrom, *Heiress of All the Ages: Sex and Sentiment in the Genteel Tradition* (Minneapolis: University of Minnesota Press, 1959), p. 16.

20. James Fullarton Muirhead, *The Land of Contrasts: A Briton's View of His American Kin* (Boston, New York, and London: Lamson, Wolffe, 1898), pp. 60–61.

21. Wasserstrom, *Heiress,* 41–42.

22. Hjalmar Hjorth Boyesen, *Literary and Social Silhouettes* (New York: Harper and Brothers, 1894), p. 8. See also Martha Banta, *Imaging American Women: Idea and Ideals in Cultural History* (New York: Columbia University Press, 1987).

23. *New York World* (7 July 1900), cited in Russell, *The Wild West,* 79.

24. Harvard Theatre Collection programme, ca. 1888. See also Wasserstrom, *Heiress,* 43.

25. Sarah J. Blackstone, *Buckskins, Bullets, and Business: A History of Buffalo Bill's Wild West* (Westport: Greenwood, 1986), pp. 85, 111. Jack Rennert concurs in *100 Posters of Buffalo Bill's Wild West* (New York: Darien House, 1976), p. 13.

26. See Mary Ryan, *Women in Public: Between Banners and Ballots, 1825–1880* (Baltimore and London: Johns Hopkins University Press, 1990).

27. Joan Wallach Scott, *Gender and the Politics of History* (New York: Columbia University Press, 1988), p. 42.

28. Dick Baldwin, "Powders I Have Known," *Guns and Ammo* 11.9 (Septem-

ber 1967):42ff. See also Albert A. Hopkins, *Stage Illusions and Scientific Diversions* (New York: Munn, 1897), pp. 309–10.

29. See, for example, "Fake Shooting Exposed," *Sunday Mercury* (New York) (15 March 1896).

30. Swartout, *Missie*, 128–29.

31. For example, Madame Bosco, Madame Card (ca. 1873–1886), Mesdames Rose and Beatrice (1880–1884), Madame Artot Roman (1886). See the boxes on magic material in the Harvard Theatre Collection's popular theatre collection; also Sidney W. Clarke, *Annals of Conjuring* (reprint, New York: Magico Magazine, 1983).

32. Dorfay, "Why Are There Not More Women Magicians," *Genii* 47.4 (April 1983):257–59.

33. Charles C. Moreau, *A Collection of Play Bills, &c. Relating to the Circus in New York City,* Harvard Theatre Collection Extra Illustrated volume (New York, 1894), p. 40.

34. *Sunday Mercury* (New York) (15 March 1896).

35. George W. Alltree, *Footlight Memories: Recollections of Music Hall and Stage Life* (London: Sampson Low, Marston [1932]), p. 89.

36. Swartout, *Missie*, 128–29.

37. Clarke, *Annals of Conjuring,* 203–4, 246; and Henry Ridgely Evans, *The Old and the New Magic* (Chicago: Open Court, 1909), p. 152.

38. Ibid., 121, 128–29, 140–41, 160.

39. Ibid., 103, 107, 254; Evans, *Old and New Magic,* 22; and Will Dexter, *The Riddle of Chung Ling Soo* (London and New York: Arco, 1955), pp. 18–25.

40. Giuseppe Pinetti, *Physical Amusements and Diverting Experiments. Composed and Performed in Different Capitals of Europe, and in London* (London, 1784).

41. Mechanical thriller feats of the late nineteenth century also enacted female imperilments. The "Human Cannon Ball," "Human Catapult," "Human Arrow" (for acrobats), and "The Limit" (originally a bicycle trick, later performed in automobiles) were done by women—or, at any rate, by performers (such as Lulu) believed to be women. This femininity was essential to their success. See Tody Hamilton, "Circus History in Thrills: The Art of Making Your Flesh Creep in the Showring," 1907 (newspaper clipping, Harvard Theatre Collection).

42. Robin Morgan, *The Demon Lover: On the Sexuality of Terrorism* (New York: W. W. Norton, 1989), p. 315.

43. Geoffrey Lamb, *Victorian Magic* (London: Routledge and Kegan Paul, 1976), pp. 67–68.

44. Clarke, *Annals of Conjuring,* 23, 82, 89.

45. Lamb, *Victorian Magic,* 114–15; see also Clarke, *Annals of Conjuring,* 185–86.

46. Milbourne Christopher, *The Illustrated History of Magic* (New York: Thomas Y. Crowell, 1973), p. 266.

47. *The Magic Circular* 15.174 (April 1921):117–18.

48. Christopher, *Illustrated History,* 268, 304–5, 422.

49. *Magicians Week* (Hewitt, NY) (March 1978):1.

50. Carol J. Clover, "Her Body, Himself: Gender in the Slasher Film," *Representations* 20 (Fall 1987):198.

51. Ibid., 198.

52. Butler excelled at trapshooting, a sport he competed in from 1876. While

touring with the Wild West, he represented munitions manufacturers and performed at local meets. He continued to compete after Oakley's retirement from show business, winning the New Jersey State Championship in 1906. "Mr. Butler's Resignation," *Forest and Stream* 29 (January 1910) (Oakley scrapbooks).

53. Mel Gordon, *Grand Guignol: Theatre of Fear and Terror* (New York: Amok Press, 1988).

54. Nancy C. M. Hartsock, *Money, Sex, and Power: Toward a Feminist Historical Materialism* (New York and London: Longman, 1983), pp. 186–230.

55. Don Russell, *The Lives and Legends of Buffalo Bill* (Norman: University of Oklahoma Press, 1960), p. 314. There is an enormous post–World War II juvenile literature on Oakley (largely ficto-biography), along with all the spin-offs from the television show, but nothing contemporary with Ned Buntline's handiwork.

56. Richard Slotkin, *The Fatal Environment: The Myth of the Frontier in the Age of Industrialization 1800–1890* (New York: Atheneum, 1985).

57. For a representative sampling of reports, see Oakley's scrapbooks at the Buffalo Bill Historical Center, Cody, WY.

58. Hartsock, *Money, Sex, and Power*, 210.

59. Ibid., 202.

60. Annette Kolodny, *The Land Before Her: Fantasy and Experience of the American Frontiers, 1630–1860* (Chapel Hill and London: University of North Carolina Press, 1984).

61. Alltree, *Footlight Memories*, 83–84.

62. Handelman, *Models and Mirrors*, 52.

63. Oakley scrapbooks.

SPENCER GOLUB

Revolutionizing Galatea: Iconic Woman in Early Soviet Culture

In Soviet culture, which has been performative and revolutionary since 1917, male hands have often roughly sculpted the female image. The Soviet Pygmalion, who remade *himself* historically, viewed his Galatea with suspicion, while desiring her with a combination of private obsession and revolutionary fervor. Meanwhile, Soviet women, who appeared often as dramatic characters and theatrical performers, political revolutionaries, and party workers in pre- and postrevolutionary society, rarely if ever served as playwrights, stage directors, or as members of the government or the party's inner elite. But although women's roles were only occasionally authorial, they were far more than merely participatory in defining the life and image of the new Soviet culture. Woman was for the Soviets a necessary and significant object through which a wider discourse was conducted.

The attempts by the revolutionary government to fold the Woman question into the Class question after 1917 concealed an insidious and long-standing strain of social and conceptual embedding that had less to do with gender than with gender-coded roles. The revolutionizing of Galatea by the patriarchal Soviet state's Pygmalion coincided with the casting in the statue's role of the "feminized" and "politically uncommitted and disempowered" artist-intellectual class. This unpublicized union ironically recast the expressed desire of decadent prerevolutionary Russian culture, which equated Woman and Art with inertia and death. As such, the Soviet aesthetic valorized a counter-revolutionary concept dressed up in the trappings of a new style and a new, more enlightened way of seeing. This tragic theme, as I will show, emerged only gradually from the historical drama, whose announced plot was the reconfiguration of Man and Woman, proletarian and intellectual, as political and cultural equals bonded together by a common cause.

I have made the transliteration consistent throughout the text and notes, except where publishers have employed different systems in rendering authors' names and the titles of their works.

In the prerevolutionary period, male and female self-engenderment (sexual role reversal, androgyny, and bisexuality) as behavioral and artistic codes defined a performative and metaphorical solution to personal and national identity crises, even as it illustrated the problem. "Systematic duality,"[1] entertaining difference while predicting spiritual union, was effaced, after 1917, in the Bolsheviks' promotion of the anonymous, largely degendered proletariat and the resolution of history into communism's all-encompassing revolutionary moment. The collective monolith of material utopianism engineered by the new Soviet state was designed to celebrate its victory over the vaguely spiritual communities nostalgic for the past that were envisioned by prerevolutionary aesthetes. Rather than attempt the impossible, the inscription of "the feminine . . . in common language," the Bolsheviks forged a syncretic vocabulary of group-speak and official acronyms. The Bolsheviks revolutionized Galatea in theory while absorbing her into a syncretic model of New Personhood for the New Society. However, while the male party leadership and Soviet culture celebrated the "New Man" for his toughness and honesty, they characterized the "New Woman" as "grim, mannish, plain and armed." Masculine consciousness continued to cast a watchful eye on feminine spontaneity.[2] Woman was attendant at the birth of the Revolution; according to Soviet history, however, Man was its birth mother.

The new Soviet regime wanted to see itself expressed in images of mastery—invention and production—rather than in terms of mystery and identity crisis. Machines and machine-men defined a man-made world of objects and materials whose rational, orderly perfection shamed "the capriciousness of [Mother] Nature." Man's universal fear of female otherness was quelled by folding the Woman question into the Class question. Sex and gender issues were demystified, even as they were pushed onto the national stage by politics and discussed by more people more often.[3]

The new Soviet culture inscribed masculine values and forms, promoting the athletic body over the aesthetic eye and mass, density, dynamism, and space over the static, painted surface that masked the prerevolutionary symbolists' inner world. This tendency was ironically predicted by elements in the prerevolutionary avant-garde. A character called "A Time Traveler" in the "trans-rational" (*zaumny*) cubo-futurist opera *Victory Over the Sun* (St. Petersburg premiere, December 1913), proclaimed: ". . . Look / Everything's become masculine / The lake is harder than iron / Don't believe the old gauges." Artist El Lisitsky's (Lazar Markovich Lisitsky) *The New One* (1920–1921), a lithographic representation of an "electro-mechanical production" for an unrealized staging of *Victory Over the Sun*, captured the newly constructed mystery of the machine age. This two-legged, two-headed, "dynamic figure built up of nonobjective shapes," with its red-square heart and overall red and black revolutionary color code and metallic frame, suggested the new order's resolved dualism, a reconstructive, dialectical consciousness that extended to gender.[4] At the same time, however, such artistic montages in various media broke up the homogeneity of visual space, and within that space, Woman's body continued to disrupt social consciousness.

The new Soviet order "presupposed socialist fellowship as a fellowship of men" and continued to distrust women as being inherently passive, inconsistent, and uncommitted to any political ideology. While few male party leaders were as openly misogynistic as Joseph Stalin, who referred disparagingly to female intellectuals as "herrings with ideas," all sidestepped the question of complete equality between the sexes. This attitude prevailed despite the fact that it was the rioting of socialist factory women that ushered in the February 1917 Revolution.[5]

Lenin, who believed that "a woman can never give herself a hundred percent to the party," certainly had the many illiterate and socially conservative women of his country in mind when he proclaimed that "a person who can neither read nor write is outside politics." However, although fewer women than men were politically indoctrinated in the early stages of the Revolution, those who were (along with a high percentage of artists and Jews) soon became responsible for improving the literacy and political consciousness of Bolshevik men. Women commissars headed the *politotdely,* the political sections of the Red Army during the Civil War. These were under the general direction of Varya Kasparova, who directed the Agitational Department of the Bureau of Military Commissars in Moscow. Women also directed the Central Executive Committee's School for Agitators and Instructors. Still others worked in the Cheka, the secret police, during this same period.[6]

There were, of course, many other women whose "support positions" consisted of little more than making the beds, cooking the meals, and cleaning the apartments of male activists. Lenin, for example, sought to cast his wife Nadezhda Krupskaya in the role of domestic madonna to counterbalance his mistress Inessa Armand's role of revolutionary muse. This ironic replay of prerevolutionary decadent iconic stereotyping backfired, however, when Lenin discovered, much to his consternation, that his domestic skills were superior to his wife's. Krupskaya's self-defined role was, at first, largely passive—not obstructing and however possible freeing her husband to do his political work. Armand, however, was Lenin's soul-mate and political confidante and, on at least one occasion, his alter ego. Lenin sent her to represent him at a revolutionary Presidium under the female variant of his pseudonym "Petrov(a)," telling her: "So, through our pseudonyms, we shall face the public united in one person—openly yet secretly.

You will actually be me." This conflation of male-female identity modeled what was to be the new fashion of anonymous revolutionary collectivism, which would nominally replace the celebrity of prerevolutionary individualism.

In the meantime, Krupskaya, whose frumpishness and unexceptional nature embarrassed her husband, evolved from being a nurturing wife to being a skilled educational propagandist. She continued, however, to be plagued by shyness, which was misread as passivity. She is but one example of how even leading female revolutionaries helped on occasion to reinforce male stereotypes of women. The widely admired revolutionary Mariya Spirodonova (who killed a provincial governor at the age of nineteen) told the American communist writer Louise Bryant that women are better martyrs than administrators because "it needs temperament and not training to be a martyr." Spirodonova and fellow revolutionary Angelika Balabanova suggested that women are held back by conscience and a lack of inner freedom that do not impede most men.[7]

"We are weak," reflected Vera Pavlovna, the proto-feminist heroine of Nikolay Chernyshevsky's novel *What Is to Be Done?* (1863), "because we consider ourselves so." This negative self-assessment is, however, inconsistent with the historical profile of female revolutionaries developed in part from the testimony of their male counterparts. The men saw them, again romantically, as being more ruthless than they, with an "almost reverent" attitude toward terrorism. Historian James H. Billington, citing examples of female revolutionaries of the nineteenth and early twentieth centuries, wrote that "their distinctive role . . . was to purify and intensify terror, not to articulate ideas," and that "this passion for purity fueled a growing desire among women revolutionaries to be the one to throw the bomb, to be sentenced to death, or even to immolate one's self in prison." One such revolutionary, Evstoliya Rogozinikova, "heavily perfumed in an elegant black dress," blew up the director of the main prison administration in St. Petersburg with "thirteen pounds of high explosives that she had packed into her bodice and used to enhance her bust."[8] Such self-empowered women were the prototypes for the revolutionary *belle dame sans merci* that the male Soviet leadership feared and respected enough to neither encourage nor develop.

Russian men in general still considered women to be objects, even as Bolshevik party leadership extended to them limited partnership as revolutionary subjects. Lenin, who spoke to the first All-Russian Congress of Women, was a sympathetic listener in the discussion of the Woman question; however, in *On the Emancipation of Women* (1919), he stated that working women must liberate themselves without creating their own separate political organizations, which he feared would divide the party and subvert the Class question. Accordingly, Aleksandra Kollontay tried to make the Women's Section of the Party (*Zhenotdel*), which she headed from 1920 to 1922, appear to be less separatist and more gender-neutral. Feminism, in place since the 1860s, was regarded by most Soviet men and women as a bourgeois enterprise. As Billington states, "Women tended to be more revolutionary than feminist in Russia." Evidence to the contrary, however, was provided by Yakov Protazanov's 1924 film *Aelita*. Aelita, Queen of Mars, seduces a brave Soviet engineer into aiding her in fomenting a workers' revolt on her planet. This plot having been accomplished, Aelita seeks to destroy the engineer, thus betraying a feminist agenda hidden within her revolutionary plan. This scenario embodied a male and party paranoia that never really abated.

The number of prominent Bolshevik women placed close to the centers of political power, though small in the period between the advent of the Revolution and the years directly following the Civil War (1917–1923), thereafter dropped precipitously. In 1922, only 8 percent of party members were female, a proportion that rose to 12 percent by 1927. Overall, only three women, Elena Stasova (functioning secretary of the party during and immediately after the Revolution), Varvara Yakovleva (director of the Petrograd branch of the Cheka in 1918), and Aleksandra Kollontay (Commissar of Public Welfare, the first female member of the party's Central Committee, and director of *Zhenotdel*, 1920–1922) belonged to the party's highest ranks. Only four women—Klavidiya Nikolaeva, Aleksandra Artyukhina, Krupskaya and Anna Kalygina—served on the Party's Central Committee between 1924 and 1939.[9] The role of women in the government was only slightly better.

Politically talented women occupied mainly mid-management positions in the new regime and competed for Lenin's attention. His benign but aloof paternalism replaced the patriarchy of the Church fathers and reinforced that of the husbands and fathers who ruled the traditional family unit. Although the political equality that radical women had expected since the nineteenth century and that the Soviet constitution guaranteed never came about, Lenin could justifiably proclaim in "Soviet Power and the Status of Women" (1919): "In the course of two years of Soviet power in one of the most backward countries in Europe, more has been done to emancipate women, to make her the equal of the 'strong sex,' than has been done during the past 130 years by all the advanced, enlightened, 'democratic' republics of the world taken together." Still, the Bolsheviks were concerned with liberating working class women more for their social class than for their gender, and Woman remained "an appendage to a broader labor problem."[10]

The Sex question was a symbolic means for the Bolsheviks to maintain the characterization of Woman as politically recalcitrant Other, so as to separate her from the goal of political common cause. A statement made by a character in Fyodor Gladkov's Soviet novel *Cement* (1925) that romance required "the muscles of a bull," "healthy nerves," and cold, calculating minds reflected the Bolsheviks' attempt to abstract sex from the realm of private emotion, to transmute it into an objective, anonymous (that is, collective) political desire. The Bolsheviks at least publicly asserted that abstinence rather than sex with contraception was most conducive to effective party work.

Aleksandra Kollontay's removal as minister of welfare was made inevitable by what Lenin viewed as her mixing of sex and politics. Kollontay was specifically reprimanded for defending her husband Fyodor Dubenko, leader of the Kronstadt fleet, against the charge of trading with the Germans. Louise Bryant suggested, however, that the unspoken charge against Kollontay was her "excessive theatricality." To this description one might ascribe her advocacy of free love, her marriage to a man some years her junior, her "feminine" insincerity and irresponsibility (the ability to play-act and the desire to do so), and her iconicity. The political patriarchy preferred the maternal, "heavy, earthy figure of Eve" to "the slim, inspired unmaternal figure" of the New Woman—the autonomous, revolutionary Salomé that Kollontay embodied.[11] The latter put the party too much in mind of the decadent Columbines who graced the stage of prerevolutionary culture in which ironic *commedia dell'arte* plays and motifs were extremely popular among the "feminized," that is, the ambivalent, alienated, and paradoxical, intelligentsia.

The Bolsheviks disliked and distrusted renegade theatricality, which escaped their design and control, whether in the form of free love or gender role reversal. For this reason, Provisional Government leader Aleksandr Kerensky, whom Edmund Wilson described as being "an emotional and ornamental orator, . . . badly spoiled by the ladies of Petrograd," saw his vanity and self-importance parodied. Nikolay Evreinov, in the mass spectacle *The Storming of the Winter Palace* (7 November 1920), depicted Kerensky escaping from the Winter Palace in drag to the exclamations of his Women's Battalion. Sergey Eisenstein, in his film *October* (1927), presented Kerensky as a preening Napoleon. As recently as the 1970s, stage director Yury Lyubimov offered an "hysterical" Kerensky to a new theatre-going public at Moscow's Taganka Theatre.[12]

Kerensky's theatrically flamboyant figure contrasted unfavorably with the unprepossessing Lenin, "who never said more than he meant" and who refused to purchase new clothing en route to the Finland Station to take command of the Revolution. Both Lenin's and Kerensky's personae were, however, developed from legitimate revolutionary models. Lenin's revolutionary asceticism—the mythical Lenin who ate only what was within reach of the common people and engaged in "nothing but the necessary"— was derived from Rakhmetov, who slept on a bed of nails to strengthen his will in Chernyshevsky's novel *What Is to Be Done?* Kerensky, with his self-dramatizing tendencies, his love affair with language, costume, and self-affirmation, could claim as his prototype the Decembrist revolutionaries of the 1820s. But the syllogistic logic that equated theatricality with femininity, femininity with weakness (seen in the earliest Russian fables), and thus theatricality with weakness proved to be too ingrained to be easily effaced. The developing Soviet state sought to "de-feminize" and de-theatricalize men and women, to strip them of all vanity and pretense (code words for individualism), to create the appearance of a uniform and a uniformly strong political collective.[13]

Romantic egoism was replaced officially by comradeship, predicated upon the assumption that "nobody is *one,* but *one of.*" The subjective "I" was symptomatic of and conducive to bourgeois nostalgia and petty sentiment. In Evgeny Zamyatin's dystopic parody *We* (1920), the male protagonist D-503, a worker on the space project "Integral" ("the endless equalization of all Creation"), rejects the sentimental and compliant o-90 for the New Woman E-330, who helps him develop a soul (*dusha,* gendered feminine in Russian). The New Man's and the New Woman's sense of having invented one another, the ideal embodied in El Lisitsky's "The New One" and partially in the D-503/E-330 relationship, is shadowed in *We* by an image from/of the past. In a glass cage, suspended in mid-air, a man and woman stand frozen in a kiss, "her whole body . . . bent backward, as if broken. This for the last time, for all time."[14]

Bolshevism was threatened by nonpolitical romantic union and by separatist politics. In particular, the party hierarchy feared the autonomous Amazon, characterized by her detractors as a "psychological freak," an unnatural hybrid of male will and female desire.[15] The model of Amazonian autonomy was the Women's Death Battalions, commissioned by the Provisional Government as "stopping detachments" in the struggle to capture army deserters and dissuade would-be defectors during the Civil War. Of the 250 members of the Women's Battalion who unsuccessfully defended the Winter Palace from Bolshevik attack in 1917, six were killed and thirty wounded. Their commander, Mariya Bochkarova, the daughter of a former serf, hated men and distrusted women in equal measure. She trained her all-female unit separately from the male soldiers, which deepened the suspicion and resentment already caused by the battalion's link to a right-wing feminist organization. When one of her female charges autonomously sought sexual union with a man, Bochkarova allegedly bayoneted her to death while in the act.

In the film *October,* Eisenstein depicts the members of the Women's Battalion in a moment of repose inside the Winter Palace. They proceed to remove their masculine uniforms, revealing their female undergarments, and to apply cosmetics. This action parodies both femininity, via homo-erotic association, and the depth of the female resolve to enact the male's activist role, a resolve the Bolsheviks considered to be suspect. At least in the fictional retelling, the Winter Palace as symbol of the decadent past became the stage upon which both Kerensky and his female defenders en-gaged in cross-dressing. Once the honest, healthy Bolshevik workers seized control of the government, the Amazons of the Women's Battalion "were ordered home and told to put on female attire because they were considered enemies of the revolution."[16]

The amount and intensity of criticism, gossip, and parodic abuse of the Women's Battalions in Russia and abroad constituted nothing short of a ritualized public humiliation. These masculinized women had not only co-opted a male social role but a male artistic prerogative. Prerevolutionary male artists expressed their embedded femaleness in female characters whom they both idealized and destroyed. The Women's Battalions trans-formed the female role from one of artistic object to that of artistic subject and dared to fetishize and perform *male* identity in the process. The fic-tional Kerensky's donning of female garments, while under the protection of his trousered female defenders, signified that the only women's skirts left to hide behind were his own. Male desire was thrown back upon itself. The anti-Bolshevik, prerevolutionary artists-intellectuals, director Nikolay Evreinov and designer Yury Annenkov, who staged Kerensky's "historical" action in the mass spectacle, would soon emigrate, their political and cul-tural disempowerment vested in the symbolic images they had helped create.

The vast majority of the five thousand women who fought in World War I and the eighty thousand who served in the Civil War (figures ap-proximate), many of whom filled the noncombatant roles of laborer, health- and food-service worker, teacher, and spy, were individuals teamed with men and celebrated in wartime propaganda.[17] The Bolsheviks produced their own heroic Amazon in the person of Larisa Reisner, the prototype for the Commissar who saves the fleet from anarchy in Vsevolod Vishnev-sky's 1933 drama *An Optimistic Tragedy.* The daughter of a St. Petersburg law professor, Reisner was a twenty-two-year-old beauty when she joined the Red Army in the Civil War. As head of the intelligence section of the Volga Fleet, she conducted spying missions behind enemy lines, but later she could not accept the moral turpitude precipitated by the Soviet exper-iment in a free market economy, the New Economic Policy (1921–1928).

Alisa Koonen, the lead actress of Moscow's Kamerny Theatre and wife of its artistic director Aleksandr Tairov, counted Vishnevsky's Commissar among her most successful professional roles (Kamerny Theatre premiere, 1933). In her performance, Koonen stressed the partially revealed feminine qualities in the Amazon.[18] Reisner, a member of the Soviet "cult of power" and the self-designated "woman of the Russian Revolution," was also an amateur poet, and she sought to intercede with Lenin to stay the execution of Acmeist poet Nikolay Gumilev. Here and elsewhere, she manifested the empathic, "contradictory and unrestrained" (that is, feminine) aspects of her otherwise Amazonian character. By rewriting the Salomé-Sphinx's calculating female laconism as constructive, Lenin-like, male laconism, the fictionalized Amazon Reisner could become the "heroine" of Vishnevsky's play. Vishnevsky wrote of the Commissar: "She does more observing than speaking because there is so much that she will have to do" (p. 206). The silent woman had been presented by prerevolutionary male artists in a deadly or death-like state, the (male) artist-destroying, symbolist Sphinx who "rules [words] by stopping them, stillborn, in the throat," and by the drowned Ophelia, the artistic object who enacts the artist's (Hamlet's) self-destructive self-adulation. In *The Optimistic Tragedy*, the translation of the female's penchant for "untransformed cruelty" and self-victimization into a thoughtful prelude to heroic action was accomplished simply by masking male character with a woman's face.[19]

If the Bolsheviks were in conflict concerning dramatically expressed female autonomy, they were likewise uncertain as to whether and how the family unit could be made responsive to Woman's and the party's nominally shared ideals. The Bolsheviks, citing *The Communist Manifesto*, believed that *bourgeois* family life would disappear with capitalism. Karl Marx linked women's liberation with the abolition of the patriarchal family structure.[20] Lenin, however, associated the family with orderliness and orderliness with the party cause. Neither the Bolsheviks nor the average Soviet citizen wanted to see family life abolished, and only the Bolsheviks wanted to see it re-defined.

Leon Trotsky had warned that the revolutionary woman, in particular the *zhenotdelovka,* a member of *Zhenotdel* (the Women's Section or Department of the Central Committee Secretariat, 1919–1930), owing to her preoccupation with the women's movement, would act as a dissolvent of family life. Throughout the country and especially in the provinces, men fought (sometimes with the aid of other women) Zhenotdel's efforts to organize and politicize their wives. For the most part, Zhenotdel concerned itself with family issues such as child and orphan care, school service and inspection, food distribution and housing supervision, preventative medicine, and public health and education. However, by investing civil powers in strong women and by giving women in general a sense of personal and

collective identity independent of their husbands, Zhenotdel helped to undermine the traditional patriarchal family structure. The assertion of an
even more dominant, centralized patriarchy under Stalin, made necessary
by the demands of intensified industrialization, led to the elimination of all
secondary loyalties and associations, including Zhenotdel. With this development, the Woman question, born in Russia in the late 1850s and early
1860s, was officially considered "resolved." Paradoxically, Zhenotdel was
originally founded by the male party leadership (and staffed in part by their
wives and relatives) as part of a propaganda campaign aimed at winning
women over to the Communist cause.[21]

The prototypical New Soviet Woman, the *zhenotdelovka* Dasha Chumalova in *Cement,* was "a woman with a red kerchief about her head . . .
burn[ing] like a flame" (p. 60) (Lenin's revolutionary newspaper was called
The Spark). She seemed "strange, not womanly" to her husband Gleb, just
returned from serving in the Civil War. Whereas in Rakhmetov's "spiritual
autobiography" (in *What Is to Be Done?*), reading precedes experience,
Dasha is first brutalized by life and only then becomes a "woman at the
table." This new, activist, sociopolitical character type sought to replace
the popular nineteenth-century image of the "woman at the window," a
male-dependent, passive nonparticipant in life. The shift from the window
to the table, while dramatic, did not, however, represent a clean break with
the past. When the student revolutionary Mariya Vetrova was lionized for
immolating herself with kerosene from her reading lamp, her martyrdom
to a self-determined fate simply recast the decadent image of Woman as
the Bride of Death.[22]

In his play *The Puppet Show* (1906), Aleksandr Blok parodied the symbolists' romantic and self-important characterization of Woman as Death.
A panel of mystics (symbolists) confuse a woman's plait (*kosa* in Russian)
with a scythe (also *kosa* in Russian). In *Cement,* one of Dasha Chumalova's
fellow *zhenotdelovki* announces her intention to cut her plait, likening it
to a noose on which women hang and that men hang on to as a romantic
symbol. The cutting of the plait, a likely reference to Blok's play, represents
the New Soviet Woman's consignment of the virgin-harlot personae to ob-
solescence. The semiotics of altered and confused identity—bobbed-haired
women and clean-shaven men—reflected the changing face of the Party as
surely as Peter the Great's (reigned 1682–1725) shaving of his nobles'
beards signified the shift from an old, insular Slavic order to a new Wes-
ternizing one.

A non-nurturing and sexually liberated mother and wife, Dasha gives
her young daughter to the collective to be raised and withholds herself
physically from a husband whose inability to listen to her she calls "un-
manly." The Chumalovs' child dies in the care of the Children's Home

"Krupskaya" (where all the girls have their hair cut like boys), symbolically leaving the future in the hands of the party workers while tacitly fulfilling Trotsky's explicit and the other Bolsheviks' implicit warning of a separate, feminist agenda. The recent consolidation of Bolshevik power in the spring of 1921 and the intra-party factionalism that commenced with Lenin's death in January 1924 required the appearance of unity that a bonded male-female model could iconically represent. Thus, Dasha, with the aid of her politically reconstructed husband, re-opens the derelict cement factory, a space of shared male-female authority and activity.[23]

Alternatively, in his 1928 drama *Inga,* Anatoly Glebov employs the mechanization of the factory as a metaphor for the suppression of personal, emotional desire and independence (if not feminism), specifically in *Woman.*[24] The proletarian Inga, a member of what a male character calls "the class of paradoxical women," is unmarried and physically unable to bear children. Her enthusiasm is for elevating the work process to an aesthetic realm, introducing art into production. This art-into-production ideal and the reference in the play to "the figure of a woman-mannequin draped in a new model dress" (p. 376) recalls the "Amazons" of art and design of the 1920s. Varvara Stepanova, Aleksandra Ekster, Lyubov Popova, and Vera Mukhina applied the constructivist principle of "the organic entry of art into life" to the factory-inspired rhythmic design and mass production of functional clothing (*prozodezhda*) and sports clothes (*sportodezhda*). They, along with fellow Amazons Natalya Goncharova, Valentina Kulagina, and Olga Rozanova, brought an "aggressive enthusiasm" to all aspects of design, including theatre, that helped dispel the association between female passivity and aestheticism/non-utilitarian art.[25]

Lacking a domestic and a sexual life, Inga forfeits her status as role model for the New Soviet Woman to Glafira, who learns to balance child-rearing with sociopolitical work after her husband leaves her. Ultimately, implies Glebov, the New Soviet Woman must satisfy the New Soviet Man, and he is threatened by a proletarian Joan of Arc like Inga, who makes no allowance for family life. The limits of female autonomy were continuing to be defined by male revolutionary culture.

Concurrently, nearly instantaneously, no-fault divorce was legislated in 1917, and in 1918 a new code recognized marriage as a matter for civil rather than religious authority. The Family Law of 1918 allowed each party in a marriage to take "that property earned by his/her labor," while the Family Code of 1926 established community property and legally recognized domestic labor as a valid claim on property rights. The 1926 code also permitted adoption, which the Revolution had abolished as a legal right. In 1920, hospital abortions performed by physicians were declared legal (this law was repealed in 1936), and throughout the 1920s, maternity benefits for working mothers were improved.

Although Glebov's Glafira rejects alimony payments from her ex-husband, most Soviet women continued to depend on male incomes. The experimental New Economic Policy (NEP) resulted in devastating unemployment among women, who comprised the major part of the nation's unskilled labor force.[26] Mikhail Bulgakov's NEP dramatic satire *Zoya's Apartment* (1926) depicts resourceful and desperate women operating a seamstress shop/brothel, a parodic reworking of Chernyshevsky's seamstress collective/revolutionary cell established by his heroine Vera Rozalskaya. Kollontay called prostitution "a scourge which falls chiefly upon the women of the working class" and sought via Zhenotdel propaganda to keep the family as social building block intact.[27] Bulgakov's brothel madam is a survivor. Her prostitutes, referred to as "mannequins," to cloak them metaphorically in the modesty of the seamstress's profession, are both male-manufactured and male-fetishized objects and revolutionary subjects. They model figuratively the Stepanova-designed and Glebov factory-produced *prozodezhda* of the real Soviet woman, who is actively engaged in her profession. In Zoya's apartment, the collective ideal yields to economic necessity; in turn, Soviet society's illegitimacy, which the state has attempted to bury with law and propaganda, is revealed.

In the early postrevolutionary years, Galatea, in the person of Woman and the marginalized "formalist" artist, was examined by the state in light of the Legitimacy question. In this scenario, historical legitimacy, which confers political authority, was determined by an ideology masquerading as an objective point of view. This legitimacy theme was represented in official art and critiqued in the countervailing perspective-seeking art of the Fellow Travelers, who were thrice damned for being nonproletarians, non-Communist Party members, and formalists. These artists revealed in their work how, in the postrevolutionary period, the decadent theme of male voyeurism in relation to female anatomy had come to symbolize the panoptic reality, conditioned by an increasingly paranoid collectivism. Although the national plan for communal housing began in earnest in 1929 under the slogan, "For the Socialist reconstruction of daily life," this Gogolian profanation of the collective ideal started earlier. In Nikolay Gogol's comedy *The Inspector General* (1836), a corrupt provincial town is made paranoid by the sudden appearance of what appears to be an anonymous representative of the geographically distant and so equally anonymous but omnipotent tsarist government. As in Gogol's play, spatial compression had foreshortened individual perspective in Soviet society so that, while external authority could peer in, the anonymous Galateas shaped by the state's voyeuristic Pygmalion gaze could not look out with any accurate sense of distance or context.[28]

The dramatic satires of Fellow Travelers Nikolay Erdman and Yury Olesha demonstrated how the state's emasculation of both intellectual and proletarian culture in its bid to consolidate power conditioned a resurgence of prerevolutionary stereotyping by men of Woman. In Soviet drama, Galatea was imbued with the male dramatic character's/artist's guilt over his powerlessness to reconstruct his own image as a New Soviet Man, while also encoding his resentment of the Pygmalion state, which sculpted him in the female statue's image.

In Erdman's play *The Suicide* (1928), the iconically named Mariya embodies the residual, longed for yet profaned soul of "Mother Russia," upon whom her unemployed husband Podsekalnikov leans for support and casts blame for his weakened state. She is in turn objectified by the proletariat in the person of Egor the Postman, who spies on her through the keyhole in the bathroom door of their collective apartment. This voyeurism is sanctioned by the state, Egor assures her, because it represents a "Marxist point of view."[29] Meanwhile, Podsekalnikov's decision to commit suicide (an idea inadvertently suggested to him by his wife) has brought forth a plague of Gogolian "sluts" and "witches," preying women, and feminized men, that is, artists, dilettantes, and intellectuals. These "former people," disenfranchised by the Revolution, are anxious to claim Podsekalnikov as a martyr to their individual causes as a means of legitimizing themselves. Finally recognizing that "I can imagine myself without a wife" but not "without me" (p. 51), Podsekalnikov unheroically chooses life.

The question of how to be or how not to be what is desired by the individual and/or by the collective in life and in art was posed by an actress costumed as Hamlet in Olesha's drama *A List of Blessings* (1931).[30] The political irresponsibility of the artist's individual agenda is (traditionally, in terms of Russian culture) represented in the protagonist's femaleness, which the other characters repeatedly observe or interpret in her anatomy and in her dreamy lightmindedness. Olesha clearly identified with his protagonist, the Soviet actress Goncharova, who leaves Russia to perform the role (Hamlet) that she, as an alienated female artist-intellectual, has, in fact, already been playing in life for some time.

While asserting that "women must think like men now" (p. 107) and while performing her certainty in public, Goncharova depends primarily upon fairy tales to bolster her low self-esteem. Her dream of being transformed, like Cinderella or the Ugly Duckling, and even her identification with the heroic proletarian, Chaplin's "Little Tramp," whom she adores as an icon of romantic humanism, is anti-Soviet. Her co-opting of the fairy-tale hero's role, generally reserved in Russian fables for men, is balanced by her simultaneous assumption of women's traditional role as the witch who impedes the hero in his quest.[31] This Hamletian self-contradiction is represented by the two lists of Soviet power's blessings and crimes that Goncharova carries with her into what becomes permanent exile. Having been played upon by capitalists, Communists, and anti-Communist emigrés, Goncharova ends as an accidental martyr to the Marxist cause when she intercepts a bullet meant for a strike leader. Although her final request is to be covered with a red flag, her corpse, appropriate to her ambivalence in life, is left uncovered.

Goncharova, like the Commissar in *An Optimistic Tragedy,* is, in a sense, a man disguised as the New Soviet Woman. She was based, in part, on the famous Soviet Hamlet and emigré actor Michael Chekhov and on Olesha, whose biography reveals his obsession with fairy tales and images of flight.[32] The impediment that Goncharova's biological femaleness creates to the fulfillment of her "masculine" goals likewise represents a male fantasy imposed upon Woman. The play also somewhat ambivalently cautions Soviet culture that biology cannot be undone, that the masculinized woman may prove as "freakish" as the feminized man (a "freakishness" the playwright himself has experienced). Although Soviet power had, in effect, legislated alienation and difference out of existence, Olesha's representation of a woman impersonating a man (Hamlet/Michael Chekhov/Olesha) suggests that the Soviet male artist's romance with the Self, a legacy derived from prerevolutionary times, required the continued services of the Other.

The state insisted that the capacity for change, for development toward the Soviet collective ideal, must be unimpeded by the paradox of self-love/self-hatred. Individuals and personal relationships were legitimized by their political, social, and cultural iconicity. Goncharova's failure to remake herself into a new Soviet citizen is signaled by her attachment to a politically incorrect icon, Hamlet, the symbol of the intelligentsia's disenfranchisement and its romance with alienation. The artist-icon affinity reveals the more profound guilt by association of the individual and her social class: Not being a proletarian by birth, Goncharova cannot be remade. In Aleksandr Afinogenov's drama *Fear* (1931),[33] a play generally studied for the political conversion of its male protagonist, the female character of Valya likewise remains untransformed, despite her marriage to a New Soviet Man. A member of the intelligentsia, Valya is guilty of iconic incorrectness. She is working on a sculpture of Venus, the goddess of love.

The woman who is remade in *Fear,* Elena Makarova, is, by contrast, not an artist but a scientist and "a rough-hewn, proletarian young woman, vital, energetic, and handsome in an unadorned style" (407). Her apartment, like Dasha Chumalova's, reflects the semiotic laconism of the true revolutionary: "Its furnishings are simple, almost severe, consisting of bare necessities" (407). The workplace is the locus of her passion for experimentation. She champions an art "borne by life itself" (p. 462), that is, the flesh-and-blood New Soviet Man, and "no clay model of some 'Proletarian in Science'" like what the newly "converted" Valya has prepared. Valya's dependence on others, for example a new proletarian husband (Makarova's ex-husband) to re-create her, transforms this sculptress-Pygmalion into a Galatea and represents not so much an individual as a class error. Her clay-footed intellectual father's (the play's protagonist's) recantation of his theory that fear rules the new Soviet order coincides with his newly sculpted proletarian daughter's crumbling into dust. Makarova's transformation is announced unintentionally in her ex-husband's statement, "It is a mistake of nature that you are a woman" (425).

The sculptor Michelangelo's words (Sonnet XXIV) preface Aleksey Arbuzov's play *Tanya* (1938): "Thus I came into the world as an unpretentious model of myself. To be born again later as a higher and more perfect creature. . . ."[34] Tanya's solipsistic love for her husband and young son requires that they both be taken from her as punishment. Thereafter, she remakes herself into a country doctor and a socialist heroine. She is, in a sense, a re-gendered mirror image of Ivan Chatsky, the proto-revolutionary hero of Aleksander Griboedov's classic dramatic satire *Woe from Wit* (1824). Chatsky, newly arrived in Moscow bourgeois society from European revolutionary culture, is sent away by his beloved Sofiya, an act partially justified by his misanthropic individualism, expressed in his antibourgeois critique. Conversely, Tanya is welcomed in from the storm by her future love, who later joins her in the pursuit of a romanticized socialism. Where Sofiya's dream fearfully predicted the arrival of Chatsky as a rampaging beast, Ignatov's (Tanya's lover's) framed Tanya in a heroically "vivid flash of lightning" (p. 485), that is, as the spontaneous yet inevitable advent of the revolutionary moment.

By the 1930s, the New Soviet Man and Woman had apparently dreamed one another into existence. But even before the nightmare of Stalinist terror and the mythologized pedestrianism of socialist realism killed the dream, artists and the state had separately and together sown the seeds for the destruction of the marriage between the New Soviet Man and Woman. The tragic irony that was for a long time implicit and that now became explicit in this drama was that Pygmalion and Galatea were being merged into the statue's role by the state. By engineering a merger that vested in itself virtually all power to create art and iconicity, the state concluded its plan not to revolutionize Galatea but to rob her of all eminence as well as of autonomy.

Before Stalin succeeded in forging men and women out of stone and steel, however, early postrevolutionary artists tested the new technology on far more subjective and paradoxical prototypes. These models updated the fear, prejudice, and self-loathing of male artists in the form of Woman as the virgin-harlot of modern technology, promising Man/the Artist increased power while threatening him with diminished control.[35]

The gynoid (to coin a dysphonic term), a staple of romantic literature (for example, E. T. A. Hoffmann, Villiers de l'Isle-Adam), can be viewed in the Soviet context as a male wish-fulfillment transformation of the autonomous, allegedly man-hating Amazon into a male-manufactured and male-dependent object. "Emotional life-likeness is psychological abstraction, a masculine impersonality," writes Camille Paglia, who, with some creative license, characterizes Wilde's Salomé as "entranced, robotlike . . . a somnambulistic android." The gynoid, traditionally passive and compliant whereas the male is aggressive and destructive, offered an artistic corrective to male social impotence in the early Soviet period.

Originally, the gynoid was designed as "humane technology," symbolic of de-gendered comradeship/equality between man and woman.[36] Even here, however, there were aspects of Amazonian "shaming" of Soviet men. Like the factory-produced "woman-mannequin draped in 'a new model dress'" in *Inga,* the gynoid encoded a mixed message.

Ivan Babichev, the counter-revolutionary hero of Olesha's novel *Envy* (1927; dramatized as *The Conspiracy of Feelings,* 1929), "dreamed of Woman as the flowering of a dead civilization blinding the new man with her light." Having lost his adopted daughter Valya to the new Soviet machine-man Volodya, Babichev invents "Ophelia" (borrowing the name of the prerevolutionary Hamlet's romantic victim), a "universal machine" programmed to corrupt Soviet technological order with bourgeois, emotional chaos. His gynoid combines the aggressiveness of the "vulgar bitch" (Salomé, *The Conspiracy of Feelings,* p. 32) with the passivity and propensity for self-victimization "of a girl who lost her mind for love and from despair" (Ophelia, *The Conspiracy of Feelings,* p. 32). Even in Grigory Kozintsev's much later Soviet film version of *Hamlet* (1964), Ophelia was presented as "a willess [sic] marionette, laced into the iron corset of court etiquette." On hearing the news of her father Polonius's death, "her puppet mechanism breaks down."

In Olesha's work, however, the plaited hair of the virgin-harlot had become steel-plated and sharpened to a point. Instead of avenging the male inventor against the new order, Ophelia emasculates Babichev by stripping him and pinning him squealing to the wall with a shining needle.[37] Babichev's Ophelia (whom he has dreamed about but not actually produced), like Hamlet's, is the product of a self-emasculating male imagination.

Beginning in the 1920s, Soviet culture displayed a "yearning for machines [which was] stronger than that for a sweetheart." As part of this movement, artists such as Meyerhold, whose career spanned the prerevolutionary and postrevolutionary periods, staged and enacted the growing cultural confusion between the productional and romantic functions of Woman and gynoid. The constructivist machinery designed by the "Amazons" Popova and Stepanova for Meyerhold's 1922 productions of Fernand Crommelynck's *The Magnanimous Cuckold* and Aleksandr Sukhovo-Kobylin's *Tarelkin's Death* expressed and exacerbated the impotence and self-torture of the plays' male protagonists in relation to women and machines and to women as machines. *Cuckold*'s jealous husband Bruno transforms his innocent young wife Stella into an adulteress. In the process of this re-creation, Bruno becomes enamored of his role as passive observer, of his wife's role as "vulgar bitch"—compliant to his "inventor's" role—and of the machinery (his jealousy) that effected the transformation. Bruno plays Pygmalion to his wife's Galatea and Galatea to his own Pygmalion-like fantasy. In Meyerhold's production, male-fetishized accessories—silk stockings and button boots—protrude from under Stella's neutral, "apron-like *prozodezhda*," combining the old and the new in the female mannequin/gynoid.[38] Meyerhold's production of *Tarelkin*, with its largely male cast, featured cross-dressing. Stepanova's "constructivist machine," "something between a barred cage and a meatgrinder," underscored the play's theme—the little man's emasculation—and her enthusiasm for the Taylorized movements of the Little Tramp, Charlie Chaplin.

In his 1926 production of Gogol's *The Inspector General* and elsewhere, Meyerhold fetishized his beautiful actress-wife Zinaida Raikh, apparently with her eager compliance. In his review of the production, entitled "Fifteen Portions of the Mayor's Wife," Victor Shklovsky said of Raikh's frequent costume changes and scene-stealing actions (both partially justified by the text), "The mayor's wife [Raikh] was on almost all the dishes offered to the audience." In Meyerhold's precisely choreographed *mise en scène*, Raikh/the mayor's wife became a beautiful gynoid, whom the automatic liar and android Khlestakov will seduce interchangeably with her daughter. In a quadrille, the two ladies are exchanged by Khlestakov and his double, his complementary part, the Meyerhold-invented Visiting Officer.[39]

Raikh has been portrayed by historians and by former Meyerhold associates as being a vain and destructive dilettante who compromised the work of her husband, which gave her artistic life.[40] Raikh represented, to her and her husband's critics, Meyerhold's forbidden, prerevolutionary obsessions set in a postrevolutionary context. She was Woman as *objet d'art*, beauty personified. As his Galatea, she represented as well the artist's self-regarding intelligence. The artist's narcissism and the model's vanity together produced a double portrait, reminiscent of Aleksandr Golovin's painting of Meyerhold dressed as Pierrot (1917), staring out at and yet excluding his imaginary audience as his mirrored reflection looks the other way. This painting referred to Meyerhold's performance as Pierrot in *The Puppet Show*, a play that, not incidentally, presented symbolically the fatal drama of another artist and his model, the playwright Aleksandr Blok and his wife, the symbolist eidolon Lyubov Mendeleeva.

In an admiring letter written to Zinaida Raikh by Michael Chekhov, whom she had impersonated indirectly in *A List of Blessings,* the actor enthused: "How rare it is to see on stage, beauty which is fully realized! You make miraculous use of your beauty."[41] What Chekhov here seemed to suggest was that the realization and the use of beauty are both two-sided. Raikh was the agent for and the artist of her beauty. She as subject helped to shape (and did not simply passively embody) Meyerhold's vision of her as object. Raikh's greatest stage triumph was as the doomed de-mimondaine Marguerite Gautier in Alexandre Dumas *fils*'s play *La Dame aux camélias* (staged by Meyerhold in 1934), a woman whose role in life was co-invented by herself and her society and whose life was destroyed by male- and self-consumption. Raikh was victimized as much by her independence as by her dependence. Meyerhold interpreted Dumas *fils*'s melodrama as a tragedy on the theme of role-playing. In the masquerade ball, which ended the production's first act, there appeared fleetingly in the crowd of guests "a mask of Death—as though direct from *The Puppet Show*—with a grinning face and a scythe in hand." As it turned out, this appearance foretold more than one death.[42]

Raikh's husband Meyerhold was arrested and disappeared into the Soviet *Gulag* (the national prison camp system) in 1939, where he was believed to have been executed in 1940 for the crime of "formalism." At the time that he was first charged with this "crime," Meyerhold was also criticized for giving his wife leading roles in his productions, which presumably she did not deserve on the basis of her talent alone. Thus, in the minds of the public and of Soviet historians thereafter, Raikh (Galatea) was associated with, even synonymous with and to some degree responsible for, Meyerhold's (Pygmalion's) formalism.

On 16 July 1939, Raikh, whom the press described as being "one of the most beautiful women in Soviet Russia," returned to her Moscow apartment after a stay at her country house. She was awakened at 4 A.M., presumably by two burglars, who entered through the apartment's second-floor balcony. Her throat was cut and her eyes gouged out, apparently as she tried to resist the intruders. Her murderers were never caught.[43]

Whether or not the murder of Zinaida Raikh was premeditated, as most believe, or to some degree accidental, there are certainly some messages encoded in the excessive spectacle and in the particular nature of her demise. The question that immediately arises asks why the more famous and ostensibly the more "criminal" Meyerhold was made into an invisible corpse while the body of the less seriously considered Raikh was made to suffer the cruel publicity of defilement? Although it would be ill advised to vest too much significance in the staging or "creation" of Raikh's death, it would be negligent not to consider possible ways of "reading" the incident. Certainly, the gouging out of Raikh's eyes and the cutting of her throat not only robbed her of the vision and voice necessary to obstruct and/or identify her attackers, it made her beauty silent, deathlike, and antique. The Meyerholdian gynoid reverted to her classical statue's role of Galatea. This fetishizing of the corpse as faux classical art, which the drama of Raikh's death invites, was and is, of course, pornographic. Read through an additional literary filter, it becomes even more so since the body as "text" becomes further abstracted from the body as person. Meyerhold adopted the pseudonym of "Doctor Dapertutto," which he used in his experimental theatre work, from a character in German fabulist E. T. A. Hoffmann's short story, "A New Year's Eve Adventure" (written 1814; published 1816). In Hoffmann's story "The Sandman" (1816), Professor Spalanzini, an inventor, and the evil eyeglass salesman Coppelius/Coppola ("eye-socket" in Italian) contest the ownership of the gynoid "Olympia" and the right to play the role of Pygmalion to her Galatea. Olympia is a singer and pianist whose beauty and purity causes the story's hero Nathanael to lose all perspective on reality, signaled by the weakening of his eyesight and culminating in his madness. Nathanael's obsessive love inflames Olympia's otherwise dead doll eyes and vests her inexpressive mind and soul with meaning and passion. Nathanael's fatal attraction is for his own Pygmalion-like artistic fantasy. His narcissism helps to animate Galatea and to destroy him. In the story's climactic scene, Coppelius steals Olympia from Spalanzini and Nathanael (who sought to marry her), leaving behind *only her bloody eyes*. Though it would be ludicrous and macabre to imagine Raikh's murderers with copies of Hoffmann's story tucked into their jacket pockets while they performed their unsavory deed, the reference does not detract from the symbolic value of the tableau created by their act.

Raikh, it seemed, was destroyed for a variety of possible reasons, all of which related to her iconicity. Her vanity concerning her formal beauty and Meyerhold's vanity regarding the formalist art he created from that beauty (and as an analogue to formal beauty) made Raikh into the simultaneously longed for and despised Olympian Eve. Not content simply to transform soulless beauty into art, Meyerhold insisted on hubristicly "shaming" his audience by making Raikh his equal and forcing them to accept her as such. In doing so, Meyerhold embedded the artist's self-love in the model's performative image, which replayed the forbidden drama of the prerevolutionary period. The state could not abide this and so, assuming the role of Coppelius, killed Olympia and stole her eyes—the windows to her soul and the symbol of the artist's vision that she modeled.

Raikh's murder also served as a ritualized warning to the living of the state's excessive rationalism and excessive irrationalism, which Stalin would draw upon and intensify in his construction of the Soviet utopia and the Great Terror. Raikh's very public death advertised and foretold the death of Meyerhold and thousands of invisible, anonymous corpses. Her death was a monument to the future.

Traditionally, Russian male artists had symbolically purchased their freedom of personal expression at the cost of Woman's life. Decadent Salomés and Sphinx-like spiritual destroyers were fetishized as idealized feminine corpses, able only to articulate their male ventriloquists' voices and not their own.[44] In general, however, the prerevolutionary male artist's voice was equivocal, reflecting what the Bolsheviks characterized as "lightmindedness." As Woman's voice developed together with the Revolution, her image as a passive, inarticulate, easily led and as easily killed "lackey of reaction," a doll in a puppet show, was slow to fade from the mind of the male party leadership. Lenin, who was greatly moved and troubled by a performance of *La Dame aux camélias* while in exile in Geneva, Switzerland, helped determine the character of the Soviet male response to female revolutionaries after 1917.[45] By Stalin's time, the Soviet Galatea had at least nominally become an object of social rather than of aesthetic beauty. Soviet art depicted her, together with her male counterpart, as an icon of restless striving, albeit paradoxically toward an already achieved end, thus re-encoding the officially discredited, decadent theme of arrested movement and the fetishizing of objects and ends. The "new" act in the drama of the female icon, coinciding as it did with the new revolutionary order, began in an atmosphere of hope; however, the state's romantic creation of the New Soviet Man and Woman disguised how it was co-opting their active roles in the new culture. The highly publicized union of Soviet Man and Woman was realized in the creation of an only nominally revolutionized Galatea, whose eyes, voice, and soul had already been stolen by the state.

Notes

1. Temira Pachmuss, trans. and ed., *Between Paris and St. Petersburg. Selected Diaries of Zinaida Hippius* (Urbana: University of Illinois Press, 1975), pp. 14–16.

2. Sandra M. Gilbert and Susan Gubar, "Sexual Linguistics: Gender, Language, Sexuality," *New Literary History* 3 (Spring 1985):516; Richard Stites, "Iconoclastic Currents in the Russian Revolution: Destroying and Preserving the Past," in *Bolshevik Culture. Experiment and Order in the Russian Revolution,* ed. Abbott Gleason, Peter Kenez, and Richard Stites (Bloomington: Indiana University Press, 1985), p. 18. See also Katerina Clark, *The Soviet Novel. History as Ritual* (Chicago: University of Chicago Press, 1985), pp. 15–24.

3. Steven A. Mansbach, *Visions of Totality. Laszlo Moholy-Nagy, Theo Van Doesburg, and El Lissitzky* (Ann Arbor: UMI Research Press, 1980), p. 31; Sheila Rowbotham, *Women, Resistance and Revolution* (1972; reprint, New York: Vin-

tage, 1974), pp. 149–50, quoted in Judith Mayne, "Soviet Film Montage and the Woman Question," *Camera Obscura* (1989):26.

4. This new order and its artistic representation passed from the abstract to the concrete under Stalin in Vera Mukhina's statue *Worker and Collective Farm Woman.* Commissioned to crown Boris Iofan's Soviet pavilion at the 1937 Paris Exhibition, the statue celebrated the union of Soviet industry and agriculture in the straining musculature and resolved striding forward of its giant hammer-wielding man and sickle-wielding woman. While El Lisitsky's avant-gardist piece capitalized on the confusion of the Civil War years (1917–1923), Mukhina's patriotic creation belied its historical moment, which was producing the Great Terror of the 1930s. Igor Golomstock, *Totalitarian Art. In the Soviet Union, the Third Reich, Fascist Italy and the People's Republic of China,* trans. Robert Chandler (New York: IconEditions/Harper Collins, 1990), p. 191; David Elliot, *New Worlds. Russian Art and Society 1900–1937* (London: Thames and Hudson, 1986), p. 151. Gail Harrison Roman, "When All the World Was a Stage: Russian Constructivist Theatre Design" (exhibition catalogue) (Louisville: J. B. Speed Art Museum, 1989), pp. 8–10; Stephen Kern, *The Culture of Time and Space 1880–1918* (Cambridge: Harvard University Press, 1983), p. 142; see Mayne, "Soviet Film Montage," 48.

5. Judith Mayne, *Kino and the Woman Question. Feminism and Soviet Silent Film* (Columbus: Ohio State University Press, 1989), p. 140; S. A. Tokayev, *Betrayal of an Ideal* (1954), p. 160, quoted in Alex de Jonge, *Stalin and the Shaping of the Soviet Union* (New York: William Morrow, 1986), p. 136; Adam B. Ulam, *Stalin. The Man and His Era* (Boston: Beacon Press, 1989), p. 25; Anne Eliot Griesse and Richard Stites, "Russia: Revolution and War," in *Female Soldiers— Combatants or Noncombatants/Historical and Contemporary Perspectives,* ed. Nancy Loring Goldman (Westport: Greenwood Press, 1982), p. 63.

6. Richard Stites, *The Women's Liberation Movement in Russia. Feminism, Nihilism, and Bolshevism 1860–1930* (Princeton: Princeton University Press, 1978), pp. 320–21, 326; V. I. Lenin, "Report to the Second All-Russia Congress of Political Education Departments," *Collected Works,* vol. 33, p. 78, quoted in Gail Warshofsky Lapidus, "Sexual Equality in Soviet Policy: A Developmental Perspective," in *Women in Russia,* ed. Dorothy Atkinson, Alexander Dallin, and Gail Warshofsky Lapidus (Stanford: Stanford University Press, 1977), p. 120; Xenia Gasiorowska, *Women in Soviet Fiction 1917–1964* (Madison: University of Wisconsin Press, 1968), p. 133.

7. Following the October Revolution, Armand became chairman of the Moscow Provincial Economic Council and later head of the Women's Department of the Central Committee of the party. Alexander Solzhenitsyn, *Lenin in Zurich,* trans. H. T. Willetts (New York: Farrar, Straus and Giroux, 1976), pp. 21, 24–29, 271; Nadezhda K. Krupskaya, *Memories of Lenin,* vol. 2 (New York: International Publishers, 1933); Edmund Wilson, *To the Finland Station. A Study in the Writing and Acting of History* (New York: Farrar, Straus and Giroux, 1973), p. 535; Louise Bryant, *Six Red Months in Russia. An Observer's Account of Russia before and during the Proletarian Dictatorship* (London: William Heinemann, 1918), pp. 164, 166, and 169; Barbara Evans Clements, "The Birth of the New Soviet Woman," in *Bolshevik Culture,* 233.

8. N. G. Chernyshevsky, *What Is to Be Done? Tales about New People,* trans. Ludmilla B. Turkevich (New York: Vintage/Random House, 1961), p. 293; James H. Billington, *Fire in the Minds of Men. Origins of the Revolutionary Faith* (New York: Basic Books, 1980), pp. 493–95.

9. Billington, *Fire in the Minds of Men,* 494; Stites, *Women's Liberation Movement in Russia,* 321, 323–34, 326–27, 332, 341, and 345; Gasiorowska, *Women in Soviet Fiction,* 177; Lapidus, "Sexual Equality in Soviet Policy," 120, 122.

10. V. I. Lenin, "Soviet Power and the Status of Women," *Collected Works,* 4th ed., vol. 30 (Moscow, 1960–1970), quoted in Lapidus, "Sexual Equality in Soviet Policy," 119; Rose L. Glickman, "The Russian Factory Woman, 1880–1914," in *Women in Russia,* 79–80, 82.

11. Fyodor Vasilievich Gladkov, *Cement,* trans. A. S. Arthur and C. Ashleigh (New York: Frederick Ungar, 1980), pp. 237, 239, and 240; Stites, *Women's Liberation Movement in Russia,* 324, 333, 359–60; Gasiorowska, *Women in Soviet Fiction,* 115, 119, 123, 126; Louise Bryant, *Mirrors of Moscow* (New York: Thomas Seltzer, 1923), pp. 111, 114–15.

12. Wilson, *To the Finland Station,* 538. Material on *The Storming of the Winter Palace* was drawn from written breakdowns of the scenario for the spectacle in the Manuscript Division of the Leningrad State Theatrical Museum; Alexander Gershkovich, *The Theater of Yuri Lyubimov. Art and Politics at the Taganka Theater in Moscow,* trans. Michael Yurieff (New York: Paragon House, 1989), p. 63.

13. Wilson, *To the Finland Station,* 449, 543–44; Chernyshevsky, *What Is to Be Done?* 229, 231, 236–37. See Gasiorowska, *Women in Soviet Fiction,* 134–39.

14. Yuri Olesha, "Human Material," in *Envy and Other Works,* trans. Andrew R. MacAndrew (Garden City, NY: Anchor/Doubleday, 1967), pp. 199–200; Evgeny Zamyatin, *We,* in *An Anthology of Russian Literature in the Soviet Period from Gorki to Pasternak,* ed. and trans. Bernard Guilbert Guerney (New York: Vintage/Random House, 1960). All references are to this edition.

15. Richard Stites, "Women and the Russian Intelligentsia: Three Perspectives," in *Women in Russia,* 56; Gasiorowska, *Women in Soviet Fiction,* 133; Mayne, "Soviet Film Montage," 43.

16. See René Fülöp-Miller, *The Mind and Face of Bolshevism. An Examination of Cultural Life in Soviet Russia,* trans. F. S. Flint and D. F. Tait (1927; reprint, New York: Harper and Row, 1965), p. 203; Bryant, *Six Red Months in Russia,* 212–13; Griesse and Stites, "Russia: Revolution and War," 65; Cathy Porter, *Alexandra Kollontai: A Biography* (London: Virago, 1980), p. 265.

17. Griesse and Stites, "Russia: Revolution and War," 64, 66, 67.

18. Alla Mikhailova, "Nine Plays Out of Many," in *Classic Soviet Plays* (Moscow: Progress Publishers, 1979), p. 12. All references to Vishnevsky's *An Optimistic Tragedy* are to this edition. Stites, *Women's Liberation Movement in Russia,* 319; Alisa Koonen, *Stranitsy zhizni* (Moscow: Iskusstvo, 1975), p. 355; Nadezhda Mandelstam, *Hope Against Hope. A Memoir,* trans. Max Hayward (New York: Atheneum, 1980), pp. 108–12.

19. Camille Paglia, *Sexual Personae. Art and Decadence from Nefertiti to Emily Dickinson* (New Haven: Yale University Press, 1990), pp. 7, 50.

20. Gasiorowska, *Women in Soviet Fiction,* 95. Actually, Marx and Engels, like their Bolshevik successors, were far more concerned with the Class question than with the Woman question, thus establishing a precedent for neglect. The Woman question was addressed by their friend and associate August Bebel in his book *Woman and Socialism* (1879). Alfred G. Meyer, "Marxism and the Women's Movement," in *Women in Russia,* 99. Alix Holt, "Marxism and Women's Oppression: Bolshevik Theory and Practice in the 1920's," in *Women in Eastern Europe and the Soviet Union,* ed. Tova Yedlin (New York: Praeger, 1980), p. 89.

21. Solzhenitsyn, *Lenin in Zurich,* 23; Lapidus, "Sexual Equality in Soviet Pol-

icy," 121–22, 125; Stites, *Women's Liberation Movement in Russia,* 339, 341–42, 344–45; Fülöp-Miller, *Mind and Face of Bolshevism,* 202.

22. Gasiorowska, *Women in Soviet Fiction,* 96; Billington, *Fire in the Minds of Men,* 648 n. 100.

23. Aleksandra Kollontay proclaimed in 1918 that "a class conscious mother should achieve the spiritual level at which she would no longer make a distinction between 'my child' and 'your child,' but would remember that all children are 'ours,' children of a Communist, toiling Russia." A. Kollontay, *Semya i kommunisticheskoe gosudarstvo* (Moskva, 1918), p. 23, quoted in Gasiorowska, *Women in Soviet Fiction,* 186. Judith Mayne argues, via illustrations drawn from Soviet silent films of the 1920s, that despite official pronouncements by the state, public (sociopolitical) space remained largely a male preserve. Women were still relegated to and trapped in private (domestic) space. See Mayne, *Kino and the Woman Question.*

24. Anatoly Glebov, *Inga,* trans. Charles Malamuth, in *Six Soviet Plays,* ed. Eugene Lyons (Boston and New York: Houghton Mifflin, 1934). All references to the play are to this edition.

25. Stepanova's husband and co-worker, Aleksander Rodchenko, designed the set and costumes for the 1929 production of *Inga* at Moscow's Theatre of the Revolution. Rodchenko and Stepanova often worked as a collective out of one studio. The other "Amazons" were likewise closely associated with male artists of various sorts: Goncharova–Mikhail Larionov, Kulagina–Gustav Klutsis, Popova–Aleksander Vesnin, and Rozanova–Aleksey Kruchenykh. See also Natalia Adaskina, "Constructivist Fabrics and Dress Design," *Journal of Decorative and Propaganda Arts* 5 (Summer 1987):144–59; Alexander Lavrentiev, *Varvara Stepanova. The Complete Work,* ed. John E. Bowlt (Cambridge: MIT Press, 1988), pp. 7, 104; Benedikt Livshits, *The One and a Half-Eyed Archer,* trans. John E. Bowlt (Newtonville, MA: Oriental Research Partners, 1977), pp. 128–29; Alexander Lavrentiev, "Experimental Furniture Design," *Journal of Decorative and Propaganda Arts* 11 (Winter 1989):157.

26. Parts I and II of the "Code of Laws on Marriage and Divorce, the Family and Guardianship," cited in R. Schlesinger, *Changing Attitudes in Soviet Russia: The Family in the USSR* (London: Routledge and Kegan Paul, 1949), p. 156; Holt, "Marxism and Women's Oppression," 89, 93, 107; Beatrice Brodsky Farnsworth, "Bolshevik Alternatives and the Soviet Family: The 1926 Marriage Law Debate," in *Women in Russia,* 140–41, 250.

27. Mikhail Bulgakov, *Zoya's Apartment,* trans. Carl R. Proffer and Ellendea Proffer, in *The Early Plays of Mikhail Bulgakov,* ed. Ellendea Proffer (Bloomington: Indiana University Press, 1972); Kollontai, quoted in Bryant, *Mirrors of Moscow,* 125.

28. As a result of this, the superhuman demands placed upon the population by Stalin in the 1930s and 1940s—for example, "Five years in four," the slogan of the economic five-year plan—became possible. Stalin was so great, the people reasoned, and they so small in terms of what they saw and knew about the enormous task of building a Communist state, that anything, even the redefinition of time, space, and personal identity, became possible. Lavrentiev, *Varvara Stepanova,* 79.

29. Nikolay Erdman, *The Suicide,* trans. Peter Tegel (New York: Samuel French, 1979), p. 42. All references to these two plays are from the editions cited.

30. In Yury Olesha, *The Complete Plays,* ed. and trans. Michael Green and

Jerome Katsell (Ann Arbor: Ardis, 1983). All references to *A List of Blessings* and *The Conspiracy of Feelings* are from this edition.

31. See Gasiorowska, *Women in Soviet Fiction,* 134.

32. Elizabeth Klosty Beaujour, *The Invisible Land. A Study of the Artistic Imagination of Iurii Olesha* (New York: Columbia University Press, 1970), pp. 89–90.

33. Aleksandr Afinogenov, *Fear,* trans. Charles Malamuth, in *Six Soviet Plays,* ed. Eugene Lyons (Boston: Houghton Mifflin, 1934). All references to the play are to this edition.

34. Aleksey Arbuzov, *Tanya,* in *Classic Soviet Plays.* All references to the play are from this edition.

35. Andreas Huyssen, "The Vamp and the Machine," in *After the Great Divide. Modernism, Mass Culture, Postmodernism* (Bloomington and Indianapolis: Indiana University Press, 1986), p. 73.

36. See the character of the Phosphorescent Woman, who visits the bureaucratic Soviet state, ca. 1930, from the twenty-first century, in Vladimir Mayakovsky's satirical play *The Bathhouse* (1930). Paglia, *Sexual Personae,* 368. The observation concerning the aggressive nature of the android versus the passive nature of the gynoid was offered to me in conversation with Professor William Crossgrove of the German Department, Brown University. The gynoid as iconic representation of an emasculated, romantic, prerevolutionary spirit also occurs in emigré dramatist Nikolay Evreinov's comedy *Radio-Kiss, or The Robot of Love* (1925). I discuss this play in "A Kiss Is Not a Kiss: Evreinov and the Illusion of Desire," in *Wandering Stars: Papers on Russian Emigré Theatre,* ed. L. Senelick (Iowa City: University of Iowa Press, 1992).

37. This predicts a theme that Elizabeth Wright correctly discovers in Heiner Müller's play *Hamletmachine* (1977), namely: "Hamlet's failure to become a revolutionary subject is contrasted with Ophelia's refusal to remain a pathetic victim of male oppression." Elizabeth Wright, *Postmodern Brecht: A Re-Presentation* (New York: Routledge, 1989), 132; Klosty Beaujour, *The Invisible Land,* 62, 69–71, 84; Andrew MacAndrew, "Introduction," in *Envy and Other Works,* xii; Yury Olesha, *Envy,* in *Envy and Other Works,* 77; Sergey Yutkevich, "Gamlet s Taganskoy ploshchadi," in *Shekspirovskie Chtenie 1978,* ed. A. Anikst (Moskva: Nauka, 1981), p. 87.

38. Gladkov, *Cement,* 115; Nick Worrall, "Meyerhold's 'The Magnificent Cuckold,'" *The Drama Review* 1 (March 1973):30.

39. Viktor Shklovsky, *Krasnaya gazeta* (22 December 1926); Konstantin Rudnitsky, *Meyerhold the Director,* trans. George Petrov (Ann Arbor: Ardis, 1981), pp. 310–11, 394, 404.

40. Zinaida Raikh was formerly married to the poet Sergey Esenin. When she met Esenin, Raikh worked as a secretary and typist for the Petrograd newspaper *The People's Cause* (*Delo naroda*). She and Esenin had two children, a daughter Tatyana and a son Konstantin, whom Esenin did not accept as his own, precipitating the couple's divorce in October 1921. Esenin later married the dancer Isadora Duncan but retained a strong love-hate for Raikh, which he commemorated in his poetry. Gordon McVay, *Esenin. A Life* (New York: Paragon House, 1988), pp. 88–89, 102. Former Meyerhold associate Yury Elagin claimed that Raikh drove away some of the best actors in Meyerhold's company with her behavior. Yury Elagin, *Temniy geniy* (*Vsevolod Meyerhold*) (1955; reprint, London: Overseas Publications Interchange Ltd., 1982), pp. 306–7.

41. Lyubov Rudneva, "Zinaida Raikh," *Teatr* 1 (January 1989):110–29.

42. While Raikh played the nineteenth century's most famous demimondaine, Alisa Koonen performed its most famous female bourgeois, Emma Bovary, in her own adaptation of Flaubert's novel (dramatization 1938; production 1941). A. S., "Actress Dramatizes *Madame Bovary* for Production by Kamerny Theatre" (newspaper title unknown), press clipping, Harvard Theatre Collection (13 April 1938); Rudnitsky, *Meyerhold the Director,* p. 509.

43. This account of Raikh's murder is taken from an unsigned article, "Meyerhold's Wife Killed in Moscow," *The New York Times* (18 July 1939), Harvard Theatre Collection. Raikh's murder eerily echoed that of Louise Simone Dimanche, the mistress of nineteenth-century Russian playwright Aleksandr Sukhovo-Kobylin, whose dramatic trilogy Meyerhold staged in separate parts—*Krechinsky's Wedding* (1917, 1933); *The Case* (1917); and *Tarelkin's Death* (1917, 1922). Though it has never been proven who killed Simone Dimanche, it was suggested that the nobleman Sukhovo-Kobylin's abandonment of her for another mistress and the Frenchwoman's foreignness and bourgeois economic and social standing doomed her in Russian society. Sukhovo-Kobylin was originally charged with the crime and imprisoned, an experience that inspired his dramatic trilogy.

44. In his film *October,* Meyerhold's former theatre student Sergey Eisenstein framed an anonymous female corpse, lying Ophelia-like on a drawbridge over water (the corpse's long hair becomes a fetishized focus when the bridge opens), between statues of Minerva and the Sphinx. This image, writes feminist film historian Judith Mayne, suggests the male belief that "the ideal of femininity is best achieved when women are corpses." Mayne, "Soviet Film Montage," 40.

45. Catriona Kelly, *Petrushka. The Russian Carnival Puppet Theatre* (New York: Cambridge University Press, 1990), pp. 203–4; Solzhenitsyn, *Lenin in Zurich,* 78.

ADRIAN KIERNANDER

The Orient, the Feminine: The Use of Interculturalism by the Théâtre du Soleil

❦ Asia, or what the West has chosen to call "The Orient," has always been a theatrical topic in Europe, the raw material for a metaphor that has often been used as a way of reassuring the anxieties of an insecurely male-dominated theatre world. Fortuitously, the earliest surviving playscript in the European tradition, Aeschylus's *The Persians,* is typical in its representation of the Orient. Asia is represented by a chorus of aged men and by the character of a weeping, tragic heroine. All these figures lament the loss of Asian manhood in the war with the Greeks, that is to say, with the same world inhabited by the audience of the play. All these Asian characters were represented on stage by male Greeks. Ever since *The Persians,* the European tradition has created a whole series of plays that deal with Asia and reinforce the idea of European superiority.

The representation of Asia in European theatre is a part of the process of Orientalization described by Edward Said.[1] The Orient constructed by this tradition is "more particularly valuable as a sign of European-Atlantic power over the Orient than it is as a veridic discourse about the Orient" (p. 6).

This reassuring construction is characterized by exotic settings and customs, enabling the world of the Orient to be useable as a representation of alterity. An interesting feature of this largely male practice is that the otherness of the Orient is emphasized by its frequent association with the female. The Other and Woman are linked.

This identification of the female as a dangerous Other is a common male practice that extends beyond the geographical boundaries of Europe and almost certainly predates any conscious "European" fear of a threat from a generalizable "Asia." Ironically, a parallel hostile attitude towards women can be found in the writings of the Persian Zarathustra. But the menacing forces of the female and the foreign, and especially those associated with Persia, seem to have been conveniently complementary in the minds of the contemporaries of Aeschylus.

For the male Greek spectators of Aeschylus's audience, the sufferings of the no-longer-male Persians can represent the destruction, lamentable (and therefore civilized, superior) but also necessary and reassuring and perhaps even inevitable, of the threat of the Other. Aeschylus does not show us on stage the actual death of the male Persian army, which might have provoked too great anxiety for the spectators; instead, we see, for most of the play, the remaining inhabitants of Persia all stripped of virility. The chorus represents the aged councillors, those too physically weak to accompany Xerxes in his pursuit of military glory. The other principal character is Atossa, the noble but powerless mother of Xerxes. The audience also sees the ghost of Atossa's husband Darius, male but stripped not only of his virility but of life itself. The presence, or rather the visible absence, of Darius shows us the male power of the Orient placed under erasure; the potency of the Orient is already a thing of the past.

At last, Xerxes himself enters. He is a general and emperor, but he enters alone. His royal robes are torn, a sign of shame according to Atossa who interprets for us, and his army is dead. Only at the end of the play, therefore, is the audience allowed, or perhaps prepared, to see a representation of the enemy, but it is without virility, a vision of a formerly hostile Other that is no longer menacing.

The play can thus be seen as a ritual of reassurance, played out by men for men. It is man, simultaneously the Greek soldier of the fiction and the Greek actor on the stage, who has the absolute power to make what is not Greek and male suffer, but gently, artistically, so that the male audience can preserve the elegant distinction between virile and brutal, between *barbu* and *barbare*.

Theatre seems to have been a commonplace locus for playing out such rituals of anxiety and reassurance in the fifth century B.C. Herodotus tells of a playwright Phrynicus who allowed anxiety to predominate over reassurance. His play, representing the capture by the Persian army of Miletus, an outpost of Greek civilization, affected the audience so deeply that they burst into tears, and the author was fined a thousand drachmae "for reminding them of a disaster which touched them so closely. A law was subsequently passed forbidding anybody ever to put the play on the stage."

The female Orient holds, in its combination of foreignness and femininity, a sort of power that continues to be unsettling. Atossa represents the vulnerable aspect of the female Other; so does the chorus, in a much more complex and problematic way, in Aeschylus's *The Suppliant Women,* a fascinating play of allegiances and shifting identifications of self and Other.

But there exists a much more directly menacing representation of womanhood. Medea is one example of the female foreigner whose passion brings destruction to the rational world of men. Herodotus provides another example in Amestris, the wife of Xerxes who lurks in the background of *The*

Histories, appearing only from time to time to perpetrate atrocities even more extreme than those of her husband—burying alive fourteen boys of distinguished family to placate the Persian god of the underworld, or, in a fit of jealousy, having her sister-in-law mutilated, her breasts, nose, ears, and lips cut off and fed to dogs and her tongue torn out.

Menacing female figures recur throughout the subsequent history of Western theatre but nowhere more clearly and powerfully than in the plays of Racine. Here, the force that threatens the masculine order of his world, of his verse, and of his neo-classical structure is frequently represented by a woman—irrational, passionate, and out of control. Dangerous foreign bodies like Bérénice, the Queen of Palestine, threaten the political stability of Imperial Rome; Phèdre, the daughter of Minos and Pasiphaë, wreaks social and personal disruption in Trézène and threatens to establish her own dynasty on the throne; or the hysterical Athalie invades the sacred male preserve of the Temple in Jerusalem.

Racine's female characters have the power to disrupt the rational social constructs of men. They are also usually closely linked with the Orient, can even become the very essence of it. In this "fabulously rich" world whose name alone evokes "the sphinx, Cleopatra, Eden, Troy, Sodom and Gomorrah, Astarte, Isis and Osiris, Sheba, Babylon . . . ,"[2] the absence of a single woman, Bérénice, can produce the oxymoron, "l'orient désert," "the deserted Orient." It is significant that the concept "Orient" can so easily accommodate simultaneously for Westerners the contradictory attributes "abundant/desert" and "populous/deserted."

To maintain its coherence, this theatrical representation of the Orient and of Woman needs a point of view that is Western and male. To maintain the sense of the strangeness of Asia, a metaphor of centrality is required—more precisely of Eurocentrality and phallocentrality. The West must be at the center of the world and of power, and the spectator must align himself with that center. Whatever is located away from the geographical center and not male can be used as a representation of the Other. For the Orientalists of the eighteenth and nineteenth centuries, this alignment was apparently easy and seemingly even natural.

Obviously, when the author and the director of a play—in other words, its two first spectators—are both women, this phallocentric alignment is likely to be called into question. The female can no longer so easily represent the Other. What is striking in the two first theatrical collaborations between Ariane Mnouchkine and Hélène Cixous is that, although both productions deal with Asia and this Asia continues to be associated with the female, the setting is no longer Orientalized in the traditional fashion.

These two productions, scripted by Cixous and directed by Mnouchkine with her company, the Théâtre du Soleil, in the late 1980s, were *L'Histoire terrible mais inachevée de Norodom Sihanouk, roi du Cambodge* (*The Awesome but Unfinished History of Norodom Sihanouk, King of Cambodia*) and *L'Indiade; ou l'Inde de leurs rêves* (*The Indiad, or the India of Their Dreams*). Both were documentary plays set in Asia, the first dealing with the history of Cambodia from the 1950s to the early 1980s, and the second focusing on the independence movement in India and the partition. Both plays made use of real historical figures, many of them still living in the case of the earlier work.

In the staging of these two productions, great effort was made to undermine the sense of Asia as a place of difference, to decenter and marginalize the West and to create an atmosphere where Asian is normal, and to encourage the audience to identify with a world that, for most of them, was largely unknown. The poster for *Norodom* was reproduced on a large scale on a huge wall in the foyer, facing the entrance. It showed a world map with Cambodia at the center, the centrality of the little-known country emphasized by concentric circles radiating outwards. The foyer itself was redecorated in Asian style for both plays and was filled with the smells of Asian markets and kitchens from the food on sale.

In the performance space, there was not much in the way of traditional stage setting for either play. Instead, there was an Eastern architecture rendered in materials that were real and permanent—bricks, plaster, silk, marble, timber. No cardboard, no canvas. An atmosphere suggesting Asia surrounded audience and actors alike, and it was solid.

Even the syntactic features of normal Western performance conventions were transformed into something more Asian, particularly in the case of *The Indiad* where, instead of a front curtain, the scenes were punctuated by small rituals in which the actors as servants spread out, quickly but very carefully, rich carpets and cushions for the ensuing scene.

A feature that contributed even more to creating a convincing Asian atmosphere was the duration of the performances. During the course of a session lasting more than four hours—eight in the case of *Norodom*—there is time to grow familiarized to the unfamiliar behaviors, costumes, customs, and rhythms of this world. The Asia of the play loses its exoticism and becomes normal.

Within these worlds, it was the European characters who seemed strange, marginalized. Dressed in inappropriate suits, they sweated in the fictitious heat, especially when they were under pressure. The gesture of wiping the brow with a handkerchief was only one of a number of identifiers of the Western characters. In these productions, the most memorable images of Europeans tended to show them as bizarre, not at all everyday. There were British soldiers in scarlet ceremonial uniform, all identical ("they all look the same"), already creatures of myth; and Henry Kissinger in *Norodom,* irascible, made almost hunchbacked by leaning over a map of Southeast Asia, was illuminated from below by the light of his map table and transformed into something like a medieval demon. It was the Westerners who finally appeared the most alien and the most threatening, and the Asians who were made the most familiar.

This process can be seen as an attempt to dislodge the "fixity" that, according to Homi Bhabha,[3] is an important feature upon which colonial discourse relies. It can be seen as a move in the direction of Babha's recommended shift of the point of intervention in colonial discourse from identification of images as positive or negative to exposure of the subjectification made possible (and plausible) through stereotypical discourse. Possibly (and plausibly) these processes can also be unmade through unstereotypical discourse.

Despite the unsettling of the Eurocentric features in the plays, the Mnouchkine-Cixous Asia has retained the predominantly female characteristics of the Orientalist stereotype, especially in the case of *Norodom*; this now-familiar Asia is still feminine compared with the images of the West in the plays. Cixous has acknowledged this use of the female:

The Khmer people are much closer to femininity than the Indian people in a certain way. By structure, in terms of *jouissance*. They are people who are much closer to the earth, a caring people, and Sihanouk is someone who is like that himself, he says so himself, because he is intelligent enough to understand that.

As far as *The Indiad* is concerned there is someone who is like that. That is Nehru, who is a character who, in reality and in the play, is not identified with the phallus. He is a personality, . . . a very strong man but by no means in terms of resistance against castration. Someone like Gandhi is much more virile than Nehru.[4]

This female quality in the representation of Asia was ironically inscribed onto the bodies of the Western, male actors, who were obliged to keep their legs shaved for over a year to be able to act Cambodians.

Beneath the carefully constructed feminine image of traditional Orientalist Asia, and what gives it its force in the imagination of the West, lies one of the motives for the fiction. The Orient is defined as feminine to render it conceptually colonizable; this feminized Asia waits ready to be taken, in marriage or in rape, by an Occident that is male and potent. The oxymorons of a declining Orient and a rising Occident are not the only paradoxes at work here—the idea of colonizability depends itself on an elegant series of paradoxes: It is *desirable* to colonize what is portrayed as feminine because it is fascinating, attractive, and weak; it is *necessary* to colonize what seems female because it is powerful, threatening, and different. The similarities and differences between the terms "female" and "feminine" can already be seen as a kind of conceptual oxymoron.

The theme of colonization is first foregrounded by the use of feminine qualities, then confronted in both these plays—in Cambodia, which is independent but in constant struggle against colonizing forces, and in India, which is in the process of liberating itself from a long period of recent history's most classic example of colonization. Sihanouk is always conscious of the danger, and he continually fights against the elements of the colonial myth in the thoughts of would-be colonizers. When the paternalistic ambassador of the United States refers to "your little country," Sihanouk responds with vehemence:

Why can't you accord us the same treatment as for countries much smaller than ours, and which you respect? Do you talk about little Belgium? Tiny Israel? It is only for Cambodia that you reserve this disdain, and whose disappearance you predict. You diminish us methodically. Look at your newspapers. First Cambodia is small, then it is very small, the next day I read that it is extremely small, then minuscule, it's a pocket-size kingdom, it's a useless remainder, an eleventh toe, a mote in your eye, a speck, a nothing! Where is it? It's going to vanish. It has vanished! . . . But I am here, Sihanouk is here, Cambodia exists! Here we are, the point of the great continent of Asia![5]

Sihanouk insists that his Cambodia is not small and weak; given the phallic metaphor implicit in his description of the country's geographical position, it also cannot be symbolically feminine. He continues, demonstrating that it is not different either. In the presence of the American, he proceeds to appropriate the most privileged place in the English-speaking world by quoting Shakespeare. His small country is thus invested with all the power and importance of the England of Edward III, "this other Eden, demi-paradise."

This Shakespearian reference acquires force because it builds on the conscious Shakespearian resonances of the full title of the play. It was first performed immediately following the Théâtre du Soleil's famous and popular cycle of Shakespeare plays, which were to be the preparation for this "history of our time."

The staging of both productions constantly emphasized the importance and force of Asia. Mnouchkine demonstrated it to her audience by incorporating Asian art, music, dance, costumes, and other theatre traditions, including the use of a mask from the traditional Khmer theatre. On the stage, the rich ceremonial of the official Cambodian meetings and the great formality of Indian political negotiations insist upon the long history of these countries, the sophistication of their civilizations, and above all their capacity to govern themselves without the intervention of the West.

Another feature of these two plays that disturbs the traditional Orientalist view of Asia is the absence of sexual desire; seductive or threatening sexuality is one of the principal characteristics of the nineteenth-century view of the Orient. Here, the audience sees briefly on stage the tenderness and complicity between husband and wife—between Sihanouk and his consort and, likewise, between Gandhi and Kastourbai. We also see close complicity between women—between Sihanouk's mother, Queen Kossomak, and a court dancer, Madame Mom Savay, who was the former king's mistress. The two of them are linked by their equal love of the dead king and by their friendship for each other. There are also two female merchants, Madame Khieu Samnol and Madame Lamné, one Cambodian and one Vietnamese, the two as good as married, inseparable and raising an adopted son. There is closeness between men, too: Gandhi and Nehru, Sihanouk and his chief adviser Penn Nouth. There is even a relationship of love between an animal trainer and his trained bear. But none of this love is expressed in sexual terms.

This absence is clearly not derived from Shakespeare. In Shakespeare's English history plays, there is no lack of sexual couples: Falstaff and Doll Tearsheet, Edward and Lady Grey, Richard and Lady Anne, Henry V and Princess Katharine, and, above all, Queen Margaret and Suffolk. But these two plays seem to express a conscious wish to avoid anything that might draw attention to sexual differentiation.

This wish stands out clearly in preliminary sketches for the scene that shows the death of Kastourbai Gandhi in prison, published as an appendix to the script of *The Indiad*. The earliest of these sketches shows Gandhi and Kastourbai as parents of a son who opposes them politically and who insists on splitting the "one flesh" of husband and wife into separate mother and father. In the second draft, the son does not appear on stage; his presence is reduced from a body to a letter read by Gandhi to the illiterate Kastourbai, but the differentiation between mother and father, male and female, is maintained in the text of the child's accusation. In the third version, the son and his accusation have completely vanished. The scene shows instead a woman in the process of dying in the arms of her husband, and the writing begins to emphasize the holiness of Gandhi, who here weeps for the first and last time of his life. One no longer sees the patriarch but a man with two roles, one private and one public; however, he still remains a man, his male body differentiated from the body of the woman dying beside him. In the final version as performed on stage, only the bereaved remains. Kastourbai is already dead at the beginning of the scene, and her female body stays offstage. Gandhi thus becomes a person alone, between male and female, lamenting the death of a partner of sixty-two years. According to the words he speaks, both partners were simultaneously parent and child. He says, "You, my mother and my baby, me, your baby and your mother."[6] The traditional male roles of father and husband are progressively occluded.

In the worlds of *Norodom* and *The Indiad*, then, there is a special vision of Asia. It remains, of course, as it always must, a representation of Asia and not the real thing, and a Western representation at that. It has many female characteristics, though its femininity is neither vulnerable nor predatory. Otherwise, it has little in common with the stereotype of the Orientalists. It is now familiar and does not represent "the Other"; it is neither menacing, nor weak, nor erotic.

Mnouchkine and Cixous have often spoken of the need to find a certain distance in art, a distance that permits metaphor. The theatrical Asia of Mnouchkine and Cixous can be seen as a metaphor of a special kind of world different from the one they and we live in. In this light, their Asian project becomes a utopian search for a type of social organization more informed by recent feminist principles.

Cixous and Mnouchkine, in these two productions, have apparently taken the Western stereotype of Asia and used it precisely because there is something in the stereotype that can provide a point of departure—the characteristic of femaleness. The female qualities in the male and female inhabitants of this construct of Asia, a female quality that is expressed both in the words of the author and in the bodies of the actors, can create the necessary conditions for the representation of a non-phallocratic world. Cixous has gone out of her way to avoid dramatic situations that would reinforce the traditional roles of man and woman, hence the absence of sexuality and the presence throughout of nonsexual forms of love.

It is not a question of replacing male power with similar female power; instead, it is a matter of struggling against binary oppositions, of focusing instead on the areas where these oppositions overlap and on the possibility of a polycentric world, which the focus on binarism conceals.

Finding a theatrical alternative to phallocentrism was begun in *Norodom,* but it was to some extent limited by the centrality of the male figure of Sihanouk himself. It must be conceded that, as played by Georges Bigot in the production, Sihanouk appeared much less male than the representation of his father, Suramarit, who was dressed in traditional Khmer costume and mask with a large moustache—the only facial hair to be seen on the stage. But like Darius in *The Persians,* Suramarit is a ghost, and the traditional male qualities he brings into the world of the play are placed under erasure, their absence made explicit by being associated with a character who is no longer part of that world. And Sihanouk calls his own gender identification into question when his admiration for Zhou En-lai makes him for a moment imagine himself as a woman, in danger of falling in love with the charm of the Chinese leader, a feature that was again emphasized in the production with the gently seductive portrayal by Andrés Pérez Araya.

Nevertheless, Sihanouk remained a male center of the play, in fact, eponymously defined that center, and it was his political enemies who were equally defined as the margin, the opposition, the Other.

It is really with *The Indiad* that Cixous started to create a convincing polycentric theatrical structure. She has said:

. . . instead of having one king, a chief, I have decapitalised it, and instead of having a Shakespearian, pyramidal system with a central character, there are 20, 30, 40 characters who are equal. There are none who are stronger than the others. That is a decision which I took. You can think of it as a dramatic economy. . . . It is not called *Gandhi*, it is not called *Nehru*, it is called *L'Indiade*. . . . For the actors it was terrible because they too are structured in a way which is, as one says, phallocentric, even if they are totally capable of femininity. But they were accustomed to having a leader, and all of a sudden each one had to be his own leader.[7]

The confrontation with binarism is not at all new for Mnouchkine and the Théâtre du Soleil. Mnouchkine has talked about a theme that can be seen in almost all her productions:

There is at least one constant theme with us, . . . and it's civil war, I mean interior war, not war against the enemy outside your frontier, but the war against the enemy who is just your brother sometimes, or even yourself.[8]

This concentration on civil war suggests that the enemy is not located elsewhere, is not the Other, that there is no "Other," properly speaking. Every struggle is really against friend, family, self. The conceptual structure based on oppositional dualities, which has been present in Western thinking at least since Pythagoras, is turned back against itself.

What might be the alternative to the view of the world as a system of binary opposition? Unfortunately, it is not enough to replace the syntax of Either/Or with Both/And. Even though the copula has the power to link distant and opposing concepts, the concepts remain distinct, and the phallocentric world view has a demonstrable capacity to withstand vacillation between various forms of fear and desire. Indeed, the presence of so much oxymoron in its discourse suggests that it may even be dependent on this ability to hold opposites together in order to avoid confrontation with its own inner contradictions.

The answer that Cixous seems to be exploring in these works—and what she has advocated in her theoretical writings—is to break the habit of creating hierarchies by dissolving, as far as possible, the structures of binary opposition through the use of Neither/Nor. In these productions, a character is neither explicitly male nor female, neither Asian nor European, neither self nor Other. These qualities remain, but their meaning vanishes along with the binary structures that valorize them. The solution is dissolution.

Using the medium of theatre makes this project more feasible, especially at the Théâtre du Soleil where the audience can observe the performers getting made up before and during the performance and where actors, both in character and out, mingle with the audience during the intervals. The dissolution of normal oppositional structures is particularly marked in a theatre characterized by ritual processes where the audience and the performers blend. The actors are not the only ones to act in this theatre, neither are the spectators inactive. All the participants perform the act of observance together, and at the end of four and a half or eight hours, there is a strong sense of unity. The roles of subject and object are dissolved, and, in the process, the concepts Occident/Orient, self/Other, male/female can begin to be redefined.

Notes

1. Edward Said, *Orientalism* (London: Routledge and Kegan Paul, 1978).
2. Ibid., p. 63.
3. "The Other Question . . . ," *Screen* 24, no. 6 (Nov.–Dec. 1983):18.
4. Interview with the author, 22 January 1988.
5. Hélène Cixous, *L'Histoire terrible mais inachevée de Norodom Sihanouk, roi du Cambodge* (Paris: Théâtre du Soleil, 1985), act 2, scene 1, 65.
6. Hélène Cixous, *L'Indiade, ou l'Inde de leurs rêves, et quelques écrits sur le théâtre* (Paris: Théâtre du Soleil, 1987), act 2, scene 1, 75.
7. Hélène Cixous, interviewed by the author, 22 January 1988.
8. Ariane Mnouchkine, interviewed by the author, 27 January 1988.

3. Dancing Attitudes

JOHN EMIGH AND JAMER HUNT

Gender Bending in Balinese Performance

❦ In the Balinese village of Mas in 1975, at a temple festival (*odalan*) honoring the ancestors and the gods, a scene from the Indian epic, the *Ramayana*, is enacted as a *Parwa* dance drama. As the metallophones and drums of the *gamelan* orchestra sound and thereby reference a well-known legendary world, two elegant and noble brothers—Rama and Laksamana, costumed in brilliantly colored and gilded cloaks and tabards that hark back to a golden age of Javanese and Balinese culture—move elegantly through a curtain and into the liminal performance space that now represents "the woods" of their exile. On the open ground before the curtain, all but surrounded by an audience of men, women, and numerous children, the "princes" slowly, with grace and calm strength, claim this space. Their hands gracefully sculpt the air as they dance in the manner typical of refined male characters: feet turned out, knees slightly bent, and hips set straight ahead. Both Rama and Laksamana are played by women.

The demoness Surapanakha now enters through the curtain—the character also played by a woman. She is "disguised" as a great beauty, and her body is wrapped in gilded, colored bands of cloth that emphasize the lines of her hips, buttocks, and breasts. Her feet are pointed straight ahead and close together, her hips sway undulously, and her head and eyes make small, precise, flirtatious movements. She is attempting to seduce the noble brothers in exile. When these impressive efforts at enticement fail, the "disguised demoness" leaves through the curtain and is instantly replaced by a male dancer masked as a hideous, fanged hag, complete with flapping, fur-tufted cotton dugs. This is Surapanakha in her "true" form. The demoness (played by a man) proceeds to assault sexually Rama and Laksamana (still played by women), only to fail clumsily and have "her" ears lopped off. Throughout this action, the audience—and especially the women in the audience—laugh uproariously at the inversions and reversals of gender and of gender-bound social situations.

Play with gender distinctions and across gender categories is a common occurrence in both secular and sacred Balinese performance; though the patterns have been changing, these inversions and cross-castings have been common features of Balinese theatre and dance at least throughout this century. In fact, Walter Spies and Beryl deZoete, in their seminal 1938 study *Dance and Drama in Bali,* describe the entrance of the widow-witch of Girah in the exorcistic drama *Calonarang* as follows: "Then she herself appears, an old woman . . . played, of course, by a man."[1] Out of context, this passing observation sounds jarring and eccentric. Why, on an island where women commonly can and do perform in the theatre, should an old woman *of course* be played by a man? Unpacking what is being communicated by the gender bending exemplified in the *Ramayana* performance at Mas—why, "of course," the old woman Spies and deZoete saw had to be represented by a man.

Balinese performances—like performances elsewhere—serve to represent, reconstitute, and otherwise play with the various epistemological structures found within the larger culture. It is in large part through these performances that the Balinese are able to reconfirm and make changes in the ways they construct and make sense of their changing world.[2] In its presentation, Balinese theatre makes use of commonly understood codes of dress, movement, and speech that denote refinement and crudity, maturity and youth, past and present, sacred and secular, and masculine and feminine. Though these codes are relatively fixed and are presented, *mutatis mutandis,* in performance after performance, there is a delicious enjoyment taken in assigning the presentation of these codes to "inappropriate" performers: little boys play warriors, old men play amorous youths, little girls play kings and queens, and mature women play exemplary men, including the God-King Rama and his brother. These casting inversions are indications that, despite the use of relatively well-fixed codes, it is a richly dynamic rather than static world that is being projected. The inversions highlight the transformative play with nature inherent in the theatre and heighten the subjunctive play with social categories such as age, gender, and status typical of the theatrical performance.

The play on notions of gender that is an active part of this process takes many different forms. Rarely is the gender of the performer completely disguised, as in traditions of male and female "impersonation" found elsewhere in the world that aim—at least temporarily—to trick the audience's perception. Though the costume may partially conceal the gender of the dancer, the actor crossing the gender line is almost always clearly recognizable as a man or a woman playing "the other."[3] Still, there are instances where, without irony, males may assume the roles of idealized females and females, the roles of idealized males. At other times, the tension between the gender of the role and the gender of the role player may be exploited for parodic purposes. In some instances, mixed messages may be deliberately given, and the gender codes grotesquely entwined and confused. All three strategies are identifiable in the example at Mas; it is their mixing that gives rise to the rich comic mischief of the scene. There is an historical dimension to this play with gender, also: A dance that may have been traditionally performed by men might be played by women, or roles once reserved for women taken by men—often with new social meaning. This essay surveys the complex play with gender in Balinese performance and tries to assess some of the societal and cultural reasons for its pervasiveness and appeal, as well as for recent variations.

The presentation of gender in Balinese performance is not always scrambled, of course. In the conservative village of Tenganan, for example, it is the custom for adolescent boys and girls to be presented to each other in an *Abuang* ceremony. Both the young men and the young women are dressed in intricately woven and patterned double *ikat* textiles that are wrapped around their bodies. Accessories emphasize their respective "maleness" and "femaleness": each of the young men has an ancestral dagger, or *kris,* tucked into the back of his costume, while the young women have tiara-like, mirrored, flower-bedecked headpieces of gilded leather set in their hair, their lithe fingers accentuated by the tightly bound cloth wrappings and an additional long front panel. As the haunting music of the old iron *selonding* metallophones is played, the young men and women dance before each other in a somewhat tentative manner. This dance is—historically at least—a courting ritual, and pride, embarrassment, and nervousness upon entering gendered adulthood are all evident. The women sway their bodies more, bending at the hip, and take slightly smaller steps, while the men tend to take more static poses, their feet turned out to form a somewhat broader base as they make more angular motions. The gendered difference in movement, while apparent, is not extreme. There is no gender bending here; yet, one can see the beginnings of the gender codes that are exaggerated, hardened, and then frequently transgressed through cross-gender play in more modern Balinese dance forms.

Legong—a "secular" form of dance theatre relatively well known in the Western world—presents one example of the historical complexity of this play.[4] Usually danced by three highly trained, pre-adolescent girls, it is regarded in Bali and abroad as a quintessentially feminine form. The story most commonly accompanying this dance and its characteristic music is that of a thirteenth-century East Javanese ruler, the King of Lasem. In abstract, stylized form, the story is told of his abduction of a beautiful maiden, Rangkesari, of his attempts to persuade and then force her into his bed, of his encounter with a bird of ill omen, and—by inference at least—of his subsequent death on the battlefield at the hands of the woman's brother, the King of Daha.[5] The story is potentially rife with sexual politics. The capture of brides was once commonplace in Bali, yet there are time-honored strictures in Balinese culture against forcing women—wives included—into sexual activities against their will.[6]

Playing in this (at best) ambiguous ethical space, the king's death is implicitly linked to his attempts to force his captured bride to his bed. Yet the story is performed with such refinement, by such diminutive and innocent players, that the complex gender politics of the story is easily lost in the abstract beauty of the dance and in the audience's wonder at the accomplishments of the young dancers as they perform all the roles—male and female, turn and turn about—without any change of costume except for the addition of gilded leather wings for the bird of ill omen. Asked why older women were not allowed to dance Legong, Balinese told Jane Belo in the 1930s that mature dancers would "infuse a disturbing element into the dance which is in its essence sexless, impersonal, acute, and pure in its stylization."[7] Mature young women are now performing this story, however—as demonstrated in a recent American tour by the STSI Conservatory of Denpasar—increasing the emphasis on the female body within performance.

The ethical ambiguities of the story, muted though they usually are for the audience, have echoes in the history of the form. Traditionally, the three pre-adolescent dancers who played all the roles in the drama were picked from the most beautiful girls in the village and bedecked in fine jewels and opulent costumes to showcase the prince's swelling wealth. The dancers were often exempt from their more strenuous domestic responsibilities. They danced until menarche, at which point, historically, they were often handpicked by the prince for marriage or, somewhat ironically, became teachers of subsequent dancers portraying this tale of failed courtship.[8]

Although the vocabulary of gesture and movement used in Legong is influenced by the archetypal—and male-dominated—Balinese dance form, Gambuh, it is also strongly rooted in the female trance tradition known as Sanghyang Dedari.[9] The sanghyang dancers, who are "smoked" with sandalwood incense and put into trance, become vessels for the heavenly nymphs' prescriptions of rituals or offerings needed to purify a diseased village or to ward off the practice of witchcraft. Chosen because they are susceptible to trance and, being pre-menstrual, considered to be purer—more "goddess-like"—the girls, while in trance, are usually considered to be inhabited by the widyadari, or female nymphs (though in Cemenggaon, the village in which Sanghyang Dedari most strongly survives, only one of the inhabiting celestial spirits is now thought to be female, and the other is considered male; the form is accordingly known as Sanghyang Dedara-Dedari).[10] The dance itself is in many of its physical aspects similar to Legong, though simpler in its choreography and costuming and ritually far more powerful; the physical movements of *Legong* are stylizations from the vocabulary of gesture and movement in *Sanghyang Dedari*.

Legong is said to have originated with a dream vision experienced by the Prince of Ketewel, in which he pictured young women dancing elegantly as celestial nymphs in the manner of the *sanghyangs*, but dressed in resplendent costumes.[11] The sacred prototype version of *Legong* that resulted, in which young girls wear masks representing the *widyadari*, is still danced in Ketewel. The unmasked secular dance that has evolved is even more languorous and fluid, accentuating sinuous, curved lines, delicate hand gestures, and bending movements from the hip. The accompanying costume is essentially one long band of gilded and brightly colored cloth that is tightly wound to emphasize the form of the swaying body (*Legong* itself comes from the root word *leg*, which means "sway," a movement typical of the dance).[12] Although these historical and stylistic factors combine to give *Legong* its reputation as a quintessentially "feminine" dance form, in the earlier years of this century there was a version of *Legong* called *Nandir* in which unmasked young boys in the town of Blahbatuh were taught to imitate the dance of the celestial nymphs. This dance, it seems, was the current *Legong*'s immediate predecessor; according to I Made Bandem, *Nandir*, which predates the popular secular version of *Legong*, was later re-choreographed for two (then three) young girls and eventually evolved into the famous modern form, with some of the *Nandir* dancers going on to become famous *Legong* teachers.[13] Emerging out of the history of *Legong*, then—seemingly the most "feminine" dance form existing in Bali—comes a stream of unsettling masculine intrusions in character roles, story lines, and the history of the genre itself and its social implications that considerably complicate the picture.

Famous as Bali is for its dance traditions, forms of "social dancing" are rare (though the burgeoning tourist nightclubs in Sanur and Kuta Beach are changing that fact rapidly). There is, however, besides the ancient *Abuang* courting dance of Tenganan, a more widespread traditional form called *Joged* that traditionally takes place within a highly charged social and sexual context. In village situations, this form is a bawdy, flirtatious dance, in which a professional woman dancer is hired and men vie with each other to match the audaciousness of her flirtatious movements. *Joged* draws its dance vocabulary from both *Legong* and the "welcoming" dances—*Gabor, Pendet,* and, most recently, *Panyembrama*—used to honor gods, ancestors, and now human guests. The *joged* first dances a solo piece based on *Legong* movements and then invites male members of the audience to join her. As with the ultra-feminine, "disguised" Surapanakha, the traditional wrappings of *Legong* here accentuate the mature female form, and shy boys are pitched forward by their friends, only to run panicked back into the crowd. Other, more daring young men—and sometimes a few older ones—tie a scarf around their waists and dance erotically close to the *joged,* sometimes barely missing her breasts with their hands, until the *joged* dismisses them with a wave of her fan and moves on to the next male clamoring for attention or pitched into the circle of dance by his excited friends. The *joged* follows the lead of her suitor/adversary, turning as he turns, swooping low with him, bringing her nose close to his, but always maintaining a slight distance. The dance takes the form of highly stylized foreplay to love-making, and the *joged* entices the male dancer with erotic gestures—undulating hips, coy gestures with a fan, and inviting smiles and winks—which, in the past, are said to have often continued beyond flirtation after the public displays of the performance.[14] This form is the ancient *Abuang* courting dance transformed into sexy sport, and the gender codes inchoate in *Abuang* and aestheticized in *Legong* are accordingly greatly exaggerated.

On an island where courting has generally been secretive, where displays of physical affection between opposite sexes are shunned, and where sex is openly discussed but clandestinely performed, the intense allure of *Joged* is understandable. As with *Legong,* these performances could also be a prelude to more permanent sexual relations. It was often the case that, along with the more chaste *Legong* dancers, the ruling prince would request the *joged* for his own—generally assigning her a lower ranking among the concubines in the royal harem—a practice eventually banned by the Dutch as a form of royal prostitution.[15]

The history of *Joged* also has its gender twist. *Gandrung* is the name of a form in which young boys, in *Joged* costumes, performed and enticed the male audience just as a female *joged* would do. Covarrubias called the now extremely rare form "decadent" in 1937 and cited examples of *Gandrung* that resulted in uncharacteristically heated reactions and even fights that could end in death among the participant/observers.[16] There was apparently no decrease in enthusiasm, emotionally or sexually, shown by the men of the village towards the boy dancers who danced *Gandrung.* Dr. Julius Jacobs, who was in Bali during the 1880s, wrote then:

You know already that they are boys and it disgusts one to see how, at the end, men from all ranks and conditions of Balinese society offer their coins to perform dances in the oddest attitudes with these children, and it disgusts you still more when you realize that these children, worn out and dead-tired after hours of *perpendicular* exercises, are required yet to perform *horizontal* manoeuvres, first stroked by one, then kissed by another.[17]

Open male homosexual activity seems to be less common in Bali during the latter half of this century than in previous eras.[18] Aside from its direct associations with homosexual encounters, though, note the erotic appeal accorded the androgynous play of *Gandrung*. Katharane Mershon, observing an adolescent boy at a *Gandrung* performance at about the same time Covarrubias was writing, saw the performance as a training ground for male adolescent sexuality—heterosexual as well as homosexual:

[Pegeg's] lips were parted as he moved smoothly to entice the *ganderung*. . . . Small beads of perspiration glistened on his forehead, his eyes shone like glowing coals of fire as he accented the music with his head. . . . His hands fluttered close to the *ganderung*'s body in an ecstasy of trembling rhythms. His boyish torso leaned forward, swerving and turning, until his maze of movement halted as he faced the child and bent toward him. Their noses nearly touched, the gesture of caress. . . . Men far older than Pegeg succumbed to the wiles of the child and danced their feeling in response to his tiny figure. Some were humorous, some stylized, some were as Pegeg—assailed by the fragile loveliness of the child-dancer. Pegeg had danced the longing and desire of a man coming into manhood. One could not perform in such a way with a woman. But a *ganderung*! He was a boy like Pegeg. He would understand.[19]

The evolution of *Legong* from sacred, ritually efficacious forms and their permutations to more secular forms and the complexities surrounding the function and portrayal of gender within this history have parallels in the evolution of other Balinese genres. *Baris,* a "warrior" dance, depicts the glory of a triumphant Balinese soldier as he encounters his opponent on the battlefield. The word *Baris* itself means "line" or "file" and refers to the traditional battle formations used in defense of princedoms as well as to the choreography of the ancient version of the dance, still performed by squads of older men on the temple ground.[20] The more popular solo version, now usually danced by young boys, was derived from this more tightly constrained and ritually occasioned group variation within recent history. As opposed to the graceful and flowing lines of the feminine *Legong* dancer, the solo *Baris* dancer is frenetic, bursting with energy, and commanding in his whirling, spectacular flashes. The *Baris* wears a costume that forces up and accentuates his shoulders. His legs are bent, his body rigid, and, all in all, there is a far greater degree of tension to his movements. Manifesting the most admired traits of the warrior—fierceness, disdain, pride, and acute alertness—*Baris* is, quintessentially, in a male domain.[21]

Into this masculine realm came one of Bali's finest dancers and most famous teachers, I Nyoman Kakul. According to Ana Daniel, he began training young girls to dance *Baris* in the 1950s because "he thought it most important for women to show their strength and took a stand by teaching young Balinese girls the power demonstrated in the *Baris*."[22] His first young female warrior was his daughter, Dawan, and among his later students of *Baris* was Sukawati, the daughter of then President Sukarno (himself half-Balinese).[23]

What appears to be two essentially opposite gender-specific forms—

Legong (a prime example of female dance, or *igel eluh*) and *Baris* (a quintessentially male dance, or *igel mwani*)—can be seen, on closer inspection,
as manifesting the twin Balinese themes of complementariness and balance.
As I Wayan Dibia points out, although Balinese musical genres, costumes,
and dance positions (*agem*) are all coded as "masculine" and "feminine,"
an important and pervasive aesthetic concept dictates that, just as percus-
sive and sustained, heavy and light, or fast and slow must be reconciled
within a musical composition or choreography, so, too, must the principles
of "masculinity" and "femininity."[24] Drums and metallophones are therefore commonly played together in "male" and "female" pairs (the "female"
being the lower pitched of the two). The *Baris* dance features the interjec-
tion of a light, feminine step (*milpil*) in the choreography to prevent it from
being "too hot." The *Legong* choreography similarly features within it a
"masculine" sudden accentuated raising of one foot (*nengkleng*) to prevent
it from being "too sweet." The idea is to bring "male" and "female" into
harmony.[25] One way to bring about this desired complementarity, then, is
to counterbalance the dominating "male" or "female" elements within a
composition or choreography with sounds or strips of behavior that are
coded as appropriate to the other gender. Another way to achieve balance
is to project the code of one gender onto the body of the other.

Stylistically mediating between the "maleness" of *Baris* and the "femaleness" of *Legong* is the relatively new form, *Kebyar*, that originated in
the north and spread quickly throughout the island. Originally choreographed to express the changing moods of an adolescent male, *Kebyar* has
been frequently tinkered with and refashioned. I Mario, the famous choreographer of *Kebyar*, borrowed movements, gestures, poses, and costumes
from *Legong*, fused them with movements and gestures from *Baris*,
adapted music that was developing in the north of Bali, added some innovations of his own, and created a distinctly new form. Young women,
then, also attempted the form. They were perfectly adept at managing the
physically demanding routine but were regarded as unable to evoke the
subtle nuances of male emotion and affectation that *Kebyar* demanded.
Several new dances were then choreographed in the *Kebyar* style especially
for females: for example, *Mergapati, Yudapati,* and *Wiranata*. One such
dance—the *Tumulilingan,* or Bumblebee Dance—features a Kebyar dancer
as a male "bee" pursuing a female "bee" in a *Legong* costume, creating a
sort of refined concert version of *Joged*. This reassertion of gendered difference did not remain stable, however; one of the more popular of these
Kebyar-style dances is now the *Taruna Jaya,* in which a mature young
woman mimics (and lightly satirizes) a preening adolescent male—the subject of I Mario's original dance. The Balinese have even created a new, inherently flexible version, *Kebyar Bebancihan* (from the word "*bancih,*"

meaning both "hermaphrodite" and "transvestite"), that may be danced by either a male or a female dancer.[26]

Many of the movements, musical scales, character types, and stories in *Legong, Baris, Kebyar,* and *Arja* are influenced to some degree by the classic, and now rarely performed, *Gambuh*. Considered to be an anachronistic holdover from the Javanese court dances of the profoundly influential Majapahit era (fourteenth century), *Gambuh* is reputed to have come to Bali with the Javanese nobility when Java fell under the sway of Islam. It is a slow-paced, ceremonial dance, considered overly sedate by many of the Balinese themselves. The *Gambuh* repertoire centers around the exploits of Prince Panji—an East Javanese culture hero.[27] Inevitably, Panji is separated from his love, the refined Princess Candra Kirana, and must endure hardship and adventure to be reunited with her. In the process, Panji is often forced to undergo a metamorphosis—into a woman, a cruder male, or even into another species—to achieve his goal. Candra Kirana, too, disguises herself—often as a male—and eventually comes to rule Bali and meet up with Panji on the battlefield.[28] Traditionally, the many characters called for in *Gambuh* stories were all portrayed by males. Slowly, though, women have infiltrated *Gambuh* from the top, frequently playing the most refined characters available—including, most notably, both Candra Kirana and Panji himself.[29]

Studying Sundanese culture on the nearby island of Java, Kathy Foley notes a similar delight in casting across seeming barriers of age and gender, and she ascribes a metaphysical dimension to this form of play:

. . . [T]he Sundanese do not demand that the gender, age, or even species of the performer and character coincide—men play women, women play men. Septuagenarians may be singled out for their fine representations of adolescent characters; and demons, gods and animals are all felt to be splendidly performable by human beings. . . . This system recognizes that the particulars of bodily life change with gender, age, and circumstances, but that souls are more comprehensive and in need of fuller exercise: the individual "soul" participates in the overall cosmic power manifest in all things continuing eternally; material "abodes"—bodies—are limited and temporary containers of this force.[30]

A corresponding world view is embraced by Balinese metaphysics and can be glossed by the Upanishadic saying, *"Tat tvam asi"*—"Thou art That"— indicating that every individual potentially contains within himself or herself the entire universe. This world view has had a profound impact on Balinese performance.[31] Still, in Balinese practice, some transformations of gender are favored over others; to understand the reasons for recurring patterns of cross-gender representation, the way in which Balinese notions of gender interact with other categorical differences must be addressed.

Cutting across the categories for gender, status, and personality types in Bali are the opposed aesthetic constructs of *halus* (refined, noble, and graceful) and *kasar* (coarse, profane, and uncultured), with *keras* being a third term for strong characters standing somewhere along the mid-range of the continuum between these opposites. The normative ideal of *halus* behavior is reinforced, verbally and kinesthetically, in many of Bali's dance forms, and *Gambuh,* especially, provides a rich field of study for the cultural construction of *halus* and *kasar.* The *halus* characters, most often the benevolent nobility, are identifiable by their falsetto voices, delicate features, and refined, restrained movements. *Kasar* characters, on the other hand, are represented by coarse voices, hairy, fat bodies, and a splay-footed gait. Alongside, and intermixing with, the binaries of pure/impure, godlike/animalistic, high status/low status, and the more problematic male/female, the *halus/kasar* antinomy provides the Balinese a means for ordering the world and structuring personal interaction.[32] The Balinese (at least nominally) strive to be *halus* in their ways, while retaining both great affection for such forthright *keras* characters as Bima in the *Mahabharata* and a fascination with the quintessentially *kasar* realm of the demonic. To behave like an animal, showing strong emotions and aggression, is to subvert the modes of this ideal behavior; thus, young Balinese adults have their teeth filed in an elaborate ceremony (*matatah*) to distance themselves further from the fanged animal world.[33] Whereas *halus* characters are generally admired, the *kasar* characters are either the most abhorred or, as in the case of the lovable, though obscene clowns, the most dearly loved. It is against this continuum that the "true" and "false" forms of the demoness Surapanakha and the gender switches involved must be understood.[34]

The *halus/keras/kasar* continuum figures prominently in the gendered aesthetics of dance roles. Although there is no one-to-one correspondence, feminine behavior is conventionally thought to be more in tune with *halus* qualities, and masculine behavior is frequently regarded as tinged with *kasar* characteristics. Thus, in traditional Balinese terms, it would usually be unfitting to have a woman playing the parts of obscene, *kasar* clowns (though recently they have taken on the *Condong*'s somewhat comic role of the *keras* interlocutor). Many women dancers perform *halus* male roles, whereas only those men most proficient at female impersonation might play the role of a beautiful princess—a cross-over that is becoming increasingly rare on the Balinese stage. As Abby Ruddick points out:

When adult men play refined women in dramas, they [tend to be] clowns who exaggerate female speech and demeanor not to pass for, but to point out their ineptness as women; audiences find these men screamingly funny. When girls dance male roles, they embody the refined and elegant hero, who is often an accomplished warrior or hunter.[35]

At the other end of this continuum, the few (but significant) *kasar* female characters—old hags, witches, and awkward, "masculinized" women—are portrayed most frequently (and in some instances, exclusively) by men. The *halus/kasar* axis thus helps establish parameters for gender-switching in the Balinese theatre that intertwine the portrayal of refinement and crudity with assumptions about gender.

These parameters are perhaps most fully evident in the typical role reversals and gender transgressions of the Balinese dance drama known as *Arja*. This form, developed first in 1825 for the funeral of the King of Karangasem, is the closest relative in Bali to Western opera, relying more heavily upon sung dialogue than do other forms of Balinese performance. The stories—often tales of East Javanese nobility and kingdoms—also possess a more prominent sentimental and romantic streak than those featured in other Balinese narrative forms. Because of this quality, and aided by its usual occurrence in the middle of the night, *Arja* has a reputation for providing an atmosphere ideal for courtship in Bali.[36] It is usually performed by four principal actor/singers and a number of secondary players, supplemented by the always necessary buffoons and clowns. Originally, *Arja* troupes were entirely male. Then, in the 1920s, all-female troupes emerged, and various experiments were made incorporating women into the previous all-male troupes. There was much debate during the 1930s as to the relative virtues of the male falsetto and female soprano voices for the *halus* principal roles, as well as debates about the endurance of female actors and their ability to indulge in ribald comedy.[37] Although at least one all-male *Arja* troupe still exists in Bali, most companies over the past several decades have combined men and women—though, significantly, the performers do not necessarily perform roles of their own gender. Thus, the young maidservant (*Condong*), Princess (*Galuh*), Protagonist Prince (*Mantri Manis*), and Antagonist King (*Mantri Buduh*) are all generally played by women, while the principal comic male servants (*Punta* and *Kartala*) and various other comic servants and eccentrics are played by men.

One character peculiar to *Arja* since its inception is the *Limbur*—a determined, strong-minded, older female character who was originally designed to satirize one of the late King of Karangasem's wives and is usually assigned the role of an eccentric mother or mother-in-law, rarely far from the center of action. Spies and deZoete noted that the *Limbur* remained a favorite for female impersonators long after women began to play the principal roles. They describe the typical portrayal as "not necessarily unsympathetic, though it generally has a nuance of intrigue, and a certain eccentricity expressed by a manly voice and commanding gestures, sudden, arbitrary accents of the wrist and shoulder, and surprising fluctuations of the body."[38] Women have recently begun to play the *Limbur* role as well.

Interestingly, the same patterns that dominated *Arja* for decades are also evident in the syncretic genre of *Prembon*, created in the 1940s by grafting *Arja* characters and characteristics onto the all-male, masked genre of *Topeng*. Here, too, young women—until very recently always without masks—might play elegant (though sometimes frail and unstable) young princes, while men continued to play the more comic, old, and maladroit female roles. Similar role divisions are regularly followed in *Parwa*, a form that blends elements of *Arja* with aspects of other, more ancient dance and puppet forms—*Wayang Wong* and *Wayang Kulit*—traditionally used to convey the Indian epics.

So far, we have been dealing with gender in Bali as though it always existed in a male/female dyad, however that dyad may be teased and tortured. But in Bali, genders are counted as three. Though not extensively documented, the hermaphrodite or *bancih* occupies an important position in the Balinese schemata and is acknowledged in ritual blessings intended to include everyone in a Balinese community—"every man, woman and hermaphrodite."[39] A palm leaf manuscript (*lontar*) attributes the *bancih*'s condition to an equal mixing of the white and red procreative substances of the male and female, respectively.[40] This blending of male and female elements has parallels in Hindu cosmology and iconography: In abstract representation, the *lingam* is not complete without the *yoni*. The Indian concept of *Ardhanariswara*—sometimes cited as embodying the perfect unity aspired to by married couples—combines the male and female essence into a single androgynous and divine form in which one half is female and the other half is male. Philosophically, such divine androgynes may also be conceived of as pre-existing a gendered world and representative of what Foley refers to above as "the overall cosmic power manifest in all things continuing eternally." Thus, in Balinese cosmology, the undifferentiated, androgynous power held to be at the root of all creation is commonly referred to as Sang Hyang Tunggal or Sang Hyang Widhi Wasa. Though the term *bancih,* in practice, is used to describe male transvestites as well as true hermaphrodites, the taking on of a *bancih*'s dress and role by a male transvestite does not necessarily indicate a change in sexual preference. Indeed, the hermaphrodite *bancih* is said not to participate in sexual activities at all.[31] The concept of the *bancih,* then, seems to reference an ontological concern with androgyny as much as a sexual one.

Jane Belo, in *Bali: Rangda and Barong,* specifically addresses the phenomenon of crossed sex roles in Balinese performance in relationship to the androgynous divine. Examining Balinese attitudes towards conception and reincarnation, she cites a cyclical merging and redifferentiating of gender. The merging of sex roles—man into woman's, woman into man's—is seen as a reiteration of the ultimate, undifferentiated male-female type, as typified by the Balinese ultimate God, Sang Hyang Tunggal, who exists before all time and is the union of all elements. Belo observes that the Balinese highly revere the undifferentiated male-female type, since it reflects the state of the ultimate God, and that, consequently, the newborn—a result of the union of the differentiated male and female parents and regarded as sexually ambiguous until birth—is considered a direct descendant from God and is likewise revered.[42] Within the cycle, though, the sexes merge in order to redivide and restore their polarity and sexual potential: Babies acquire gender, mothers and fathers resume differentiated lives, and even the godhead assumes male and female aspects—for example, Siwa and Parwati. The theatre, like the *bancih,* can provide remainders of ultimate oneness as well as mimic the cycle of union and redivision through cross-gender casting of idealized male and female roles and their grotesque opposites.

These phenomena are especially salient in *Arja* and are also characteristic of the scene from the *Ramayana* presented at Mas. It is important to stress, though, that, whereas Rama, Laksamana, and the *Mantri* characters present a divine fusion of gender characteristics, the *Limbur* and the demonic form of Surapanakha, with their grotesquely scrambled gender traits, do not present images of an androgynous ideal but of its total inversion. For the Balinese, such a grotesque reversal of the androgynous ideal can produce generous laughter or, in cases to be dealt with next, signify ritual danger.[43]

Complex play with gender is also evident in those forms meant more to exorcise than to entertain. While observing an exorcistic performance that seems to have recycled the form of *Joged* within its dramatic development, Margaret Mead described the following transformation of mood: ". . . a charming street dance in which a little pre-adolescent girl dances to delight the men of the village, represents the desirable and irresistible in woman, [then] takes a doll, turns it into a witch and crushes its head under her foot to kill it."[44] This sequence of events illustrates well the Balinese abhorrence of and fascination with all things related to witches, black magic, and evil spirits. The prime theatrical manifestation of the witch in Bali—*Rangda*—is both a key participant in the famous confrontation between herself and the floppy dragon/lion known as the *Barong* (more precisely, *Barong Keket*)[45] and the focal point of the exorcistic drama known most commonly as *Calonarang.*

The dramatic showdown between *Rangda* and *Barong* has sparked the greatest amount of interpretation and subsequent controversy among Western scholars of any of Bali's dance forms. Perhaps because it is often perceived of as a ritual contextualization of "Good versus Evil," or as a means of documenting the trance-induced self-stabbing, or as a spectacular articulation of the fantastic or the archetypal, it has rarely escaped the interpretive eyes of cultural ethnographers. These ritual confrontations also contain essential information about Balinese constructions of gender that both support the performances and are sustained by them.

Like so many of Bali's performance texts, the story of *Calonarang* that most frequently provides a narrative platform for the adversaries' encounters has its roots in quasi-mythical, traditional Javanese legend. The variations on the plot are myriad, but Stephen Snow sums up the source succinctly.

[It is] a drama created from the lontar (palm leaf) manuscripts which relate the legend of the eleventh-century Balinese prince, Erlangga. Rangda, in the story, is first known as Mahendradatta, a Javanese princess who married the Javanese raja, Dharmodayana. Erlangga is their son. In the legend, Dharmodayana banishes Mahendradatta to the forest because he suspects her of practising witchcraft. Dharmodayana then dies and Mahendradatta becomes a widow (a *rangda*). She gathers a band of pupils about her and trains them in the art of Black Magic. She seeks revenge on her son's kingdom because none of the noblemen will marry her daughter as they fear she too may be a witch. Rangda, now known as Calonarang, sends plagues to kill the people. She goes to the cemetery and digs up the corpses, drinking their blood and bedecking herself with their entrails. Erlangga cannot prevail against her, and he finally sends for Mpu Bharada, a famous holy man. Mpu Bharada dispatches his son or assistant (depending on the version of this narrative, of which there are several), Bahula, to marry Ratna Menggali, Calonarang's daughter. Bahula discovers from his wife that the witch's power comes from a little book, which he steals for Mpu Bharada. . . . With the power of the book, Mpu Bharada restores life to the victims of the witch. In the end, he kills Calonarang, not once but twice: first in her supernatural form as Rangda, and then in her human form . . . in order to absolve her of her many sins.[46]

As Roma O'Neill points out, the legend represents the forces of good on Erlangga's side as mostly male characters, who are pitted against the forces of destruction—primarily female characters.[47]

Though this already gender-laden story is performed in infinite variety, in the most typical version, *Barong* enters first and performs an introductory dance, displaying the virtuosity of the two male dancers animating the mythic beast. Then (as in *Gambuh*), the *Condong*, or maidservant, enters and provides the narrative background; Bandem and deBoer note that, up until very recently, this maidservant has also been portrayed by a male.[48] Next enter four to six of *Calonarang*'s female pupils, the *Sisyas*—always played by women—whose eerie dance, white, draped costumes, and loose, flowing hair are unique to this form. Finally, the old Widow of Girah (a fictionalized version of Mahendradatta) enters in human form—Matah Gede, "the Great Uncooked One"—played, "of course," by a magically powerful (*sakti*) male. Translated by the *Condong*, "she" instructs the *sisyas* in spreading pestilence and, in doing so, explains both how to perform *and* combat black magic—an extremely dangerous task since it undermines the power of real life witches in the village. After a comic interlude, King Erlangga enters, commands Mpu Bharada to kill *Calonarang,* and escorts him to *Rangda*'s dwelling. The *sisya*s then reenter and perform a dance in which

> . . . [t]he girls cover their faces with pieces of white cloth, their loose hair hangs free in front. Some of them immediately begin to mime picking up dead babies from the ground, while they all howl with laughter. Dolls wrapped in white cloth provide very realistic properties. The sisya mime eating the little bundles, and then they dance again, shaking their breasts obscenely and jumping from side to side while in a squatting position. They wiggle their buttocks with an ugly motion. In general it may be said that they defy every customary aesthetic principle of Balinese dance.[49]

Another comic interlude usually involves *Rangda*'s daughter, who, like Surapanakha, may appear in both enticing and grotesque forms, played respectively by female and male performers. As the dramatic tension rises, sometimes a spiritually powerful or *sakti* man will assume the role of a corpse and agree to spend the night in the graveyard. This act is a show of great bravery, for the cemetery is the haunting ground of the evil spirits.[50]

Finally, the old widow-witch herself enters—now in her horrific form of *Rangda.* Mpu Bharada may now attack *Rangda* and attempt to stab her with his ceremonial dagger (*kris*). Because *Rangda*'s magic is so powerful, however, the blade does not penetrate, and *Mpu Bharada* is thwarted. *Rangda* may next challenge the local practitioners of black magic to a duel. In a frequently performed variation, *Mpu Bharada* may use his own magical power to transform himself into the *Barong.* When this occurs, the *Rangda* and *Barong* are understood to be *pamurtian*s—horrific representations of the embattled protagonists and their powers.[51] Just as the *Barong* seems to be defeated, selected men of the village, deep in trance, rush upon *Rangda* and atempt to kill her with their *kris*s. But *Rangda,* once again too strong, brandishes her magical white cloth, forcing the men to turn their swords upon themselves.[52] In the frenzy of self-stabbing that follows, the *kris*s do not puncture the men's skin, for they are protected by the *Barong*'s magic and the depth of their trance. It is not unusual for the women of the village to enter trance, but the women never attack *Rangda*; they only partake in the self-stabbing.[53] Eventually, all those who have become entranced are brought out of their frenzy by being sprinkled with holy water, frequently from the human beard of the *Barong.* One of the characteristics that has made this dance drama so intriguing to Western scholars is the seeming lack of climax to the enactment of the story. The *Barong* (here depicting *Mpu Bharada*) does not kill *Rangda,* and the confrontation often ends with neither one victorious and with several members of the village, the two dancers of the *Barong,* and the dancer of *Rangda* all (though not always) going into deep trance.

The *Calonarang* can vary widely; this is only one version—albeit a common one. The figure of *Rangda* is particularly complex in its symbolic resonance. Drawing upon past Western scholarship and Balinese responses, Jane Belo noted that *Rangda,* as represented in *Calonarang,* is a laminate of cultural values:

> To the anthropologist and student of Eastern religions, *Rangda* is Durga. . . . To the historian she is Queen Mahendradatta. . . . To the student of theater she is the angry widow. . . . To the contemporary ethnologist she is a mother figure. . . . To the psychologist she is Fear. . . . *Rangda* must have in its make-up a deeply complex, laminated structure, layer upon layers of meaning reaching down to the present out of a foggy or accurately recorded past, for the most part deeply comprehended but not articulately stated by the people whom it most directly concerns.[54]

To add further complexity, the *Rangda-Barong* confrontation (referred to in Balinese as a *Mapajar*) can be set within a variety of narrative contexts, or performed quite apart from any specific narrative. An account of one such non-narrative performance of a *Mapajar,* witnessed outside Pura Ulu Siwi of Jimbaran in January of 1991, may reveal some of the complex play with gender at the core of these performances.[55] The *Barong* enters from the temple where it is stored and proceeds past a gamelan to the far northern (sacred) end of a cordoned-off street. Following the *Barong* are a group of costumed men who are most commonly referred to as *telek*s in Bali (though in Jimbaran they are called *sandar*s); they are wearing smiling white masks and elaborate gilded and painted costumes. The sexual identity of these figures is confused, since the masks are without facial hair, and they carry fans in their hands as well as swords on their backs. The *halus,* swaying movements of their group dance reinforces a sense of femininity, and elsewhere in Bali (in Ubud and Sanur, for example), *telek*s are danced by women or are referred to as *jauk luh*—female *jauk*s.

The *jauk*s themselves (termed *omang*s in Jimbaran) come next—sporting heavily mustachioed red, orange, brown, black, and white masks with bulging eyes and flared nostrils and glinting, mother-of-pearl teeth. Costumed almost identically to the *telek*s, but without fans, they are clearly male. As the *telek*s form in a group and fan themselves, the *jauk*s begin to come up from the southern (profane) end of the road, jockeying amongst themselves for power and making individual sallies past the centrally located *gamelan* and towards the *telek*s. One by one, starting with a comic old man and continuing through a series of vigorous, warrior-like personae, they approach the files of *telek*s in a *keras* manner, vaingloriously strutting, pointing with two fingers in the mode of royal command, and trying to gain entrance into their fan-fluttering ranks. One by one, they retreat and give way to the next pretender for power and control. Finally, one of the *jauk*s penetrates into the *telek*s' territory and seems to take control of the group, forcing one of the *telek*s to kneel submissively as the other *jauk*s approach. From behind, though, this would-be master of the *telek*s is struck down by the blow of a fan, and he is carried off, perhaps mortally wounded, by his fellows. At this point, with the masculine *jauk*s and more feminine *telek*s once more in separate camps, the *Barong* (danced by two men) approaches from the (sacred) north, where he has been stationed with his back to the action. Moving through the ranks of the *telek*s and towards the *jauk*s, his dance seems to bring reconciliation and unites the embattled factions; the *jauk*s and *telek*s join together under the *Barong*'s influence and return to the temple ground. The *Barong* moves back towards the north, playfully dancing and snapping at children in the audience with his bearded jaw.

A male priest dressed in a saffron cotton shift and wearing a yellow female mask with small fangs moves along the road, tossing rice at the onlookers. *Rangda*'s apprentice, Rarung, and her grotesque, comic maid-servant, Jero Luh, now enter from the temple and take up the *jauk*s' former station at the south end of the road, where Rarung cackles and howls. Both of these female characters are played, as always, by men. Both carry "magic cloths," and Rarung's red kerchief, in particular, is established as a baby's sling by the way she (mis)treats it. They taunt the *Barong* and make it chase its own tail. *Barong* snitches the red cloth with its jaws, but Rarun, aided by Jero Luh, swipes it back. If the masculine and feminine principles represented by the *jauk*s and *telek*s, respectively, had been reconciled by the *Barong*, this reconciliation has proved fleeting. This time, though, the more aggressive challenge seems to come from the feminine side.

Rangda herself enters and conducts a screaming, screeching colloquy in ancient Javanese with Rarung. Eventually, Rarung and Jero Luh depart, and *Rangda* herself confronts the *Barong*. Then, from the extreme north end of the street, the *Barong*'s followers—all men—charge at full speed with their *kris*s drawn, They throw themselves onto *Rangda,* but, as in *Calonarang,* their swords will not penetrate "her" body. *Rangda* withdraws to the temple, seemingly victorious, and the man who has been possessed by her spirit takes off the mask and, still in trance, rips the head off a chick with his teeth. The *Barong*'s followers alternately turn their *kris*s upon themselves and cry their frustration into the *Barong*'s open jaws. While this frenzy of self-stabbing and lamentation continues, they are sprinkled with holy water—first in the street and then in the temple yard—until they—and those who have played principal roles—are finally brought out of trance.

Though the performance lends itself to more than one interpretation, clearly tensions between principles coded as male and as female are prominent in this all-male exorcistic performance in which the health of the village is held to be at stake. The aim, it seems, is not to defeat the *teleks*, the *jauks*, *Rangda*, or the *Barong* but, rather, to recognize and engage the sources of power that each possesses and to contain these powers within some larger, re-balanced whole.

The figures of *Rangda* and *Barong* themselves partake of this play with gender and gender-laden values. Margaret Mead was the first to suggest that there were aspects of the *Rangda* figure that were ambiguous in their sexual coding; noting that *Rangda* had the pendant breasts of an older woman and a hairy body characteristic of an older man, Mead hypothesized that *Rangda* represented a curious combination of male maturity and female maternity.[56] Mary LeCron Foster examines the sexual iconography of both *Rangda* and the *Barong* more extensively and uncovers more pervasive evidence of androgyny. As Foster observes, although *Rangda* is the widow past childbearing years whose envy of fertility causes her to seek revenge through witchcraft, she is also kinesthetically linked to the archetypal male—the *Baris Gede* warrior—in her posture (*agem*), gesture, and costume. The *Barong* is often referred to as *Banas Pati Raja*, alluding (in part) to a shamanic "Lord of the Forest";[57] yet, he moves in sinuous, circular, and flowing patterns and is portrayed as playful, gentle, and, for the most part, unaggressive—all considered female characteristics. Indeed, the *Barong* in Jimbaran is named *Dewa Ayu*—an unusual combination of *Dewa*, or male god, and *Ayu* (literally "pretty"), a female princess.[58] Foster describes the net effect accordingly:

[T]he bad characteristics of both sexes have been assigned to *Rangda* and the good to *Barong*. She embodies male aggressiveness, female old age, desexualized intellectuality or infertile wisdom, hatred and destructful greed which is death dealing. He embodies female lack of aggression, youthful sexuality of both sexes, female-animal-childlike playfulness, and unthreatening animal appetite which is life giving.[59]

But it would be a mistake to think of *Rangda* as simply representing "bad characteristics" associated with both the male and female genders. Whatever else she represents, *Rangda* is both a figure for and the possessor of a power known as *sakti*. Neither inherently good nor evil, *sakti* is subject to the will of the user. Thus, in Balinese theatre, the male gods Siwa and Wisnu can take the horrific *pamurtian* form of *Rangda* to display their *sakti*, which generally functions as a protective power. Although *sakti* significantly derives from the Sanskrit term for active/feminine energy—hence the appropriateness of *Rangda*'s gender—either males or females may come to possess it by inheritance, prayer, or study.[60] When used for benevolent purposes, as by the spiritual healers called *balians*, *sakti* is deployed for healing power or to cleanse ritually. As a weapon, though, *sakti* has the potential to cause illness, to lure the opposite sex, or to dominate the will of others. This power lies in the domain of black magic, hence the appropriateness of *Rangda*'s role in *Calonarang* as the Queen of the Witches who feeds on corpses, babies, and human entrails and commands legions of evil spirits (*leyaks*) that frolic in the graveyard and spread disease and pestilence. This same connection, however, accounts for the appropriateness of her paradoxical, apotropaic function as Monarch of the Temple of Death (*Pura Dalem*) and protector of the village from local black magic practitioners—most of whom are women;[61] for, when in a performance of the *Calonarang* the male performer playing *Rangda* challenges local practitioners of black magic to attack her, "she" defuses the magical danger to the village—a danger perceived as coming primarily from women.

Though there are male witches, there is an undeniable pervasive association in Bali between the practice of witchcraft and the female sex. This association seems to fly in the face of the assumption that women are more naturally *halus* noted while detailing the gender switches that are most common within more secular forms. It is as though that normative assumption carries with it a dark underside. This inconsistency should not be so surprising; black magic—in Bali as elsewhere—works by inversions of norms. Moreover, as Abby Ruddick suggests, women may be more prone to practice witchcraft in part *because* they are identified as the physically weaker, less outwardly aggressive sex: "Connected with this weakness is the association of women and witchcraft, and the assumption that a woman is more likely to succumb to the temptations of black magic which must be studied before white magic can be mastered, and become a *leyak*."[62] Another strong connection between witchcraft and women is created through Balinese notions of sexuality and procreativity. Young female witches are reputed to have rapacious sexual appetites.[63] *Rangda* and her legions of *leyaks* work nightmarish inversions on the connections of women to childbirth. Not only do *Rangda* and Rarung carry white cloths (*anteng*), which resemble slings for carrying babies, but in *Calonarang* there are frequently grotesque humorous scenes of pathetic, pregnant women (played by men) giving birth in a graveyard to stillborn babies that are then stolen by the *leyaks*.[64] As Mary Douglas has noted, where women are symbolically subordinate to men—which is true in many areas of Balinese life—there likely results a great deal of ritual danger associated with feminine sexuality.[65] *Rangda*, as a widow, is particularly dangerous as a carrier of *sakti* since she is sexually knowledgeable but outside the social grid.

This association between women and witchcraft in many ways supports Sherry Ortner's argument that women, universally, are culturally defined as closer to "nature," whereas men are considered the representatives of "culture." Though often mediating between nature and culture, women are commonly identified with something that society devalues or fears—in this case witchcraft—and are thus subordinated to men.[66] Ortner bases her argument on three significant "universal conditions":

> It all begins of course with the body and the natural procreative functions specific to women alone. We can sort out for discussion three levels at which this physiological fact has significance: (1) woman's *body and its functions,* more involved more of the time with "species life," seem to place her closer to nature, in contrast to man's physiology which frees him more completely to take up the projects of culture; (2) woman's body and its functions places her in *social roles* that are in turn considered to be at a lower order of the cultural process than man's; and (3) woman's traditional social roles, imposed because of her body and its functions, in turn gives her a different *psychic structure,* which like her physiological nature and her social roles, is seen as being closer to nature [her emphasis].[67]

Although universal programs are notoriously unreliable, it does seem that the Balinese have constructed their own categories of gender along similar lines.

One of the ways in which a woman is associated with untamed nature—and therefore touches off the sort of chain reaction that Ortner outlines—is through the bleeding of menstruation. Any form of bleeding is seen as an attraction to demons and therefore places the bleeder in a state of ritual pollution—of being *sebel.* A woman is *sebel* every month due to menstruation and thus may not enter a temple, granary, kitchen, or well. She may neither prepare religious offerings nor attend religious festivals and feasts. The wife of a high priest (*pedanda*) is forbidden to speak to her exalted husband, and, supposedly, a wife must sleep apart from her husband. Sex during menstruation is prohibited for fear that a deformed child or "freak" will be produced, a disastrous omen for a village.[68] Christiaan Hooykaas lists ten impurities that upset daily harmony, one of which is purchasing food in the marketplace that is sold by a woman who is *sebel*—presumably one who is menstruating.[69] The complex Balinese calendrical system, which determines auspicious religious occasions, makes no compromises for the monthly cycles of a woman; thus women are often barred from important religious festivities.[70] Even *Rangda* cannot dance on the days calculated for her period. Foster explains menstruation as a failure to incorporate the male seed, resulting in a condition analogous to death, since no life has been conceived.[71] Given the high cultural value that the Balinese ascribe to conception, menstruation, signifying lack of conception, takes on a negative value and may help to explain the cultural construction of menstruation as pollution.

In her study of gender and healing in Bali, Ruddick suggests,

> Menstrual pollution differs from other kinds of ritual pollution because it occurs predictably and regularly. Unlike pollution due to an external event involving other

people, it comes from within the woman herself. . . . Women know that their inherent, unavoidable, and cyclical pollution can interfere with ritual and ceremonial
activity, and prevent them from sacred undertakings ranging from handling *lontar*
to preparing offerings. The regulations for high caste women are even more strin-
gent than those for commoners. Menstruation helps account for women's inferior
strength in comparison to men's; it is seen as a weakening factor.[72]

This overall concept of *sebel* or ritual pollution is restricted neither to
women nor to procreativity but is a pervasive element in Balinese religion
that can also afflict men.[73] The braided concerns of sexuality and ritual
pollution make women particularly dangerous in this regard, however.

Concentrating on the *Sanghyang Dedara-dedari* ritual in Cemenggaon
but necessarily paying attention to the *Calonarang,* Roma O'Neill observes
"a need to emphasize the destructive female chthonic aspect as particularly
apparent in Cemenggaon, with its regular performances of the *Calonarang*
legend."[74] After noting that female characters are assigned both the life-
giving and life-destroying roles in the drama, O'Neill goes on to suggest
that, as a result, not only must there be a reunification of the chthonic with
the celestial and the destructive with the creative but also a unifying of
male with female—imperfect and temporary though it might be—in order
to attain the supernatural power necessary to dispel malevolent influences.
The ritual, then, ultimately reaffirms the co-existence of these oppositions,
especially as they affect creativity and destructiveness.[75] Accordingly,
Rangda must always be played by a man who is ritually powerful (*sakti*)
enough to withstand the great dangers of wearing such a magically potent
mask.[76] The performances in which such male adepts allow themselves to
be the vehicle for the *sakti* emanating through the Rangda mask can be
seen as elaborate strategies to re-harness feminine energy within a fundamentally male-ordered society.

As the conflation of many symbols and oppositions—male/female, good/
evil, white magic/black magic, celestial/chthonic—*Rangda, Barong,* and
their confrontation realign those imbalanced elements that have caused a
village to need a ritually cleansing performance such as *Calonarang.* As
Bandem and deBoer point out, the Balinese often perform *Calonarang*
when local incidences of black magic and sightings of *leyak*s are dangerously high and threaten a village.[77] In other words, when there is an "ex-
cess" of unmitigated, female-associated disturbances, male dominance,
structure, and "normalcy" reassert themselves through the enactment of
the *Calonarang.* Since the ultimate powers of reproduction and destruction
are controlled by women, these feminine powers must therefore be controlled by men in order to perpetuate the patrilineal social order. The
Balinese bracket procreativity within the fear-inspiring Calonarang performance in order to re-express its symbolic manifestations within the

male, social domain. The fear of feminine power is thus appropriated, sub-sumed, and contained. From this perspective, within ritually efficacious, metaphysically directed genres of performance, the merging of male and female characteristics not only restores their polarity, as Belo and O'Neill assert, but also re-establishes male dominance and the male-centered, pa-triarchal social structure.

If these ritual forms serve such a conservative function, though, the more secular forms afford space for grappling with—and sometimes even en-couraging—social change. There is a pattern evident in the constellation of the *Sanghyang Dedara-Dedari,* a village-based exorcistic dance, *Legong,* a court-sponsored dance form, and, finally, *Joged,* a thoroughly secular, popular form. In moving from the *Sanghyang Dedara-Dedari* to the *Le-gong,* there is increased attention to aesthetic factors—to the dancer and to the dance. As the dance form becomes less efficacious, it is regarded more in terms of entertainment, for the human audience as well as for the gods and ancestors, and the play with age and gender loses much of its ritual significance and becomes part of this aesthetic field of accomplish-ment. In *Joged* and its transvestite companion form, *Gandrung,* the play with gender is aggressively brought back to the surface as content—what the piece is "about"—and the dancer is accordingly appreciated as a vir-tuoso in the portrayal of gendered sexuality. The same pattern can be no-ticed among, say, *Calonarang, Gambuh,* and *Arja.*

In general, as secular theatrical forms become more popular in their orientation, the overt play reclaims traditional categories of gender latent in ritual drama, but this traditional use serves for very different effect since the narratives and accompanying jokes encompass social situations that contain sexual situations. Thus, the gender bending found in the *Parwa Ramayana* performance at Mas helps expose the sexual dynamics at work in the scene while rendering them at a joking remove. In the continuum of dance forms from ritually efficacious, religiously powerful, and village-centered domains, to court-sponsored, public, and quasi-secular forms, to popularly based dramas and dances, there is a noticeable increase, first, in virtuoso performing that blurs gender distinctions and, then, in the fore-grounding of overt sexual content, accompanied by a fluid use of gender-bending play. In performances such as the one observed in Mas, there is an increased emphasis on a social—as opposed to metaphysical—domain of experience. In such performances, the Balinese may subvert and playfully reconstruct traditional notions and behavioral patterns concerning sex-uality and gender within the confines of aesthetic play.

The historical evidence seems to suggest that most of the secular theatre and dance forms were originally performed by all-male companies and that only later were females incorporated. This seems to be true for *Arja,*

Kebyar, Baris, Gambuh, and, more problematically, for *Legong* with its prototype of *Nandir.* All of these transformations seem to have been effected this century. During this time, the Balinese have been barraged with new and conflicting images of appropriate sexual roles and behavior. Dutch colonialism, tourism, nationalism, family planning, and, perhaps most influentially, film and television (available since 1975) have all potentially disrupted traditional gender categories (on a recent trip to Bali, *Pretty Woman* was the most popular film in the capital of Denpasar). During this time, women have also entered the public domain as teachers, health facilitators, and even laborers.[78] It is surely no coincidence that women are also now performing artistic roles previously denied to them, appearing as shadow puppeteers (*dalangs*), musicians, and occasionally even wearing *topeng* masks. At the same time, as Martha Logsdon points out in her study of gender depictions in Indonesian elementary school textbooks:

The ideal family that is presented in these texts is headed by a father who gets the most respect. Mother stays at home in the kitchen with her daughters. . . . In presenting Indonesian society as more "sexist" than it really is, we find parallels with gender role descriptions in Western elementary textbooks.[79]

Perhaps, by shifting and altering traditional categorizations of gender in performance, the Balinese are playfully destabilizing traditional social constructions of gender, playing one construction off another, sparking humor and recognition, affirming some configurations while ridiculing others, and helping to forge new relationships in the process. It will be interesting to note whether, in the future, there is a breakdown or significant re-definition of gender divisions in Balinese social domains as a result. There are recent indications, such as the transfer of the *Limbur* as well as *Condong* roles to female actresses in *Arja,* the growing tendency to have *Legong* danced by more mature female performers, and the passing out of fashion of *Gandrung* and the female *Baris,* that a more literal parceling out of gendered roles might be asserting itself. Whatever the outcome, though, as the Balinese redesign their culture under the pressures of modernization, the shaping and articulation of gender within the subjunctive procedures of performance will no doubt continue to play a formative role in the process.

We have basically differentiated the multiplicity of forms into two main categories: those that are magically oriented, religiously powerful, and regarded as ritually efficacious, and those that are intended more as entertainment, are focused more in the social world, and that (often) are regarded as having greater aesthetic value. In the first case, the occurrences of gender anomalies are characterized by a merging or fusing of gender-specific characteristics to reassert paradoxically the importance of polarities. These performance forms—intended to dispel malevolence and disease—function to contain the threats to life that are primarily associated with female powers and to subsume them symbolically within a male-centered structure. The most secular forms, on the other hand, either re-deploy gender switching as an aesthetic accomplishment or—in the most popularly based forms—use such play with gender to make satirical comments on activities in the social sphere. Such forms mischievously juggle perceptions of appropriate behavior and, perhaps in the process, serve to encourage a re-evaluation of traditional conceptions of gender. Play with gender in Balinese theatre and ritual has provided a powerful set of tools with which the Balinese have many times taken apart their world and put it back together again—for survival and for fun.

Notes

1. Beryl deZoete and Walter Spies, *Dance and Drama in Bali* (1938; reprint, Singapore: Oxford University Press, 1986), p. 120. The authors gratefully acknowledge debts to I Made Bandem, Rucina Ballinger, Hildred Geertz, and Garrett Kam, who read this essay in an earlier draft and made many helpful comments. Fredrik deBoer, I Wayan Suweca, I Nyoman Wente, I Nyoman Catra, I Nyoman Sedana, I Wayan Dibia, I Made Wiratini, and Ni Masih also provided helpful assistance. Mistakes, of course, remain our own. One seeming mistake concerns the use of the term *Parwa* for the *Ramayana* performance cited; by definition, this term is usually reserved for performances of *Mahabharata* stories, whereas the *Ramayana* is usually performed as *Wayang Wong*. In this case, though, a *Ramayana* story was being performed by a Parwa troupe, using the conventions of that form.

2. This statement is a gloss of recent findings in the anthropology of performance. For works that have established this statement as a premise and that discuss the theoretical issues involved, see Clifford Geertz, *The Interpretation of Cultures* (New York: Basic Books Inc., 1973); Victor Turner, *The Anthropology of Performance* (New York: PAJ Publications, 1986); Richard Schechner, *Essays on Performance Theory* (1977; reprint, New York and London: Routledge, Chapman and Hall, 1988); and Bruce Kapferer, *A Celebration of Demons* (Bloomington: Indiana University Press, 1983).

3. Balinese cross-gender play is more akin to observations that Roland Barthes makes, writing (not quite persuasively) about the Japanese *onnagata*: "The Oriental transvestite does not copy Woman but signifies her," and "[T]ransvestism here is the gesture of femininity, not its plagiarism." See *The Empire of Signs* (New York: Hill and Wang, 1970), pp. 53, 89.

4. *Legong* is "secular" in the sense that it is appropriate for presentation at a temple ceremony for the entertainment of a human audience as well as for the gods and ancestors. In Balinese terminology, it is a *bebali* genre—less bound up with ritual observance than the sacred *wali* forms but more so than the *bali-balihan* genres intended exclusively for human entertainment. Often sponsored by the traditional royal courts, it has frequently been performed outside of ritual contexts—on tours and for audiences of paying tourists.

5. See Star Black and Willard A. Hanna, *Guide to Bali* (Hong Kong: APA Productions, 1985), p. 244; deZoete and Spies, *Dance and Drama in Bali*, 218–31.

6. See Andrew Duff-Cooper, "Notes about Some Balinese Ideas and Practices Connected with Sex in Western Lombok," *Anthropos* 80 (1985):411–12, 417.

7. "A Study of Customs Pertaining to Twins in Bali," in *Traditional Balinese Culture,* ed. Jane Belo (New York: Columbia University Press, 1970), p. 18.

8. See I Made Bandem and Fredrik deBoer, *Kaja to Kelod: Balinese Dance in Transition* (Kuala Lumpur: Oxford University Press, 1981), pp. 76–80; and Miguel Covarrubias, *The Island of Bali* (1937; reprint, Kuala Lumpur: Oxford University Press, 1973), p. 222.

9. See deZoete and Spies, *Dance and Drama in Bali,* 228. For a more detailed assessment of the historical and stylistic relationship of *Legong* to *Sanghyang De-dari,* see I Made Bandem, "The Evolution of Legong: From Secular to Sacred Dance of Bali," *Dance Research Annual* 14 (1983).

10. See Roma Sisly O'Neill, "Spirit Possession and Healing Rites in a Balinese Village" (unpublished Masters thesis, University of Melbourne, 1978), p. 1.

11. Bandem and deBoer, *Kaja to Kelod,* 76.

12. Bandem, "The Evolution of Legong," 1.

13. Ibid., 5.

14. See Bandem and deBoer, *Kaja to Kelod,* 97–107, for a discussion of *Joged* and its variants.

15. Ibid., 100.

16. Covarrubias, *The Island of Bali,* 229.

17. Cited in Bandem and deBoer, *Kaja to Kelod,* 98 and 116n. The italics are Dr. Jacobs's.

18. See Duff-Cooper, "Balinese Ideas and Practices," 415–16.

19. Katharane Edsom Mershon, *Seven Plus Seven: Mysterious Life-Rituals in Bali* (New York: Vantage Press, 1971), pp. 136–37.

20. See Bandem and deBoer, *Kaja to Kelod,* 19–22; a more detailed description of *Baris Gede* and its variants is in deZoete and Spies, *Dance and Drama in Bali,* 56–66. There is a growing tendency to have this dance performed by young boys, perhaps as a way of preserving the tradition; elements of the flashier solo dance tradition described below are being included in the choreography.

21. See Black and Hanna, *Guide to Bali,* 246; Bandem and deBoer, *Kaja to Kelod,* 93–94. In *Baris Melampahan,* now rare, martial stories are enacted by troupes of *Baris* dancers; see Spies and deZoete, *Dance and Drama in Bali,* 165–73.

22. Ana Daniel, *Bali: Behind the Mask* (New York: Alfred A. Knopf, 1981), p. xviii.

23. Even earlier than the 1950s, deZoete and Spies noted the existence of two female *Baris* dancers, one in Selat and the other one in northern Bali, the latter of which also assumed a role in the *Legong.* They attribute this, rather summarily, to the tendency in the north to create hybrid forms just because they are "in vogue." See *Dance and Drama in Bali,* 172–73.

24. I Wayan Dibia, "The Symbols of Gender in Balinese Dance," *UCLA Journal of Dance Ethnography,* 13 (1990), pp. 10–12.

25. Ibid., 12–13.

26. See Bandem and deBoer, *Kaja to Kelod,* 80–84.

27. See W. H. Rassers, *Panji the Culture Hero* (The Hague: Nijhoff, 1959), pp. 1–62; S. O. Robson, "The *Kawi* Classics in Bali," *Bijdragen tot de Taal-, Land-en Volkenkunde* 128 (1972):307–29.

28. Cf. Claire Holt, *Art in Indonesia* (Ithaca: Cornell University Press, 1967),

p. 274. For summaries of *Gambuh* stories, see deZoete and Spies, *Dance and Drama in Bali*, 286–89 and 134–43. The dramatic action of *Gambuh* is analyzed in greatest detail by Bandem and deBoer, *Kaja to Kelod*, 28–48.

29. According to Ana Daniel, this created some controversy. Dawan, Kakul's daughter, went on to portray Panji, but "even though there was no official restriction on the casting of this heroic character, who possesses the power to transform his sex, his species, or even his corporeal form at will—and even though Dawan was highly respected in this role, criticisms of Kakul's daring innovations continued." See *Bali: Behind the Mask*, 98.

30. Kathy Foley, "My Bodies: The Performer in West Java," *Drama Review* 34, no. 2 (1990):64.

31. See John Emigh, "The Domains of *Topeng*," in *Art and Politics in Southeast Asia: Six Perspectives*, ed. Robert van Neil (Honolulu: University of Hawaii Center for Southeast Asian Studies, Southeast Asia Paper 32, 1989), pp. 65–96. See also, Fred B. Eiseman, Jr. (I Wayan Darsana), *Bali: Sekala and Niskala*, vol. 2 (Scottsdale, AZ: privately printed, 1986), pp. 270–71.

32. See L. E. A. Howe, "Gods, People, Spirits, and Witches," *Bijdragen tot de Taal-, Land- en Volkenkunde* 140, no. 2 (1984):204. Howe suggests that there is a continuum of typologies ranging from the gods (*dewa*), at the one end, who exhibit the most meritorious characteristics, through humans (*jalma*), malevolent spirits (*buta-kala*), witches (*leyak*), and finally to animals (*buron*) that exhibit characteristics antithetical to the Balinese ideal.

33. See Eiseman, *Bali: Sekala and Niskala*, 2:387–93.

34. Cf. Richard Wallis, "Balinese Theatre: Coping with Old and New," in *What Is Modern Indonesian Culture?* ed. Gloria Davis (Athens, Ohio: Ohio University Center for International Studies Southeast Asian Series, no. 52, 1976), pp. 37–45; Benedict R. O'G. Anderson examines the application of a similar normative typology in the *Wayang Kulit* shadow theatre of central Java, stressing a paradoxical tolerance towards different ways of being engaged in life. See *Mythology and Tolerance of the Javanese* (Ithaca: Cornell University Southeast Asia Program, Data Paper 27, no. 1, 1965).

35. Abby Ruddick, "Charmed Lives: Illness, Healing, Power and Gender in a Balinese Village" (unpublished Ph.D. diss., Brown University, 1986), p. 123.

36. Covarrubias, *The Island of Bali*, 249.

37. Contrasting opinions about this debate are given in Covarrubias, *The Island of Bali*, 249; deZoete and Spies, *Dance and Drama in Bali*, 196; and Bandem and deBoer, *Kaja to Kelod*, 90–91.

38. deZoete and Spies, *Dance and Drama in Bali*, 197. See Bandem and deBoer, *Kaja to Kelod*, 90–92, for an account of the initial 1825 production in Karangasem.

39. I Nyoman Kakul, "Jelantik Goes to Blambangan: A *Topeng Pajegan* Performance," *The Drama Review* 23, no. 2 (1979):47.

40. Ruddick, "Charmed Lives," 109.

41. Duff-Cooper, "Balinese Ideas and Practices," 417. More generally, see Wendy Doniger O'Flaherty, *Women, Androgynes, and Other Mythical Beasts* (Chicago: University of Chicago Press, 1980).

42. Jane Belo, *Bali: Rangda and Barong* (Seattle: University of Washington Press, 1949), pp. 57–58.

43. This may occur in real life, as well. The *bancih,* even as Belo was writing, was evidently not so revered in the real world as in the divine one. Frequently subjected to the taunts of the villagers, the *bancih,* Covarrubias noted, was commonly

regarded as "characteristic of Gods, but ridiculous amongst humans." See *The Island of Bali*, 145. Ruddick suggests that when the *bancih*, like the *Limbur*, elicits laughter, it is not so much a reclaiming and reconciliation of the "feminine" that is perceived but, rather, an exaggeration, in stylized form, of "female" behavior. Thus, the *bancih* is sometimes viewed as a negative example, exhibiting an awkward blending of male and female characteristics to which human beings should not aspire. See Ruddick, "Charmed Lives," 110; cf. James Peacock, "Symbolic Reversal and Social History: Transvestites and Clowns of Java," in *The Reversible World*, ed. Barbara Babcock (Ithaca: Cornell University Press, 1978), p. 222.

44. Margaret Mead, *Male and Female* (New York: William Morrow and Co., 1949), p. 232.

45. A *barong* is more generically any theatrical figure created by stepping into a large, body-disguising costume with attached mask. Many of these *barong*s represent animals (boars, tigers, etc.) and are manipulated by two men. The lion/dragon *Barong Keket*, or *Barong Ket*, is the most important and best known of these figures and is commonly called *Barong* in both Balinese and Western literature. Several commentators have cited similarities with the dancing lions found in the Far East, and examples may also be found of such animals (*prabhas*) used on festive occasions in eastern India. See Belo, *Bali: Rangda and Barong*, 32.

46. Stephen Snow, "Rangda: Archetype in Action in Balinese Dance-Drama," in *Themes in Drama*, vol. 5, *Drama and Religion*, ed. James Redmond (Cambridge: Cambridge University Press, 1983), pp. 273–74.

47. O'Neill, "Spirit Possession," 72.

48. Bandem and deBoer, *Kaja to Kelod*, 135.

49. Ibid., 137.

50. See Ibid., 125–26.

51. See John Emigh, "Dealing with the Demonic: Strategies for Containment in Hindu Iconography and Performance," *Asian Theatre Journal* 1, no. 1 (1984):21–39.

52. In an interesting variation, this action is sometimes repeated with the *Rangda* mask taken off—presumably showing the ability of the male performer to sustain the *sakti* he has appropriated. This variant—as well as variants following the bloody repression of 1965 when men turned their blades against each other—is shown in the Hartley film, *Mask of Rangda*.

53. Belo, *Bali: Rangda and Barong*, 40. Gregory Bateson and Claire Holt note that in the process of self-stabbing, the men generally bend backwards with the *kris* against their body, whereas the women tend to bend forwards from the waist, with the *kris* held below. See "Form and Function of the Dance in Bali," in *Traditional Balinese Culture* (New York: Columbia University Press, 1970), p. 326. Also see the Bateson and Mead film, *Trance and Dance in Bali*.

54. Belo, *Bali: Rangda and Barong*, 18.

55. An extensive study of such encounters in Jimbaran—though without emphasis on gender—appears in Eiseman, *Bali: Sekala and Niskala*, 2:344–86. The authors' debt to this study is gratefully acknowleged. Also see deZoete and Spies, *Dance and Drama in Bali*, 86–105.

56. Mead, *Male and Female*, 232.

57. J. Stephen Lansing, *Evil in the Morning of the World* (Ann Arbor: University of Michigan Center for South and Southeast Asian Studies, 1974), p. 82.

58. See Eiseman, *Bali: Sekala and Niskala*, 345–46.

59. Mary LeCron Foster, "Synthesis and Antithesis in Balinese Ritual," in *The*

Imagination of Reality: Essays in Southeast Asian Coherence Systems, ed. A. L. Becker (Norwood, NJ: Ablex Publishing Corp., 1979), p. 188.

60. See Ruddick, "Charmed Lives," 33.

61. See Bandem and deBoer, *Kaja to Kelod,* 122–23, 141–42; also, Emigh, "Dealing with the Demonic," 21–39.

62. Ruddick, "Charmed Lives," 118.

63. Duff-Cooper, "Balinese Ideas and Practices," 416.

64. See Gregory Bateson and Margaret Mead, *Balinese Character: A Photographic Analysis* (New York: New York Academy of Sciences, Special Publication 2, 1942), p. 167; deZoete and Spies, *Dance and Drama in Bali,* 88–90, 120.

65. Cited in Leora Nadine Rosen, "A Theoretical Approach to the Study of Ritual Pollution Beliefs," *African Studies* 32, no. 4 (1973):237.

66. "Is Female to Male as Nature Is to Culture?" in *Women, Culture, and Society,* ed. Louise Lamphere and Michelle Rosaldo (Stanford, CA: Stanford University Press, 1974), pp. 72–73.

67. Ibid., 73–74.

68. Covarrubias, *The Island of Bali,* 126, 156.

69. Christiaan Hooykaas, "An Exorcistic Litany from Bali," *Bijdragen tot de Taal-, Land- en Volkenkunde* 125, no. 3 (1969):363.

70. Mead, *Male and Female,* 166–67.

71. Foster, "Synthesis and Antithesis in Balinese Ritual," 181.

72. Ruddick, "Charmed Lives," 108.

73. Ibid., 106–7; see also J. Stephen Lansing, "In the World of the Sea Urchin," in *The Imagination of Reality,* ed. A. L. Becker and Aram Yengoyen (Norwood, NJ: Ablex Publishing Corp., 1979), p. 80.

74. O'Neill, "Spirit Possession," 117.

75. Ibid., 125.

76. The dangers are regarded as quite real. The mask has been known to "turn on" the unprepared wearer, leaving him severely ill. See Geertz, *Interpretation of Cultures,* 115.

77. See Bandem and deBoer, *Kaja to Kelod,* 139.

78. See Ruddick, "Charmed Lives," 103.

79. "Gender Roles in Elementary School Texts in Indonesia," in *Women in Asia and the Pacific,* ed. Madelaine Goodman (Honolulu: University of Hawaii Press, 1985), p. 257.

JUDITH LYNNE HANNA

Tradition, Challenge, and the Backlash: Gender Education through Dance

❦ Feminist perspectives generally posit that patterns of dominance/submission and inclusion/exclusion based on gender favor male dominance to the detriment of women. Patriarchal societies permit men to enjoy higher status and more benefits than women. Even matriarchal societies often give special privilege to a woman's male kin. Throughout time, most history, philosophy, religion, and art have been crafted/managed by men in support of their status.

Jaggar[1] has classified the multifarious feminist views into four categories, each of which has different presuppositions and implications. Of these categories, the liberal feminist perspective is most germane to a discussion of images of gender in dance. In simplistic terms, the liberal feminist perspective views nonfeminist women as victims of their socialization or sex-role conditioning. The implication is that educational reform is necessary to eliminate discrimination against women so that they can achieve liberty and equality.

The issue of socialization raises questions about the inevitability of sex roles in society—What is nature, and what is nurture, or culturally patterned? How do cultures create, maintain, and challenge divisions? What might be the intent and consequence of dance performance in this process? What are the implications of male dominance in dance and the contemporary danced images that convey what makes up a man and a woman?

This essay will focus on the social and cultural nonverbal communication on gender in Western theatrical dance of the twentieth century, a period during which hierarchies of dominance have been challenged significantly.[2] I summarize aspects of the visual language of the "high" culture of ballet and its succeeding genres (what is called modern and postmodern dance) based on perceptions of critics and dancers, cultural history, and long-term, researcher-participant observation as a dance student and audience member.

Dance is a language-like social construction of reality and a medium of socialization. Researchers have demonstrated in diverse parts of the world that dance nonverbally communicates identity, social stratification, and values.[3] For example, among the Ubakala Igbo of Nigeria, dance group participants make statements about their gender identity, role, place in society, and values.[4]

Ubakala Igbo youth of both sexes use relatively similar dance movements in terms of their use of time, space, energy, and body parts. Elderly men and women also have similar dance patterns. However, when the two sexes are relatively similar in age but very different in biological and social roles, the dance movement patterns diverge most markedly. There is a strong contrast between the women as life-creating and nurturing and the men as life-taking and conquering warriors, actually or symbolically, in the domains of movement and social structure. Whereas men dance in a circle extrusively, stepping in and out, leaping up and down, and moving on the ball of the foot, the women use the circle intrusively, keeping a more homogeneous spatial level and moving predominantly on the whole foot. Rapid speed and varied spatial use represent destruction just as slow speed and limited spatial use represent construction. The warrior's killing thrust is swift; he ventures abroad. The woman's gestation and nursing period of about two and three-quarter years somewhat restricts her mobility.

The gender language[5] of dance images calls attention to a compelling issue of human life in our time: the continuing social and cultural reconstruction of gender roles and meanings. In the United States, dance is no longer the province solely of elite, ticket-paying theatre-goers and critic-reading audiences. Now a melange of dance genre can reach nearly an entire nation through television and can convey images and models of masculinity and femininity. Many of the kinds of dance I refer to have appeared on such series as "Dance in America" and "Live from Off Center."

Kinetic Language

Dance requires the same underlying brain faculty for conceptualization, creativity, and memory as verbal language. In a dance performance, as for spoken and written languages, we may not see the underlying universals and cultural structures and processes but merely evidence of them. Structures are a kind of generative grammar, that is, a set of rules specifying the manner in which movements can be meaningfully combined. Referring again to the Ubakala Igbo, the men's structural dance patterns of tension, rapid tempo, and linear and angular spatial patterns generate bourrée, lunge, and slash movements. By contrast, nontense effort, slow tempo, and curvilinear space generate the wave walk, contract-release, and hip shift movements of the women's dances.

Semantics refers to the meaning of movement, whether the style itself or some reference beyond the movement. As in language (with its words, sentences, and paragraphs), dance has movement vocabulary (gestures and locomotion) and phrases that may comprise realistic or abstract symbols. Moreover, dance has at least six devices and eight spheres for encoding and decoding meaning, for example, metaphor and metonym.[6]

The devices for conveying meaning are as follows: (1) An example of a *metaphor* would include a fairy tale romance between animals to denote the situation between human lovers. (2) A kiss standing for a love affair or a romantic duet representing a more encompassing relationship, such as a marriage, are *metonyms*. (3) A *concretization* is movement that produces the outward aspect of something, as in a courtship dance that shows potential lovers' advance and retreat tactics. (4) The *icon* is illustrated by a Haitian possessed by Ghede, god of love and death, who manifests his presence through dancing; Haitians treat him with genuine awe and gender-appropriate behavior as if he were the god rather than a human dancer representing Ghede. (5) A *stylization* encompasses arbitrary and conventional gestures or movements, such as the *danseur* pointing to his heart as a sign of love for his lady. (6) An *actualization* occurs, especially in theatrical settings where there is no rigid boundary between performer and spectator, when dancers express their own sexual preferences through dance (heterosexual or homosexual seduction of a spectator), and the audience member accepts or rejects the dancer.

These devices for conveying meaning in dance operate within one or more of these spheres: (1) the dance *event,* as when people perform and attend the ballet to be seen socially or to signal sexual or marital availability and find partners, dancing itself being incidental; (2) the total human *body in action,* as in woman or man self-presentation or audience watching; (3) the whole *pattern of* the *performance,* which may emphasize form, style, feeling, or drama; (4) the sequence of *unfolding movement,* including who does what to whom, and how, in dramatic episodes; (5) specific *movements* and how they are performed, as when a male dancer parodies a woman *en pointe;* (6) the *intermesh* of movements *with other* communication *modes* such as speech or costume; (7) dance as a *vehicle for another medium,* like dance serving as a backdrop for a performer's poetry recitation; and (8) *presence,* the emotionality of projected sensuality, raw animality, charisma, or "magic of dance."

Note that dance is *not* a universal language but many languages and dialects. Peter Martins, co-director of the New York City Ballet, believes that classical ballet and modern dance are the same language with different dialects.[7] By contrast, classical Indian dance is a different language.

India's Bharata Natyam dance is probably the most codified and prose-like of dance languages; each gesture or movement has meaning and, when combined, can tell stories. Western dance usually assembles its linguistic-like elements in a manner that more often resembles poetry, with its suggestive imagery, rhythm, ambiguity, multiple meanings, and latitude in form. Modern dancer Martha Graham believed the kinetic discourse of dance is "like poetic lyricism sometimes, like the rawness of dramatic poetry; it's like the terror—or it can be like a terrible revelation of meaning."[8]

Another groundbreaking innovator, Merce Cunningham, who rebelled against Graham's psychological drama and heralded the postmodern dance movement, made dances that paralleled modernist innovators in literature such as Gertrude Stein, James Joyce, and T. S. Eliot. Cunningham remarked, "It goes from paragraphs, to sentences, down to words—and now to words themselves separated, so you don't have even a whole word, you just have part of a word. . . . I have many references, many images, . . . because I could just as well substitute one image for another, in the Joycean sense of there being not *a* symbol but multiple symbols."[9]

Socialization

Expressions of sex and gender evolve physically and socioculturally during one's lifetime as a way of knowing about oneself and others; these expressions serve in all societies as a basis of dominance/submission and inclusion/exclusion. Ideas are encoded in public symbols, literary texts, art, drama, religious practice, and *dance,* a kind of cultural text. These forms, through which people represent themselves to themselves and to each other, are accessible to observation and inquiry.

Both the reality and illusion of performance are socially constructed through individuals producing, choreographing, dancing the dance, watching it, and writing about the performance.[10] Active physical beings create images that are read and felt by performers and audience members whose social beings then play a role in shaping the consciousness and reflexivity of these images.

Everyday precedents for meaning in nonverbal communication are so well established in a culture that they are part of the choreographers'/dancers'/spectators' inheritance. Seeking signs and symbols from their culture, choreographers take the everyday patterns and transform them for their aesthetic purposes. Signifiers of gender differences appear in contrasting posture, precedence, elevation, movement quality, and touch. For example, people generally understand the meaning of a shoulder shrug, a shaking head, and tense posture. Males take precedence and are more expansive and forceful than females. The occurrence of sex-associated movement contributes to the information dancers and spectators draw upon when making and viewing performances.

Nearly everywhere, everyday movement conveys historically male-dominated cultures in the same way that spoken and written languages do with their terms of address and pronouns of power. From the quotidian and special occasion, dance takes needs, habits, and other actions and transforms the material into spotlighted kinetic illusions and realities, as illustrated in the following sections of this article.

According to Bandura's social learning theory,[11] an individual tends to reproduce attitudes, acts, and emotions exhibited by an observed live or symbolic (for example, film or television) model. The behavior may be cognitively registered and used or may remain in subconscious memory until a relevant situation activates it. Because dance is part of the cultural communication system, modeling of gender-related dominance patterns may occur through observing in dance who does what, when, where, and how, alone or with whom.

Similar to nonhuman ritualized displays and human ritual, theatrical dance frames messages and thereby bestows power on them. Dance can be understood as a medium through which choreographers/directors/producers manipulate, interpret, legitimate, and reproduce the patterns of gender cooperation and conflict that order their social world. Through it, one can witness courtship, climax, male chauvinism, feminist theory, interpersonal exchanges, group interaction, casual relations, and stable associations. Dance images might reinforce ongoing models, evoke new responses, weaken or strengthen inhibitions over fully elaborated patterns in a person's repertoire, and facilitate performance of previously learned behavior that was encumbered by restraints.

Because learning to be properly gendered members of society is a lifelong process, viewing dance images is potentially telling. Being distanced from the everyday, the dance performance permits safe exploration of dangerous challenges to the status quo without invoking the penalties of everyday life. When moving images created by dancers violate expected male and female roles and their conventional expressions, the novel signs onstage charge the atmosphere and stimulate performers and observers to confront the possibility of altered lifestyles.[12] As a medium of gender education, dance can both reflect and influence society, transmit or transform a cultural heritage.

Moves

The history of ballet begins with Louis XIV (1643–1715). This French tradition bespeaks a patriarchal discourse. At first, men not only managed dance productions, but they even performed women's roles. Later, women danced their own roles; they gained ascendancy on stage by the eighteenth century. The French and Industrial revolutions had dealt serious blows to the prestige of dance among males. Among the sociopolitical elite, physical activities became associated with moral laxity and impediments to economic productivity. During ballet's Romantic era, the ascendancy of the female by 1840 contributed to the revulsion against male dancers and the discovery of the charm of *danseuse en travesti*. Women danced female and male roles. Their female roles were generally the untouchable, elusive sylph or the earthy, sexual peasant, but not chattels for male enjoyment. There were also erotic, macabre *wilis,* vengeful ghosts of betrayed unmarried women; they danced faithless men to death as in the nineteenth-century ballet *Giselle,* still popular today. Men, however, continued backstage as managers, choreographers, and ballet masters. Before long, they reasserted themselves as popular performers.[13]

Traditional dance defamiliarizes the ordinary social and sexual experiences of women as people and creates a social object, a representation of a desired feminine type. By becoming objects, women subject themselves to men. Classical ballet relies on conventionalized understandings of the roles of men and women that are deeply embedded in courtly roots of romantic attachments. The *pas de deux* partnering roles are often analogues of patronage by the stronger of the weaker sex, portrayed onstage as virginal, disembodied sylphide or wanton and referred to offstage by men as vulnerable child-woman, kitten, or siren. The woman "looks up" to the man, rises *en pointe* to meet him. Rising onto the tip of the toes in some positions renders the dancer insubstantial. Unable to stand alone, the male supports or assists her. When a man carries a woman draped around his shoulders like a scarf, the chauvinistic overtones are unmistakable.

Enchanting fantasies of beautiful ladies, gallant men, and Gothic and exotic situations gloss the lack of women's independence and point to her eventual submission to a man. When a woman was unattainable onstage, she was often portrayed as an ethereal creature.

Merely being onstage and the target of public gaze often reflected a woman's social reality offstage. Thought to be part of the demimonde until the third decade of the twentieth century, a female dance career was an avenue of social mobility for attractive, talented, lower-class females who preferred the glamour of dance to the factory sweatshop, agricultural labor, domestic work, or whoredom in a less exclusive setting. With economic success limited for female dancers, they were usually fortunate if they became mistresses of wealthy men.[14] There were also families in performance.

Contemporary ballet choreographers and directors, almost always male, continue to dictate to women. Today, they "mold ballet's young women to the ideal of feminine that equates beauty and grace with excessive thinness," an aesthetic that is "both punitive and misogynist."[15] Relentless pursuit of the unnatural "ideal" female body arrests puberty, imbalances hormones, contributes to hypothermia and low blood pressure, and often leads to psychosomatic disorders of starvation, vomiting, and use of laxatives. Anorexia and injury are interconnected.[16]

New Moves

Modern Dance.   At the end of the nineteenth century, a rebellion, taking the form of what was called "modern dance," began against ballet and all that it represented. Given birth and nurtured primarily by women, modern dance was in part a reaction to male domination in both dance and society at large. Female modern dancers' aggressiveness paralleled women's late nineteenth- and twentieth-century questioning of patriarchy, which resulted in change in the conventions surrounding choice of a spouse, a rise in higher education for women, and middle-class women's entry into the labor market during and after World War II. Modern dancers extended women's fight to gain control over their own bodies. Twyla Tharp even served as artistic associate for the American Ballet Theatre from 1988–1989. She continues to choreograph for the company.

Women looked to themselves for inspiration as they chose to be agent rather than object and formed female-dominated dance companies. They developed innovative movement vocabularies, themes, costumes, production patterns, and schools. Viewing femininity in ballet as patriarchy's way of marking a portion of the population for secondary status and in the service of men, women danced without partners, used weight and strength, created images of women as neither virginal nor siren but whole and complex individuals, and even caused women's dancing in public theatres to become respectable. Asserting themselves against traditional female destiny, groundbreaking modern dancers such as Loïe Fuller and Isadora Duncan through onstage images helped de-corset the wasp-waisted women and open up changes in female education, health, and professional opportunity. Braless, corsetless, and barefoot, the modern dancer's free style of dress symbolized physical freedom and a renewed, diversified self-image.

Women heralded new moves as part of the women's liberation effort. Men, too, participated in portraying women in ways that diverged from the traditional. They choreographed into the modern dance idiom images of women in a manner similar to the feminist portrayals.

Modern dance has influenced ballet and its male participants. The genres now often blend. Modern and postmodern choreographers, such as David

Gordon and Laura Dean, are even invited to choreograph for classical ballet companies.

New Female Roles.   Not until ballerina Anna Pavlova (ca. 1881–1931) "does the idea of combining the two temperaments of virgin and bacchante in one ballerina achieve force." Pavlova was both in *La Bayadère*.[17]

The turbulence of the 1960s, with its black power and women's and gay liberation movements, signaled a greater acceptance of the body, emotion, and alternative lifestyles. This acceptance created a climate for a spectrum of images onstage that offer informal teaching and learning about gender. Since the 1960s, in contrast with the earlier ethereal (humanlike nonhuman), wanton, and virginal traditional images and the combination of two temperaments in one woman, choreographer Kenneth Macmillan has provided roles of stature for women in a number of his ballets. Examples include *The Burrow* (based on the Anne Frank story), *The Invitation* (from Lorca's play *The House of Bernarda Alba*), and *Romeo and Juliet*.

A woman's stature can appear through her symbolic dance style. Although George Balanchine, ballet's foremost twentieth-century choreographer, who created more than 150 dances during his fifty years in the United States, comes from the old world of Russian ballet, his neoclassic ballet in the new world sometimes reflects a contrasting ambience. "His women do not always live for love, and their destinies are seldom defined by the men they lean on. Sexual complicity in conflict with individual freedom is a central theme of the Balanchine *pas de deux,* and more often than not it is dramatized from the woman's point of view." The "Diamonds" section of *Jewels* performed by Suzanne Farrell is illustrative: "Off-center balances maintained with light support or no support at all . . . divergently shaped steps unthinkably combined in the same phrase, . . . invisible transitions between steps and delicate shifts of weight . . . based on risk."[18] Merrill Ashley's portrayal of the modern liberated woman was not an illusion but a fact that she demonstrated "when Robert Weiss became disabled in the middle of 'Ballo della Regina' and she finished the performance without him."[19]

Martha Graham, having created modern dances over nearly six decades, bequeathed to future generations a history refocused in dance from a woman's point of view. Transgressing conventional norms, she gave women new roles as guiltless protagonists. Almost every one of her dances contains a dagger or a bed, because "'those objects are so close to life. We sleep in a bed from the time we are born,' she explains, gliding serenely over the sexual issue that her dances grapple with so forcefully, 'and while we don't, perhaps, actually *use* one, there are many times when we do wield a dagger in speech, or surreptitiously in our hearts.'"[20]

Graham's dances speak of the woman's struggle for dominance without guilt. The women in her treatment of the legends of Oedipus, Jocasta, and Orestes become human protagonists, whereas previously they had been "the pawns of gods and men."[21] For Graham, a traditional feminine stance could be adopted only as a weapon or a sign of weakness. She seldom found a way for men and women to be equals.[22]

Female choreographers also recount the anguish women face as females, being victims of love, bodily violated by men in the battle of the sexes. In Graham's work women are identified with such images. Her 1984 *Rite of Spring* shows the female as sacrificial victim of rape and death. Coming from Germany and from a younger generation of women who grapple with oppressive male dominance, Pina Bausch's *Rite of Spring* offers "no promise of rebirth. The only one who dared to love becomes the victim, and falls seemingly dead."[23]

Equality. Kinetic visualizations of men and women in relationships without dominance and subservience appear now, in the era of equal rights for women. The older hierarchical opposition between the two sexes is dissolving. For example, choreographer Eliot Feld "uses technique to say something about how the people in the ballet are feeling and how they are related to each other. . . . Boy and girl are more nearly equal here, . . . men and women partner each other to share something, . . . the partners adapt to each other rather than dominate each other."[24] In many of his pieces, modern dance choreographer Paul Taylor sends "his dancers hurtling through space and into and out of each other's arms with no regard for the conventions of partnering or sexually determined dynamic modulation."[25]

Ulysses Dove's *Episodes,* premiered in 1990, depicts both sexes explosively battling with relentless speed, desire, rejection, and aggression in an era of alienation. The dancers hurtle, leap, lunge, and spin. Women may collapse at a lover's touch only to spring onto his shoulder. Although men and women are equally combative, men are more violent against the women.

Lesbian Relations. Women have choreographed dances about female bonding and lesbianism. *Les Biches* (meaning the little does; colloquially, young women or little coquettes), created in 1924 for Diaghilev's Ballets Russes, is Bronislava Nijinska's daring ballet that presents a clear though delicate lesbian relationship in a duet performed by two women. The ambiguous boy-girl figure of the "garçonne" in the ballet was created by the French novelist Victor Margueritte. His novels were forbidden fare for adolescent girls in the 1920s. The ballet work reflects the easy amorality of the twenties and augurs the new morality heralded by the sixties.

The Dance Exchange in Washington, D.C., 29 March 1985, featured Johanna Boyce's choreography, *Ties that Bind,* based on life history interviews with lesbian performers. These two women performed an autobiographical, contact improvisation (a form of modern/postmodern dance) duet about their relationship, its intimacy, and outsiders' curiosity about them.

Male choreographers have also made affectionately sororal pieces. In *Antique Epigraphs,* New York City Ballet choreographer Jerome Robbins, inspired by the Sapphic *Songs of Bilitis,* had eight women strike figural poses, lift each other, and grasp each other's waists or buttocks.

Gender Role Reversal and Androgyny. These yet other forms of new concepts and moves in dance imaging challenge the status quo as they reinscribe notions of bipolar opposites—of masculinity over and against femininity. It is more common for women to be like men than the reverse in both gender role reversal and androgyny (the expression of male and female possibilities within us all).

During the 1960s, a reaction, called postmodern dance, occurred against modern dance psychological themes and narrative stories. Movement in and of itself became a predominant concern. Moreover, choreographers at times turned gender upside down or deemed it irrelevant. By incorporating both typically feminine and masculine movement characteristics, men are freed to enjoy the emotional rewards conventionally found in women's domain, and women are freed to enter men's competitive arenas.

Intentional Divisions/Implicit Connections, conceived by Bill T. Jones and choreographed in conjunction with Julie West, is a jolting reminder of changing social patterns in the United States. Jones, a large, muscular black man who exudes strength, danced with West, a petite white woman. Jones threw West over his shoulder, not an unusual act onstage; however, moments later, in a reversal noteworthy for the dramatic contrast in the two dancers' looks, the diminutive woman flipped the man, who is at least twice her size and weight.

Gender role reversal in movement also appears in contemporary ballet. Jiri Kylian's *Symphony in D* is illustrative. In an about-face from the classical ballet in which women "fly" through the air into the arms of men who catch them, Kylian has women break the flight of an airborne man. Three women extend their arms to catch the prone body of a man as he terminates his leap. Two women lift a man. Later, a man joins a woman's dance and displaces her in the women's group of partners lined up in a row.

Originated by black males in the United States, tap dance used to be for men only. Some white men and women developed a different style of tap. Nowadays, quite a few young white women are displaying techniques learned from the black male dancers of former generations. Both gender and racial patterns are thus reversed.

In her modern dance choreography, Senta Driver often reveals androgynous attitudes. She bowdlerizes the notion of gender as being at all relevant to use of one's mind or body; either sex is capable of intellectual, aesthetic, and physical accomplishments. In her dances, not only do men lift women but women lift men, wrap them around their bodies, and carry them.

Asexual Female Images. Because women have historically been perceived as sex objects, any denial or downplaying of female sexuality conveys a strong statement about women's choice and autonomy. For example, Yvonne Rainer's *Trio A* is the "doing" of a thing rather than the "performing" of it "toward a removal of seductive involvement with an audience. The performers . . . , for instance, never confront the audience; the gaze is constantly averted as the head is in motion or deflected from the body if the body happens to be frontally oriented."[26]

Countermoves

Women's liberation through dance has its glitches. New images that "teach" alternative gender roles for women are offset by old and yet other innovative images. Women's preeminence onstage in ballet and in the creation of challenging dance forms and thematic images provoked a backlash. Men made efforts to reassert their dominance as well as to derogate women with images of calculating bitch, clinging vine, and castrator. Another countermove was the creation of several male travesty companies that spoofed the feminine in ballet as they undermined convention.

Athleticism. One of the early modern dance pioneers, Ruth St. Denis, married Ted Shawn, who studied with her and became her husband, co-choreographer, and co-founder of the Denishawn School. Later, Shawn founded his own all-male company. Self-styled "Papa" of American modern dance, Shawn proclaimed that male dancers were necessary; he could not conceive of a symphony played only by piccolos and violins. Reflecting a prevalent male chauvinism as well as a turbulent personal relationship with St. Denis, he wanted to restore male dancing to the dignity he believed it possessed in Greece. He presented the male dancer as "jock" and proselytized dance through championing athletics (his dances include fencing, dribbling a ball, and shooting baskets) and "virile" dancing.[27]

Resuming the Spotlight. Rudolf Nureyev's defection from the Soviet Union and his six-digit income brought to a head a brewing reaction against nineteenth-century ballets that were fixated on the ballerina at the expense of the male dancer. He modified these ballets at a time when males were ready to recapture their early stature onstage. Nureyev's career can be understood in part as "an attempt to gain and hold center stage without a repertory that places him there. So he has become the usurper, encroaching on the ballerina's territory with extensions of the Prince's role or taking over 'roles that were more fantastic.' "[28] The dance boom with its economic viability for male dancers, increase in dance companies and touring and television opportunities, political activism of gay men, and promotion of men in dance contributed to the move against the preeminent place of women onstage.

In his staging of *Romeo and Juliet* for the San Francisco Ballet, Michael Smuin created more significant roles for male dancers and more boy-boy scenes than is customary.[29] Houston Ballet choreographer Ben Stevenson's *L* is an all-male, percussion jazz piece in which men hold each other's arms and flip each other as they might flip women.

The male takeover of female roles has gone so far as to allow male dancer Satoru Shimakazi, in 1982, to restage and perform pioneer Isadora Duncan's two Scriabin works, her 1929 *Mother* and 1922 *Revolutionary*.[30] In 1988, Clive Thompson performed Duncan's solo to Tchaikovsky's *Marche Slave*.[31] Men also retake the spotlight through gay themes and travesty.

Gay Themes.   Ballets with homosexual themes and love duets began to emerge following the Nijinsky forerunners in the 1920s, but only with great tact and usually disguised as something else.[32] Gay male themes tend to present fewer images of women in dances or present them negatively.

As in theatre and cinema, the theme of the unhappy homosexual was an early one in dance. *Monument for a Dead Boy*, choreographed by Rudi Van Dantzig, was one of the first ballets to deal with the making, life, and death of a homosexual.[33] During the seventies, there were ballets such as *The Goldberg Variations, Weewis, Mutations,* and *Triad* that showed the joy and tenderness of different ways of love.

Parodies.   Travesty appears in the several all-male dance companies with the word Trockadero in their titles. The men dance as females as well as males. Most critics recognize Les Ballets Trockadero de Monte Carlo as entertaining burlesque that lovingly and excellently parodies the act of performance, specific ballets, and particular styles through informed in-jokes. The Trockaderos differentiate styles among ballets and know the ballets they make fun of so perfectly that they ably portray roles and roles within roles. Raymond argues, however, that men who appear as women "rape women's bodies by reducing the real female form to an artifact, appropriating this body for themselves."[34]

Derogation of Women. Erik Bruhn, a great *danseur noble,* refused to dance the classic ballet *Swan Lake* until he had choreographed a "corrective" version in which the evil magician Von Rothbart is supplanted by evil females. In Bruhn's countermove version, the mother is portrayed as bullying, and the villain has become a woman called the Black Queen, "alter ego of Siegfried's domineering mother."[35]

The antiwoman messages in Jerome Robbins's *The Cage,* premiered in 1951 by the New York City Ballet, continue to astonish audiences. The story of female spiders who kill their lovers after using them for impregnation is "angry, . . . decadent in its concern with misogyny and its contempt for procreation."[36] The piece was theatrically alive in the 1980s.

William Forsythe's *Love Songs,* premiered in the United States in 1983 by the Robert Joffrey Ballet, presents a view of man-woman relationships wherein the women are deserving of the violence committed against them.

Unisexuality and Role Reversal. Though feminists use unisexuality, the erasure of sexual identity, and role reversal in dance to convey equality between the sexes, men's use of unisexuality and role reversal might be viewed as attempts to eliminate the specific positive character and contribution of women. This may be the case even when their motives accord with some feminist perspectives. Alwin Nikolais, a pioneer in eschewing male and female polarized stereotypes, uses costumes and movements that prevent distinguishing the sexes. He was accused of being dehumanizing. In defense, he responded to the criticism: "I work with the human figure as affected by an environment I set up for it to move in. . . . I've always abhorred the idea of male and female as opposed, as if we were all walking around in heat. Modern society forces you to be a sexual object rather than a person."[37]

Conclusion

As in verbal language, dance can be read in different ways. As metaphor, dance has ambiguities. Are dance pieces indictments of societal injustices or contemptuous put-downs? Viewers read kinetic texts from their own vantage points; however, the current male backlash against female advances in dance does coincide with conservatism in the United States—the efforts to control women's reproductive rights, promote traditional values, and censor the arts.

To recapitulate, we recognize the constitutive role of verbal speech and writing in the production of ideology—in notions of power and knowledge. Images, too, have a role in this informal education as a medium of socialization. Danced images evolve from and resonate with the contextual past, present, and future. The images both reaffirm what is in society and suggest what might be; that is, they question the status quo. Dance is sometimes like myth, an idealized disguise to hide unorthodox practice or an ideal that is achieved by none. By weaving prevailing attitudes toward gender before our eyes, dance also entices us with alternative lifestyles: unisexuality, homosexuality, asexuality. Apart from the real world, the stage of "pretend" and "play" allows adventure without the consequences of the quotidian.

Socially constructed kinetic discourse conveyed male dominance in the ballet tradition beginning with Louis XIV. Modern dance, birthed by women contesting the patriarchy of ballet and the broader society, gave females new gender images of independence, stature, and leadership, and even eliminated gender with androgyny and role reversals. Losing out to the ballerina in the spotlight during the nineteenth and early twentieth centuries and to the modern dance matriarchs in the first half of the twentieth century, men reasserted themselves onstage. Their choreography featured men and even men alone; moreover, they appropriated movements formerly categorized as female and performed both sexes' roles, as well as derogated women.

Onstage today we see a host of sexual and gender motifs in a smorgasbord of dance. Theme and variations range from the sublime to the ridiculous through revivals of past choreography and presentations of the avant-garde. Traditional and backlash-neoconservative dance convey the Christian image of the superiority of the virgin and the danger of the siren. Not only are there displays of male chauvinism but, at the same time, other images embody feminist thought. Audiences watch the battle of the sexes play itself out. This spectrum of images, including the risible, may make the ideology of gender difference difficult to sustain.

Because it uses the body—the signature key of sexuality, essential for human survival and desirable for pleasure—dance is eye-catching and engaging. It is a riveting way of continually reconstituting gender roles and meanings. When dealing with gender, dance bears on the perpetual human struggle with questions of self-identity and interpersonal relationships.[38] In this era of challenges to dominance hierarchies and the onset of genetic engineering, an attempt to understand gender relationships is of special significance. If gender is a social construct, it is modifiable and can be deconstructed and reconstructed.

Notes

1. Alison M. Jaggar, *Feminist Politics and Human Nature* (Sussex: Rowman and Allanheld, 1983).
2. This is a revised version of papers presented at the Special Session on Non-

verbal Communication of the Georgetown University Round Table on Languages and Linguistics, 11 March 1986 (proceedings, *Journal of the Washington Academy of Sciences* 77, no. 1 [1987]:18–26); and the Fourteenth Annual Conference on Social Theory, Politics and the Arts, 1988, American University, Washington, D.C. I appreciate the helpful suggestions of Laurence Senelick and Joan Frosch-Schroder on this essay. Judith Lynne Hanna, *Dance, Sex, and Gender* (Chicago: University of Chicago Press, 1988), amplifies the points on the communication of gender made herein and considers gender patterns in non-Western culture.

3. See Judith Lynne Hanna, "Movements toward Understanding Humans through the Anthropological Study of Dance," *Current Anthropology* 19 (June 1979):313–39; "The Anthropology of Dance," in *Dance: Current Selected Research,* vol. 1 (New York: AMS Press, 1988), pp. 219–38; "Dance and Semiotics," in *Semiotics in the Individual Sciences,* vol. 10 (Bochum, Federal Republic of Germany: Studienverlag Brockmeyer, 1990), pp. 352–76, for state-of-the-art assessments of dance research, including reasons for the neglect of the study of the cognitive dimensions of dance. See also Hanna's *The Performer-Audience Connection* (Austin: University of Texas Press, 1983); *To Dance Is Human* (Chicago: University of Chicago Press, 1987); *Dance, Sex, and Gender* (Chicago: University of Chicago Press, 1988); *Dance and Stress* (New York: AMS Press, 1988) for a theoretical approach to dance as nonverbal communication and language-like.

4. Hanna, "The Anthropology of Dance-Ritual" (Ph.D. diss., Columbia University, 1976); "African Dance Frame by Frame," *Journal of Black Studies* 19 (June 1989):422–41.

5. Having said that dance is a language—and recognizing that Western culture has an exaggerated esteem for language and its prerogative for describing and defining reality—I must add that there are alternative ways of knowing. The nonverbal, too, glosses experience and formulates ideas, attitudes, and a sense of relatedness. Howard Gardner, *Frames of Mind* (New York: Basic Books, 1983), points out that there are different types of competencies, including bodily kinesthetic competence. Michael Gazzaniga, "The Social Brain," *Psychology Today* (November 1985):32, argues that "the normal person does not possess a unitary conscious mechanism where the conscious system is privy to the sources of all his or her actions. . . . The normal brain is organized into modules. . . . All except one work in nonverbal ways such that their method of expression is solely through overt behavior or more covert emotional reactions."

6. Judith Lynne Hanna, "Toward Semantic Analysis of Movement Behavior," *Semiotica* 1–2 (1979):77–110; Hanna, *To Dance Is Human*; Hanna, *Dance, Sex, and Gender.*

7. Diane Solway, "City Ballet Moves to an American Beat," *New York Times* (24 April 1988):H1, 40.

8. Martha Graham, "Martha Graham Reflects on Her Art and a Life in Dance," *New York Times* (31 March 1985):H1, 8.

9. Quoted in Nancy Vreeland Dalva, "The I Ching and Me: A Conversation with Merce Cunningham," *Dancemagazine* (March 1988):58–61.

10. See Peter L. Berger and Thomas Luckmann, *The Social Construction of Reality* (New York: Doubleday, 1966).

11. Albert Bandura, "Modeling Theory," in *Recent Trends in Social Learning Theory,* ed. Ross Di Parke (New York: Academic Press, 1972), pp. 35–61.

12. Judith Lynne Hanna, *Dance and Stress* (New York: AMS Press, 1988).

13. Richard Philp and Mary Whitney, *The Male in Ballet* (New York: McGraw-Hill Book, 1977).

14. Ivor Guest, *The Romantic Ballet in Paris* (Middletown, Conn.: Wesleyan University Press, 1966).

15. Suzanne Gordon, *Off Balance* (New York: Pantheon, 1983).

16. Ibid.

17. Arlene Croce, *Going to the Dance* (New York: Alfred A. Knopf, 1982), p. 283.

18. Arlene Croce, *Afterimages* (New York: Alfred A. Knopf, 1977), pp. 127–29.

19. Croce, *Going to the Dance*, 278–79.

20. Toby Tobias, "A Conversation with Martha Graham," *Dancemagazine* (March 1984):62–64.

21. Marcia Siegel, *Watching the Dance Go By* (Boston: Houghton Mifflin, 1977), pp. 203–4.

22. Ibid., 204–5.

23. Anna Kisselgoff, "Dance: Bausch Troupe Makes New York Debut," *New York Times* (14 June 1984):C20.

24. Marcia Siegel, *At the Vanishing Point* (New York: Saturday Review, 1972), pp. 74–79.

25. Jennifer Dunning, "Women Depicted in Dance Come in Many Guises Today," *New York Times* (9 September 1984):H8.

26. Jill Johnston, *Marmelade Me* (New York: Dutton, 1971), pp. 39–40.

27. Walter Terry, *Ted Shawn, Father of American Dance* (New York: Dial, 1976).

28. Croce, *Going to the Dance*, 165–66.

29. Siegel, *At the Vanishing Point*, 179, 134.

30. Jennifer Dunning, "Ballet: Satoru Shimazaki," *New York Times* (9 January 1982):13.

31. Deborah Jowitt, "In Memory of . . . ," *Village Voice* (4 October 1988):107.

32. Clive Barnes, "Homosexuality in Dance," *New York Times* (3 November 1974):D8; Barry Laine, "Trendy Twosome," *Ballet News* (August 1985):22–25; Graham Jackson, *Dance As Dance* (Ontario, Canada: Catalyst, 1978); Joseph Mazo, *Dance Is a Contact Sport* (New York: Dutton, 1974).

33. Jackson, *Dance As Dance*, 38.

34. Janice Raymond, *Transsexual Empire* (Boston: Beacon Press, 1979).

35. Siegel, *Watching the Dance Go By*, 104–6.

36. John Martin, "Ballet by Robbins in Local Premiere," *New York Times* (15 June 1951):17.

37. Quoted in Jennifer Dunning, "Alwin Nikolais, a Dance Patriarch," *New York Times* (13 June 1985):C33.

38. Hanna, *Dance and Stress*.

ANN DALY

Dance History and Feminist Theory: Reconsidering Isadora Duncan and the Male Gaze

❦ Isadora Duncan (1877–1927) is inarguably one of the seminal figures in twentieth-century American dance.[1] Her importance lay neither in the extension of an existing form, as did George Balanchine's, nor in her progeny, as did Ruth St. Denis's, but rather in the fact that she created an entirely new form of dance. Duncan's choreography offered her spectators a new kind of meaning and demanded from them a new way of seeing. She ennobled the previously suspect image of the human body and succeeded in her bid to legitimize dance as high art. As an international celebrity who lived out her beliefs in the corsetless figure and in voluntary motherhood, Duncan is commonly held to be an exemplary feminist, although she never explicitly labeled herself as such.[2]

Duncan has been set forth as a symbol of the feminist impulse since Floyd Dell's *Women As World Builders: Studies in Modern Feminism*. Published in 1913, this book was the first of many written by Dell, a radical intellectual and assistant editor of *The Masses,* the quintessential Greenwich Village magazine. He astutely realized that the woman's movement was in large part a product of nineteenth-century evolutionary theory, "which, by giving us a new view of the body, its functions, its needs, its claim upon the world, has laid the basis for a successful feminist movement."[3] In his chapter devoted to Duncan and writer/crusader Olive Schreiner, he wrote that Duncan expressed "the goodness of the whole body."[4] This new view of the body, he believed, was "as much a part of the woman's movement as the demand for a vote (or, rather, it is more central and essential a part); and only by realizing this is it possible to understand that movement."[5] Since Dell, scholarly and popular critics alike—many less perspicacious than he—have painted Duncan as the larger-than-life symbol (sometimes the caricature) of Woman, who is casting off her corset, taking on lovers as she chooses, bearing children out of wedlock, and generally flouting the last-gasping strictures of oppressive Victorian culture.

Duncan did, of course, invite her status as a feminist spokeswoman. She began to articulate a specifically female dancer very early in her career in her famous "The Dance of the Future" manifesto, delivered in 1903 to the Berlin Press Club. (It was here that she first encountered—and embraced—the extraordinary power of the reported word as a rhetorical adjunct to her dancing.) The following passage is one of the most often quoted in dance:

[The dancer of the future] will dance not in the form of nymph, nor fairy, nor coquette but in the form of woman in its greatest and purest expression. She will realize the mission of woman's body and the holiness of all its parts. She will dance the changing life of nature, showing how each part is transformed into the other. From all parts of her body shall shine radiant intelligence, bringing to the world the message of the thoughts and aspirations of thousands of women. She shall dance the freedom of woman. O, what a field is here awaiting her! Do you not feel that she is near, that she is coming, this dancer of the future! She will help womankind to a new knowledge of the possible strength and beauty of their bodies and the relation of their bodies to the earth nature and to the children of the future.
    . . . O, she is coming, the dancer of the future: the free spirit, who will inhabit the body of new women; more glorious than any woman that has yet been; more beautiful than the Egyptian, than the Greek, the early Italian, than all woman in past centuries: The highest intelligence in the freest body![6]

Those words have become a large part of the Duncan mythology, which has grown as unwieldy as the woman herself. For a number of reasons—the lack of a film record of her dancing, the lack of a codified technique, the anecdotal nature of much dance history, the colorful drama of Duncan's personal life, and her own Irish flair for the well-spun tale—Duncan's career as a choreographer/dancer has been distorted in the American imagination. For one thing, there is no single "Isadora" to be embraced. Her dancing and her rhetoric changed over time, as did the meaning they held for her spectators. The popular image of Duncan as a liberated woman and an advocate of free love (embedded in the popular imagination by Vanessa Redgrave in the film *The Loves of Isadora*) may be more a product of our own social and political desires than a reasonable historical interpretation of her significance for American audiences during her own day.

Up until the last decade or so, dance history, which is a young discipline, consisted largely of the accretion of personal anecdotes, memories, impressions, and interpretations. The Duncan history is no exception; developing out of recycled interpretations rather than primary sources,[7] it has followed two broad veins: the first, a romantic celebration of her liberated ways (usually by women); and the second, a classical dismissal of her antitechnical "dilettantism" (usually by men). Both interpretations oversimplify her artistry and concentrate on her personality.

In large part, the Duncan history began with the posthumous publication of her autobiography, *My Life,* a few months after her tragic, well-publicized death in September 1927.[8] The autobiography, the first of two projected parts, is clearly written from the perspective of a middle-aged woman who realized that her era had passed. "My Art was the flower of an Epoch," she had written to Irma Duncan in 1924, "but that Epoch is dead and Europe is the past."[9] She made it no secret that she was writing the memoirs for the money. A strictly commercial venture, the book necessarily stressed the personal rather than the professional and was indeed successful in terms of its international sales and newspaper serialization.

My Life clearly belongs more on the side of fiction than history.[10] It tells us much more about her psychic state in 1926–1927 than it does about the course of her lifetime. But it made a legend out of Duncan's love life, thus setting the tone for much of the Duncan history. Most of what has been written about Duncan since her death focuses on her sexuality, as it was "revealed" through the book. Yet Duncan's love life was not reported in the American newspapers during her lifetime until her very last tour, in 1922–1923, when she was accompanied by her properly wedded young Russian poet lover, Sergey Esenin. Duncan's own sexuality did not provide the primary framework for understanding her dances, yet it has taken interpretive precedence in much of the Duncan history.

In the hands of balletomanes, *My Life* has become the basis for a critique of Duncan's dancing. "The Sexual Idiom," Rayner Heppenstall's notorious essay on Duncan still circulating today in a dance anthology text, serves as prototype. A British essayist and balletomane, Heppenstall baldly reduces Duncan to an erotic, bare-legged spectacle:

Isadora's Art was, in effect, then, merely an art of sexual display, and I would stress the "merely." Isadora was not conscious of the fact. Nor, I suppose, were most of the spectators. She and they thought they were enjoying a spiritual experience. Perhaps they were, but it was only in the mass stimulation of private phantasies. There was no communication, or no communication in terms exact enough to be terms of art. . . . Her art was aphrodisiac.[11]

Heppenstall criticizes her for a lack of theatrical clarity and legibility. She stands for "Phantasy," while he values "Tradition." She does not mediate her body (her self) through the self-sacrificing, external objectification of a traditional *form,* that is, balletic technique. In Heppenstall's explicitly Freudian terms, she did not adequately "sublimate" her sexual impulses, which would have transformed them into art.[12] The British balletomane blithely accepted the myth that Duncan was improvising and that her dances were a spontaneous outpouring of inner emotion. In fact, they were choreographed;[13] they were rooted in a technique; and, they had form, although a different form than ballet's.

In a sense, this reaction is part of a willful denial of Duncan as *choreographer,* as creator—in a traditionally male domain. Instead, she is defined (even by sympathetic writers) as a *dancer,* emphasizing only the immanence of her body—a traditionally female domain. From here, it is a short leap to the conclusion that Duncan was merely acting out an erotic fantasy: "Isadora Duncan was not concerned to dance, not concerned with any clarity of plastic forms," concluded Heppenstall. "She was concerned with the Dance only as part of her primarily sexual phantasy."[14]

As extreme as Heppenstall's rhetoric is, it is not atypical. The tension between an elitist ideology of the sacrifice of self to tradition (ballet) and a democratic ideology of the expression of self through an original form (modern dance) still runs deep. In 1986, close on the heels of Gelsey Kirkland's stinging critique of the Balanchine aesthetic as oppressive and inexpressive, Balanchine apologist Lincoln Kirstein dredged up the very same rhetoric in a *New York Times* article entitled "The Curse of Isadora."[15] From Heppenstall to Kirstein and beyond, all sorts of imaginatively revisionist writers have made out of Isadora a suspect female who capitalized on her near-naked body in the guise of art.

Between the balletomanes' outright dismissal of Duncan as a dilettante and the more sympathetic, feminist claim for her as the mother of us all, where is the reality of Duncan's significance to her American audiences? What role did gender play in her dancing? It is time to revise the revisionists.

Although it is the youthful gamboling that most people associate with Duncan, her choreography, as well as its meanings, changed significantly over the course of her lifetime. Her American tours can be separated into three distinct groups: her initial tours (twice in 1908, 1909, 1911), during which spectators learned to "read" this new art form; the second group of tours (1914–1915, 1916–1918) during World War I and after the much-publicized deaths of her children, during which she came to symbolize motherhood and nationalistic pride; and the third group (1922–1923), when she returned from Soviet Russia with a young poet husband to a suspicious and increasingly hostile audience. I am interested here in examining her initial American tours, when her dancing was a startling phenomenon.[16] Given the sexual interpretations often connected with her dancing, it would seem appealing to use the "male gaze" theory of representation as a framework for analysis.

Contemporary American feminist criticism was developed, in the mid- to late 1970s, through the discourses of psychoanalysis, semiotics, and film theory. It concerned itself mainly with a series of dichotomous relationships: the male and female of the Oedipal construction; the subject and object of the performer-spectator relationship (the male gaze); and the verbal and nonverbal phases of human development. The male gaze, as much a theory of Western cultural communication as anything else, refers to the way in which the structure of representation is gendered. The subject (spectator) and the object (performer)—each assumed to have a stable position in their encounter—operate in two dimensions, on a linear basis of binary opposition. The spectator, the one who looks (who consumes, who possesses), is in the position of power: a traditionally male position. The one who is looked at—the performer who puts her/himself on display for the gaze—is in a passive, traditionally female position. Much of the early feminist project in performance, as in all the arts, was to deconstruct how this model of binary opposition had rendered women secondary in—and even absent from—representation.

Before long, however, feminist critics began calling for more than just *de*construction. They sought to *re*construct a feminist subject[17] in representation. It has become clear that the logic of binary opposition and its corollaries—the singular subject and the male gaze—though they have been crucial in understanding how the present system works, are not terribly useful in advancing beyond the problem; for, if patriarchy were truly so monolithic, then there would be no room within it for a feminist subject. And, seductive as they are, utopian visions of a world "elsewhere" are cultural and theoretical impossibilities.

Asking whether or not a choreographer such as Duncan managed to "subvert" or "break" the male gaze will neither advance the feminist project nor necessarily tell us anything about Duncan. In fact, the male gaze theory forces the feminist dance scholar into a no-win situation that turns on an exceedingly unproductive "succeed or fail" criterion. We expect the choreographer to topple a power structure that we have theorized as monolithic. The dancer or choreographer under consideration will always be condemned as a reinforcement of the patriarchal status quo, despite any transgressive behavior, because, by definition, whatever is communicated arises from within the fabric of culture, that is to say, within patriarchy.

This view really leaves little room for the work of the dance scholar: The outcome of analysis—whether the dancer or choreographer in question is a "success" or "failure" from a feminist point of view—is decided before the analysis is even begun. She will always be a "failure." Historical study is left in an especially problematic situation, because the male gaze has been theorized as a trans-historical model for Western culture, impermeable to the specifics of time and place. But as we clearly know, the body and its meanings, as well as the nature of display (and, concomitantly, the gaze), do certainly change with period and culture. Furthermore, the metaphor of representation as a "gaze" is not as suited to dance as it is to static visual media such as cinema and art. Dance, although it has a visual component, is fundamentally a kinesthetic art whose apperception is grounded not just in the eye but in the entire body.

The case of Isadora Duncan is much too rich and too complex to be reduced to a *fait accompli*. To understand the significance Duncan had to her American audiences from 1908 to 1911, a new theory of representation is required: one that includes within its very structure the capacity for change. I propose that we shift the terms of our inquiry from the two dimensional to the three dimensional. We need to understand culture as a full space (not an empty one) that encompasses transgression without necessarily co-opting it, or else we are doomed to a history without change.

A number of feminist theorists have already devised space-intensive models of representation: Laura Mulvey's emphasis on the carnival as a ludic space,[18] Teresa de Lauretis's notion of the space-off,[19] Jessica Benjamin's use of the concept of intersubjective space,[20] and Julia Kristeva's model of the chora.[21] Mulvey, whose "Visual Pleasure and Narrative Cinema"[22] largely initiated the inquiry into what E. Ann Kaplan dubbed the male gaze,[23] has criticized her own groundbreaking essay precisely because of its dependence on binary logic: "The either/or binary pattern seemed to leave the argument trapped within its own conceptual frame of reference, unable to advance politically into a new terrain or suggest an alternative theory of spectatorship in the cinema."[24]

Julia Kristeva, in *Revolution in Poetic Language,* sets forth a theory of representation, really a semiotics of art, that provides an excellent framework within which to analyze the cultural significance of Duncan's dancing body. Kristeva starts with the notion that the self is not a thing situated in one position and unchanging over time; rather, the self is a process that fluctuates through space and through time. In other words, we are always in the process of becoming, a phenomenon Kristeva calls a "subject in process/on trial."[25]

She criticizes traditional semiology because it is based upon the static model of information theory, which emphasizes the message as the final *product* of codes.[26] Kristeva instead posits semiotics as a *process* of communication whose complexity and subtlety exceeds any simple transfer of information. She therefore conceptualizes literature, or any signifying practice, not as a monolithic structure of simple communication but rather as consisting of two inseparable, simultaneous realms: the semiotic and the symbolic.[27]

The realm of the symbolic is linear and logical; it is social and syntactical. By participating in these rules of order, we are able to communicate easily with one another. But the semiotic realm, on the other hand, is a kind of "underground" communication. It is a pulsing, kinetic, heterogeneous space whose meanings are much more fluid and imprecise, yet no less powerful. Kristeva describes this realm as a "chora" (from the Greek for enclosed space, womb), a term borrowed from Plato's *Timaeus,* defined as "an invisible and formless being which receives all things and in some mysterious way partakes of the intelligible, and is most incomprehensible."[28] The chora denotes something "[i]ndifferent to language, enigmatic ... rhythmic, unfettered, irreducible to its intelligible verbal translation; it is musical, anterior to judgment."[29]

All signifying practices contain both the semiotic and the symbolic, although one realm usually suppresses the other. Thus a *potentially* subversive element is posited even in the most traditional signifying system. The extent to which the semiotic is pulled out to rupture the symbolic—thus pulverizing, imploding, infinitizing its meanings—determines the potential "production of a different kind of subject, one capable of bringing about new social relations."[30] This is the "revolution" to which Kristeva refers in the title of her book. Revolutionary art need not be overtly political in content; what is more important is that it demand a new means of perception on the part of its spectators. The subject in process/on trial can thus be fundamentally transformed. Change here, at the level of individual consciousness, is a necessary element of social change. Seen in this way, the arts are not merely *reflective* of social relations but are *productive* of social relations.

For a feminist dance historian, this schema is particularly congenial, for several reasons. First, Kristeva's theory conceives of representation as a process, not as a vocabulary, syntax, and grammar of discrete units like letters or words. Dance, an art by definition in constant evolution over time and through space, cannot be explained through linguistic semiotics, as a building-block arrangement of fixed units. Unlike many theories generated from nonperforming arts, Kristeva's processual semiotics is suited to dance *sui generis*.

Second, the schema recognizes representation as historically embedded. Because the theory is based on positionality rather than essence, what constitutes the symbolic and the semiotic changes with period and culture. Positions shift, and codes evolve. The body does not remain static; it is as potentially semiotic as it is potentially symbolic.

Third, Kristeva's theory explains art as a process that is intelligible in its unintelligibility; that is, although some poetry, abstract art, or nonnarrative dance may not operate through normative codes of communication and may not be expressible in words, it is still meaningful. We can still "understand" it. Although there is no single fixed language of dance (indeed, one of the great things about modern dance in particular is that it is constantly re-creating itself), it is eminently understandable. At its best, when the realm of the semiotic prevails, dance's power to indicate meaning far exceeds its capacity to be reduced to the symbolic, that is, into a message expressed through the ordinary structure of language.

This paradox is what the theory of the male gaze cannot accommodate: that what is ineffable, what consequently poses a threat to the ordered realm of the symbolic, can be rendered intelligible without being co-opted by the symbolic, even though the symbolic to some degree is engaged. The semiotic and the symbolic realms exist in precarious, paradoxical relation to each other, and a large part of the appeal of Kristeva's framework, for me, is that it accepts and indeed poises itself at the center of paradox. For dance scholars whose job it is to render what is nonverbal into words, paradox is a familiar state of being.

Fourth, the idea that all signifying practices contain both the semiotic and the symbolic is an especially important one for dance, because dance is commonly conceived of as purely primitive, "pre-verbal," idiosyncratic, infantile, female, and uncoded, in opposition to the civilized, social, adult, male reasoned code of language. The nonverbal, and with it the body and dance, have become the "other"—marginalized and feminized—to the privileged signifying system of language. Kristeva challenges this opposition by positing that all signifying practices, literature and dance equally, include both the semiotic and symbolic realms. Like literature, most dance does emphasize the symbolic, following the codes and conventions that render the nonverbal very "readable."

The term "pre-verbal" has always been a subtle way of marginalizing movement, of relegating it to the negative role of "other" in a world supposedly constructed solely in language. This marginalization of the nonverbal in Western culture has been institutionalized in (among other places) psychoanalysis, which theorizes infant development before the acquisition of language as a great wash of nonsubjective symbiosis with the mother. The self as a separate entity is constituted only with the entrance into language. Because psychoanalysis has been the basis of so much feminist theory in literature and cinema,[31] it has been difficult for dance scholars to appropriate those logocentric models.

Daniel Stern, however, has refigured some of the basic psychoanalytic assumptions that pit the verbal against the nonverbal in a developmental hierarchy. By reconsidering psychoanalytic theory in light of what developmental psychologists have learned empirically about infancy in the past decade, he has defused the rhetoric of the "pre-verbal" by suggesting that (1) the infant progresses not from symbiosis to differentiation but from differentiation to relatedness; (2) the infant does relate as a sense of self to others through movement before learning to talk; and (3) these bodily senses of self and their corresponding nonverbal means of relatedness persist even after the acquisition of language. Whether verbal or nonverbal, these various means of relatedness are not temporal "phases" that are eclipsed with each developmental step; rather, they are spatial "domains" that accumulate into a full complement of adult interpersonal processes.[32]

Stern's revised psychoanalytic model suspends the classic binary opposition between the verbal and its negative term, the "pre-verbal" (that is, the body, movement, nonverbal behavior, dance). Furthermore, it renders unfounded our culture's romantic, and sexist, notions of pre-verbal existence as the feminine realm of the Other. Nevertheless, the cultural marginalization of the nonverbal is deeply ingrained. The nonverbal stream of our everyday encounters, Stern observes, are eminently deniable. We cannot deny our words, but we can always deny the "body language" with which we deliver them. Similarly, Kristeva sees gesture as highly marginal.[33] Ideally, gesture (and dance, by extension) is an excessively semiotic process— a trace, really—whose significance we can understand without its being embedded in literal meaning. It lives in between and across the semiotic and the symbolic, testing the outer limits of what it takes to produce signification.

That which is so marginal as to be deniable has obvious subversive potential. Kristeva's project of paradox is to appropriate marginality— whether it be femininity, race, or class—for subversive ends: "to make intelligible, and therefore socializable, what rocks the foundations of sociality."[34] It is only by working through the semiotic, she suggests, that we can implode the symbolic. The study of gesturality, which may be as close as one can get to a pure chora, would be "a possible preparation for the study of all subversive and 'deviant' practices in a given society."[35] It is partly because dance (which is, after all, culture's aestheticized gesturality) had such a marginal status in American culture at the turn of the century that Isadora Duncan was able to manipulate it so successfully as a means of social critique and that her spectators were able to appropriate it so successfully as an enactment of their respective agendas. To her liberal yet mainstream Progressivist spectators, she embodied an optimistic belief in the reformability of the social and political system. To her radical spectators—including suffragists, anarchists, and socialists—she enacted a paradigm of complete social rupture.

When Duncan toured America in 1908, 1909, and 1911, her reputation as the "Barefoot Classic Dancer" had preceded her from Europe. Newspaper accounts had reported on her rise to fame and her colorful lifestyle ever since her first Parisian appearances in 1900. Broadway producer Charles Frohman initially imported the dancer as a Broadway novelty in late summer 1908, pushing up the original September debut in order to preempt the appearances of Duncan imitators who were spreading across two continents. She fared poorly in the summer Broadway venue, whose audiences expected light entertainment. When her subsequent Frohman tour also began badly, she released the producer from his contract in order to tour with the esteemed conductor Walter Damrosch and the New York

Symphony Orchestra, beginning with a second "debut" in November, this time at the Metropolitan Opera House. The Duncan/Damrosch tour was a success, as were her subsequent American appearances when she traveled primarily to large northeastern cities. Duncan's repertoire included the dance interludes from Gluck's *Iphigénie en Aulide,* scenes from Gluck's *Orpheus,* Beethoven's seventh symphony, a Bach/Wagner program, as well as selections from Chopin and Tchaikovsky. Her encores included Schubert's *Moment Musicale* and the ever-beloved Blue Danube Waltz by Johann Strauss.

What did Duncan's American audiences see onstage during those early tours? What did it mean for them? Although Duncan's bare limbs were certainly an issue for her audiences, I am not willing to begin with the premise of the male gaze theory, that what they saw was first and foremost an objectified female body. That may be what we, from the late twentieth century, would see, but our way of seeing was not necessarily their way of seeing.

Just because Duncan's limbs were bare does not mean her performance was necessarily seen as erotic. Her bare legs and feet were as potentially distasteful to some as they were titillating to others. Her homemade, nip-and-tuck tunics were anything but glamorous. They emphasized an abundant figure, quite the contrary of the hourglass curves that were then the erotic ideal. The tunics were quite modest, because attached inside the shoulders of each one was a leotard-style undergarment, made of the same cloth as the outer tunic. Furthermore, Duncan danced with her entire body, as an integrated whole; she did nothing to isolate and thereby heighten the sensuality of her breasts, legs, or pelvis.

Without exception, newspapermen (primarily music critics) felt compelled to make immediate comment upon whether or not the barefoot dancer was indeed a proper sight. The public was ripe for indignation, in no small part because Duncan's American debut came in the midst of an epidemic of Salome acts—no less than twenty-four in vaudeville in October 1908.[36] But reviewer after reviewer stated unequivocally that there was nothing "sensational" about Duncan's dancing; it was, rather, quite "chaste."[37] *Current Literature* reported that:

Miss Isadora Duncan has not given the Salome dance in her present tour through the United States. She refuses to sacrifice her art to the sensationalism and the vulgarity of the hour. In her dance the purely physical plays no part. She dances scantily clad, remarks a writer in the New York *Sun.* "The fact that her feet and legs are unclothed is forgotten. It is part of the picture. Miss Duncan therefore does not rely upon physical charms to add to her success, as do some of the so-called dancers who are at present doing various sorts of stunts on both sides of the water. Her success comes through her grace and ease of movement, not on account of her ability to kick or wiggle or do acrobatic tricks."[38]

Even before her actual appearances, it was clear that Duncan offered something different, if only for the reason that no one else had ever devoted an entire evening to dancing solo, without respite of song, skit, or recitation. Before they set foot in the theatre, the public was predisposed to accept Duncan on legitimately artistic terms for two main reasons. First, she placed herself within the Hellenistic tradition, which was then considered the pinnacle of genuine artistry. Second, she had been acclaimed by European royalty, artists, and intellectuals. At a time when America was struggling to develop a cultural tradition of its own, the imprimatur of European high culture held ultimate authority. It did not hurt, either, that this high priestess of the Terpsichorean Art could be claimed as one of America's own daughters.

That is not to say, however, that Duncan's reputation as a barefoot dancer was not in some cases a drawing card for the curious and for the erotic appetite. Since the 1880s, images of ballet girls and actresses ("stage beauties") had functioned as pinups in dubious publications such as the *National Police Gazette* and even in more respectable ones such as *Munsey's*.[39]

Whatever her audience's expectations, they were confounded by the dancer's actual performance. Duncan's dancing was different than anything that had previously hit the American stage. She did not construct herself as a visual spectacle, as her contemporaries did, performing a string of steps in mechanical time in some thematic costume, complete with backdrop. Ballet girls and vaudeville dancers were step dancers; their legs were their stock-in-trade, and not much of interest happened in the rest of their bodies. They operated in a pictorial mode, striking pose after pose or performing trick after trick. This was entertainment, whose appeal lay in the shapeliness of the female form, the successful (maybe even graceful) achievement of physical feats, and the novelty of the mise-en-scène. This image was what filled the pages of the *Police Gazette*. In Kristeva's terms, the entertainment was the countenance of the symbolic realm of early twentieth-century dance.

Because Duncan's dancing did not conform to these easily readable conventions, many of her reviewers found themselves at a loss for words. (Dance criticism, it should be noted, was only in its infancy. The first full-time dance critic would not be appointed for twenty years.) The critics spent a lot more space rhapsodizing on the aesthetic beauty of her dancing rather than describing how she achieved her effects. Although they knew not exactly what she was intending in some of her dances, they assured their readers that it was a "poetic" experience all the same. Interestingly enough, Kristeva's own term for the expression of the inexpressible was the same one used widely in Duncan's time by critics of theatre and art to denote the same thing: an expression that is beyond the grasp of conventional communication, whose meaning is deeper, more oblique, and more profound. Other critics voiced that same feeling in stronger terms, declaring outright that the exquisiteness and depth of Duncan's expression defied being put into words at all. She was revealing something about the powers of the dancing body that had never been enacted on stage before, and neither her audience nor the critics had discovered the vocabulary to articulate this strangely ephemeral, transcendent, elusive vision.

In the meantime, they turned—quite reasonably—to the discourse on the academic nude, rooted in the classical visual arts.[40] It gave the critics at least some way to discuss the beauty and nobility of her dancing body. By this late date, however, the Victorian discourse was fraught with hypocrisy. It often functioned as a thinly disguised sanction of erotic spectacle in the name of "art." Despite the use of this suspect rhetoric in Duncan's reviews, it is clear from their uniformly serious and respectful tone that she did appeal to them on artistic grounds. Unfortunately, the only language they possessed to discuss this phenomenon was one that belied the nature of their experience.

The line between the chaste and the erotic is hardly a solid one, anyway. "The barriers between what is deemed licit and illicit, acceptably seductive or wantonly salacious, aesthetic or prurient," Abigail Solomon-Godeau has written, "are never solid because contingent, never steadfast because they traffic with each other—are indeed dependent upon each other."[41] Just as Solomon-Godeau has shown that, for photography in late nineteenth-century Paris, the "chaste" had become "erotic," so, for a brief time when Duncan's choreographic invention was new to America, the "erotic" became "chaste."

The press's reaction is typified by the *Chicago Daily Tribune*'s description of her debut there in 1908:

Of Miss Duncan's dancing it is not the easiest thing in the world to write. It is so elusive, so fine, so delicate in its grace, and so perfect in its technic that it needs to be seen rather than read about. To say that she appears with bared feet, legs, and arms, and so gauzily draped for many of the dances that the whole form is clearly defined, is to suggest to the reader something of the sensational and possibly the prurient.

Nothing could be further from the truth. Miss Duncan, when she is dancing, gives no hint to the onlooker of her being in anywise naked or unusually bared. The idea of sex seems wholly obliterated when watching her. The spirit of youth and of joyousness seems embodied for the moment before you, and there is nothing more of sex in her appearance than there is in boyhood or maidenhood.

When the dancer comes forward to acknowledge applause she is unmistakably feminine—girlish, perhaps, but essentially of the woman conscious and confident. But when she is dancing, the fact of her being a woman and of her feet and limbs being bare never makes itself realized. This is sincere commendation of her art and in fullest justification of her manner of dressing for her dances.[42]

Duncan had made it a rule never to perform in vaudeville houses or music halls.[43] She played in legitimate theatres, concert halls, and opera houses, where she transformed the stage into a mythic space. She effectively metamorphosed the stage, paradoxically, by *not* attempting to make it into something other than itself. There were no illusionary sets or props. A simple set of tall, voluminous, blue-gray curtains surrounded the stage on three sides, and there was a similarly colored carpet underfoot. Having dispensed with the harsh glare of the footlights, Duncan placed the light sources in either wing. They were soft tones—ambers and pinks mostly, but never stark white—that gently mottled the stage in shadow and light.

Into this awaiting space, unmoored from any particular time and place, flooded the sound of the orchestra. It always played for a while first, sometimes as much as the first movement of a symphony. Only after the space had been enshrouded in melody and rhythm would the dancer slip through the shadows into the audience's awareness. She did not play characters *per se*; instead, she preferred to function as did the Greek chorus, allowing the movement to convey universal emotion. In this dim radiance, Duncan surged and floated, gathering inward and spreading outward, without a hint of self-consciousness. Duncan looked a vision, her tunic as alive as her body, the garment's light gauze catching the force of her curving, swaying, onrushing motion.

Her vocabulary was simple. She used basic ambulatory steps, adapted from the social dances of her childhood. She stepped, skipped, hopped, and jumped; but that was merely *what* she did to get from here to there. It was *how* she moved (and sometimes how she stood still) that distinguished her dancing, that imploded the conventional syntax of the ballet girl or chorine.

First, Duncan's body was always moving of a single piece, the torso and the limbs integrated seemingly without any effort. Gesture and pantomime (she was a very talented mime) were never isolated; they were always woven into the flow of bodily movement. There was a strong oppositional pull in her movement—her torso twisting to the left while her arms motioned to the right, for example—that gave her a potent dynamism. The impulse of her movements visibly originated from the center of her body (the solar plexus), and that energy flowed freely outward, like a wave, through her head, arms, legs, and into the furthest reaches of space. She achieved a kind of groundedness at the same time that her arms floated—a rare mixture of strength and grace. While the ballet girl's arms etched static lines, Duncan's were always carving out sculptural space in three dimensions. And unlike the typical dancer of her day who went mechanically from pose to pose, Duncan's movements melted one into the next, into the next, into the next, with seamless ease.

She was extraordinarily sensitive to the dynamic qualities of movement. In fact, much of her effect was communicated through her genius for choreographing the drama of the kinesthetic—the sense of intentionality communicated through activated weight, the attentiveness signaled through spatial sensitivity, and the impression of decisiveness or indecisiveness gained through the manipulation of time. Today we take for granted the expressive potential of these formal means of movement, but in Duncan's day, they were revolutionary. Her powers of focus and concentration—her ability to stay fully alive inside each moment—produced a compelling sense of presence.

Duncan had an uncanny instinct for musicality, which is the temporal expressiveness within the way music unexpectedly stretches out or rushes ahead. Instead of dancing squarely on the beat, she played with the elasticity of her accompaniment's rhythm, embedding hesitancy, fear, longing, or a whole host of inner states by variously quickening or suspending her movement through time. Paradoxically, although Duncan revealed her flesh in unprecedented quantity, she effectively dematerialized her body in the expressive force of the music.

Reviewers constantly articulated this distinction between what they *perceived* in Duncan's dancing and what they actually *saw*, because the stuff of her dancing was not physical. It was virtual;[44] that is, there was more happening on stage than a dancer simply moving her body parts. As writer/reformer Bolton Hall wrote:

It is not dancing, tho' dancing is of it. It is vital motion, expressing emotion. Unlike the ordinary dancing, it has no set pattern or subordinate motif increasingly repeated.
It has structure and design, but so closely allied to its beauty and grace that it can only be perceived, not seen.[45]

Duncan gave the impression of dancing spontaneously, even though her dances were choreographed.[46] As Hall wrote, there was "structure and design," but spectators could not discern it while they were experiencing the dancing. They were not meant to discern it. The choreography was very simple, usually a gently repetitious, symmetrical scheme supporting the kinesthetic drama of the piece, primarily through the use of body level (up and down) and floor pattern (side to side, front to back, diagonal to diagonal). Again, as with her vocabulary, structure served only as a framework, meant to recede from view as the work was performed.

Thus, for her American spectators between 1908 and 1911, Duncan's body effectively dissolved in the act of performance. H. T. Parker of the *Boston Transcript* (a fine writer who worked as a theatre, music, and dance critic) described this phenomenon as "this innocence, this spontaneity, this idealized and disembodied quality in her dancing."[47] A perceptive, anonymous critic from the *Philadelphia Telegraph* wrote similarly that Duncan was "an absolutely rare and lovely impersonation of the spirit of music, more like a sweet thought than a woman, more like a dream creation than an actual flesh and blood entity."[48]

Duncan's dancing was a paradigm of the late nineteenth-century symbolist aesthetic, captured in Walter Pater's dictum that "all art constantly aspires towards the condition of music." Unfettered by character, plot, mise-en-scène, or the conventions of the ballet girl, Duncan stirred the imagination with her poetic, nonrational form of communication. In Kristeva's terms, she was enacting the chora, tapping into a realm of meaning that was not linear, not logical, not mimetic. When Duncan began dancing, whether her spectators' preconceptions were sacred or profane, it was clear that she was neither an entertainer nor a performer in the theatre's realistic tradition. She was, instead, as a number of reviewers called her, a "symbolic dancer," whose capacity to communicate meaning went beyond that of apparent convention. (What they called symbolic at that time is what Kristeva called semiotic almost a century later.) The poet Shaemas O'Sheel wrote that:

Isadora Duncan's dancing is no less than an interpretation of life in symbols. Watching her I have felt that I was watching the Soul of Man moving in the Dance of Destiny. The term "dance" has a very different and very much more serious significance when used to indicate Miss Duncan's work than it has when standing for even the most talented and delightful of ordinary stage dancing. It connotes not merely something pretty and happy, something to beguile and amuse; it is an expression of the impulse which is a dream of all beauty; it is a questioning, an aspiration, a thrill with hopes and fears, desires and joys and melancholies, and ever with wonder.[49]

What was so extraordinary about Duncan for those early, American audiences was that she made visible the inner impulses, stirrings, vibrations of the soul. When Duncan initiated a motion from her solar plexus, then successively lifted her chest and raised her head heavenward or threw it backward Dionysically, it was a stunning embodiment of Nietzschean Will. Ongoing movement became a metaphor for what they then termed "soul," what we call the self. The dancing body was no longer a product—of training, of narrative, of consumption—but rather a process. The dance was about becoming a self (the subject-in-process/on trial) rather than about displaying a body.

Duncan essentially played out the drama of a self yearning for something, or somebody—an ideal, really—that continually obsessed her. All her life she was dogged by the inability to integrate all the different aspects of herself, and her early choreography was about a person—not necessarily a woman, not necessarily a man—yearning and searching and, in that process, finding beauty and pleasure. Even today, the choreography is not taught as a series of steps but as narratives of someone moving forward but being pushed backward by an unseen force, for example, or of someone repeatedly looking here and there for something beyond reach. Those were the virtual forces that drove the choreography; and, at a time when America was obsessed with finding for itself a national selfhood, a cultural identity, and a means of individual self-expression, spectators were primed to participate in this dancing subject-in-process.

America was poised on the threshold of modernism, a moment when corporate organization threatened the primacy of the individual and mass production threatened the uniqueness of the individual. According to cultural historian Jackson Lears:

For many, individual identities began to seem fragmented, diffuse, perhaps even unreal. A weightless culture of material comfort and spiritual blandness was breeding weightless persons who longed for intense experience to give some definition, some distinct outline and substance to their vaporous lives.[50]

Duncan's dancing provided that intense experience, connecting with the innermost reaches of the soul. As a teenager, she had been infuenced by Delsartism, which was absorbed into the larger physical cultural movement at the turn of the century. Delsarte and physical culture manuals[51] (forerunners of the contemporary self-help guide) circulated widely, promoting the idea that the individual *did* indeed have control over her fate through physical activity, whether calisthenics, dance, or sport. The message of these manuals spread through popular magazines and women's clubs: Outward behavior could be changed as a means of improving one's inner being.

The origin of the self was thus effectively relocated from God to human. The self could be constructed and reconstructed through behavior, which became a conspicuous mark of identity that embedded the theatrical into everyday life. If you changed the way you carried yourself, the way you walked, and the way you gestured, you could then bring about fundamental changes: physical health, moral improvement, aesthetic grace. In effect, you could be whomever you wanted to be. America soon found its longed-for identity in the "self-made man."

Duncan was one of America's first self-made women. She was constantly re-imagining herself, both onstage and in her interviews. (*My Life* was only the last in a long line of autobiographical narratives.) She embraced the importance of this connection between the internal and the external, and out of it she created a new art of the dance. Dance was no longer about the spectacular display of the legs for entertainment's sake; it was now about the self's inner impulses made manifest through the rhythmic, dynamic expression of the whole body. To Duncan, freedom meant being able to give presence to those otherwise invisible stirrings (consequently, she did away with the studio mirror, because it emphasized external image rather than inner impetus). Her dances of the early period were essentially about the self in formation. Constantly ongoing movement provided the perfect metaphor for that fluid identity.

Moreover, hers was a kinesthetic experience in which the spectators actively participated. From the mythic stage space to the familiarity of the music, from the accessibility of the vocabulary to the flow and ease of her movement style, Duncan constructed a literal and metaphorical theatre environment that included the spectators. Her Progressive-era audiences were filled with marginalized Americans—women, artists, radicals, intellectuals—whose vision of a new social order was marked by unchecked optimism. They moved *with* this universal being onstage, this subject-in-process whose unspecified longings they could fill in with their own specific agendas. One writer recalled:

I remember when I first saw her. . . . I shuddered with awe. In this . . . free, simple, happy, expressive, rhythmic movement was focussed all I and a hundred others had been dreaming. This was our symbol, the symbol of a new art, a new literature, a new national polity, a new life.[52]

Duncan started with the known, normative discourses of the symbolic—Greek sculpture, physical culture, even the leg show—and took her spectators to what was unknown inside themselves: "This solitary figure on the lonely stage suddenly confronts each of us with the secret of a primal desire invincibly inhering in the fibre of each, a secret we had securely hidden beneath our conventional behaviors, and we yearn for a new and liberated order in which we may indeed dance."[53] She activated the chora, creating in the theatre a fluid, porous, pulsing space of representation that invited spectators to engage in the dancing as a subject-in-process. She created a space of intelligibility into which the unintelligible—in this case, the kinesthetic and all its attendant emotions—erupted. For a time, her spectators reveled in this freely moving self, for it offered them the possibility "to make intelligible, and therefore socializable, what rocks the foundations of sociality."

Notes

1. Drafts of this essay were delivered at the 1990 annual conference of the Association for Theatre in Higher Education as well as at a fall 1990 installment of the Women's Studies Research Seminars at the University of Texas at Austin. I appreciate the insightful comments offered to me in those arenas. In particular, I

would like to thank Mark Franko, Peter Jelavich, and Amy Koritz for their perceptive responses. Also, thanks to Lori Belilove, Julia Levien, and Hortense Kooluris for sharing their understanding of Duncan dancing and technique. Any shortcomings in the essay, however, are my own.

2. Historically, the term and concept of "feminism" only began to supplant "woman movement," the nineteenth-century phraseology, in the 1910s. However, "feminism" (whose proponents distinguished it from "suffragism") was not entered into the *Oxford English Dictionary* until its 1933 supplement. Duncan spoke mostly in universal terms, rarely referring to specific political situations or movements such as suffragism. See Nancy F. Cott, *The Grounding of Modern Feminism* (New Haven and London: Yale University Press, 1987).

3. Floyd Dell, *Women as World Builders: Studies in Modern Feminism* (Westport, CT: Hyperion Press, Inc., 1976), p. 44.

4. Ibid., 49.

5. Ibid.

6. Isadora Duncan, *Der Tanz der Zukunft* (Leipzig: Eugen Diederichs, 1903), pp. 25–26.

7. Elizabeth Kendall's groundbreaking study of early American modern dance, *Where She Danced: The Birth of American Art-Dance* (New York: Alfred A. Knopf, Inc., 1979); and Nancy Lee Chalfa Ruyter's study of Delsartism, *Reformers and Visionaries: The Americanization of the Art of Dance* (New York: Dance Horizons, 1979), are notable exceptions. They mined important new historical evidence and made fresh connections between Duncan and American culture. Ironically, however, their originality has now become grist for the mill of recycled history.

8. Isadora Duncan, *My Life* (New York: Boni and Liveright, 1927).

9. Isadora Duncan to Irma Duncan, 10 June 1924, Irma Duncan Collection of Isadora Duncan Materials, Dance Collection, New York Public Library, New York City, New York.

10. That is not to say that the book is an untruth or useless. The work of Duncan's autobiography as historical evidence is not so much in the "truths" it imparts as in how Duncan constructs her vision of those "truths." Without the pretense of being an historical record, *My Life* offers us the seeds of a history, which we must take responsibility for sowing.

11. Rayner Heppenstall, "The Sexual Idiom," in *What Is Dance?* ed. Roger Copeland and Marshall Cohen (Oxford, Toronto, Melbourne: Oxford University Press, 1983), pp. 272–73.

12. At the root of Heppenstall's elaborate objection to Duncan is a near-paranoid fear of female sexuality. Although Heppenstall faults Duncan for being transparently sexual, he builds his own supposedly disinterested theory of dance on implicit models of male versus female orgasm:

He [the dancer] commits rape and begets lovely forms in his own body, with continual increase of power. His material, the field of his creative experience, is his own muscular and nervous being. And his fulfilment is in the *externalised joy of movement, the release, the building up of inherent tensions into a powerful system of release.* This is the only true freedom. It is the kind of joy and freedom we call dancing. Not the joy of *an inward, an unprojected ecstasy,* which can only be communicated through erotic empathy and sympathy between the Dancer and the onlooker. (Ibid., 288, emphasis mine)

13. The term "choreography" is a twentieth-century phenomenon. A very early,

if not the earliest, use of the term was in an article on Duncan entitled "Emotional Expression": "Her sister reads the poem which she is to interpret choreographically, and an accompaniment harmonizing with the words and sentiments is played on the piano" ("Emotional Expression," *New York Herald* [20 February 1898]). The article was reprinted in *The Director,* a magazine of "dancing, deportment, etiquette, aesthetics, physical training" ("Emotional Expression," *The Director* 1, no. 4 [March 1898]:109–11).

14. Heppenstall, "The Sexual Idiom," 272.

15. Lincoln Kirstein, "The Curse of Isadora," *New York Times* (23 November 1986), section 2, pp. 1, 28.

16. A Californian by birth (and temperament), Duncan had originally plied her art in the East, in high society venues, but she went to Europe in 1899 to make her name in the world of legitimate theatre. The American tours beginning in 1908 were in effect her "first" appearances here.

17. I borrow the term "feminist subject" from Teresa de Lauretis. It recognizes the postmodern feminist's dilemma in wanting to posit a female subjectivity while also recognizing the myth of the singular subject. See Teresa de Lauretis, *Technologies of Gender: Essays on Theory, Film, and Fiction* (Bloomington and Indianapolis: Indiana University Press, 1987).

18. Laura Mulvey, "Changes: Thoughts on Myth, Narrative and Historical Experience," in *Visual and Other Pleasures* (Bloomington and Indianapolis: Indiana University Press, 1989).

19. de Lauretis, *Technologies of Gender.*

20. Jessica Benjamin, "A Desire of One's Own: Psychoanalytic Feminism and Intersubjective Space," in *Feminist Studies/Critical Studies,* ed. Teresa de Lauretis (Bloomington: Indiana University Press, 1986).

21. Julia Kristeva, *Revolution in Poetic Language,* trans. Margaret Waller (New York: Columbia University Press, 1984).

22. Laura Mulvey, "Visual Pleasure and Narrative Cinema," *Screen* 16, no. 3 (Autumn 1975):6–18.

23. E. Ann Kaplan, *Women and Film: Both Sides of the Camera* (New York and London: Methuen, 1983).

24. Mulvey, "Changes," 162. Not unrelated to this turn toward space as an organizing metaphor is a renewed interest in the body, which creates the very field in and around it, whether on the micro level (social interaction, choreography) or the macro level (culture). But in studying the body and the meanings it generates, feminist and cultural theorists vary widely in their willingness to confront the body as a material as well as symbolic object and to deal with the body as the ground of perception. Dance studies have much to offer feminist and cultural studies precisely because the object of study is the body, that crucial site where culture and nature intersect. The dancing body provides a kind of living laboratory for examining the production of the body: its training, its image, its story, and its ways of creating the world around it.

25. Kristeva, *Revolution.*

26. Julia Kristeva, "The System and the Speaking Subject," in *The Tell-Tale Sign: A Survey of Semiotics,* ed. Thomas A. Sebeok (Lisse, Netherlands: The Peter De Ridder Press, 1975). Julia Kristeva, "Gesture: Practice or Communication?" in *The Body Reader: Social Aspects of the Human Body,* ed. Ted Polhemus, trans. Jonathan Benthall (reprinted from *Semeiotike: Recherches pour une semanalyse*; Paris: Seuil, 1969).

27. Kristeva, *Revolution*.

28. Quoted in Léon Roudiez's "Introduction" to Julia Kristeva, *Desire in Language, A Semiotic Approach to Literature and Art* (New York: Columbia University Press, 1980), p. 6.

29. Kristeva, *Revolution*, 29. It should be noted that the semiotic realm is *not* a "feminine" one. The chora corresponds to the pre-Oedipal realm, and the symbolic, to the emergence into language. The chora, therefore, cannot be coded as "feminine," because sexual difference does not exist in the pre-Oedipal realm. Kristeva is a staunch anti-essentialist whose idea of the "feminine" is one of position (which is relative) rather than of essence. In fact, those figures whom she cites as exemplary writers of the semiotic (e.g., Artaud, Mallarmé) are men.

30. Kristeva, *Revolution*, 105.

31. Kristeva's theory of the chora is rooted in psychoanalytic theory; the contours of the semiotic and the symbolic are modeled on Lacan's scheme of the imaginary and the symbolic. (Since the publication of *Revolution in Poetic Language*, Kristeva has become a psychoanalyst, and her writings have intensified in that direction.) The problematic question of how her theory of the chora serves both to affirm and to marginalize the nonverbal is extremely complex and beyond the scope of this essay.

32. Daniel Stern, *The Interpersonal World of the Infant: A View from Psychoanalysis and Developmental Psychology* (New York: Basic Books, Inc., 1985).

33. Kristeva, "Gesture."

34. Kristeva, "System," 54.

35. Kristeva, "Gesture," 272.

36. "The Vulgarization of Salome," *Current Literature* 45, no. 4 (October 1908):437–40.

37. The analysis of Duncan's reviews in this article is based on the extensive collection of clippings in the Isadora Duncan Reserve Dance Clipping File at the New York Public Library Dance Collection, as well as those from other archival and library collections across the country.

38. "Vulgarization," 440.

39. Mark Gabor, *The Pin-Up: A Modest History* (New York: Bell Publishing Company, 1972).

40. T. J. Clark, *The Paintings of Modern Life: Paris in the Art of Manet and His Followers* (New York: Knopf, 1985).

41. Abigail Solomon-Godeau, "The Legs of the Countess," *October* 39 (Winter 1986):104.

42. W. L. Hubbard, "Girl's Art Dance Airy As Her Garb," *Chicago Daily Tribune* (1 December 1908).

43. There were a few exceptions, notably her 1908 Frohman-produced run at the Criterion Theatre in New York City. At this point, she was in urgent need of money for her school.

44. See Susanne K. Langer, *Feeling and Form* (New York: Charles Scribner's Sons, 1953), p. 175. She asserts that virtual gesture is the essential sign of dance:

The primary illusion of dance is a virtual realm of Power—not actual, physically exerted power, but appearances of influence and agency created by virtual gesture.

In watching a collective dance—say, an artistically successful ballet—one does not see *people running around*; one sees the dance driving this way, drawn that way, gathering here, spreading there—fleeing, resting, rising, and so forth; and all the motion seems to spring from powers beyond the performers.

Duncan is an embodiment of this principle. Ironically, due to the prevalent modern dance bias against Duncan at the time Langer wrote this passage (Graham and Humphrey and others wanted to distinguish their formalism against what they claimed was Duncan's self-indulgence), she used Duncan as a negative example of the misguided idea that dance is essentially a handmaid to music.

45. Bolton Hall, "Isadora Duncan and Liberty," quoted in *Dionysion,* 1914 performance brochure.

46. Besides Duncan's genius as a performer was her genius as a choreographer. She created that feeling of spontaneity through precisely calculated means. Her technique, while it appeared easy, was actually a physically strenuous and performatively sophisticated one, requiring years' work to perfect.

47. H. T. Parker, *Motion Arrested: Dance Reviews of H. T. Parker,* ed. Olive Holmes (Middletown, CT: Wesleyan University Press, 1982), p. 59.

48. "Triumphs Again," *Philadelphia Telegraph* (24 November 1908), Isadora Duncan Reserve Dance Clipping File, Dance Collection, New York Public Library, New York City, New York.

49. Shaemus O'Sheel, "Isadora Duncan, Priestess," *Poet Lore* 21 (1910):482.

50. Jackson Lears, *No Place of Grace: Antimodernism and the Transformation of American Culture 1880–1920* (New York: Pantheon Books, 1981), p. 32.

51. An extensive variety of these manuals, consulted in research for this essay, are at the Library of Congress.

52. W. R. T., "Classical Dancing in England," *T.P.'s Magazine,* Isadora Duncan Dance Reserve Clipping File, Dance Collection, New York Public Library, New York City, New York.

53. O'Sheel, "Isadora Duncan," 481.

KARL TOEPFER

Speech and Sexual Difference in Mary Wigman's Dance Aesthetic

❦ Historians of modern dance tend to associate that art form with an heroic effort to release human identity from "unnatural" constraints imposed upon the body. The "modern" body is "free" of oppressive regulation by archaic, "unprogressive" codes and signifying practices, and dance becomes the sign of this freedom when it refuses to subordinate the body of the dancer not only to the stagnant codes or textualizations of ballet but also to the master encoding of perception itself by language.[1] Modern dance is modern because it lacks a specific "language," a unified "vocabulary." Moreover, the history of modern dance presents this emancipation of the body primarily in relation to the liberation of *female* bodies. Men, of course, made powerful contributions to the development of modern dance, but the fact remains that the bodies of those who *performed* modern dance were overwhelmingly female. The appeal of modern dance for so many women was due to the perception of an heroic moment when women could pursue an unprecedented opportunity to redefine female identity and the feminine.

Thus, while modern dance liked to present itself as a transcendence of the rigorous sexualization of identity cultivated by ballet, sexual difference nevertheless controlled perception of this region of modernism. Sexual difference operates through attitudes toward the relations between language and dance. *Performance* of modern dance, largely the achievement of women, "naturally" excludes speech; but *writing about* modern dance was, in the early decades of this century, largely the achievement of men. Though few might doubt the therapeutic value of dance for the dancer, to obtain credibility as an art, modern dance had to sustain the interest of spectators, and it was overwhelmingly the published language of men that defined this interest and articulated the identity of the spectator until well into the 1930s.

A pervasive attitude throughout the world's modern dance culture assumed that dancing was a "feminine" activity and that discourse about dance, the power to ascribe significance to this "feminine" activity, was a "masculine" phenomenon. The justification for this assumption came from the huge preponderance of female bodies in dances and to the equally huge preponderance of male bodies responsible for published statements about dance. No doubt, "cultural conditioning" plays a large part in explaining this sexual difference, but modern dance has been reluctant even to acknowledge the difference with the result that even today it is difficult to persuade men that they might have something to "say" as dancers. Since the 1930s, women have become far more active in articulating the spectator's perspective; still, language and speech *in* dance remain essentially alien to modern dance culture. Whenever a dance incorporates writing or speaking, people assume that the performance belongs to the realm of the postmodern. The efforts of a great pioneer in modern dance, Mary Wigman (1886–1971), to incorporate speech into some of her dances thus complicate the perception of sexual difference in modern dance culture and subvert the assumptions about "masculine" and "feminine" identity associated with the production of "modern," emancipated bodies. At the same time, however, the extraordinary complexity of these efforts helps explain why the public felt far more comfortable with far less ambiguous agendas of modernized identity and sexualization through dance.

Of course, the motive for a sexual difference between spectating and performing, between "masculine" speaking and "feminine" silence, begins to dissolve when we consider the voice as part of the body rather than separate from it. A completely emancipated body cannot suppress or exclude an organ that it obviously possesses. Yet the extreme rareness with which modern dance does include the voice indicates that the pursuit of complete emancipation is by no means a simple matter. That dance was hardly "free" of language was perhaps more obvious in Germany than elsewhere during the early years of modern dance, for Germany, the great center of modern dance in Europe until 1940, produced more writing about dance than any other country and was the site of initial efforts to incorporate speech into dance. Yet even in the free-wheeling, experimental climate of the German dance scene, the structures of sexual difference that reinforced the "modern" relations between the "language" of the body and the "body" of language itself were never challenged.

The great theorist of bodily movement, Rudolf Laban (1879–1958), did experiment with speech accompaniments to dance. But the obscurity and tentativeness of these experiments, which tended to push dance toward pantomime, have overshadowed the fact that, for Laban, it was the language, the rhetoric one used to define or describe dance (not dances or dancers), that produced a new value and a new appetite for dance culture. More than anyone else, Laban linked an expanding, liberating dance consciousness to the theorization of human movement, not to dances themselves. In numerous theoretical writings, therefore, he strove to establish a vocabulary, a kind of grammar, culminating in the Labanotation system, for identifying the signifying potential of the body.[2] These writings profoundly changed the way people spoke *about* dance. Laban went much further than eurhythmics pioneer Émile Jaques-Dalcroze in offering a vocabulary through which choreographers and dancers could communicate with each other. Specific, "modern" modes of speech were consequently much more significant in constructing modern German dance performance than a study of performances alone would ever indicate. In other words, because *dances* include very little, if any, speech hardly means that dance itself designates a zone of signification that is "free" of language. On the contrary, modern dance was such a mysterious and deeply stirring phenomenon in Germany that, between 1919 and 1935, more publications, more *writing* on modern dance appeared in German than in any other language before or since. The dance bibliography from the period is enormous and suggests that, far from being an art that is "outside" or "beyond" linguistic control, modern dance functioned as a great provocation to say something, in words.

More precisely, the perception that modernity was being signified through dance seems to have acted as a provocation for digging deeply into language for "explanations" of a phenomenon that could display serious "misunderstanding" of the body as a sign of emancipation. Probably the fact that the overwhelming majority of modern dance bodies were female contributed much to a need for literate, rational explanations of the emancipatory impulse. Because of its very appreciation of the body's power to sustain aesthetic feeling (desire), this impulse always risked being perceived as a threat to the power of language, to sexual morality, and to the authority of institutions, such as theatre, to "contain" the body while simultaneously empowering it.

In any case, it is difficult to ignore the suggestion that sexualization regarding the relation between language and bodily movement shaped the evolution of German modern dance: Women do most of the dancing, and men do most of the writing about dance. Although women occasionally contributed small articles on dance to magazines and specialist periodicals, men pervasively dominated the mechanisms for forming and transmitting language about dance. Before 1935, when Mary Wigman published her memoirs, *Deutsche Tanzkunst,* only a couple of women dancers, Grete Wiesenthal and Valeska Gert, produced any books on dance, and both of these were autobiographies that dealt more with the formation of personalities than with dance itself.[3]

The sexualized difference between the voiceless movement of the (feminine) dancer and the motionless (inscribed) "voice" of the (masculine) spectator existed primarily in relation to "dances" performed for the public. In relation to dance as an activity encompassing more than mere dances, however, the sexualization process becomes yet more mysterious.[4] Mary Wigman, for example, cultivated a very complex attitude toward language. "Dance is speech," she observed, "communication, language of the body in motion."[5] Her perception of dance as a "language" was not entirely metaphorical, but neither was it stabilized by any powerful theoretical framework.

Wigman began her dance career during World War I as a student of Laban, from whom she learned to regard art as an heroic endeavor and to appreciate the value of a heightened critical perspective in developing confidence as an artist. She also seems to have learned from Laban the great importance (as far as success in dance is concerned) of cultivating a "mysterious" persona, which simultaneously transmitted an aura of heroic aloneness and a charismatic magnetism capable of attracting many disciples. She was over thirty before she achieved (1918) any public recognition as a dancer. But from the end of the war until her death, she remained the most prominent figure in modern dance, not only in Germany, but in Europe. The end of the war coincided with her "divergence" from the master, Laban. For Wigman, the freedom sought by the "modern" body depended on more than hygenic purity, eurhythmic energy, or physical strength. Freedom entailed *expressive power*; it entailed a right to signify the "inner life" of humans—intense and complex feelings. If modern dance was to achieve "serious" consideration from the public, therefore, it could not remain afraid to project a tragic dimension.

To achieve this ambition, she introduced all sorts of innovations into the "expressive dance" (*Ausdruckstanz*); she brought the body closer to the surface upon which it danced; she experimented with costumes, masks, light, and complex rhythmical structures; and through her fascination with percussion sounds, she detached the signifying power of movement from its previous dependence on melodic musical structures. She maintained an ambivalent attitude toward narrative: Some of her dances told a sort of story, but many were quite "abstract" in that they concentrated less on exposing the motives for emotions than on the power of emotion itself to move the body. As a result, the modernist public could acknowledge that dance was capable of signifying and constructing highly complex psychological states. By the mid-1920s, she had become a kind of high priestess of a powerful European dance cult, headquartered in Dresden. She extended her influence to America, first through tours in the early 1930s, then through her disciple, Hanya Holm, who emigrated to New York before the outbreak of World War II. With the advent of the Third Reich, Wigman was not able to sustain the level of innovation she had enjoyed during the

Weimar Republic. Consequently, until her death, she focused the bulk of her energy on trying to institutionalize her ideas, into building a pedagogical apparatus that would preserve the emancipatory legacy of *Ausdruckstanz* for future generations of modern dancers.

Wigman's connection to the German literary world was not nearly as close as that of Grete Wiesenthal or even of Valeska Gert, yet her interest in language was much more literary than that of nearly any other dancer of the era.[6] Language, both written and spoken, was very important to her in creating dances. She wrote out scenarios for her dances and incorporated into the manuscripts sketches, marginal comments, and cryptic movement notations, sometimes employing different colored inks and pencils.[7] She was fond of drawing pictures that included words in the imagery, such as a sketch she did of New York City in 1931 that, in collage fashion, consisted entirely of words from signs she saw on the streets of the city.[8] She kept notebooks and a diary in which she included sketches that disclose her inclination to label or caption her images.[9]

Apparently she "saw" the dances she created through a process of inscription. The image of language gave her the image of movement. In rehearsal, she was not content to watch and comment nor even to interrupt the performance by her commentary; she liked to talk to the dancers *while* they danced, telling them, in highly metaphorical language, not what movements to make but what feelings they should experience, what effects they should produce. The urge to speak compelled her to enter the dance, but she would shout out isolated words and phrases rather than complex or even complete sentences.[10] Occasionally, she published brief articles in dance journals; in these pieces, her language remained consistently metaphorical and polemical rather than analytical. She was at her best when she wrote autobiographically, when she connected attitudes toward dance (rather than significations themselves) to specific events in her life. Unlike her teacher, Laban, she was never able to articulate a *system* for encoding and decoding dance. All her writing seems fragmentary, completely dependent on knowledge of her dances to give it significance.

Whereas Laban sought, through theoretical language, to detach the significance of bodily movement from specific dances, Wigman saw language and dance as interactive phenomena that revealed an utterly unique personality: The significance of dance for her could not be understood independently of the dancer, and understanding of the dancer depended on significations that made a specific performing body "different" from other bodies. The difference between Laban and Wigman in incorporating sexual difference is not clear, however, because dancers (who were mostly female) and dance spectators (both male and female) seemed to have regarded both artists as "correct" in establishing the identity of modern dance. Yet these two modes of modernity in dance contradict each other, and this contradiction, which no one at the time articulated very clearly, if at all, emerges from the sexual difference in attitudes toward the body as a sign of modernity. The sexual difference "hides" behind a somewhat more obvious difference in attitudes toward the relation between language and movement. In other words, the difference between "theoretical" ("masculine") and "poetic" ("feminine") uses of language to describe and motivate dances conceals a sexual difference in the meaning ascribed to the "modern" body. For Laban, modern identity is an abstraction of the body caused by imposing theoretical controls on signifying choices; abstraction "liberates" the body from sexual difference. For Wigman, however, modern identity implies a heightened condition of exposure, vulnerability, a mode of nakedness, insofar as dance results from "an inner, indefinable, undeniable urge that desires a visible, definable expression."[11] Conditions of exposure "liberate" the body from its abstraction, not so much by theory but by unarticulated mechanisms of ideology. From Wigman's perspective, a body was "free" to the extent that it neither hid nor effaced its sexuality nor remained imprisoned within a premodern "image" of sexual difference, such as ballet tended to perpetuate.

Wigman's "poetic" perception of relations between language and dance tended to remain embedded in her method of creation rather than in her dances themselves. The idea that "dance is speech" lacks motivating power as long as it is *merely* a metaphor. Dance loses its subordination to language (the thing to which it is compared) only when we see dance *as* speech and speech *as* dance, which effectively means seeing dance *in* speech and speech *in* dance. Wigman seems to have been preoccupied with achieving some sort of movement from the metaphorical to the literal in her perception of relations between speech and movement. In 1930, she published an article in *Der Tanz* in which she declared:

. . . the combination of the dance and the spoken word is scarcely known to us. That it is possible we know both from reports on civilizations that have vanished and from contemporary experiments that have brought this fundamental problem of histrionic art to the forefront of critical discussion. . . . Only when it had got rid of the dictatorship of music was [dance] free to assume fresh shapes and to form new combinations with kindred arts.

The problem of the relation between music and dance may be regarded as solved. But the connection of the spoken word and the dance, with its unlimited possibilities, is still an open question—a question so urgent that it can no longer be answered by theories. It must be worked out in practice and stated as a creed.

In recent years I have been repeatedly approached with the request to help solve this problem of the union of the dance with drama and poetry. I never felt able to comply, for the dancer within me remained insensible to the appeal. It was only when I got to know Albert Talhoff's work that all scruples were overcome.[12]

Despite the "urgency" of the "problem," Wigman was very cautious about developing any synthesis of speech and movement in her dances. She first used speech in dance in her *Seven Dances of Life* (1921), which a Frankfurt opera dramaturge, Hanns Niedecken-Gebhart, urged her to do. In this allegorical piece, the Speaker is a shadowy male who never dances. He begins the work by reciting an expressionistic, free-verse poem that reveals the motives for the ensuing eight dances (Dance of the Girls, Dance of Longing, Dance of Love, Dance of Lust, Dance of Suffering, Dance of the Demon, Dance of Death, Dance of Life). The poem indicates that each dance signifies a more intensified, daring state of freedom for the female dancer:

> But the dancer
> did not heed the King
> and danced past him
> the Dance of Suffering
> And then she danced
> the dark dance
> of the Demon
> stirring up all forces
> hidden beneath the threshold of life.[13]

The poem, written by Wigman herself, presents dance as a great encounter with or risking of death performed by women. The piece as a whole associates death simultaneously with speech and with maleness. In the spoken prologue, the Speaker narrates the story of a king who has life and death power over a slave woman, whom he expects can "unravel life's meaning" through dance. Each of the "seven dances of life" represents an escalating condition of freedom for the woman, which depends on the danced signification of emotions that are otherwise repressed or "unspeakable." These emotions, this "tearing asunder all fetters / and transcending all confines," challenge the authority of the king to confine the woman within his own definition of her as a "slave." This challenge provokes the king to condemn her to death, but the "silent" Dance of Death presents death as an effigy of the king, to whom the black-veiled dancer bows in submission.

> But the king
> kissed the dancer's forehead
> and said:
> "Your dance conquered Life
> and it conquered Death.
> Live now and be free!"[14]

The recited poem that begins the work is only a fragment of the scenario as a whole. The scenario describes each dance using "poetic" language to evoke the actions and feelings that the dance, rather than the voice, should "say": "Her feet laugh and lure like the summer songs of the birds when the sun awakens them. Her white arms fly through space in blissful undulation and caress the air as sea gulls would touch the waves of the ocean. 'I love you,' the dancing body speaks."[15] In other words, the language of the written scenario, which shifts between present and past tense, absorbs the spoken language of the prologue and the "unspoken" language that motivates dance signification. The scenario functions as a commentary on or re-telling of the spoken story that motivates the dance movement. The dance movement then becomes a commentary on the language of the scenario. The relation between language and movement is therefore much more complex than a performance of *The Seven Dances of Life* alone would indicate. Dance is "language" or "speech" to the extent that it decodes an image that encodes itself through inscription. To decode is to expose or make naked what language, the text, hides (encodes) or "says" when it remains external to the *bodies* that *speak it,* through voice or dance.

The male Speaker enters the dance again about halfway through, at the end of the Dance of Suffering. "Out of the dark," he "recites" (rather than sings) the Song of the Demon. The Speaker assumes a different persona than the one he projected in the prologue. He does not speak in the manner of a mythic figure telling an archaic fable; instead he addresses the Dancer:

> You became aware of me
> on one day of your life.
> Shapeless, I wafted
> through the spheres
> of the world.
> But you created me,
> You gave the form
> in which I now
> dwell in your life.
> What could make you
> fear me?[16]

But this "demonic" voice is not really external to the Dancer; it is "inside" her for it signifies a region of desire that drives her to "say," through dance, "those lost hours when life is silent," which conquers death:

> Why are you frightened
> of the creation of your own
> fantasy?

"You will no longer be without me," the Demon remarks, and then he indicates that the *erotic* relation between speech and movement, Demon and Dancer, disembodied voice and voiceless body, is *vampiric:*

> Beloved!
> The smile of horror
> around your red lips
> makes me thirsty
> I feed
> on your warm blood—
> Now I am quite close to you![17]

The male voice, in the dark, *inside* the body of the dancer, apparently is heard rather than "seen," for the Dancer does not dance (or at least move) *to* the words; instead, cowering on the floor, she "absorbs their life" and thus acquires the strength to perform the ensuing Dance of the Demon, "full of trembling lust and distorted beauty." The speech of the Demon is, nevertheless, some sort of dance, which is feeling, desire itself, an "invisible" phenomenon perceptible only when the Dancer's "eyes have learned / to see more than can be seen":

> Do you feel
> how the invisible dance
> of my limbs holds you embraced?[18]

"Like" language, feeling has no body of its "own"—it "feeds" off a body, and this "feeding" is the motive for "demonic," danced signification by the body. Speech does not expose the body but veils it with darkness, moves it toward death; and proper movement toward death, which is dance, is ultimately ecstatic, since dance then signifies a "triumph" over death insofar as it is freedom from fear of death, the great theme of Wigman's choreography in general.[19] As Hedwig Mueller observes in relation to Wigman's *Ecstatic Dances* (1918), movement toward freedom implies "the transformation of the physical into the metaphysical," a transcendental condition that achieves its most dramatic signification through the body's power of movement to signify the immanence of death, "the unity of desire and destruction," the end of pulsation as such.[20]

It may seem that Wigman has objectified, through the use of the male voice, a conventional, sexualized attitude toward speech and movement: The speaking body is male, the dancing body is female. But Wigman complicates the identity of this voice by her theatrical treatment of the body that speaks. Not only does the male body assume two distinct personas through speech, but the choreographer inscribes the voice into her scenario, the language of which is a motive for dancing. The scenario, as a "literary" text, then becomes a commentary (or image) of this motivating language, "saying" what speech and language cannot "say" in themselves. Thus, for Wigman, the phenomenon of speaking involves the body in more complex significations than those produced by the voice alone. This complexity arises from Wigman's inclination to perceive ecstasy, a supremely desired movement of the body, as a kind of "perfect" (utterly fearless) encounter with death, that supremely motionless condition of the body. From this perspective, in which the artist sees dance as movement toward ecstasy, dancing (rather than dance spectatorship) implicates the body simultaneously in modes of "saying" and "not saying." What Wigman's aesthetic suggests is that it is not attitudes toward language that account for the operation of sexual difference in dance, neither for the "feminine" identity of dance nor for the "masculine" identity of dance spectatorship. Rather, it is attitudes toward ecstasy and death that account for the "difference." Ecstasy is "feminine" insofar as it is a *performance* in response to death, to an "invisible" mode of being for which disembodied speech is *merely* a sign. Ecstasy is "masculine" insofar as it is a response to a performance, to something seen, to signs that "expose" or make "visible" even death. Apparently, these attitudes toward death and ecstasy function independently of language's "power" to construct identity.

Wigman somewhat complicated her attitude toward speech-movement relations in her next work employing speech, *Totenmal* (1930), for which the Swiss author Albert Talhoff wrote the words. Though the piece failed to gain much critical approval, Wigman regarded it as the most successful statement of her perception of speech-movement relations.[21] The eight-part "dramatic choral vision for word, dance, and light" calls for six separate choirs who represent, respectively, the spirits of fallen soldiers and their wives, mothers, sisters, and lovers. The eight parts or "compositions" include five "halls" and three interludes.[22] Of the six choirs, one, the Celebration Choir, consists of two parts: One part speaks within the "halls," and the other part, situated around two "light altars," speaks in close proximity to the color organ. A female dance choir (Tanzender Chor I) and a male dance choir (Tanzender Chor II) never speak and only dance. A Speech-Orchestral Choir, like the Celebration Choir, contains voices of both sexes. The Celebration Choir and the Speech-Orchestral Choir occasionally speak in unison and also form as many as ten "groups" of voices from within either the Celebration Choir or the Speech-Orchestral Choir.[23] One of these groups consists of a boy choir. The Instrumental Choir, which plays percussion instruments (drums, cymbals, bells), sometimes speaks or "screams." From out of these choirs come eight figures who speak numerous verses solo.[24] Another five figures dance without speaking; these include a male Demon and a female Dance-Play figure, which Wigman herself performed.[25]

In this huge dance, literary language does not construct "characters" in any way that we might expect of a dramatic text. Instead, Talhoff's expressionistic verse turns the bodies that speak into abstractions, or, rather, language becomes a sign of modernity by its power to expose the body, which speaks as an abstraction. Whether in a choral or a solo mode, the speaking body always projects an anonymous, generic identity.[26] The language creates different "communities" of voice that nevertheless speak the same *types* of language and (pacifist) sentiments. No one body seems powerful enough to speak any sentiment unique unto the speaker. Each body (and voice) seems but a *fragment* of a larger, even more abstract communal identity. Despite the communality of desires signified by the numerous, interlocking choirs and solo speakers, the dominant mood of the piece is one of profound loneliness, of the living (mixed sexuality) separated irrevocably from the dead (male) and the dead separated from the living. The distribution of speech among so many choirs, groups, and soloists creates an extremely complex, antiphonal sound world. Wigman treats this sound world much like a musical accompaniment to dance movements. Though the choirs and speakers are by no means static, the piece strongly differentiates between their movements and those of the nonspeaking dancers. Choirs sway, undulate, or extend their arms but otherwise never move with the freedom or complexity ascribed to the Demon or the two Dance-Play figures. Just as the realm of the dead is immutably "other" than that of the living, so speech remains in tension with movement. Because, however, the text motivates dance, one must assume that, in this case, language "controls" movement or shapes it according to its own rhythms. But the text does not make clear how bodily movement "translates" the spoken language that accompanies it. The free verse wildly shifts rhythms from speaker to speaker. For example:

SPEECH AND GESTURAL FIGURE II
No!!
from the ten million dead
                    the dead
                    the dead
for you is the path out of hate and need assigned
all their peoples
make them holy
holy
beacons of this planet (*Darkness.*)
CELEBRATIONAL CHORUS:
And no one guesses
that now at last before God and world
without question
and for murder
hammer of death
falls on all those of this earth—!
INSTRUMENTAL CHORUS:
VOICES:
oh save
save

the light of the world!
light of the world!
the world
world
. . . .
. . . . 27

Do relations between words and relations between words and space on the page "motivate" unique relations between speech and movement in performance? Even the Labanotation of the piece does not provide an especially accurate answer to this question.[28] But if we consider Wigman's dependence on writing to create her dances, we might suppose that she believed that the rhythms of *language,* not speech, "control" rhythms of the body. In *Totenmal,* however, speech rhythms, treated as musical accompaniment, must have the same sort of impact on bodily rhythms that music "normally" does. Rhythms of speech, language, and the body must somehow "mirror" each other; yet Wigman keeps speech out of the dancing body and makes it always "other" than the "language" of movement.

To intensify the anonymity and abstraction of the body, all the performers wear masks; but whereas the costumes and masks of the males are uniformly identical, those of the females are differentiated according to eight archetypal ("feminine") emotions or moods.[29] Mask type determines movement type. Performing before the various choirs is a lone, unmasked woman (Wigman), whose dances attempt, unsuccessfully, to resurrect the dead. Speech, of course, does not issue from her or her counterpart, the shrouded male Demon, but from choirs and figures whose text consists of Talhoff's verse lamentations for the dead, messages from the dead, and occasional exhortations to the audience not to "forget" the dead. Integrated into Talhoff's language are fragments of actual letters written by English, French, and German soldiers who died in World War I. The solo speakers of these fragments are male and "invisible," because they speak, individually, from concealed booths.

In her detailed reconstruction of *Totenmal,* Susan Manning discusses the political ambivalence of the piece, its murky blend of pacifism and reverence for "heroic" sacrifice.[30] My purpose here is to observe that the formal and political complexity of the work indicates how Wigman's perception of speech-movement relations had changed subtly in the ten years since *The Seven Dances of Life.* Speech emanates from visible and "invisible" bodies, but unlike the earlier dance, speech here is not entirely synonymous with death. The voices neither sing nor speak but adopt a kind of *Sprechstimme* or chanting style of delivery.[31] The drum-and-cymbal music (by Talhoff) also emanates in part from "invisible" bodies (Instrument Choir), but because it supports the movement of all the choirs, the spectator associates it with the aural-visual network of signs for both "life" and "death," whose "normal" sign, of course, is silence.[32] Performance entails a complex interaction between the lone, unmasked woman dancer, the figures, the movement choirs, the male and female speech choirs, the mixed choirs, and the "invisible" bodies of those who produce speech and music.

A further mode of interaction occurs in a more subtle way. The "author" of the performance text is not synonymous with authorship of the scenario, for *Totenmal* is as much Wigman's creation as Talhoff's, and Wigman herself credited sculptor Bruno Goldschmidt's eerie masks with controling much of the meaning of the piece.[33] But whereas the male "authors" remain "invisible" during the performance, the female "author," Wigman, is a focus of visual perception, and her body signifies a vortex of resurrecting energy.[34] Obviously, it is not accurate to say that the construction of sexual difference operates through an opposition of visible and invisible patterns of signification. Not only does the piece require movement choirs of both sexes and male and female speech choirs, but the speech of the speech choirs makes explicit (even accusatory) reference to the "invisible" audience, whose sexual identity the performance text assumes is "mixed," a sexually transcendent "you" (e.g., "The curse of terror and of shame / Be on you all").[35]

The sixth episode concludes when Wigman, having apparently revived the dead by persuading the male movement leader to imitate her movement, becomes separated from her partner by the appearance of a sinister male Demon (masked), who compels her, through dance, to retreat into the shadows. The final (eighth) "composition" does not involve bodily movement at all: The male and female speech choirs stand rigidly with arms upheld as a color organ bathes the scene in blazing red light. The Celebration Choir thunderously exhorts the audience to believe that God's love will triumph over destructive human impulses toward war. The final "Amen" produces a strange ending. The lone woman seems to have exhausted herself "to death" trying to revive the dead through her dance; yet the sign for "triumph" over death is a tableau-like image of monumental stasis, with a multitude of bodies "frozen" in the almighty refulgence. In the end, light and sound are dynamic, not the bodies.[36]

These complications in Wigman's perception of speech-movement relations inhibit the assertion that tensions between speech and movement objectify tensions between masculine and feminine attitudes toward the body. In *Totenmal*, speech signifies a kind of "deadness," but not Death, for Death here has a "demonic" male *body*, which *dances*.[37] The (male) dead themselves appear statically uniform, but Death is dynamic. The dance of Death is indeed of such power that it vanquishes the woman dancer, overshadows the dance of Life; yet it is the woman's dance that invites or provokes the appearance of Death. I therefore read the woman-demon dance as Wigman's effort to show that Death is a kind of male shadow of the feminine body: Dance does not "conquer" death but drives the dancer toward it, "heroically," as do the episodes and all the dances when they culminate in the completely static male and female bodies of the speech choirs, the absence of the woman dancer and the movement choirs, and the dynamic configuration of "bodiless" light accompanied by "bodiless" dead voices. If we can't see the woman, we can't "see" death; all we can see is the dead, that final condition in which language, speech, and voice are all coordinates of a triumphantly immobile, rather than invisible or repressed, body. Death is movement toward a "final" stasis.

Dance, then, is not a release from death—it is an exposure of it. Still attached to her eurhythmic heritage, Wigman perceives the phenomenon of "exposure" in relation to movement rather than in relation to the body. Movement makes us see what is otherwise hidden from us, namely the "view" that death is *in* life rather than opposed to it. For the feminine body, death is masculine insofar as it is demonic, a figure of desire, "another" body "exposed" by the dancer's effort to use her body to bring things to life.

The monumental complexity of *Totenmal* undermines the reduction of sexual difference to a conventional set of equations in which "femininity" signifies life, movement, silence, a spectaclized body, physicality of being; and "masculinity" signifies death, stasis, speech, a spectating subject, metaphysicality of being. Because for Wigman heightened bodily movement (dance) simultaneously signifies life and death, the dancing body is the locus of contradictory pressures and therefore has no "essence." These abstract contradictions "veil" the body to such a degree that the nudity of the body is, by implication, merely an illusion of "authentic" being. *Movement* is what makes the body naked, not flesh, because movement is what "reveals" the contradictory energies "hidden" within the body.

To call attention to the movement, Wigman "veils" bodies through the use of masks, hoods, capes, gownlike costumes, and startling contrasts between light and shadow. At the same time, she "strips" music of its power to "blind" or weaken visual perception; she relies entirely on percussion sounds. Movement is in tension with speech in the sense that speech belongs to a body that is "other" than the body that dances. Yet the meaning of the dancing body is not complete without the words spoken by these "other" bodies; speech itself is a sign of otherness in relation to movement. Dance, then, as movement toward death, exposes "other" bodies that remain "invisible" when perception focuses too narrowly on *the* body.

The lone dancing body of the woman motivates a multiplicity of "other'

bodies that are communal, male and female, speaking and moving, historical yet archetypal, dead yet alive, physical and metaphysical, choric yet
suffused with a profound sense of being alone, abandoned or "forgotten"
by either the dead or the living. All these "other" bodies are masked, for
the Other is in itself the mask of identities "hidden" within "the" body,
that body that is "most naked," the unmasked body of the lone woman
dancer. By keeping her face unmasked and by wrapping the rest of her body
in a medieval-like gown, Wigman effectively dramatized the perception of
the "real" or "authentic" body as an intensely death-conscious vortex of
tension between exposure and concealment of itself. The chief sign of lone-
ness is nakedness (of the face); the chief sign of otherness is speech; and
the chief sign for signifying the dissolution of difference between lone being
and the "others" is movement.

After *Totenmal,* Wigman continued to explore relations between movement and the voice (though not speech), but her work remained confined
to the choreography for operatic and choral works, beginning with the
production of Orff's *Carmina Burana* (1937) in 1943.[38] *Totenmal* was the
most complex effort to involve speech in dance during the Weimar Republic, yet its preservation of the idea that speech belongs to a body that is
"other" than the dancer's inhibited the piece from more significantly im-
pacting the German dance scene. Wigman's approach left intact the great
reluctance of modern dance to regard speech, the voice, as a part of the
body that "moved" or exposed a liberated relation between desire and
action. In modern dance, the modern body reached the limit of its modernity when it could not subvert the structures of sexual difference controling
the differentiation between the "speaking" spectator and the "speechless"
dancer. *Totenmal* challenged (1) the notion that an emancipated body is
"free" of language; and (2) the notion that sexual difference operates
through a tension between a speechless order of "feminine" being (dance)
and a speaking order of "masculine" being (dance theory).

But the challenge was too idiosyncratic to alter the course of modern
dance. Both men and women, within and without the modern dance world,
were too comfortable with overly reductive perceptions of sexual difference
to embrace a more complex and more demanding construction of language-
body relations. Wigman did not seek to "transcend" sexual difference
through dance; indeed, *Totenmal* implied that sexual difference drives
other social, cultural, historical, and economic differences that lead to war
and catastrophic "misunderstandings," especially when we see difference
as something "other" than the body instead of internal to it. She instead
detached sexual difference from the difference between the dancing body
and the voiced body. For her, sexual difference manifested itself through a
tension between movement and Death (masculine), and neither movement

nor Death were "beyond" the power of language to "contain" them, to make them internal to itself. But these ideas were too dark and too intricate for the time in which they appeared, and perhaps for our time as well, for we do not yet trust ourselves to speak anything worth saying while we are dancing.

Notes

1. A recent, typical example of this perspective is Inge Baxmann, "Stirring up Attitudes. Dance as Language and Utopia in the Roaring Twenties," *ballett international* 11 (February 1989):13–18, which claims that "the new dance was a criticism of spoken language as well as of the dominance of one type of rationalism [visual] characteristic of western cultures" (p. 14).

2. Perhaps the most comprehensive statement of Laban's notion of dance as a "grammar" or vocabulary of bodily movements is his *The Mastery of Movement* (London: Macdonald and Evans, 1984), a revision by his disciple, Lisa Ullmann, of his 1950 *The Mastery of Movement on the Stage*. The effort to describe the grammar itself is in Albrecht Knust, *Kinetographie Laban*, 2 vols. (London: Macdonald and Evans, 1979), which, however, describes techniques for notating (or "spelling" on paper) thousands of human movements (or "words") without discussing meanings attached to any particular combination of movements.

3. Grete Wiesenthal, *Der Aufstieg. Aus dem Leben einer Tänzerin* (Berlin: Rowohlt, 1919); Valeska Gert, *Mein Weg* (Leipzig: Devrient, 1931), a little book of only fifty-five pages. Olga Desmond's *Rhythmographik* (Leipzig: Breitkopf und Härtel, 1919), is scarcely a book, but a pamphlet of a handful of pages. A few major dancers of the 1920s did publish larger works after World War II; these include Grete Wiesenthal (a novel), Valeska Gert (two more memoirs), Niddy Impekoven (memoirs), Grete Palucca (dance technique), and Trudy Schoop (dance therapy).

4. Rudolf Laban perhaps had the strongest grasp of dance as a metaphor when, in *Die Welt des Tänzers* (Stuttgart: Seifert, 1920), esp. 156, he refers to the "dance of constellations" or the "dance of cultures." From this perspective, it is language rather than the body or objects that constructs dance.

5. Mary Wigman, *The Mary Wigman Book* (Middletown: Wesleyan University Press, 1984), p. 87.

6. Wiesenthal was close to Hugo von Hoffmannsthal and his circle; some literary works "inspired" her dances, but neither her dances nor her writings make any explicit connection between language and bodily movement. See Leonhard M. Fiedler and Martin Lang, *Grete Wiesenthal* (Salzburg and Wien: Residenz, 1985). Gert knew many writers in Berlin and was very busy as a film actress whose experience in dance allowed her to give very distinctive, memorable dramatic performances. But her cabaret parodies of *Ausdruckstanz* (and Wigman) appealed to a literary audience without really revising perceptions of relations between language and dance. See Frank-Manuel Peter, *Valeska Gert* (Berlin: Fröhlich und Kaufmann, 1985). Neither of these "literary" dancers saw dance as an "appropriation" of literary language.

7. Many of her manuscripts appear in facsimile fashion in Dietrich Steinbeck, *Mary Wigmans choreographisches Skizzenbuch* (Berlin: Hentrich, 1988).

8. Hedwig Müller, *Mary Wigman* (Berlin: Quadriga, 1986), pp. 174–75.

9. See, for example, in Müller, *Mary Wigman*, 173, a drawing of the New York skyline, devoid of any human figures, in which she prints at the top of the paper, *in the image*, the word, "NEW YORK," then writes at the bottom of the page, *out of the image*, the phrase (in German), "View of New York from the St. Moritz Hotel." It is not just the relation between title and image that is mysterious here, but the relation between the image and the movement of the hand that names the image it has created.

10. Evidence for the interjections comes largely from a documentary film (on video) about her: A. F. Snyder and Annette Macdonald, *Mary Wigman, When the Fire Dances between the Poles* (Pennington, New Jersey: Princeton Books, 1991 [1982]).

11. Wigman, *The Mary Wigman Book*, 87.

12. Ibid., 116.

13. Ibid., 73.

14. Ibid., 74.

15. Ibid., 75–76.

16. Ibid., 78.

17. Ibid., 79.

18. Ibid., 79.

19. See especially her remarks on *Dance of Death* (1926), which are such a complex tangle of ideas that it is understandable why she decided not to include them in her *Die Sprache des Tanzes* (Stuttgart: Battenberg, 1963); they do appear in *The Mary Wigman Book*, 97–104.

20. Müller, *Mary Wigman*, 186.

21. Wigman, *The Mary Wigman Book*, 116.

22. The "compositional" organization of the piece is as follows: Komposition I—Raum des Rufs (Hall of Calls); Komposition II—Interludium I; Komposition III—Raum der Vergessenheit (Hall of Forgetfulness); Komposition IV—Interludium II; Komposition V—Raum der Bannung (Hall of Expulsion); Komposition VI—Interludium III; Komposition VII—Raum des Gegenrufs (Hall of Echoes); Komposition VIII—Raum der Andacht (Hall of Devotion).

23. It is not clear from the text, Albert Talhoff, *Totenmal* (Stuttgart: Deutsche Verlags-Anstalt, 1930), what the total number of voices is for either the choirs or the groups within them. Moreover, some of the groups appear to consist of voices from more than one choir. The idea, apparently, is that neither the language nor the voices that speak it belong entirely to any one "community" or even body. It is a very complex perception of voice. However, Talhoff's text does not offer any great distinctions between voices spoken within it—all the language is in a swollen, "expressionistic" mode. Thus, the strongest differentiation between "voices" within the text is that between Talhoff's language and the quoted language of the actual letters written by the soldiers who died.

24. The "figures" include: Tanz- und Spielfigur I and II; Sakralfigur; Sprech- und Gebärdenfigur (Speech and Gestural figure) I, II, III, IV, V; Agierende Sprechfigur (Moving Speaking figure) I and II; Dämon; Signalfigur I and II.

25. It is not clear to me from either the text or the documentation of the performance if these nonspeaking figures are ever part of the choirs or "communities." Wigman used numerous blackouts in transitioning from scene to scene.

26. Even the "real," dead soldiers bear generic identities, such as "One who fell at Verdun," "One who fell in Flanders." Yet despite this intense abstraction of

identity, Wigman's personality dominates the piece so completely that no one has attempted to stage it since the 1930 performances at the Munich Dance Congress. This situation contrasts greatly with the fate of Oskar Schlemmer's *Triadische Ballett* (1912–1929), which features an even more radical abstraction of human identities—bodies as pure, abstract, virtually robotic forms. This work, which has no speech, has been revived repeatedly since Schlemmer first staged it in 1922. See Dirk Scheper, *Das Triadische Ballett und die Bauhausbühne* (Berlin: Akademie der Künste, 1988), pp. 33–58. For Schlemmer, abstraction is the image of modernity, which treats the body as a mysteriously mechanical phenomenon. But for Wigman, abstraction is "modern" to the extent that it is a sign of death; it is language that is central in bringing about the equation of abstraction with death, with an identity "other" than the body or "life."

27. Talhoff, *Totenmal*, 71.

28. According to the 1930 edition of the text, a Labanotated version was to appear in 1931, but I have not been able to verify such a publication. Large audiences saw the piece in Munich, and abundant criticisms of it in the press do not seem to have diminished public fascination with the work. English language translations of Talhoff's text appeared in the United States in 1930 and 1937. The idea of a Labanotated version of *Totenmal* was apparently in response to public interest in more precise information about the performance. Thus, the failure of this version to appear was more likely due to insurmountable difficulties in notating the piece, in clarifying relations between speech and movement.

29. For example, "First Figure (Gestalt): Every movement is a scream . . . Mask: mouth open, eyes without focus. . . . Second Figure: She walks as if behind a casket. . . . Mask: mouth paralyzed, eyes closed. . . . Third Figure: She walks transfigured. . . . Mask: Eyelids barely open; vacant look," and so on. These indications come from yet another version of the text, published in 1930, which contains somewhat more stage directions than my copy. Susan Manning quotes them in her reconstruction of the piece, "Ideology and Performance between Weimar and the Third Reich: The Case of *Totenmal*," *Theatre Journal* 41, no. 2 (May 1989):211–23, esp. 217.

30. Manning, "Ideology and Performance," presents an "ideological critique" (p. 211) of the production, which to her "seems a token of [modern dance's] stagnation" in Germany (p. 214), because its strange blend of pacifism and veneration for the war dead constitutes a "strategy which can be termed protofascist" (p. 220). But it is difficult to see how a work assumes "protofascist" qualities or "prepares" its audience for Nazism merely because it does not make sharp differences between left-wing and right-wing attitudes toward the war dead or because it does not present Nazism as a subject of critique, even at a time of Nazi ascendancy. I fail to see how a work is protofascist because it projects a bourgeois idea of apolitical meaning, with apolitical referring to the failure of the work to adopt a "correct" ideological position in regard to its social context. Nazis condemned *Totenmal* as vigorously as left-wingers, and one can even suggest that the complex ambiguities of the work polarized its audience to a greater degree than any objectification of the polarization in the performance. Far from being a sign of "stagnation" in German modern dance, *Totenmal* represents a spirit of adventure that had suddenly disappeared as economic hard times set in and multitudes of modern dancers struggled for professional survival by seeking conciliation with ballet, conventional eurhythmics, or *Freikörperkultur*. See Horst Koegler, "Tanz in den Abgrund—Berliner Ballett um 1930," in *Theater in Deutschland 1928–1938*, ed. Wolfgang Haus (Berlin: SFB-Werkstatthefte, 1981), pp. 23–35.

31. It is not, however, a Schoenbergian or Bergian *Sprechstimme,* which operates within an intricate, notated system for determining the sound of the voice. Wigman and her collaborators developed an improvised (uninscribed) method for creating this "strange" voice.

32. Indeed, it is striking that, in a piece so obsessed with death, moments of silence or even quietude are absent. Both Wigman and Talhoff thought of death as having a very "large," unmelodic voice. Bodies and voices "scream" throughout the work.

33. Other important collaborators included Adolphe Linnebach, a pioneer in the development of theatrical projection systems, and Karl Vogt, a well-known choirmaster.

34. *Totenmal* is not a text that one "interprets" through performance; rather, it is a performance of several concurrent or "parallel" texts, which are the result of a collaborative authorship, as the subtitle indicates: "dramatisch-chorische Vision für Wort Tanz Licht." But obviously Wigman made the whole thing happen; without writing anything, she became the dominant author within the collaboration.

35. Talhoff, *Totenmal,* 48.

36. Actually, the stage directions indicate that "the entire space swings now in rhythm to the bells, burns in the victorious glow of the light altar." But an eyewitness to the performance, quoted in Manning, "Ideology and Performance," claims that the "mourners stood straight with their arms held high in a token of victory and belief" (p. 220). At any rate, light and sound project a greater sense of power than any movement of bodies.

37. The "body" of language inhabits and "deadens" many human bodies, but death itself apparently has *one* body. The dance of this (male) body adopts a highly measured dynamic. When in Komposition V the demon appears, the stage directions describe his movements with considerable, if somewhat contradictory, precision: "In a powerful movement the demon suddenly throws himself between the two forms [Tanz- und Spiel Figuren I and II] and stands there motionless, threateningly. Each movement that he gives is short, barely visible, and yet loaded with surprising power. He is law. In vain, Tanz- und Spiel Figur I [Wigman] attempts to vanquish him. The first sign of the demon deprives her of strength . . ." (p. 33). At the end of this Komposition, after much thunder from the Speech-Orchestral Choir, the demon slowly and "strangely" begins to move. "Crawling, laden with entirely animal, elementary strength," Tanz- und Spielfigur I repeats "movements" and "signs" given her by the demon, but these repetitions render her powerless and push her up the ramp, "where she collapses and falls into the abyss. The demon is without gesture, without gaze. Only a terrible grin pulses from his mask. Darkness" (p. 36). The danced signification of death's power therefore emerges through slow, simple movements given tremendous weight, not only through mask and costume, but through their "crawling" repetition by another dancer. Death appears "suddenly" but does not move quickly; power belongs to that body that is not in a hurry yet changes other bodies all of a sudden.

38. Prior to *Totenmal,* Wigman had done choreography for productions of *A Midsummer Night's Dream* (Dresden, 1922) and Pfitzner's opera *Die Rose von Liebesgarten* (Hannover, 1921). But, of course, in both these productions, dancing was an interlude and did not attempt to "appropriate" language or the voice. Of the five vocally significant productions she staged between 1943 and 1958, two were scenic cantatas by Orff, two were operas by Gluck, and one was an oratorio by Händel. It seems, then, that she was not entirely sure which "other" genre was best for further exploration of relations between speech and movement.

4. Voicing Experience

ELAINE SAVORY FIDO

Freeing Up: Politics, Gender, and Theatrical Form in the Anglophone Caribbean

Many of my calypsoes were written from stories that women themselves told me. I try to write about the sufferings of women as much as I can. When I first started out it was the women who criticised me most. Now look how time change eh. Women's clubs and so invite me to speak. When my calypsoes don't make a hit it is as if I am lettin them down.
CALYPSO ROSE, first female calypso National Monarch of Trinidad and Tobago[1]

❦ To discuss gender and performance in the anglophone Caribbean requires first that the context in which the performance takes place is understood.[2] Performance here is not only the play, which is a relatively confined form of theatrical work that is limited in audience. Performance in general includes the whole range of Caribbean orature: verbal and musical forms such as calypso, reggae and dub, and dance, as well as less formal but nevertheless recognizably theatrical forms such as the sermon, public political meetings, and rituals and festivals (most importantly, Carnival). Performance forms, then, have been developed as fundamental aspects of the political expression of Caribbean peoples.

The Caribbean is a theatrical culture. It has often been noted that theatricality permeates modes of social interchange in Caribbean societies. People meeting at the bus stand, at the stan'pipe (communal water tap), in the rum shop, at the cricket match, at the market, at the schoolyard, at the local festivals engage in conversations, tell stories, and express opinions in modes that draw on old traditions of telling and demonstrating, consciously or unconsciously. This continuum of theatricality, from informal performance on the street to formal, structured dramas on the middle-class theatre stage provides a tremendous variety of options to the dramatist or performer.

To speak of gender issues in performance is thus to speak of a newly conscious strand of political life developed through aesthetic channels. The growth of the women's movement in the anglophone Caribbean has brought more opportunities for women to be involved in performance arts, in more central ways and ways more sensitive to women's issues, although this development is still limited and unevenly distributed. As Derek Walcott, the justly celebrated West Indian dramatist and poet, has said, there is a long step between the theatrical and the theatre, and that step, successfully made, depends upon the theatrically talented being able to find the creative space in which to develop their work. For the female dramatist in the colonial and newly postcolonial Caribbean, such space is being won with difficulty.

It is the contention of this paper that gender is impossible to separate from race and class in the Caribbean context, and that the area's performance forms are mainly responsive to a popular culture that is hardly at all progressive in terms of gender, with a few notable exceptions. Nevertheless, these exceptions and the development of a middle-class, fairly intellectual experimental theatre dealing with women's issues contribute to the establishment of a freer environment for the presentation of gender issues. They also continue the consciousness-raising process that the women's movement has been steadily developing for the past two decades.

Caribbean women have, of course, always been involved in performance in informal and relatively unstructured ways, like telling stories or teaching Biblical texts to children within the household. They have also participated in more ritualized ways in cults, rituals, church services, and festivals within the boundaries of various traditional ethnic and class expectations as to the proper role of women.[3] Women's influence on the development of the modern Caribbean is central, and there are many stories of unusual female lives, such as that of Nanny, the famous Maroon heroine of Jamaica.[4] This influence has been pervasive despite their relatively limited access to direct national political power.

No history of an art form in the Caribbean can ignore the shaping force of the major social experiences of the region: the colonization of the islands by succeeding waves of Europeans who displaced or killed the native Amerindians; the importation of Africans as slaves to work the sugar plantations and, later on, of Indians as indentured laborers; the arrival of small, generally mercantile communities of Chinese, Jewish, Lebanese, and Syrian peoples; the struggles for independence from colonial government; the development of local forms of socialism; the as yet unfinished struggle for economic power on the part of the African majority.[5] All forms of structured performance have taken their places within this context. The history of women's involvement in theatrical performance in the region is thus intertwined with the history of the fight for autonomy, equality, and opportunity for disadvantaged Caribbean people, most especially the African majority, and the transformation of English into Creole.

Feminism in the anglophone Caribbean is a complex interaction of gender, racial, and class issues that is necessarily centered in attempts to assist the development of poor women, especially the very large number of mothers who are heads of households. Although the region suffers from a lack of educated women in positions of direct power and influence[6]—an issue the feminist movement is starting to address[7]—nothing is more urgent than alleviating the "feminization" of poverty, resolving the difficulties faced by the large number of women who are raising children alone and without skills to protect them in the workplace. As Peggy Antrobus, one of the most important voices in Caribbean feminism, and Lorna Gordon put it: "The life of the low-income Caribbean woman is a constant struggle for survival—a feminist struggle, although the term is never used because it is not part of the vocabulary."[8]

Certain important differences between feminism in the Caribbean and in, say, the United States need to be noted because they so greatly influence the participation of women in theatrical performance. Seventy-five percent of all Caribbean women are mothers (having an average of 4.5 children), and motherhood is still viewed as a most important role for women by both women and men. Many women begin childbearing at a very young age, and many older women assist in the rearing of children not their own (grandmothers, aunts, friends of the family). Caribbean society is still very conservative regarding sexual roles and preferences. Lesbian and gay people tend to stay underground, and there is little overt expression of their experience of Caribbean society or their own considerable cultural contribution. Additionally, the very complex ethnic diversity within the Caribbean makes many generalizations difficult to sustain for all circumstances.[9] For example, Indo-Caribbean women, both Hindu and Moslem, have until recently been little known outside their immediate family circle and community. Although there are a number of leading radical Indo-Caribbean feminist women active now in the region,[10] there is still relatively little Indo-Caribbean female presence in many spheres of public life, including the arts.

The term gender is used here to signify a viable and separate cultural identity, though no woman's culture exists entirely outside dialogue with the corresponding male culture of a particular place, economic condition, and time. Within Caribbean society, gender relations within the wider cultural context are to a greater or lesser extent characterized by alienation or ambivalence. Pat Ellis, in speaking of male-female relationships in the region, explores the latter:

On the one hand girls are taught from an early age strategies to ensure their survival and that of their families whether a male is present or not. This creates a sense of independence—hence the image of the strong Caribbean woman who can cope with anything. At the same time they are also taught that it is not only desirable, but important, to have a male partner; that in the male-female relationship the man is dominant and that the woman is not free to do as she wishes, but must defer to her mate.[11]

Sexism is still very prevalent in the Caribbean, despite a recently strong and resourceful women's movement and the establishment by governments of policies and departments designed to define and protect women's rights. Gender tensions still arise from women's sense of their economic and political powerlessness, as well as from male resentment at perceived excesses of domestic power, which characterize, to their way of thinking, the women who raised them, most often as single parents.

In such a cultural context, it is not surprising that gender-focused performance has arrived only very recently as the result of the consciousness-raising effect of the women's movement, to which, of course, this kind of theatre, in turn, contributes. The involvement of women in theatrical performance, as singers, actors, dancers, oral poets, calypsonians, continues to be inhibited greatly by two factors: the difficulty of earning a living or even establishing a career as a professional theatre person in the Caribbean,[12] and the degree to which women are centrally involved in child-rearing during most of their adult lives. Popular plays in the Caribbean, performed both in theatres and on television, still often portray scenes that are very much enjoyed by both men and women but that serve only to deepen the stereotyping of the Caribbean woman. Such scenes include public physical fights between women or portray the woman as a slatternly shrew.

Caribbean theatre and drama, as has already been suggested, reflect a historical experience, itself formative of Caribbean culture. Whereas many festival and ritual forms, most often African in origin and sometimes giving powerful roles to women,[13] survived and changed as a result of their context (as when the African kalinda drums were silenced by the colonial authorities in Trinidad and steel-pan was born from discarded oil drums translated into instruments), plays put on in theatre buildings have often shown a strong colonial character even up to now. To this day, the Caribbean has a politically radical, theatrically experimental tradition of performance that began outside the theatre building in the culture of the poor when theatres were virtually class and race segregated. The area also maintains a politically inert tradition of reproducing foreign or local plays. Some of these are commercially successful, well-crafted farces, which, being set in foreign cultures, offer an escapist appeal.[14]

There is very little possibility that an actor, director, or playwright who lives and works in the Caribbean can become a full professional in the sense of obtaining training and earning a living through theatrical work. Government subsidies for the arts are small and uncertain and are often granted for particular occasions as opposed to being sustained over a period of time, although there are exceptions. The pre-eminence of Jamaican theatre in recent years was largely due to the establishment of government-supported schools for the arts. The survival of small, self-supporting theatre companies is usually only possible because few members of the company are paid or paid reasonably fairly for their work, and because the company only performs serious works in between commercially successful productions, which must have a wide appeal. However, feminist productions have proved to be well supported by the general public, though in general actors and theatrical workers who produce them are forced to remain amateur, that is, unpaid. Given these considerations, as well as the limitations on evening work that often control the lives of single mothers in the region and the fact that women's involvement in theatre and public festival (such as Carnival) was frowned upon until relatively recently, it is obvious why only a few Caribbean women have been able to sustain a committed involvement in theatre over the years.[15]

What must be remembered, however, is that the colonial period, with all of its gender, race, and class divisions and restrictions, ended not much more than two decades ago. Both the women's movement and the movement to effect cultural and political decolonization were stimulated by the civil rights movement in the United States and by the general climate of the 1960s. A few women were part of the first generation of West Indian writers, coinciding with the anticolonial movement towards independence. Cicely Waite-Smith wrote formal plays at the end of the colonial period. Her play, *The Impossible Situation* (1966)[16] presents two women, one light-skinned and middle-class and the other her dark-skinned cook, and centers on the inevitable intersection of gender, race, and class in a Caribbean context. But women working as writers or directors have been relatively rare.[17]

Until recently, male dramatists were not concerned in any serious way with the role and image of woman, since their societies were not concerned with such questions. The best-known West Indian dramatist, Derek Walcott, has rarely provided an actress with a central, satisfying role, more often celebrating or examining the male cultural experience in the Caribbean as if it could stand for the whole. The more recent work of writers such as Earl Lovelace and Rawle Gibbons[18] has more often incorporated women however.

Lovelace's *Jestina's Calypso* (1984) portrays an extremely plain, economically independent woman who writes to a man she has never met, a "pen-pal" living in America, sending a picture of her attractive friend Laura instead of her own image. The play opens as the man is about to arrive on his first visit. By interweaving the stories of three women, Jestina, Laura, and Prettypig, Lovelace explores the theme of the meaning of female beauty in Trinidadian society. Laura, for example, expresses to Jestina the burden of being beautiful: "I have envied you the freedom to be, to be a failure, to be without talent or charm or grace, to be vulgar and ignorant, . . . [t]he freedom you had to go out into the real world and move and dance and feel hurt."[19] Given the usual stereotypical and misogynistic portrayals of women in comic drama in the Caribbean, the women in *Jestina's Calypso* are remarkably fresh and alive. Jestina's last speech captures the exuberant irreverence of Caribbean street talk while confronting prevailing macho attitudes to women: "Watch me and laugh. Laugh. I am the ugly duckling, the swan, the queen, who only a prince could kiss and turn into a princess. But they ain't the man yet, with the love yet, and the courage and the beauty to get me. So kiss my arse."[20]

But the play is still contained within the relatively conventional world of gender relations that characterizes the Caribbean. Sexuality is strictly conceptualized as between man and woman, for example, and a woman's single status is a necessary evil caused by the failure of the search for male love. Caribbean feminism has begun to tackle homophobia and the odd juxtaposition of beliefs in "respectability" and permanent male-female bonds, despite the number of female single parents; but Caribbean cultural identity is still often traditional and relatively conservative. The women's movement has also had to deal with economic crisis, that is, the conditions in which the majority of women live and work. An overly simplistic radical feminism is often very insensitive to the context of Caribbean women's lives. For example, though religion frequently confines women, for many poor Caribbean women, the social contact it brings provides a much-needed support and relief from stress. As Caribbean societies move further from the colonial period, all aspects of freeing culture from repressive elements are revealed as deeply interrelated and sometimes self-contradictory.

Rawle Gibbons's recent *I, Lawah*[21] explores a historical moment in Trinidad in the late nineteenth century. It relates a story of a group of jamettes[22] and their fight to keep their own cultural expression alive through Carnival forms in the face of colonial repression. The central motif of the work, which is not so much a play as a piece of Carnival theatre,[23] is the revitalization of the community through women, one a French Creole with a love of dancing and of Afro-Caribbean culture, and one a brilliant dancer who works as a domestic servant in the French Creole household. Again, then, race, gender, and class intersect. Probably the most unusual aspect of the work is the way in which Gibbons presents the white Creole girl as a self-immolating sacrifice, whose death rekindles a desperately needed energy in Sophie Bella so that she can revitalize the jamettes and revive their sense of their own identity.

Women have been importantly and consistently involved in the decolonization of anglophone Caribbean theatre, even when this effort was not intentionally feminist, not specifically focused on women's issues. An early pioneer of oral performance, Louise Bennett (Mis' Lou)[24] is a remarkable actress and writer of Jamaican Creole poems, which she performs alone. Born in 1919 and a writer from her youth, she has become an institution in Jamaica. It was her observations of the community in which she grew up that gave her her material and her determination to create a place for the often rejected or despised "dialect."[25] She describes how she came to make her very first poem:

When I was on the tram that day, there were no seats in front, so I decided to go in the back. Well I was fourteen and portly and was dressed up so I didn't look like a fourteen year old. So one woman said to another woman,
   "Pread out yourself, one dress a woman a come. Pread out."
   And me dear everybody start pread dem apron all over de seat dem. And I wrote the first set on this, when I went home I wrote it. The next day I tried it out in school and it sweet them.[26]

What is important here is the linkage between women's culture and the beginnings of Mis' Lou's writings. Although her work has ranged over many different social issues and is often simply wittily entertaining, she has produced a good deal of affirmative poetry about women. Most importantly, her very presence as a major figure in Caribbean theatre has centralized a positive image of woman, as well as privileged her love of the speech of the ordinary person in Jamaican society. Her first collection of poems, *Jamaica Labrish,* utilizes the idea of gossip or women's talk in the title. Louise Bennett's commitment to her art and her immense achievement in establishing "dialect" poetry as successful public performance are decolonizing developments in themselves.

Perhaps the most startling aspect of the development of postcolonial Caribbean art has been that the most ordinary and normal aspects of daily life for the majority of the population became radical form when adopted by artists because of the colonial opposition to indigenous, and especially African, culture. Beryl McBurnie, leading practitioner of dance in Trinidad for many years, remarks: "Dance is my form of nationalism. They say it's politics. They frighten for Beryl";[27] and again, "A lot of people thought it was politics, but it was pride."[28] She thought that a particular rhythm can underlie a whole culture: "The basic rhythm of our culture is syncopated, a calypso rhythm and if you are building a culture you must come back to the ritual."[29]

It was through Beryl McBurnie that folk dance, just as neglected as the "dialect" that Louise Bennett restored to the status of an important public treasure in Jamaica through her work, became once more respected and honored in Trinidad. As with Louise Bennett, McBurnie was, in actuality, restoring pride in the culture of African-Caribbean people. Just as importantly, she and Bennett were drawing on the particular experience of women as a major part of that culture.

One of the cornerstones of the Jamaican effort to establish local theatre after the 1930s was the Jamaican pantomime begun in 1941 by Greta Fowler, a form that became one of the foundations of the Jamaican Little Theatre Movement. A number of women have been significantly involved with the composition and/or direction of pantomimes since then, including the novelist Sylvia Wynter,[30] theatre activist Marina Maxwell (who experimented with a form called "Yard Theatre," an informal attempt to reflect popular cultural/political images), and, recently, the witty and incisive writer/director Barbara Gloudon.

Pantomime, like the term musical, has a more politically significant meaning in the Caribbean than in Europe or America. Both Caribbean forms seek to reinforce "folk" material—topical issues, songs, dancing, music, and clever word-play—bringing together different moods and tones and appealing strongly to the enjoyment of oratory that is so strong in the Caribbean. Pantomime can be seen as both a popular entertainment and an outlet for political and satirical comment, similar to the highly developed social commentaries of the calypso. In Barbados, Daphne Joseph-Hackett[31] was a pioneer of a pantomime show called "Bimshire." Her work in developing enthusiasm for indigenous art forms on the island was similar to that of the Little Theatre Movement in Jamaica. On both islands, there needed to be a movement away from colonial influences and towards more participation in staged performances by the African-Caribbean community.

It is the growth and strength of the women's movement in the Caribbean, however, that has done the most to bring gender issues into theatrical work. The relation between form and content is crucial in any attempt to shape a theatre that encourages decolonization. Just as earlier important practitioners of experimental theatre and drama in the Caribbean often sought out better forms by examining those traditions that were still genuine (as opposed to spurious versions of tradition performed for tourists, for example), so there has been an effort within politically conscious women's theatre to rediscover those aspects of old custom that particularly reflect women's roles and participation in society. This search is still too occasional and limited, but certain aspects of form have become appropriate for gender-based work.

This rediscovery of form has happened in a number of ways. The general encouragement that the movement has brought to women to try new areas of achievement has opened up previously male preserves, such as the calypso, to women. Not all the women who sing calypso are feminist, and obviously not all are equally skilled in composing witty, clever lyrics with social significance as well as possessing a good stage presence and vocal capacity to deliver the songs. But there have already been some remarkable calypsoes, such as Singing Francine's 1979 "Run Away," advising women to leave violent men. It remains true, however, that women are still among the staunchest supporters of sexist calypsoes. As Carol Boyce Davies comments:

Themes pertaining to male ego maintenance, sexual prowess and conquest have been present throughout the calypso's history. . . . Throughout the history of the calypso (a) sexual war was waged in an ongoing attempt to put the independent Caribbean female in her place.[32]

Gordon Rohlehr, whose recent excellent study of pre-independence calypso has done much to retrieve the history of the form, remarks that the relation between men and women imaged in calypso was a reflection of gender tensions in the society itself. Men felt a "sense of Ego" perpetually under attack from other men and from women, "the most extreme example of the Other."[33] Nevertheless, women were present in the tradition of early calypso or kaiso, but as colonial values penetrated the Caribbean, they disappeared as singers until relatively recently. Calypso Rose, quoted at the beginning of this paper, was a pioneer in contemporary times and had to face a great deal of opposition from her family when she decided to become a professional calypsonian.

Another avenue of development has been the growth of greater social consciousness about women, which the women's movement has spread to entire societies. The effect of this awareness has been to make women's issues topical and politically important, despite the constant undertow of entrenched sexism. Theatre and drama can thus become constructively controversial by including women's issues in their work or by choosing from among classic Caribbean playscripts those emphasizing the role and meaning of woman in society.

Some male writers and directors have consequently become interested in working more creatively with women's theatre,[34] but the development has not yet led to the appearance of many women playwrights. Where women are working in the theatre to create plays, they seem to be more interested in improvisation as a way of writing as a group rather than in writing a script as a single author. There have, however, been some examples of formal plays that have dealt with what are still largely perceived of as women's issues, such as rape, abortion, motherhood.[35] Much of this writing is polemical and intends to introduce an issue as controversially as possible while retaining a relatively familiar, formal structure for the play.

This new consciousness has also been extended by the use of various kinds of theatre and drama. Government departments that must disseminate information about women and work towards change—for example, in reducing rape and minimizing its traumatic effects on women—have turned towards the idea of improvisational theatre and documentary film

as a medium for reaching a wide audience. The research necessary to bolster such work is just becoming available, for the University of the West
Indies has launched a women's studies research and teaching program.[36]
Conferences on women's affairs always include a cultural event or two,
most often involving poetry readings[37] or sometimes calypsoes. In the small
communities of Caribbean islands, news travels fast, and the women's
movement has the advantage there of being able to sustain a visibility that
would be harder to achieve in a large country.

There has been a serious attempt to create a new kind of theatrical form,
a women's theatre, built out of group work and reflecting a collective, focused female consciousness. This very important collective, called Sistren
and established in Jamaica, has rightly gained international attention for
the radical ways in which it has documented the lives of working-class
women in Jamaica. The project was begun, in 1977, when a trained theatre
professional, Honor Ford-Smith, came together with thirteen working-
class women employed as street cleaners. Ford-Smith, a white, middle-class
Jamaican, has made it clear that she is aware of the class difference between
herself and the women who formed Sistren's first acting company. There
is also, of course, a difference in race. Nevertheless, her role in Sistren has
not been to explore explicitly that difference and to discover how to cross
it, but to become the group's first, though not only, director, the script-
writer of the improvised scenes that came out of group work, and the editor
of the excellent collection of testimonies by Sistren women, *Lionheart Gal*
(1986).[38] She has, over time, articulated how the extraordinary company
came into being and what aims and principles guided the creation of their
productions. Sistren, established in 1977, developed out of the desire of
the women to express as story their consciousness of themselves as triply
exploited (via gender, race, and class). One woman, Ford-Smith tells, described working in a factory for a very small wage and the beginnings of
industrial action for better conditions and pay. This attempt to unionize
was discouraged by the factory. The woman got no maternity leave when
she had a baby. From this kind of raw material, the theatrical performance
is gradually developed.

The method was to draw out stories from the women, to shape them by
using group exercises, then to make them into a production. Sometimes
the result would be a major production, like the successful *Bellywoman
Bangarang* (1978),[39] produced in a commercial theatre—the Barn Theatre
in Kingston. This work, made up of dramatic verbal scenes interspersed
with game-playing, masking, and mime, richly conveys the stress, joy, vulnerability, and contradictions of poor African-Jamaican women. Teenage
pregnancy and relations between mother and daughter, between young
girls, and between young girls and young men provide the context within

which the traumas of poverty, birthing, and parenthood are mingled with religious ritual and survivals of African custom. It is a powerful work and, at the time it was created, was an original and new kind of approach to the lives of poor, urban, working-class black women. It empowered them to make their own stories and to develop their own relation with a world that oppressed them. When Sistren began its work, its vision was unusual and very important, nothing less than the ending of a silencing of a huge group of women whom the actresses represented. The language of the work is the Creole that the women speak, itself decolonizing and authentic, thus having an immediacy that frequently fails to emerge from middle-class versions of working-class speech. Here, a young girl complains about the treatment her boyfriend has given her since she got pregnant:

How clothes fe de baby and myself a buy and wid out me nuh get some arguement me nah move from de gate tonight. Sey what? Me fe go put on de government clothes? What a facety dutty crab louse boy. If anybody did tell me you'd a do me dis me'd a tell dem say a lie. When you used to come a me gate blow prap prap, me tidy sweet no bitch an gone een your motor car. Anything me want fe eat and drink, dat deh time me get it. Now not even de dust offa de motor car me can't see.[40]

Sistren sometimes gives workshops designed for participatory involvement by a particular group of women, urban or rural, and to further popular education. The workshops themselves then provide further raw material for reworking into theatre, which in turn becomes a vehicle for consciousness-raising in the wider society. Despite the fact that Ford-Smith has stated that methods are not as important as political consciousness in shaping work,[41] she has contributed greatly to the shaping force of women's forms in theatre.

In addition to the theatrical work of the group, Sistren also became a center for craftwork. The collective was interested in pooling women's resources to help each other. Through its public voice—the performance—the group became a very important symbol of the imagination and creativity of working-class, formally uneducated women. Sistren is therefore the most advanced experiment in gender-oriented theatre with a political agenda to come out of the anglophone Caribbean.

But there have been other, less radical attempts to explore feminist visions of society. Barbados theatre witnessed a phase of feminist productions, from American writer Ntozake Shange's successful choreopoem *for colored girls . . .* (1982)[42] to the improvisation-based *Lights* (1985 and 1986),[43] but has had no sustained development of a womens' vision of theatre, and there is no female company existing there. *Lights*, which was based on a combination of improvisations and adaptations of excerpts from women's writing from the Caribbean and elsewhere, suffered from a lack of a strong writer to pull the production into a coherent whole. It skipped lightly over too many major themes, each worthy of a production in itself: mothers and daughters, female maturation, menstruation, giving birth, rape, marital violence, race, class, lesbianism or love between women, ageing. Also, the male director, trying to respond to women's issues, created a first set that was a huge womb enclosing the stage—an image which offended some women as being too close to the cliché of Woman as mother, which so strongly endures in the Caribbean.

This kind of production, however, based as it was on six months of research both into the conditions of women in Barbados and into literary texts, is really a form of information-gathering as well as a theatrical experiment. The director, Earl Warner, stated that the work was not a play, and clearly many of the most innovative theatrical developments in the Caribbean recently have stepped around the colonial form of the play as much as possible. Instead they have chosen to advance an innovative, local form of performance through improvisation and verbal play, music, dance, mime, and song.

More conventional in terms of form, the Trinidadian play *Desiree*[44] by Norman dePalm was produced in 1985 in Barbados and was a one-woman performance, portraying the conflicts of a young mother. Such productions have sought to extend and consolidate awareness of women's issues and have had, therefore, a direct political intention, but their contribution has also been important in terms of experimental aspects of performance style and shape. This work was noteworthy because it attempted to undermine the myth of the happy, all-resourceful Caribbean mother by showing maternal violence and the deprivations of a young woman's life who is too soon a mother. This characterization might seem a very limited questioning of women's options, but, within the conventions of contemporary Caribbean theatre, the play aroused a good deal of interest, largely because it unusually featured a single actress.[45]

As is clear from the foregoing account, women's theatre in the anglophone Caribbean is just beginning to develop a vocabulary and style of its own. Clearly, in the absence of female playwrights, there will continue to be a focus on collective creation of theatrical works that reflect women's experience without seeking to explore character particularly. Character becomes a strategy for the actress to interpret a facet of a collective vision, and it is that vision that lies at the center of the work, as opposed to the traditions of formal Western plays. This kind of theatre joins very easily with the revitalization of communal forms such as Carnival, religious ceremony, possession, masking, and children's games, thus extending the prevailing experimental theatrical movement in the Caribbean and uniting secular, dramatic work with traditional theatrical forms.

Despite the existence of a strong male tradition of play-writing in the region, there is no reason to suppose that women will follow that route. Perhaps our women's theatre tradition will become a true alternative, reflecting the communality and complexity of Caribbean women's roles and both sharing and reinforcing women's community. We have yet to see.

But as the decolonization process in theatre proceeds and creative opportunities become more various, it is likely that there will be a number of different kinds of theatrical work that is gender-focused in the region. One development, for example, that is long overdue is to unify the Caribbean culturally, so that to speak of separated linguistic zones (i.e. anglophone, francophone, hispanic) would no longer make sense. The feminist theatres of the region would then be able to cross-fertilize each other more freely than they can now. What seems certain, however, is that gender-based theatre is going to be a major experimental wing of Caribbean theatre, continuing its role as part of a radical freeing of consciousness in the region.

What must be remembered is that the region has something very important to offer the world and that feminism forged in the Caribbean may not be the same as that made of other cultural confluences. Certainly, the challenge of resolving inequalities based not only on gender but on race and class prevents any simplistic oppositional positioning of female and male, and the tremendous ethnic complexity of the region prevents simplicities about racial separatisms as much as it warns of over-idealizing visions of integration. Although there must be a greater freedom for differing sexual preferences, expressed as cultural identity and contribution, to become visible within Caribbean theatre, this change, like other changes, has to come from within. Already, the term feminism itself has been reshaped within the region. Peggy Antrobus, in defining a feminist as anyone, woman or man, who perceives the oppression of women and works against it, is responding to the plain fact that the Caribbean must find ways towards unity to survive, as opposed to greater fragmentation. In this way, theatrical performance seeks to reflect Caribbean reality and not other cultural images of political radicalism. Thus, gender as a shaping principle of Caribbean theatre must take note of race and class as well as of the ever-present threat of Caribbean cultural autonomy being absorbed into cultural influences from economically powerful neighbors like the United States. The most significant experiments in gender-focused theatre in the Caribbean so far have drawn on the popular, folk forms of art, which have developed as a result of the historical experiences of the region and frequently were the result of intensely fought opposition to oppression.

Gender thus comes as a late but vital addition to the art forms of the region, representing a spirit of creative confrontation with denial, inequality, and prejudice. The possibility exists that greater interaction may occur in the future between the Caribbean communities of the United States, Britain, and Canada and the region itself. With more government or private funding available, much more women's theatre could be achieved. What is certain is that gender-focused theatre in the region is developing, despite all the difficulties, as a powerful aspect of the women's movement and of the decolonization process in the Caribbean, although it would be premature to predict or prescribe it in any heavy-handed manner.

Notes

1. Quoted in Nesha Haniff, *Blaze a Fire: Significant Contributions of Caribbean Women* (Toronto: Sister Vision Press, 1988), p. 66.

2. This paper deals only with the theatrical world of the anglophone Caribbean, which is not much in touch with the francophone and hispanic Caribbean, unfortunately.

3. The vexed question of what relation between tradition and modernity best facilitates the development of women, as well as the protection of Caribbean cultural identity, is central to defining a feminist's particular position within the politics of decolonization and of cultural sovereignty at this time. Caribbean women have always been both conservatives and radicals, the latter responsible for many important social changes.

Ethnic differences make differences in women's conceptions of progress and freedom for themselves. For example, black women in the Caribbean have always worked and, since the systematic undermining of the black family during slavery by plantocracy, have often been heads of households. They have thus had a good deal of domestic power but no economic power in the wider society, and they have had to deal with racism and the resentment of black men articulated as crude sexism. In the slavery period, they had to contend with the lust and arbitrary emotional attitudes of planters and overseers. In the Indian community, women have to deal with inherited traditions of Islamic or Hindu religious culture. They may wish to reject all of their inheritance or to work within their religious culture to free women from sexism, which is the result of temporal corruptions of the religion rather than the religion itself. The Indian woman is contained within a rather strict and protective family structure, which until recently effectively prevented her from having much of a public role in society as a whole. Caribbean feminism thus has to take account of racial and religious differences in shaping goals.

4. See, for example, Michelle Cliff's *Abeng* (Trumansburg, New York: The Crossing Press, 1984) for a feminist treatment of Nanny. The maroons, or communities of escaped slaves formed in the Caribbean, Latin America, and the United States, are particularly well known in Jamaica. See Richard Price, *Maroon Societies* (Baltimore and London: Johns Hopkins Press, 1979).

5. See Gordon Lewis, *The Growth of the Modern West Indies* (New York and London: Modern Reader Paperback, 1968); Franklin Knight and Colin Palmer, ed., *The Modern Caribbean* (Chapel Hill and London: University of Carolina Press, 1989); Peter Roberts, *West Indians and Their Language* (Cambridge: Cambridge University Press, 1988).

6. There have been some striking exceptions, such as the prime minister of Dominica, Eugenia Charles. A number of women have held ministerial or high gov-

ernmental office, such as Billie Miller in Barbados, Jeannie Thompson in the Bahamas, and Lucille Mathurin-Mair in Jamaica. But at every level of the professions, women are enormously in the minority at the higher levels of authority and complain often of sexual harassment and of invisible but powerful blocks to their advancement. Dame Nita Barrow, the first female governor-general of Barbados, came to world prominence as an administrator through predominantly female organizations and her original profession of nursing. Many of these women are single, are not mothers, or are divorced, reaffirming the fact that motherhood is the most likely detour and marriage another significant one in a woman's professional life during her vital years, and that these factors are especially operative in the Caribbean.

7. The term feminist is a difficult one in the Caribbean. Progressive organizations like the Caribbean Association for Feminist Research and Action (CAFRA) have adopted the term and defined it for their own context. Many Caribbean women associate it with white, northern, middle-class women, with whom they feel little natural affinity. Most importantly, adopting the term is seen as declaring a political activism on behalf of women but as referring the term always to Caribbean realities and situations. See the discussion on feminism and womanism in Carole Boyce Davies and Elaine Savory Fido, eds., *Out of the Kumbla: Caribbean Women and Literature* (Trenton, N.J.: Africa World Press, 1990).

8. Peggy Antrobus and Lorna Gordon, "The English-Speaking Caribbean: A Journey in the Making" in *Sisterhood Is Global*, ed. Robin Morgan (Harmondsworth: Penguin, 1985), p. 125.

9. Since the majority of the population is of Afro-Caribbean descent, many generalizations are based on Afro-Caribbean culture, but this culture in itself is complex since it varies depending on the admixtures (English, French, Dutch, Amerindian, Indian, etc.) that prevail in different territories. Of course, each island or territory has a cultural and linguistic identity of its own.

10. This activism is, of course, most evident in the two countries with a large Indo-Caribbean community, that is, Trinidad and Tobago and Guyana.

11. Pat Ellis, "Introduction," in *Women of the Caribbean*, ed. Pat Ellis (Kingston, Jamaica: Kingston Publishers, 1986), p. 8.

12. Caribbean women performers who live overseas are sometimes more easily able to establish themselves, as in the case of Jean "Binta" Breeze, who became known for her oral performances in Britain. Particularly excellent is her performance of "Riddym Ravings: The Mad Woman's Poem," included in *Voiceprint: An Anthology of Oral and Related Poetry from the Caribbean*, ed. Brown, Morris, and Rohlehr (Harlow: Longman, 1989). In the Caribbean, Lorna Goodison has established a reputation for fine readings of her own poems. See particularly, *Heartease* (London: New Beacon Books, 1988), especially if the poet can be heard reading it.

13. For example, in Etu, a Jamaican African ritual celebration of the dead, the participants are usually female. Women also play an important role in Haitian Voudon, as do female goddesses.

14. For example, the plays of the British writer Alan Ayckbourn are popular in Barbados.

15. Colonial mores have much to do with this. Carnival was originally a French Creole festival, then became the creative territory of ex-slaves who imbued it with their own African rituals and forms. It became, however, associated with low-class vulgarity (a colonial slur, for it was a source of rebellious attitudes and alternative cultural forms). Women were thought, by the colonial and colonized middle class,

to be immoral and low class to be involved in it. This attitude had the advantage of leaving Carnival a creative space in which new art forms could be developed without middle-class respectability interfering with them. When the middle class decided finally to involve itself in Carnival, many of the old traditions were abandoned, but have now been retrieved by serious theatre practitioners as important cultural expressions and excellent theatrical resources.

Similarly, the involvement of women in ritual has produced inspiration for modern theatrical performance. Cumina or Kumina, a Jamaican cult, membership of which is a matter of birth, is a strong link with African culture. The Kumina families are assumed to have kept a link with African religions. A Kumina Memorial dance has among the principals a "Kumina Queen" and a "Mother of the Cumina." The Kumina Queen dances for the ancestors and the recently dead being remembered in the ceremony. The Mother of the Cumina sings, dances, and is possessed during the ceremony. The outstanding contemporary Jamaican dancer and choreographer Rex Nettleford shaped one of his most recent works around the Kumina dance for his Jamaica National Dance Company, involving a real Kumina Queen who, as an elderly woman, displayed not only dancing ability but an ability to continue for a long while, all the time balancing a glass of water on her head. See, for a description of Kumina, George Eaton Simpson, *Religious Cults of the Caribbean* (Rio Pedras, Puerto Rico: University of Puerto Rico, 1980).

16. Cicely Waite-Smith, *The Impossible Situation* (Mona, Jamaica: University of the West Indies ExtraMural Department, 1966). Her best-known play is *Uncle Robert* (Mona, Jamaica: UWI ExtraMural Department, Caribbean Plays Series, 1967).

17. In the immediate postcolonial period, a number of women directors and writers were foreign-born, often Caucasian. The reasons for this are fairly clear. Foreign-born women usually have no family opposition against their involvement in theatre, beyond their husbands, if they are married. They may bring with them an intensely radical feminism and no inhibition about being involved in the theatre. Additionally, they are usually middle class and able to find the time and financial support to participate in theatre, sometimes as a result of not being able to work because they came to a Caribbean territory as wives of temporary residents and were not allowed to take paid jobs. If they had theatrical skills, therefore, they could find opportunity to use them. Their time of prominence, however, is probably over, as more and more women are becoming involved in feminism and in theatre, and the theatre itself is more and more reflective of local cultural nuances difficult for an outsider to reproduce.

18. Both of these writers come from Trinidad and Tobago, where the feminist movement is quite strong and visible. Also, Zeno Obi Constantine shaped a play in Trinidad for Indian schoolgirls on the subject of teenage motherhood: *The Ritual* (produced 1978). This play caused a great deal of controversy at the time and was banned from Trinidad and Tobago television. See Keith Noel, ed., *Caribbean Plays for Playing* (London: Heinemann, 1985), pp. 51–75.

19. Earl Lovelace, *Jestina's Calypso* (London: Heinemann, 1984), p. 21.

20. Ibid., 41.

21. Unpublished. See Elaine Savory Fido, "Finding a Truer Form: Rawle Gibbons' Carnival Play *I, Lawah*," *Theatre International* 13, no. 3 (1990):249–59.

22. "Jamettes," from the French "diametre" meaning outside, were inhabitants of poor housing areas or yards in urban areas first settled by freed slaves.

23. Carnival theatre is a prevalent, recent form of theatre in the Caribbean,

incorporating dance steps, music, and song drawn from Carnival traditions and the very form of Carnival itself as an episodic festival. Helen Camps and Rawle Gibbons in Trinidad and Earl Warner in Barbados have been most associated with this form.

24. See Louise Bennett, *Jamaica Labrish* (Kingston, Jamaica: Sangster's Bookstores, 1966).

25. "Dialect" is now an abandoned term. Creole is recognized as a continuum of language usage, ranging from the lightest to the heaviest, the former closest to international English (or French, Dutch, etc.). It is now recognized that Creole is a series of languages forged by a people from different linguistic origins, whereas dialect was regarded as a poor version of a metropolitan, colonial language. This shift in perspective is a major aspect of decolonization in the Caribbean.

26. Haniff, *Blaze a Fire,* 58.

27. Ibid., 84.

28. Ibid. The meaning of "frighten for" in this context is that McBurnie frightens the group termed "they."

29. Ibid., 82.

30. See Sylvia Wynter, *The Hills of Hebron* (Harlow: Longman, 1984). Wynter is also one of the most exciting of contemporary Caribbean intellectuals.

31. Joseph-Hackett was a pioneer of postcolonial theatre in Barbados and encouraged many young people to become involved in serious theatre. As a black woman, a teacher, and a theatrical innovator who began to be involved in plays when they were still mainly performed by expatriate British colonials, she became a role model for many women in theatre in Barbados, encouraging local forms and new ideas.

32. Carole Boyce Davies, "Woman Is a Nation: Woman in Caribbean Oral Literature," in *Out of the Kumbla,* 175, 179.

33. Gordon Rohlehr, *Calypso and Society in Pre-Independence Trinidad* (Port of Spain: Gordon Rohlehr, 1990), p. 276.

34. For example, Earl Warner (Barbados) and Rawle Gibbons (Trinidad).

35. Pat Cumper's play, *The Rapist* (produced 1978; as yet unpublished), was original in looking at reasons why a man might rape in the context of Caribbean social attitudes at the time (the man had been brutalized by his mother) but was conventional in form. She uses a skilled interplay of linguistic registers in the play, reflecting more and less middle-class Jamaican speech. She has recently been working with the Sistren group as a writer.

36. This field is developing in the three campus territories of Trinidad, Barbados, and Jamaica and has already produced a significant amount of research material on Caribbean women. The program is titled "Women and Development Studies" to emphasize the integral link between women's issues and those of the whole region as a disadvantaged economic community. The nature of development is crucially central to women's issues. For example, industrialization, or the exploitation of cheap, often female labor by foreign multinationals, is not a desirable aspect of Caribbean development.

37. Christine Craig, who is now known as a poet, *Quadrille for Tigers* (Sebastopol, CA: Mina Press, 1984), began her public career with a reading at a symposium on women and culture held in Barbados in 1981 as part of the Caribbean cultural festival (CARIFESTA). Rawle Gibbons's play *I, Lawah* was staged at the Commonwealth Institute in London as part of a Caribbean Writers Conference in late 1986, itself a part of the nationwide, British celebration of the Caribbean, Ca-

ribbean Focus. For that event, a special pan-Caribbean company was formed, but after the production in London and two performances in Barbados, it was disbanded for lack of funding.

38. Honor Ford-Smith, "Sistren-Women's Theatre—A Model for Consciousness-Raising," in *Journey in the Shaping,* ed. Margaret Hope, Report on the first Symposium on Women in Caribbean Culture, CARIFESTA, Barbados, 1981 (Bridgetown, Barbados: Women and Development Unit, n.d.), p. 58. See also Sistren, with Honor Ford-Smith, *Lionheart Gal* (London: Women's Press, 1986). See also, Honor Ford-Smith, "Sistren-Women's Theatre: A Model for Consciousness Raising," *Jamaica Journal* 19, no. 1 (February-April 1986):2–12; Honor Ford-Smith, "Sistren at Work," *Carib* 4 (1976):55ff.; Rhonda Cobham, "The Function of Ritual Framework in Sistren's *Bellywoman Bangarang,*" *Theatre International* 15, no. 3 (1987):239–49.

39. As yet unpublished, although an edition of Sistren's scripts, co-edited by Honor Ford-Smith and Rhonda Cobham, is forthcoming.

40. Unpublished playscript, p. 36.

41. See Elaine Savory Fido, "Finding a Way to Tell It: Methodology and Commitment in Theatre about Women in Barbados and Jamaica," in *Out of the Kumbla,* 331–44; also Elaine Savory Fido, "Radical Woman: Woman and Theatre in the Anglophone Caribbean," in *Critical Issues in West Indian Literature,* ed. Erika Smilowitz and Roberta Knowles (Parkersburg: Caribbean Books, 1984), pp. 33–45.

42. Ntozake Shange, *for colored girls who have considered suicide when the rainbow is enuf* (New York: Bantam Books, 1980). This choreopoem, written by an African-American poet, was adapted for performance in the Caribbean.

43. The full title of this production was *If You Wait Until the Lights Are Green, You'll Never Get into Town,* a quotation from a woman interviewed during the research process for the production. She was commenting on her feeling that women have to get on with their lives and not wait for times to change or things to get easier.

44. As yet unpublished.

45. One man was heard to comment before the play that no woman could hold an audience for a whole night alone.

MEGAN TERRY,
JO ANN SCHMIDMAN, AND
SORA KIMBERLAIN

Gender Is Attitude

❦ [*Editor's note*: The Omaha Magic Theatre (OMT) has been on the theatrical cutting edge in its home state of Nebraska and on the road nationally for over twenty years. Founded by Jo Ann Schmidman in 1968, the theatre has consistently declared its mission of opening "windows to new ways of perceiving and thinking, putting the audience in touch with contemporary themes of immediate personal relevance." The creative troika currently in charge is made up of Artistic Director Jo Ann Schmidman, Playwright-in-Residence Megan Terry (with the theatre since 1970), and Designer-in-Residence Sora Kimberlain (with the theatre since 1980). The artists of OMT do not work within any predefined framework of feminist thought; their productions do, however, deal with issues of gender both in subject matter and the use of cross-gender casting.

[In *Babes in the Bighouse* (1974), a piece that explored the mechanisms needed to cope with life in a woman's prison, the female inmates were portrayed by both men and women. *Goona Goona* (1979) exposed the problem of domestic violence within the context of a comic Punch-and-Judy show. *Sea of Forms* (1986), "a large-scale performance/sculpture event," was designed around the styrofoam works of sculptor William Farmer. It dealt with ways of taking responsibility for one's own life. *Headlights* (1989) celebrated the ability to read, write, and think through exploring the problem of illiteracy in America. *Body Leaks* (1990), OMT's most recent collaboration, takes self-censorship as its point of departure. In the following discussion, the artists at OMT reflect on the way in which these plays have touched on gender issues and offer experienced insight into the practice of cross-gender casting.]

MEGAN TERRY (MT):   Ever thought about gender in our work?
JO ANN SCHMIDMAN (JAS):   No. I don't think of what we do as playing "characters" of any type, either. The voices inside, the different personalities a performer projects are what's essential. What I'm interested in doing with the experiences I've had, the interesting people I've seen, or

essences I've absorbed of my grandmother, my grandfather, or someone I respect, what I want to do as a performer is to be able to pull out and project these essences or experiences at will, in either performing or writing.

MT: When you play on stage . . . ?

JAS: When you play on stage—those selves, those personalities come out through the rhythms they speak and the attitudes they project, but they don't have to be always female just because we happen to be women.

MT: For instance, in the 270 Foot Woman speech, the dickhead speech in *Body Leaks,** are you gender specific males or females? Who are you? How do you think of yourself, or how do you think of the images you play?

JAS: Not necessarily as women, right?

SORA KIMBERLAIN (SK):   I'd never thought about it.

MT: They're such wonderful spirits, but they're not like everyday women or everyday men or anyone that we have met before; but the audience cues into them right away and responds to them so well.

JAS: They're lookers inside; they could be either male or female.

MT: And they're gleeful spirits, they're full of fun.

JAS: But they're essentially on a journey; they're questioning each other. They're different parts of the one, and they're certainly not exceptional at all.

SK: They're one person, one attitude.

JAS: They wear the same glasses.

MT: There's that word attitude.

JAS: They get insights from constantly looking at the garbage of the world.

MT: When I have to play something that is not close to myself, I assume the attitude of that person or that essence. Since we are able to play things like wind or the prairie grasses—animals, creatures—it's not very difficult at all to play a gender opposite. I just assume the attitude of a specific male I know very well. When I play David in one scene in *Body Leaks,* I'm playing a combination of a teenage boy and a very, very old man from the nursing home. I project these males by taking on their attitudes, and then another kind of voice comes out of me. That's what I mean when I say gender is attitude. By assuming an essential attitude, I can play anything, a mole, a warm breeze, a llama, or an old man.

SK: Makes you think.

MT: When you play that military person . . .

JAS: The one with the steel plate in his head . . .

*See appendix to this chapter.

MT: Who are you there?

SK: It's a feeling I have. I think about my grandfather because it's his story.

MT: When you play that person, your body changes, your chest takes on a whole different angle. These are behaviors that I've observed. You hold your head in a different way.

JAS: Also, it's how you think he felt because he had to be so concerned with his shield, this armor he was wearing. It's like this feeling of his that you empathized with as his granddaughter. Whether he showed you that feeling or not, you empathized with it.

SK: Yes, that's interesting too, because he's a storyteller. But this story happened to be true. I always had trouble deciphering—I believed everything when I was real young. I started questioning his stories later. I confronted him one day. He had a real twinkle in his eye, and he knew the last story he told wasn't true. And he knew I knew it wasn't true, but it was all OK. But then I found out that the steel plate in the head story really was true.

MT: What war was your grandfather in?

SK: I don't remember things like that—just this kind of energy or feeling I got from him.

MT: The energy of "the male" or the energy of your specific grandfather?

SK: My specific grandfather.

MT: I think of my stepfather and how he patterned himself exactly after John Wayne. Talk about assuming the attitude of a role model—he thought like him, he used his arms like him, he had this chivalrous attitude toward women, and he was very shy and wouldn't kiss anybody. He learned his whole masculine trip from the movies—and anyone of us can.

SK: I never thought of myself as a guy there; it's interesting that you bring it up.

JAS: The stereotypes! Look, I can't identify with what's thought of as a feminine—play the ingenue, play the character lady . . .

MT: It's harder for you to play an ingenue than a masculine character?

JAS: No, I just don't personally identify with *any* of the stereotypes thought of as feminine *or* masculine. So why would I ever be interested in playing them on stage?

MT: When I play the men in our show, I don't think of myself as a man, I think of myself as presenting this masculine attitude. It's this male attitude that comes through my instrument. I don't first convince myself I'm a man to play a male—I simply assume the attitude of a male or several males I know or have observed acutely.

JAS: I think we all have masculine and feminine attitudes within us. For instance, masculine certainly feels more linear to me, more angular, not even angular but more controlled and less circular than . . .

MT: Than the possibilities for playing a woman?

JAS: Right! And I can pull those parts out of myself. I don't have to look at somebody else to get a male essence. I'd rather pull it from myself than look at some guy next door.

MT: How many different males and females did you two play in *Headlights*? You transform back and forth between children, boys and girls, older people.

JAS: I didn't plan it as a director or a performer—I gave over to the writing. If the writing is good writing, the gender and the age is in the *rhythm* of the writing: a seven-year-old as opposed to a seventeen-year-old as opposed to a seventy-year-old, male or female. Males have different verbal rhythms than women. It seems to me that's the writer's job. If it's written right, then as a performer or as a director you don't do anything but give yourself over to realize those words, you connect with the essence of the speaker. When you connect with that essence, then age and/or gender is projected with ease, but not in terms of age or gender or . . .

SK: It's funny, in *Headlights,* when I was supposed to walk over the chairs, it was the grandfather who did that. You said that I was in a room and I was really talking to myself out loud. Now that we are talking about it, I think in my mind I pictured what the guy looked like who would be walking in that room and talking to himself. But it was also as if *I* was talking to him, the grandfather, which was the man in my mind, but *I* was *not* the man. I pictured him in that room, and then I groped for anything from the human condition, any experience that I could relate to, whether it was pride or shame, in order to play it.

JAS: The only thing that we did work on with that in mind is what I've observed about the way men cover their shame as opposed to the way women cover their shame. The covering of shame is true for men or women but, as I think about it, it is different the way they project it.

MT: In *Goona Goona*, you played a teenage boy, a male surgeon of forty-two, his mother who was around sixty-two, and a hyperactive girl of five years. When you went back and forth playing those parts, what sort of thing did you reach for inside? Did you let the writing carry you?

JAS: Yes. And the rhythm. But it's the giving over as a performer to the writing—it's the writing. I know it's the writing—I think the attitude comes from the writing.

MT: Connecting with the attitude of the character?

JAS: Yes. Certainly a five-year-old boy or girl couldn't say those Grandma Goon lines, there's no way. Nor could a woman say Granville's [the forty-two-year-old male] lines, there's just no way.

MT: You certainly convinced the Eagles' Forum you were a male. They claimed you had an eight-foot penis, which you exposed in Evanston, Wyoming. We got cancelled in Gillette because of your masculine exhibition. What were they looking at on the stage?

JAS: Well, they were looking at essence and attitude. Certainly in *Goona Goona,* which was a lot of fun, I got to play with the male strut, the way a man holds himself.

MT: Phyllis Schlafly's Eagles' Forum women were convinced you actually were a man. They seemed to have no idea you were really a woman impersonating a man.

JAS: Amazing, and my costume changes were made in front of the audience's eyes. They saw my long hair come in and out of the helmets. It was the lawn watering scene that so disturbed them. Dr. Goon was trying to make time in that scene with the woman next door, as demonstrated by his physical attitude. That attitude evidently made them see all sorts of things that weren't there.

SK: How were you using the hose?

MT: As if she was watering, . . . she had a piece of plastic tubing about eighteen inches long.

JAS: It was really a musical instrument. But I was cocky about it; I was leading with the hips.

MT: The ability to take on essences allows us to transform and to play anything, so we're not limited or confined to physical givens. One of the marvels of this is we're not held to having to go out and hire people of specific gender to play specific parts like many theatre companies who limit themselves in that way. We can decide to do any kind of play, and we can cast it any way we want to, because the actors we choose are able to call up these essences in themselves.

JAS: It's horrifying to think about being limited in that way. The college I went to limited us like that.

MT: To play only women?

JAS: To play only *thin* women. To play only blondes. They made the students feel that if they were not five feet, eight inches tall with blue eyes they could never act.

SK: How much is dependent on the writer, and how much is dependent on the director?

JAS: The way I look at theatre, the writer starts it. But there are many shared contributions in the beginning stages of the way we work at Omaha Magic Theatre.

MT: When we begin to create a new piece?

JAS: We three—a designer, director, and writer—come together and play around with ideas. In the case of *Body Leaks,* which explores self-censorship, after some preliminary discussion we said, "That interests me. . . . It interests me, too. . . . It interests me. . . ." That's where the beginning is with us. But in most situations, it's the writer who throws an entity into the ring; usually the director picks it up next and starts to dream on it, then takes it to another level and interprets the writer's words.

SK: When they interpret it, that's explaining what the gender meant to them and who wanted to play what, not knowing what the writer had in mind.

JAS: That's how I see theatre. And then the designer takes that thing that's been tossed into the ring at nearly the same time that the director does. I don't feel that they even have to talk, at least at first. Both pick it up, and the designer interprets from her point of view.

MT: For instance, Sora, when you made the costume for the person with the plate in the head in *Body Leaks,* did you two talk about that?

SK: I don't think we did; we talked about many other aspects, but I don't think we talked about that.

MT: It was Sora's idea that that person was going to wear armor to present an essence?

JAS: I have a difficult time saying that the words write a performance. Words are one part of it. I feel the images I create with performers and the choreography is also writing. The designs that appear on the wall, the headdresses the performers might wear, or a placement between the projected image on the wall and the performer—the relationship between the two, which is created by both Sora and me—that's also writing. That's what I mean when I say we all write. But it's the writer who determines things like gender, I think.

MT: The writer may indicate gender in the language used, but the director or actor could cast opposite to that—the actor could choose to play in opposition to the given lines, to see the action or the writer's ideas from another point of view. For instance, when we did *Sea of Forms,* no character was gender specific except at certain points when there were little stories, but two-thirds of the play's characters were essences or spirits. Were they masculine or feminine spirits?

JAS: I don't know. But I don't know that about *Body Leaks* either, except the play feels round to me. But so did *Sea of Forms.* It was a very feminine, meditative piece.

MT: The overall feeling of the piece was feminine to you even though half the company was male?

JAS: *Headlights,* too. I wouldn't say *Headlights* was about men and women.

MT: It's about the mind grappling with breaking the code, with the struggle involved in reading and writing.

JAS: It's about signs, it's about the translation of those signs.

MT: In the seventies when we did *Babes in the Bighouse,* the characters were specific women, but half the company who played them were men. In fact, more than half the company were men at the time. And the men wanted to play women; they studied women and the feminine in themselves to play the women in *Babes.*

JAS: What it was like to be woman, emotionally.

MT: They didn't camp the women they played, they *became* the women they played.

SK: Did you explore the differences between how women and men would, for example, react differently to situations?

JAS: . . . What a woman would feel like being taken away from her children and locked up. In essence, it was about women in prison.

SK: So you did explore her emotion?

JAS: *Babes in the Bighouse* was about how to maintain sanity. . . .

MT: . . . when other people impose their will upon you, and you have to survive.

JAS: [*an aside*] How do *we* survive?

SK: So you were at your greatest challenge at that time?

JAS: Right. We found it often involved turning off the exterior reality and playing another tape inside your head. What that tape might be was the main exploration for the performer and director in workshop and rehearsal. The main structure of the piece was the movement in the corridors between the cell block and the Warden's Office, the laundry to the kitchen. . . .

MT: . . . to the medical complex.

SK: So, you showed how you could positively program yourself or essentially brainwash yourself into doing what the outside world required, but at the same time not lose yourself to their world?

MT: Yes, how you *could* survive in that world. What you had to do to maintain your self-respect. When we performed that piece, many men in the audience said they finally understood what the women's movement was about for the first time in their lives. Because they were shocked by the performance, they could empathize with the men on stage in dresses, who were in a prison and also in society's cage. They finally got what it might be like to be female in our culture.

JAS: Earlier, we'd seen how young males react in other instances when we performed in a prep school. No matter the level of performance, if a male spoke on stage, the young boys in the all-male audience would shut up and prick up their ears. Women would interact on stage—chaos. It was a parochial boys' school; they were used to priests standing up in front and demanding attention. Mom does it, forget it. It was amazing.

MT: We'd played this piece many, many times, and we knew where all the jokes were, but this audience would only laugh at something a man said.

JAS: You can see it when you perform in a male prison.

MT: We played prisons all through the sixties, seventies, and early eighties.

JAS: There's no question they'd get it. But the way the males in prison respond to women, until they *hear* what you say, is phenomenal. "A piece of ass," is the initial response, until they happen to listen by mistake, then the whole thing changes. But after performances of *Babes in the Bighouse* to our regular audience, men said, "I realized seeing men dressed up in dresses, I chose to look at the men not the women and finally I could understand what women have been saying about what they've been going through because this male was *doing* it."

MT: And they realized how controlled women are by men and how women's images are controlled by men.

JAS: Isn't it amazing to realize how this happens and amazing to confess such a thing, too. But it would be very interesting to do *Body Leaks* in prisons, because there is no gender.

MT: The gender shifts. You can take your choice whether it's a male or female from the audience point of view. I got a lot of credit for having women play the Viet Cong in *Viet Rock*.* It was a directorial choice because the men in our company were getting outside jobs that paid money all the time, and they were always taking off from the rehearsal process. I never had enough men. So I said, "To hell with this, I'm having the women play the Viet Cong because they're small, pretty people anyway." It was like the first time people saw something like that in New York. Even though there's been a tradition of men playing women, women playing men is still startling. It was very startling in the sixties. When the women came out playing the Viet Cong in *Viet Rock,* it had a double whammy. Recently, I had the occasion to see some Cambodian dancers at the TCG conference present the Cambodian Court Dances. This is dance that's been going on for hundreds of years. Women played men, and they've been doing this for centuries. They played elaborate love scenes, incredible flirtation dances, marriage dances—and all the parts are played by women. The women who demonstrated and lectured to us told us that, when these dances were danced for the king, he would get very excited—this would really turn him on erotically. In other cultures, people shifting from one gender to another has been going on for hundreds of years—depends which culture you're looking at.

SK: Why is it so odd in our culture?

---

*Editor's note: Megan Terry's *Viet Rock* was produced in 1966 by the Open Theatre in New York City.

MT: We're stiff in many ways. We have such a difficult time with sex. Look at all the censorship problems coming down now.

JAS: Look at corporate America. Women wear suits to work.

MT: We see them downtown here with their leather brief cases and their little silk ties . . .

JAS: . . . their straight skirts and jackets.

SK: Do they have a dress code?

MT: Yes, and there's even a secret dress code. To get up into the proper echelon you have to wear dark jackets. The darker the color you wear, the more authority you are perceived to have, no matter who you are. [*To JAS*] There was something you wanted to say about being a woman.

JAS: The self-censorship that women experience.

SK: Women's reaction to it, our emotions about it?

JAS: I think it did have to do with the writing in this case. With *Body Leaks*, it *is* different. I think males self-censor, but they hide it—it's almost deeper than women's self-censorship. We may be having trouble with being honest and feeling bad about who we are, but it feels to me like males are so boarded up. Working on *Body Leaks*, I found out incredible things about myself. Obviously, people in the audience connect with various speeches and images from the reactions they shared with us afterwards.

MT: Men seem to connect just as much as women. Fights the men and women are getting into with one another as they go out the door are amusing too. [*To JAS*] Recount that argument you happened to hear.

JAS: Essentially it was what we were just talking about. The man said the show has more to do with what it's like being a man, and the woman said, "No, no, it's clearly about how we women feel about self-censoring." They went around and around, and then they asked me. I had to think about my choices, and obviously males aren't excluded. I think some of the strongest feedback about the show has come from men, as strong certainly as from women, wouldn't you say?

SK: I never thought about it, I can't say that.

JAS: At our public discussions, males always talk more, but so many women came up after the show or returned several times.

MT: Right, I would talk to women *after* the discussion, because I would see them wanting to talk and not letting themselves. I would go to them and say, "I saw your face, and I saw your hand go up and then come back down. What is it you wanted to say?" Then a ten-minute outpouring would come.

JAS: Wouldn't you say it was equal then, even though the men pushed their way in at the public forum more?

MT: Equal response?

JAS: Yes, identifying—anyway, that was what the argument was about—the man said, "It was for me," and the woman said, "No, it was for me."

MT: It was a big surprise to me that so many men connected with it—and at a very deep level.

SK: If we can convey gut honesty the way we tried to about the human condition, then there shouldn't be fighting about who it's about. It's about human beings.

MT: Then maybe our work is getting past testosterone and estrogen and going directly to the essential soul of the individual?

JAS: That's a real interesting thing, too, when you think about gender and the questions, "Who am I?" "Who do you think I am?" "I am who I think you think I am." And if the *you* is a male, if you play that out, I am who I think you think I am; or if the *you* is a female and you play that out—if that's how you live your life.

MT: Some critics say that it's impossible to get beyond the male gaze, that you're always playing into male expectations or the male gaze. Have we done enough work that we can get beyond the superimposed or internalized male voice and gaze?

SK: Or the intense thought patterns going through the air? I have to fight off that consciousness because it's so prevailing. Every time men open their mouths, their thought patterns go through the air like light waves.

JAS: And our mothers raised us to protect us with that in mind, too.

MT: We've been working here twenty-two years. In the last two years, we've changed our method to open a production only when we believe it's ready, right?

JAS: If the research and workshopping on a piece goes very well, it can take six months. Regional male theatres do a show a month. They feel grateful to have four weeks' rehearsal.

MT: Three weeks; if they have four, it's a luxury. Do you think the kind of work we've been doing with ourselves has helped bring this about?

JAS: It's been a combination of hard work and taking the time to bring it to fruition. Realizing intellectually that we *can* do it. We finally see that nobody is standing with a gun to our heads, demanding we open a show a month.

MT: It's the gun from the outside world that we are in the process of getting rid of. There's only a trigger left—we got rid of the handle.

SK: There's still a trigger.

MT: Getting this all out has taken a good fourth of our lives hasn't it—when you look at it that way.

JAS: Yes, and that's why most people hold onto things like gender. They feel safe if one can be identified as a male or female. I can clearly see you're a male, and I know males only feel a certain way, otherwise they're perverted. Females only feel another way, otherwise they're perverted. But when I'm onstage, I can be very commanding and show control, and yet they look at me and I have breasts and clearly I'm a woman. And we wear dresses in the show. On the surface, it looks safe to come see our plays, which is part of the reason we're threatening to certain groups.

SK: It's attitude like you were talking about in the beginning.

MT: Your attitude about yourself.

JAS: Can I climb that mountain?

MT: Your power—the power you give yourself.

SK: As long as we don't take on the negativity of the power that's put out by the power structure.

JAS: Right, and we don't. *Goona Goona* did show both sides of Dr. Goon, the poet and this horrible abuser—the healer and the abuser. In domestic violence, the abuser is generally male, and he acts out in the way Dr. Goon did, for the reasons he did. On the other hand, June Goon, who was played by a male, is clearly a victim—and it's not that males can't be victims, but they seldom are in a domestic situation—it was financial, emotional . . .

MT: The doubles and triples that we got out of it by having you, Jo Ann, play the man and James Larson play the woman were enormous. The audience had to go through a lot in their heads and in their hearts.

JAS: Again, it was making it unsafe, even though it was clear. Again, it took the lines and softened the separations between. If a female plays a male and a male plays the female, it's the same thing as we do in *Body Leaks,* taking on that male essence and holding yourself in that way. You can't clearly say that's white and that's black.

MT: By doing that, it wasn't putting the whole rap on the males or the whole rap on the females. The audience can concentrate on the action— the behavior that's hurtful and negative.

JAS: I'm saying that for the audience the clarity of, "Oh, that's a woman, and now she's doing male things and that's bad." But, if they can't see that clearly, then they feel a little on the edge. And in *Body Leaks* they can't, because often it's women performing male stories.

SK: The roles may be a little more clearly defined in *Headlights* or *Goona Goona.*

JAS: Not in *Headlights,* but in *Goona Goona* they're defined.

SK: I'm talking about character.

MT: They *are* traditional characters in *Headlights.*

JAS: But it did the same thing—because if a woman played a male character, it's the same thing really as a woman taking on a male essence, even if it's just for a little bit of time. Still, the audience was challenged:

"What's wrong with this picture?" They really have to look at it. They have to look at the emotional stakes, and they have to look at who's saying what. Is it appropriate or inappropriate? Suddenly, action is put in high relief. That's why they can see it better. It's not ordinary. It's not only a woman who's doing her thing.

MT: Then the audience's eye is focused on the action and behavior rather than being asked or coerced into taking gender sides.

JAS: Right, they're engaged.

SK: They aren't immediately compartmentalized.

MT: And it stops people from generalizing and stereotyping.

JAS: And then they open up to themselves and the work. Certainly we're seeing a new kind of excitement in our audience.

Appendix: From Body Leaks, *by Megan Terry, Jo Ann Schmidman, and Sora Kimberlain*

[A thirty-gallon aluminum garbage can with an electric light bulb inside is carried on stage. Light is visible through large holes drilled in the garbage can. Two performers rush to look into can.]

FOUR: Can you go into the center if you shave your head?

ONE: Can you go into the center of your brain if you shave your head?

FOUR: Can you go into the center of your body if you shave your head?

ONE: Can you be a Barbara Hepworth sculpture with a piercing void if you shave your head?

FOUR: Can you see clear through to China if you shave your head? Can you see Hong Kong? Queen Kong? Or is it the 270 Foot Woman who can crush entire cities of dickheads with a single blow?

ONE: She's touring the globe leaving no city untouched.

FOUR: It is she

ONE: That I will see

BOTH: When I shave my head.

[They exit with can.]

NOREEN C. BARNES

Kate Bornstein's Gender and Genre Bending

❦ When Kate Bornstein (who was, at the time, Al Bornstein) first announced to her (then his) mother that she (then he) was going to undergo a change of gender, her (then his) mother's response was: "You've been an actor all your life—are you sure this isn't just another role?"

Albert Herman Bornstein was born forty-three years ago and remains enchanted by the fact that he entered this life as a double Pisces in a town called Neptune (and, appropriately enough, now collects art and jewelry depicting mermaids). Bornstein grew up just outside Asbury Park, New Jersey, as the second son in an upper middle-class Jewish family, which was conservative but not terribly religious. His father was a doctor, his mother, a schoolteacher, with combined Russian/Dutch ethnic backgrounds.

Since the age of about four, Bornstein possessed not only an attraction to, but an identification with, females, and from the time he was a young boy, he secretly cross-dressed. As a teenager, Bornstein attended a private boys' school, and, although the school was Methodist, he sang in the choir. Not only did he have a good voice, but he loved wearing a gown.

Bornstein also distinguished himself in athletics, in public speaking and debate, as editor of the yearbook, in the National Honor Society, as the senior class president, and as an actor in several plays. He entered Brown University as a pre-med major (encouraged to follow in his father's profession) and also planned to be on the crew team. A bout of mononucleosis forced him out of college sports, and after recovering, Bornstein found that the only extracurricular activity in which he had any interest left was theatre. He (literally) carried a spear in several productions, then began to get larger roles throughout his time at the university and was the first student to graduate with a degree in Theatre Arts in 1969.

Bornstein's impressive resumé attests to the variety of parts he (and, later, she) has played. While pursuing a career in graduate, community, and professional theatres on the East Coast, Bornstein appeared in such Shakespearean roles as Prince Hal and King Lear, in the musical leads of Mack in *Threepenny Opera,* of the king in *The King and I,* of Herbie in *Gypsy,* as Nagg in *Endgame,* and as the Marquis de Sade in *Marat/Sade.*

Briefly intent on pursuing an M.F.A. in acting at Brandeis University and determined on a course of self-discovery, Bornstein, through a haze of drugs and alcohol, found a way out of being drafted, dropped out of school, worked on a ship, and launched himself into a series of marriages and a long-term involvement with a cult. When his gender questions began to surface, Bornstein declared himself transsexual, became clean and sober, reentered the theatre, and found a stronger and more personal spiritual path to take.

In Philadelphia in the early 1980s, Bornstein began living as a woman, started taking hormones, and, after some searching for a sympathetic surgeon, had penile inversion surgery. Bornstein had difficulty not in finding a doctor who would perform the operation but in finding one who would do so knowing Bornstein's intent to remain sexually involved with women—*as* a woman. Kate Bornstein was the first transsexual on the Mayor's Commission on Sexual Minorities and was the co-founder of the women's theatre company, Order Before Midnight. She moved to San Francisco in 1988, and her performance career there has been associated with both Theatre Rhinoceros, the oldest gay and lesbian theatre in the United States, and Outlaw Productions, a company devoted to giving voice to sexual minorities through performance.

When Bornstein made her San Francisco theatrical debut in Theatre Rhinoceros's 1989 production of Genet's *The Balcony,* directed by the late Leland Moss, the press noted the presence of three well-known drag performers—Doris Fish, Tippi, and Miss X—in the production, but to Kate's surprise, there was no speculation about her performance as the Judge (whom she played as a female character). Bornstein expected commentary such as, "Who is that playing the Judge?" She notes that, although she functions "socially as a woman, I don't think of myself as a woman." But neither does she think of herself as a man; rather, she considers herself as being in a kind of neutral territory as far as gender is concerned, thus giving her a great deal of freedom in gender-play in performance as well as in real life. On this life-long journey of discovering true self-expression, however, she acknowledges that it is frightening at times not to feel female or male. She also observes that transsexuals have not played transsexuals in the theatre (or film), and that "transgendered people have been exoticized" by the media (she notes, for example, John Lithgow's performance in *The World According to Garp*). It is with Outlaw that Kate realized her autobiographical *Hidden: A Gender,* in which she has starred and toured since November 1989 with co-performers Sydney Erskine and Justin Bond.

Bornstein views San Francisco as a "safe haven" vital to her growth and sense of self, having discovered a good deal of support here that does not exist elsewhere. She has a high profile in the community as an arts writer, is a popular personality in the local "queer culture" scene, speaks frequently at conferences, participates in readings and panels, and has, literally, been in the national spotlight as a guest on both the "Geraldo" and "Donahue" television shows. In addition to continuing to write for several publications and lecturing, Bornstein is also working on several scripts, including a multicharacter solo endeavor about transsexuals, and is collaborating with other writers and actors.[1]

She has a number of acting students in the Bay Area and has taught Gender in Performance workshops at the Dell Arte School of Physical Theatre in Blue Lake, California, and at the National Gay and Lesbian Theatre Conference in Seattle. At the latter conference, she worked with both male and female actors, and at Blue Lake, she coached an ensemble of non-United States women. For both, she focused on transforming one gender into another (very different from drag or impersonation) by using a gender attribution system (cues) and applying them to performance. The work explored the continuum between the opposite genders. Bornstein notes that the initial attempts of the young female actors at Blue Lake were "burlesques of men" and that it took them time to develop a real sense of male attributes and to find compassion for their male characters. She continued to work with them on shifting between male and female in physical comedy in order "to create a putting off-balance—enough uncertainty about gender so that when the truth is presented, it's very powerful—a kind of emotional earthquake."[2]

The critical question of "Who am I?" is at the center of Bornstein's life and work (and is certainly a central concern of *Hidden: A Gender,* though it is more often phrased by the characters as "What am I?"). Bornstein herself questions whether she is male, female, or other and is surprised when other people do not. But she is content with what she is doing and feels clear about ethics, morals, her career, her personal path. For her, "the gendered body is an accomplishment."[3]

First, the Practice

Hidden: A Gender parallels Bornstein's own story with that of the nineteenth-century French hermaphrodite, Herculine Barbin. Barbin has already appeared as a character in fiction, film (*The Mystery of Alexina*), and several plays, including Caryl Churchill and David Lan's *A Mouthful of Birds*; her memoirs, edited by Michel Foucault, served as the basis for Bornstein's extrapolations on Barbin's brief life.

Bornstein and I originally worked together as playwright and dramaturg, then moved into the roles of actor and director. The play was first produced by us, as Outlaw Productions, in association with Theatre Rhinoceros in the fall of 1989. It then went on to represent the theatre at the Gay and Lesbian Theatre Festival in Seattle in the summer of 1990, to tour the East Coast throughout the fall, and, in 1991, to reopen as a mainstage production back at Theatre Rhinoceros. It then ran briefly with Outlaw's second touring production, Catherine Harrison's *Permission,* in Santa Cruz in June 1991.

As we began our collaboration, it became evident that Bornstein's initial concept of a one-person, multicharacter performance would have to change and that it would be necessary to work with several other actors to serve her vision effectively. We asked Justin Bond and Sydney Erskine to work with us. Bond is a gay man who plays Herculine as both the girl she thought she was and the young man (re-named "Abel") that the medical profession and the state determined her to be; Erskine, a lesbian, plays a heterosexual man, "Herman Amberstone" (a version of Bornstein's own name), who becomes "Kate," a transsexual lesbian. Bornstein plays Doc Grinder, a heterosexual man (and sometimes a woman, though that shape-shifting is not acknowledged by the actor) who serves as Master ("or is it Mistress?") of Ceremonies, narrator, talk show host, and foil to Erskine's characters.

One of the many layers of the performance is Grinder's insistence that the audience "buy" the idea of a bipolar gender system through purchasing his miracle elixir "Gender Defender," while Grinder him/herself alters gender. The hidden agenda is that Grinder really has no gender yet sells the heterosexist formula in "the pink bottle for the girls and the blue bottle for the men."[4]

While doing some early research for the character of Grinder, we concentrated on late nineteenth-century sideshow carnival barkers, moral lecturers, and pitchmen/quack doctors. Bornstein and I quickly realized that, just as the contemporary equivalent of the freak show is the television talk show, the parallel to the barker/pitchman today is the tabloid talk show "host." We did preserve a few remnants of the historical popular entertainment format (including the occasional pitches for Gender Defender and the title of "Doc"), but we brought them into a contemporary perspective by merging the long-standing traditions with their modern-day media counterparts. Bornstein consciously exploits the notion of the freak and the freak show, of course—but with a twist. Once inside her carnival tent/television studio, the audience finds itself not merely seeing the freaks but listening to what they have to say as well. She has given voice to those who have been without one for centuries.

The piece, in writing and performance, remains fluid in structure, style, and genre, with form necessarily reflecting the content of the work and the internal progress of the characters. The character of Herculine is played within a nineteenth-century realistic mode. Grinder invites the spectators to watch Herculine but cautions, "Do not interrupt her, or she will disappear."[5] Only at the end of the final monologue does Herculine/Abel break the fourth wall convention to speak to the audience; otherwise, the character speaks to those unseen—while praying, at confession, reading a letter, at the bedside of the beloved (and unconscious) Sara, and during a torturous physical examination. In contrast, Herman/Kate emerges from his/her assigned performance space to confront Grinder and finally to appropriate Grinder's territory. Erskine and Bornstein use a kind of Brechtian direct address and talk to individual audience members.

Herculine begins in an upstage-center space and gradually moves downstage through her story, until she addresses the audience in the final graveyard scene. Grinder and Herman/Kate play off each other from opposite downstage areas, and the act of crossing that space ("clearly defined lines") becoming symbolic of their struggle for power. Grinder controls the action from a stage right stool, while Herman relaxes in his father's easy chair.

Within this basic structure are other scenes, running the gamut of theatrical styles: all three actors in a parodic Marx Brothers sketch about two doctors refusing to perform a sex-change operation for Herman (an incident drawn from Bornstein's experience); the surgery, itself, performed by Erskine as a Julia Child-like cook demonstrating "genital conversion technique"; Bond and Erskine as themselves, frantically trying to sweep "gender" up from the stage; Bond and Erskine after gender transformation, as Abel and Kate, meeting on the metaphysical plane in a surreal dance—a dreamlike sequence shattered by Grinder's manipulation; and the television game show, "What's My Gender?" With each scene change comes a corresponding shift in the performer/spectator relationship. While several critics have found this sequencing of performance styles "theatrical gimmickry" that was frequently "jarring,"[6] the blending of genres into one piece is a structural device common to several other recent works to come out of the gay and lesbian theatre, such as Split Britches' *Little Women* and Sky Gilbert's *Drag Queens in Outer Space* (performed by Toronto's Buddies in Bad Times Company). I would posit that what these playwrights, directors, and performers have created is a distinct style of fluid form and content in a move "towards a queer theatre," which demands in turn a fresh critical reception for such work.

The comic element is particularly critical to how Bornstein imparts information. Doris Fish, in the San Francisco *Sentinel,* observed that the way Bornstein "maintains such humor about her life without trivializing it is remarkable."[7] The juxtaposition of pathos and parody, often in a quick succession that prevents the audience from responding to one or the other, became crucial in the play's staging. For example, Herculine's horrific medical examination, in which her vagina is leeched (and in which only the actor's face is lit), is followed immediately by the same actor's voice as a television game show announcer in a blackout, and lights quickly come up on Herman as a contestant waiting for the entrance of Grinder as the show host. It's part of the punch of the play that, as Fish noted, "hits between the eyes and often below the belt."

Doc Grinder's opening monologue sets the stage and the rules of the action to follow. Grinder introduces Barbin and Amberstone—one as unfortunate victim, the other as offensive practitioner—as "creatures from a world with which I hope you seldom have any contact," that of "Gender Blur."[8] It's all part of a pitch to sell gender rather than a particular product, while pointing out that sex and gender are the most effective marketing ploys: "You'll buy anything to relieve the nagging feeling that you're not quite a man, not quite a woman. You'll buy anything, because you want to be secure in your gender identity."[9]

What follows are the parallel stories of Herman and Herculine, on display as those with the disease of "gender blur," interspersed with Grinder's commentary. The determination of the devout Herculine's gender comes from an authority to whom she must submit: "He is saying I am a man and I must obey him for I am nothing if I am not obedient."

Herman, in contrast, makes his own decision to change his gender. Herculine places blind faith in the higher power of the nuns, priests, and doctors; however, Herman's journey takes him away from placing trust in others (from teachers to the "Church of Diabology"), until he finally realizes that having faith in oneself is more important. Herculine names her officially designated male self Abel—"child of peace, victim of aggression, loved by God, mourned through the ages"[10]—but literally does not survive the enforced transformation of her life. For Herman, after becoming Kate, comes the realization that there are still many questions left unanswered. In her final confrontation with Grinder, who threatens to write her out of the show, Kate takes over the stage, eulogizes Herculine/Abel, and asks, "As to being a man or a woman, must I be one or the other?"[11] and claims that she is "constructing myself to be fluidly gendered" despite Grinder's arguments. The character of Kate concludes:

I don't consider myself a man, and quite frequently I doubt I'm a woman. And you, you still think gender is the issue! Gender is not the issue. Gender is the battlefield. Or the playground. The issue is us versus them. Any us versus any them. One day we may not need that.[12]

When Bornstein began to collect material for the play (based on observations about gender cues and pieces of monologues from a variety of roles she has played "serendipitously" throughout her career), she realized that what the play concerned, as a result of weaving her own biography with that of Herculine Barbin, was "fucking with gender attribution."[13] The ethnomethodological term "gender attribution" means simply that we always make a decision, whether consciously or not, about people's gender, usually the first thing we notice when we meet people. If their gender is in question or isn't clear from all the gender "cues" we have been conditioned to read, we stop and think, do a double take, look at that person again. Uncertainty disrupts the notion of two distinct genders that fall neatly into two prescribed categories of attributes. Bornstein notes that "once we attribute gender, it's difficult to change the attribution,"[14] and it is, in fact, disturbing to do so.

In *Hidden: A Gender,* Grinder discusses the concept of gender attribution with the audience, in the character's first appearance in a female persona and during the character's seduction by the preoperative Herman, an actor:

HERMAN: . . . the women lined up. They just lined up outside my dressing room door. They wanted that stud. And I learned to be that stud. They wanted the leather jacket and they wanted the eyes they couldn't see and I wanted them so that's who I became.

I wanted every one of those women. And one by one I fucked them, they fucked the character they had just seen on stage, and I fucked them over. And every night the lines outside the stage door got longer and every woman on that line convinced me I was a man. I learned. I was that stud. I learned. I had the Marlboro Man by the balls and I could fuck like the best of the boys. I learned. So I couldn't be a woman. Not if I loved women so much. I learned. How could I be a woman? How could I?[15]

Bornstein then enters as Grinder, with the same basic costume of black formal jacket, white shirt, and black tights but this time with obvious eye makeup, earrings, and, in place of the red tie, a soft flower print scarf. The actor's voice and movement are also quite different. Herman is now referred to as a "poor victim" rather than a "twisted creature"—the shock tactics of a Geraldo Rivera have become more like the appeal for pity and pathos of a Sally Jessy Raphael:

GRINDER: Yes, strange as it seems, he still feels like a woman. That's gender blur. We don't think about our gender day and night. Not like these poor victims. No, it doesn't even cross our minds. Not until someone [*to woman in audience*] calls you "sir" again. Not until someone [*to man in audience*] says you're behaving far too effeminately. Experts agree that we don't even think about gender in terms of ourselves. No, it's not until we see someone walking down the street and we can't tell if it's a man or a woman. Ever wonder why you can't stop staring until you decide one way or the other? It really bothers you, doesn't it?[16]

But this feminine manifestation of Grinder, while spouting Doc's manifesto, displays quite a different physical response to Herman. Revulsion transforms into attraction, and Grinder is unsettled by Herman's gaze (inscrutable in sunglasses). Meanwhile Grinder speaks to the audience and even seeks a temporary refuge amongst the spectators before being seduced by Herman, the actor who had learned "to get women."

The shape-shifting of Grinder from male to female persona, from moral lecturer to junior high school English teacher (delivering a monotonous speech on gender and pronouns), is a conscious part of Bornstein's larger role than that of "your friendly neighborhood transsexual s/m lesbian sha-man."[17] Of her shamanism, Bornstein considers her transsexual journey "like any path of Shamanism. Any death and rebirth is shamanistic and I've lived many different lives. We all have. I find the people who acknowl-edge those deaths and births are usually more comfortable with me."[18]

In his review of the play, critic Wendell Ricketts wrote that it "redeemed my conviction that theatre ought to be risky business—quirky, prickly, a triumph of substance rather than of form, even a bit subversive." It was "one of the most remarkable pieces of organic theatre to come along in some time," he asserted, "and is all the more significant for being, so to speak, home-grown."[19] It is with a bit of irony that Ricketts uses the term "organic" to describe a piece that is, essentially, a construction *about* a construction.

Gender is the "flexible framework" upon which Bornstein has draped the content of her work. Her identity as not only a transsexual but as a lesbian has been intriguing to most people and problematic for some. On his show, Geraldo Rivera attempted to bait her with, "So you became the thing you loved," to which Bornstein replied, "Yes, and I loved what I became."[20]

Bornstein, whose own "dream role" is that of Virginia Woolf's *Or-lando,* finds that, when rehearsing, "fear is the first signal that means I'm on to something" and that a feeling of "danger is the signpost I've ar-rived."[21] In dealing with the gender system as a subject in theatre, Born-stein addresses "that area you can't put your finger on because it's fluid. And gender, because it's a social construct, is quicksilver."[22]

The performances of *Hidden: A Gender* throughout the country have brought with them critical commentary, interviews, and theoretical re-sponses to Bornstein's work, and Bornstein herself has wrapped a theory of gender construction around her theatrical practice.

The Theoretical Response (to and by) Bornstein

Bornstein's exploration of gender in performance was initially revealed at a presentation at the Women and Theatre Pre-conference (of the As-sociation of Theatre in Higher Education) in San Diego in 1988. She per-formed three monologues: as Tolin from Ann Jellicoe's *The Knack,* as the

Master of Ceremonies in Brecht's *Happy End,* and as Sue from Jane Chambers' *Last Summer at Bluefish Cove.* The progression from playing a womanizing, heterosexual man, to drag role, to lesbian woman—all roles that Bornstein had actually performed in full productions—mirrored her own journey. She played Tolin in college when she was Al Bornstein. The performance in *Happy End* was the last before her sex-change surgery, and the part in *Bluefish Cove* was her first role after surgery.

During her presentation, Bornstein stated:

I was a woman who was a man playing a man written by a woman using a man's voice directed by a woman and coached by a man. Then I was a woman who was a man playing a woman written by a man, using a man's woman's voice directed by a man coached by a woman. And finally I was a woman who was a man playing a not-man/not-woman in a woman's voice written by a not-woman/not-man and directed by myself. And I hope that clarifies it.[23]

Erika Munk reflected that this performance of Bornstein's "sex identity vertigo and role critique" was that of a "woman playing former straight male self playing gay man playing straight woman."[24] Jill Dolan's perspective was that:

Bornstein performed a noncoincidence of body and language, a Brechtian, postmodern dissociation of presence and discourse. Her monologues traded among shifting, constructed identities, layered on a body that has experienced all of these constructions. Bornstein hired a surgical knife to allow her to play the gender role she desired in a body that would look the part. Confined by gender construction, Bornstein opted to reconstruct her body to fit herself in gendered discourse. Or did she subvert gendered discourse by her choice to tamper with biology? Watching her perform, I was unsettled by my awareness that Bornstein has no neutral body, that even her biology is not immutable but constructed. Is this the death of character? Where is the truth in this experience?[25]

Bornstein acknowledges that some feminist critics who examine the intersection of theory and performance are disturbed by her work and that Dolan is quite right in her observation that Bornstein "has no neutral body." Bornstein has, however, been able to set her own course, unencumbered by the need for academic approbation, celebrating, instead, an outlaw status that has drawn a diversity of groups to her performances and readings. These audiences, with gender agendas of their own, have discovered a great truth in her experience with which they have been able to connect.[26] Ironically, academic scrutiny itself has taken a turn, for gender studies classes at three universities have added *Hidden: A Gender* to their required reading lists.

In an interview in early 1989 with Lila Wolff-Wilkinson, Bornstein articulated what was to be the basis of *Hidden: A Gender,* which she was in the process of developing:

There was at first in my life a construction of male. Then a deconstruction of male and a construction of what I assumed female was. Now currently there's a deconstruction of that socially accepted "this is female" and a reconstruction of me. It's not that I'm just taking parts. I don't consider myself androgynous. Androgyny is as rigid an assumption as a bipolar gender system. In fact, androgyny assumes bipolar, it assumes a scale along two poles. And to me, I see gender as flux, it's what life is about. It's gender as layers, and sometimes we want to express gender in one term and sometimes in another. The word gender simply means "class."[17]

In an essay, "Fuck Gender Anyway," Bornstein proposes "a call to action, and in acknowledgement of the work of my camping compatriots, because I'm furious with the injustices, the cruelties, and the bigotry committed by reason of the existence of gender." Regarding gender as essentially a constructed, two-class system in which one class has more power than, and thus oppresses, the other, Bornstein claims that this idea needs to be completely discarded. She claims that "doing away with gender is key to doing away with the patriarchy. . . . There *is* no gender inequity that doesn't first assume there *is* gender—and only two at that."[28]

Of gender—the obsession in Bornstein's life and art—she says that the "universal truth" underlying it is the concept of "us versus them." It is adversarial in nature and concerns power. She makes a clear distinction between genderism and sexism. The former occurs when one is discriminated against for not acting according to the code of one's assigned gender. In contrast, sexism is discrimination against women just for being biologically female. She believes that what is often perceived as homophobia is actually genderism (not "gender-fucking" but "fucking with gender").

Beyond discussing gender as a system that demands definition, Bornstein the transsexual assails the cultural "myth" of transsexuality:

It's also called "gender dysphoria." Look—everyone has some kind of bone to pick with their own gender status, gender role, gender assignment, or gender identity. And when this dissatisfaction can no longer be glossed over with good manners, or cured by purchasing enough gender-specific products or services—and when this dissatisfaction cannot be silenced by the authority of the state, the medical profession, the church, or one's own peers—then the dissatisfaction is called "transsexuality." . . . We're all of us dissatisfied. Some of us have less tolerance for the dissatisfaction, that's all.[29]

What frames Bornstein's "notes for a manifesto" is commentary on camp—the "folk art of the genderless":

It's frightening to be genderless. What makes it easier is a sense of humor, and that's where camp comes into the picture. Camp points out the silliness, exaggerates the roles, shines big spotlights on the gender dynamic. Camp is only possible when there is no fear of humiliation, and at that point, social control becomes very difficult. Camp is, in fact, the leading edge in the deconstruction of gender, because camp wrests social control from the hands of the fanatics. . . . [It] is the safety valve that can keep our activism from becoming fanaticism.[30]

At the Outwrite '90 conference of gay and lesbian writers, Bornstein's remarks for the playwrights' panel (now published in *High Risk: An Anthology of Forbidden Writings*) harkened back to the content of her haunting play—and then back some more:

I've come to see gender as a divisive social construct, and the gendered body as a somewhat dubious accomplishment. I write about this because I am a gender outlaw and my issues are gender issues. . . . I write . . . because I don't want to hear "You're not welcome in this bar," "You're not welcome at this party," "You're not welcome in my home," and I say I don't know why separatists won't let me in— I'm *probably* the only lesbian in this room to have successfully castrated a man and gone on to laugh about it on stage, in print and on national television. My ancestors were not shunned. They were celebrated. . . . Current theatrical forms reflect a rigidly bi-polar gender system. They aren't fluid enough for what I want to say, and I feel that form and content in theatre, as in life, should be complementary, not adversarial. So I work on my own gender fluidity and sometimes it works and sometimes it doesn't. And I work on the fluidity of my theatrical style—and sometimes it works and sometimes it doesn't. My life and my theatre—my form and my content—sort of do as I say and do as I do. Like my ancestors.[31]

Her recent concerns stemming from her activism and writing include assimilation ("I am afraid to belong to this community because I'd have to pass as a gendered person," she told the audience at the Outwrite '91 conference) and the concept of freaks as both commodity and community:

Used to be, freaks were the holy people. Some freaks. A long, long time ago. And then with the coming of a market economy, it seems we became a commodity. We became the sideshow. We were what the people came to see. We pulled those people into the tents. And we were silent, while the circus barker or the medicine hawker pitched the wonders of our lives to people who hadn't found the freak in themselves, and so they sought their freak in us. . . . I'll be on television helping Phil [Donahue] sell his sponsor's stuff. Because I need my voice to be heard. I need to be there for one suffering freak like I used to be who may tune in to that program. I need to be on that show because that show marks a big change in this culture's treatment of freaks. Television shows like that are on the border line between freaks as commodities, and freaks as community.[32]

Bornstein also connects gender and the power intrinsic to it to sado-masochism, and cites S/M as a union of power and gender through consensual sexual play:

When the play reaches the point of almost purely dealing with power, then gender in fact has been done away with. That probably accounts for the taboos on S/M by leaders of some branches of feminism, as well as by the patriarchy. They're too invested in maintaining the genders and gender system which defines their own ideologies.[33]

Bornstein also explores gender in performance through another kind of play, a use of humor that is—in contrast to most "gender-bending" art—not denigrating to women. Most observations about gender confusion are about the loss of status; they are therefore about sex (and are sexist) and not gender. For example, the man disguised as a woman loses status as a result, and the woman who disguises herself as a man gains status but then loses it when she is ultimately "unmasked" and revealed as a woman. Bornstein plays with gender and power in her writings, but power is never lost because of gender.

Ultimately, for Bornstein, the ideal is to be able to transcend gender:

I've got an androgynous appearance, and an androgynous voice, and there are several male (gender) cues that I have, as well as several female cues. I found that insisting that I was a woman, or trying to pretend that I always was one, was ridiculous. I was never "a woman trapped in a man's body." That is just so much horseshit. There may be fluidity towards gender role, or gender expression, that I was not able to, through social patterning, express, but I was never a woman trapped in a man's body. Yet, I know that I'm not a man, that much I'm very convinced about. The part that gets confusing is that I don't always feel like a woman. It bothers me when I have to fill out forms: "Sex: Male or Female?" I always want to respond, "Well . . . yes!"[34]

Notes

1. Bornstein and I have written a full-length musical, *Three Dollar Bill Opera*, a futuristic, "queer" version of *The Beggar's Opera*, in which killings to be made in a high-tech marketplace are at stake, the political atmosphere is dominated by a fundamentalist right-winger, gay and lesbian activists attempt to revive the historical gains the homosexual community won—then lost—in the late twentieth century, and heroine Polly begins as Paul and Mac is a lesbian into leather. Bornstein's solo work, *The Opposite Sex is Neither,* explores the variety of transsexual lives. It was produced in 1992. Bornstein and Sydney Erskine are also collaborating on a performance piece on politics and appearance in American culture.

2. Noreen C. Barnes, "Neutral Territory," San Francisco *Bay Area Reporter* (11 May 1989):29.

3. Ibid.

4. Kate Bornstein, *Hidden: A Gender,* unpublished manuscript, p. 28.

5. Ibid., 4.

6. The wording of Gene Price of the *Bay Times* (January 1990) and Bernard Weiner of the *San Francisco Chronicle* (5 December 1989), respectively.

7. Doris Fish, "Men, Lesbians and Transsexuals," *San Francisco Sentinel* (11 January 1990):14.

8. Bornstein, *Hidden: A Gender,* 2.

9. Ibid., 3.

10. Ibid., 42.

11. Ibid., 54.

12. Ibid., 55.

13. Barnes, "Neutral Territory," 29.

14. Ibid.

15. Bornstein, *Hidden: A Gender*, 14.

16. Ibid., 15.

17. Lily Braindrop, "Kate Bornstein: Gender Bender, Mind Bender," *Taste of Latex* (Summer 1990):26.

18. Caitlin Sullivan, "You Can Still Catch Kate Bornstein's Act at the Festival," *Seattle Gay News* (6 July 1990):27.

19. Wendell Ricketts, "Gender Agenda: Learning to Count Higher than Two," *Bay Area Reporter* (7 December 1989):28.

20. Bornstein appeared on "Geraldo" in February 1989, on a segment entitled "Transsexual Regrets: Who's Sorry Now?" (as the one guest who did *not* have regrets about her transsexuality).

21. Barnes, "Neutral Territory," 29.

22. Lila Wolff-Wilkinson, "Gender Is a Hoot: An Interview with Kate Bornstein," *Theater,* Yale School of Drama/Yale Repertory Theater (Spring/Summer 1989):34.

23. Remarks during presentation at Women and Theatre Pre-conference, ATHE Convention, San Diego, 1988.

24. Erika Munk, "Cross Left," *The Village Voice* (6 September 1988):82.

25. Jill Dolan, "In Defense of the Discourse: Materialist Feminism, Postmodernism, Poststructuralism . . . and Theory," *The Drama Review* (Fall 1989):66.

26. Bornstein actually has maintained a connection to the academy through lectures and performances of *Hidden: A Gender* at such institutions as San Francisco State University, Stanford, Brown, and George Mason University.

27. Wolff-Wilkinson, "Gender Is a Hoot," 32.

28. Kate Bornstein, "Fuck Gender Anyway: Notes for a Manifesto," unpublished paper, 1990, p. 2.

29. Ibid.

30. Ibid.

31. Kate Bornstein, "Transsexual Lesbian Playwright Tells All," in *High Risk: An Anthology of Forbidden Writings,* ed. Amy Scholder and Ira Silverberg (New York: Plume, 1991), p. 261.

32. Comments excerpted from unpublished paper, "Freak Show," delivered as part of a panel held to benefit the publication *Frighten the Horses,* San Francisco, 6 April 1991.

33. Bornstein, "Fuck Gender Anyway," 2.

34. Braindrop, "Kate Bornstein," 36.

JOHN PRESTON

The Theatre of Sexual Initiation

❦ The places where sex happens are often as important as the sex itself, at least if sex is defined as more than the simple achievement of orgasm. The context within which sex takes place adds meaning to it—a fact certainly true of sex between gay men in public places. The public nature of many sex acts between gay men betrays their nature as theatrical, in the sense of being an exhibition. If there is no audience, the goals cannot be accomplished.

A therapist approaching gay public sex with a reductionist simplification would examine gay male sex acts as psychologically motivated exhibitionism and voyeurism. Although that analysis might be true for some performers, that's too narrow a definition to encompass all actual motivations.

Public sex between gay men fulfills one of the most often overlooked aspects of gay sex; that it is male sex essential, the encounter of two or more males with one another in the sexual arena. Popular stereotypes may present gay men as "less than" real men; actual behavior shows that gay men are often acting out masculine behavior with a vengeance. In fact, the stereotype of their being less than totally manly may lead many gay men to feel a need to perform public displays of traditional masculinity in order to allow them to integrate a self-image of manliness.

The recent promotion of a "men's liberation movement" has added a new dimension to this expression of masculinity. Robert Bly has written what appears to be the first manifesto of the masculinist crusade, *Iron John: A Book about Men* (Reading, Mass.: Addison-Wesley, 1990). One of the points basic to his thesis is that young males need to be initiated into adult manhood. There must be, Bly and others contend, a rite of passage, and it must be communally recognized.

Of course, there are several ways that men in modern industrial societies gain their acceptance into adult male group identity. Though these mechanisms may not be as efficient or as effective as the masculinists would like them to be in the transmission of appropriate gender identity, activities such as athletic competition and rotation through the military are examples of how gender rights can be earned. It is worth noting that most gay men feel barred from these initiations, either culturally (they don't engage in sports because the physical contact with other men might engage an erotic response they're unwilling or incapable of expressing at that time) or legally (laws prohibit known homosexual men from entering the armed forces, even in time of war). Gay men are most often, then, kept from undergoing what might be seen as a necessary ceremony in the achievement of their adult being. The masculinists claim all men will remain underdeveloped unless they find a way to progress through this ritual.*

There is another element to gay male sexuality that pressures these men toward performing masculine acts in public as part of their sexual expression. Gay men report a nearly universal repression in the early parts of their lives. They express a need to break through that repression and offset it with a public act. The very concept of "coming out" carries with it a need to articulate publicly one's sexual preference. Privacy is an obstacle. The public act is seen as so vital that many gay activists now insist on "outing" people—bringing their sexual behavior to the public's attention—insisting that it is a communal prerogative to do so and not something the individual can control.

These different factors present a scenario that makes the public performance of sexual behavior a significant part of the gay male experience. It is so important that it has spawned amphitheatres where the display of male behavior can be displayed. Sometimes it is presented as athleticism. At other times, it is demonstrated as a test of physical endurance. There are often religious undertones to the highly ritualized activity.

To see some of the dynamics most clearly, I invite you to examine The Mineshaft, a now legendary sex club in New York. I knew the place intimately. Not only was I one of the regular attendants, I was a journalist during the height of its popularity, covering the club's activities for a national sex magazine. I was the ultimate participant/observer of the life of this club whose habitués, with only a few rare exceptions, were all gay men.

Other companies preceded The Mineshaft, but they were not nearly so professional, and their histories are only kept in anecdotes and personal

---

*It is intriguing to note the old pseudo-Freudian group diagnosis that male homosexuals are all examples of "arrested development," trapped in their adolescence. Though the masculinists wouldn't accept Freudian definitions of appropriate masculine behavior, their analysis of what is missing in modern manhood strikes a parallel with the Freudians. There is an "arrest" in the development, not just of gay men, but of all men. There is no adequate rite of passage to announce the transition from adolescence into adulthood. Jungian psychology has an equally strong statement to make about the need for men to recognize the "archetypes" of masculinity. In all these philosophies, a man, and certainly a male homosexual, cannot achieve maturity without a public embracement of male icons.

letters. Whatever they might have been, the earlier companies did not begin to approach this one in the style, substance, following, verve, and even religious passion of its actors and audience.

Everything about The Mineshaft was part of the event, part of the enviroment that the founder—a man named Wally Wallace—deemed necessary. Wallace, always vaguely drunk or high, knew enough to depend on the talents of his staff and co-workers when he opened The Mineshaft. The debut came during the winter of 1976–1977, I have been told by gay historian Michael Bronski. There were only certain parts of the stage setting that Wallace, himself, demanded. When others told him of some detail they thought important, he took their suggestions into account. This was an ensemble happening, not a star's turn. This was communal sex, even communistic. It was insurgent theatre; it was meant to offend bourgeois sensibilities, if people who held them ever mistakenly walked through the door. But the real purpose of The Mineshaft was determined by the action that was to be witnessed within the tribe of gay men. The activities were devoted to initiating males into the camaraderie of the group, something that had to be observed by the group. Given these goals, expense was no issue. Only a few parts of the costume or stage props were not affordable to anyone who was interested in and capable of taking part. Inherent talent was more important than anything that could be purchased. (In fact, many of the uniforms of The Mineshaft were decidedly working class, and the man who owned these costumes "authentically"—the man who worked for a utility company, was a construction worker, was a member of the military, and so on—was valued much more than the man who wore this clothing only as part of the make-believe.)

To enter the arena, you had to travel through Manhattan's meat-packing district, just south of Fourteenth Street, close enough to the Hudson that you could feel the wind off the water. If you arrived on foot, you could even feel a *frisson* of danger as you walked the poorly paved and poorly lit side streets. Arrival in a limousine (not nearly so rare as you might think) or a cab might provide some separation for a while, but the meat-packing houses, with their stink of spilt blood and sawdust and their visually stunning empty metal hooks on their loading docks, still pervaded your consciousness. The effect was impossible to defend against. You were entering a place where flesh was the common denominator. In this place, bodily fluids were so powerful they couldn't be covered up. In fact, it was against the aesthetic of the arena even to try. In the Spanish bullring, the horses wear brocade so the crowd will not have to see the wounds the bull makes. But this theatre had more *verité* than that. Here, there would be no silk coverings, nor any velvet curtains to keep the audience from seeing the actors out of costume.

When you got to the door—it had no sign, for knowing the correct address was part of being one of the initiates—you had to walk up a flight of stairs. Although the establishment held the street floor as well, part of your entrance into the theatre was to ascend a staircase, the first of many proscenia.

A guard stood at the top of the stairway to collect an entrance fee and to make sure that no one who entered would work against the purpose of the evening. Perfume was the greatest offense, and the most basic. It would offend the action to admit any but bodily odors or to allow other unnatural smells that could desecrate the air. Leatherwear with its pungent scent was fine; tobacco, especially in fetishistic cigars, was encouraged; but perfumes like after-shave lotions were, according to this creed, examples of society's feminization of men.*

There were some styles of clothing that were not allowed, but what was unacceptable was a highly subjective ruling. While someone would have no recourse after being barred because of floral fragrance, he could make an appeal on a ruling over his costume. He had only to articulate its function in his act. What was counterculture here was defined in reference to a unique outlook on what constituted culture. He could probably enter, even if he were wearing a three-piece suit, if he claimed to have it on for the sake of his performance.

Once past the doorman, you entered what appeared to be a traditional gay bar. This room was actually a place of transition. Here, a man could buy and drink a beer, a cocktail, even a soft drink, and stand around while he prepared himself to walk onto the stage. Some activities that were common to gay bars were allowed in this room. There could even be idle conversation (though there were limits; I was once ejected because my companion and I were talking about something unrelated to the place in a tone of voice loud enough to be heard by the other patrons). There was no pressure to perform sexually at all.

The final proscenium was a doorway covered with a leather curtain. Anyone who had passed the initial auditions could pass through it at will. The light changed dramatically in the further room; the light bulbs had reddish tones to them. There was hardly any conversation to disrupt the mood, and that was held in whispers. An occasional cough, once in a while a shared laugh, might seem disruptive, but what theatre doesn't have to contend with those?

The music was strikingly different here than in the first room. It helped heighten the sense of being in a place different from those you usually ex-

---

*I never smelled incense at The Mineshaft, but it would have been fitting. The staff would not have worked against it; they probably would have helped a supplicant light his incense if they were convinced he was using it with the correct attitude.

perienced. There might be a Baroque organ piece, perhaps an unusual African-American jazz duet, occasionally a New Age fugue. Whatever the sounds, they were deep, reverberant, almost always nonverbal. Words mixed with the sound effects would have been too specific for the experience, just as verbal communication limited what might happen.

Once in this room, the specialization between audience and actor began to be more apparent, though it could shift. Members of the assembly could become players as they desired, if they could find others to join their performance piece. There were, for one thing, spotlights that you could move into or out of. They shone on certain pieces of equipment—props, if you will. The major feature of this room was a leather sling suspended from the ceiling by four lengths of chain. After having found a partner, a man could climb into the sling, attach his feet to stirrup-like appendages that lifted his limbs up and apart, and offer his exposed anus to his accomplice. It was an invitation to fist-fucking, a specialty act that was sure to attract a crowd. The other men in the room would move closer, anxious to see the act performed, wanting to make sure it was done correctly, to ensure veracity. It would not have been acceptable to fake this exhibition.

There were other spotlights in the room that simply created focal points for the personae of some stars. Who would take the illuminated section of the stage was self-determined, but it was expected that he add to the ambiance of the place. His costume should be the most perfect, his stance the most expressive, his actions the most consistent with the action. He was supposed to be so appealing and so close to an ideal that he could attract a conspirator to affirm him and his hypermasculinity by assuming another role, that of apprentice to his masterdom.

The next room was for more group-oriented action. The lines between audience and performers were even more blurred here. The intent was to create an anarchistic atmosphere. Men knelt and sucked, others stood and moaned while they were sucked, roles were switched with great freedom. In fact, a willingness to accept role-reversal was almost required of all the participants.

There were stairs down to the street-level rooms. The descent intensified the feeling that you were entering a more critical arena. The smell of mold, urine, leather, and dirt were all more acute on this floor. The first chamber had rough concrete floors, still another indication of how coarse the action was supposed to be. Here, too, just as upstairs, the action was mainly oral sex, but there were new sound effects as well. Often there would be loud smacks of leather belts against naked skin or at least of palms against nude buttocks. There were more likely to be groans as men allowed themselves to be challenged to new heights of performance and found this stage more arduous.

The central room was, for many, the climax of the place. It, too, had spotlights. The most prominent accented an ancient bathtub. Actors could climb into or out of it. Once in, they were fair game for any of the other participants, who were invited to urinate on them. Some men could be divas and spend an entire night in the tub, though they risked the anger of other aspirants.

Finally, past a few small cubicles where more private performances of all types could be going on, there was a room where those who were tired from the stage could rest. Once again there were refreshments served, and the music was louder here. But, since all the attenders would have had to run the gauntlet to reach this place, there was also more respect for what might happen. After all, to get back out of here, you had to go back through the maze of arenas, and whoever you might talk to in this final room could be one of your co-players on your journey back up the stairs.

Perhaps because it was peopled only by those who had gone through the entire initiation, this room was where many virtuoso acts were performed. The room had a dais. Though most rooms of The Mineshaft had permanently placed fixtures, the props on this stage would change. There were occasionally stocks not unlike those the Puritans used in colonial New England. A man's head, arms, and feet were captured in wooden slats manufactured with suitable holes to bind him very effectively, making it impossible to escape whatever punishments or tortures his fellow performers might choose to inflict on him. At other times, there were chains hung from the ceilings with manacles for both wrists and both ankles, again for securing a man to them. I saw a cross there once; it was used for crucifixions—though with rope, not nails. Another time there was a platform upon which a man could be bound hand and foot, spread-eagled.

Whippings were the specialty here. They were not unheard of in the other spaces, but this room was the preferred realm for them. It only seemed to intensify the action that they took place in one of the few rooms where there was no other constant sexual activity going on.

The Mineshaft lived for nearly a decade. It spawned many competitors in New York and other cities in North America and Europe, but only a few like The Slot in San Francisco achieved anything close to its mythic status.

It was quite decidedly a theatre. One proof of this assertion was its professionalism. Not even the first cast of characters who walked through The Mineshaft understood that many of the players were professionals. I don't mean that they were simply male prostitutes. Wally Wallace actually hired men to set the tone of the place when it first opened. They were characters who live on in the imagination of many of the people who paid to make their own appearances. Wallace and his staff had wandered through Greenwich Village and Chelsea and had chosen the men who most fit their own projection of what The Mineshaft should be. They were paid to present themselves and the public personae they had developed to the rest of the clientele. They had the well-designed attire, the muscularly powerful bodies, and the carefully cultivated attitudes. They were not there just to be the stars, they were there to enable others to enter into the mood. They were coaches, paid to show the novices the ropes, to let them see how the right kind of roles should be played.

The Mineshaft was a success throughout most of its nearly ten-year run. It didn't close because the theatre had gone stale; it closed because of AIDS. Those bodily fluids, once such an important element in the establishment of drama, had become the means of transmitting a deadly disease whose horror invaded the play too realistically.

Most people assumed that such a theatre could never exist again, at least not with the same veracity, and, in fact, The Mineshaft and its rivals disappeared from the scene in New York and the rest of the world for a period of time. The need for this theatre did not disappear though. It began to reemerge in "safe sex" clubs, meetings where naked or near-naked men could masturbate together, using one another's visual and verbal stimulation to get the job done.

The safe sex clubs were minor league compared to The Mineshaft. Rather than being in the big time, they were only provincial companies. They did not exist so much for what was actually going on in them as for their ability to conjure up memories of other times. Grown men found themselves thrown back to their romanticized memories of innocent adolescence, jerking off in groups in settings that often were designed to look like their high school gymnasium. Even the little bits of clothing that were allowed in these clubs were throwbacks to teenaged years: sneakers and sweat socks, athletic shirts and jock straps, sweat bands and jockey shorts.

Safe sex clubs, because they only facilitated orgasms, could not fulfill the real demands that had made The Mineshaft such a success. They were a necessary transition, though. They allowed the audience and the actors to see ways to present their plays with only a few conversions to accommodate the new health realities. "Sex itself does not transmit the HIV virus; certain sex acts transmit the virus" is the credo of the safe-sex movement. Having learned ways to circumvent the danger of infection, men have gone back to sex clubs as a way to meet their needs. Sex that tempts death is a concept that may be attractive to a few pseudo-existential writers, but it isn't what most of the participants are actually interested in. Suicide through sex might appeal on a conceptual level, but as a performance art, few are willing to commit to it.

A number of new sex clubs have appeared in New York, San Francisco, and a few other cities in the past few years. They once again offer the same intense trip through sexual reality that The Mineshaft had excelled in. Though they are not as elaborate as The Mineshaft in its glory, the players report that these new clubs actually have a greater intensity since there are fewer amateurs interfering with the action, the lines are better understood, and the actors know how to use the props more efficiently.

Word about the new clubs is spread through a grapevine, usually by telephone. The owners are not as professional as Wally Wallace; they do not actually pay men to come to their clubs and perform. They do, however, roam the bars in the same neighborhoods and hand out free passes to those who look and act the way they are supposed to. Not only will these men again set the tone for the new clubs, they'll spread the word of the unadvertised establishment to the *cognoscenti*.

Outsiders seldom see all that is contained in the scripts that underlaid The Mineshaft or the new sex clubs. They see only men who gather in spaces where they can achieve anonymous orgasms, titillated by shared fetishes and excited by communally held icons. But much more is going on here.

The most striking element in the sex clubs is the extent to which the participants are encountering and challenging their previous repression. Since gay sex was forbidden in any form for most males as they were growing up (and is still prohibited in most places even today), the very expression of sexual identity was as controlled as the demonstration of any genital sexual drive. There is no differentiation, often, between a gay sexual identity and an interest in or desire for what would be considered much more deviant behavior than simple homosexuality. Picture the men in the bathtubs at The Mineshaft. One of the new rules of safe sex says that urinating on someone is not dangerous, as long as the urine is not ingested. The bathtub is rebaptized, the piss queen is reenthroned; after all, once you have entered this arena, you embrace the identity of the outlaw so fervently, there is no reason to establish boundaries.

To display overt gay sexual behavior, then, can often mean exhibiting grossly aberrant deportment. It is not too different from a process observable in many transvestites who are gay men. According to this logic, if you go so far as to challenge the male stereotype by admitting and demonstrating your homosexuality, you might as well go all the way and reverse the expression of your gender. You have already attacked the assumptions of your gender by being homosexual, so there is no reason to stop with just sexuality. This is certainly the position of many transvestites who infuse their cross-dressing with political motivations, and it is the attitude expressed by "radical faeries" who engage in an explicit attack on gender with their dress and ideology.

But many male homosexuals are not interested in challenging the masculine archetypes. In fact, they want to incorporate them. Being free of the distraction that the masculinists ascribe to male/female relationships, the gay man is actually in a perfect position to embrace masculinity, but he needs to engage with other men, or another man, to accomplish his goal.

While all these drives were apparent in The Mineshaft, I think the most important aspect of these public displays has to do with the masculinists' observations of the need for ritual. Without doubt, sadomasochistic behavior has many roots; there is no question that a public display of sado-masochistic behavior comes from many dynamics similar to the ones I just described. But the public display of gay male sadomasochistic sex acts is primarily an exhibition of the gay man going through the rite of passage. It is the way many gay men accomplish their gender needs of leaving adolescence and entering male adulthood.

What is most important is to understand how much of the sex in places like The Mineshaft and its successors has to do with endurance. The men who climb into the sling to be fist-fucked are *enduring* the act, and they have an audience to prove that they passed the ordeal. Though many participants report great pleasure in taking a fist up their ass, it is impressive to note that many men report that the act has to be witnessed for it to have meaning for them.

This endurance factor is even more apparent when dealing with whippings. Obviously, the person being flagellated is *enduring* a punishment. It is not sufficient to analyze that action as the expression of a poor self-image or other psycho-babble. The whipping performance has many models in the same aboriginal societies that the masculinists admire and cite in their literature. This act is the Sioux Indian enduring hooks in his chest; it is the walk across hot coals in Polynesia; it is the way a male can enter manhood.

Cocksucking is one of the most elemental homosexual acts, but even this action takes on new meaning when performed in a public space. There are many native cultures where the consumption of an adult man's semen is part of the adolescent rite of passage. Again, in the sex club, not only is the male undergoing his ritual, but he is doing it with a congregation gathered to watch him.

The language of the sex clubs underlines much of this observation. A player is "man enough" to suck cock in public. He doesn't hide his proclivity. He doesn't claim to be other than his real self. He invites the audience to watch as he gets on his knees in front of another man dressed in the attire of overt masculinity: the leather of the biker, the uniform of the military man, the outfit of the athlete, the garb of this community's expression of masculinity.

Bondage, so vital to the actions in a sex club, becomes another means for men to free themselves. The contradiction is easily understood when you watch the transformation that a male undergoes and listen to the dialogue between himself and his captor when he is placed in stocks or chained. After the more than symbolic restraints are attached, the submissive male is invited to admit that he really wants "it" done to him. He really wants to be beaten, doesn't he? the captor insists. He won't get fucked until he admits that he needs to feel "it." He won't be allowed to reach his own orgasm unless he confesses his desire to be a cocksucker, an asslicker, or a bootkisser.

In one way or another, that dialogue is repeated in all these public sexual acts. Even bondage becomes a vehicle for shedding societal restrictions. By allowing himself to be pressed into a form of servitude, the man achieves his liberation.

There are other elements to the masculinists' theory that fit surprisingly well into this analysis of the sex club. Another fascinating element is the masculinists' insistence that, not only does a young man need to go through a transformative experience, but he needs to do it with the guidance of an older man.

When gay liberation first merged with liberalizing sexual codes, there was a wave of pornography that presented the ideal sexual object as a young, blond man, as young as the laws would allow the photographers to present. I am not sure how this particular archetype was decided upon; I suspect it was a literal translation of heterosexual iconography—the blond bimbo as ultimate object—into the gay experience. It didn't last long.

In the past two decades, there have been some marked changes in that ideal figure. He has certainly gotten a great deal older. A cynical observer could note that the producers of the pornography, who tended to be on the first wave of gay activists, have gotten older as well, and that they are simply projecting themselves as desirable. That idea has some appeal and probably a great deal of truth to it. But the liberation of gay men's erotic imaginations and their impressions of their masculinity now reflect some of the masculinists' doctrine. For at least a decade now, one of the sexual ideals presented by magazines such as *Drummer,* the publication most responsible for the codification of the icons of the sex clubs, has been "The Daddy."

Daddies stand ready to initiate their "Boys" into adulthood. The classifieds of *Drummer* and many more mainstream gay male publications are proof of the appeal of this image. A spanking at the hand of a Daddy in a sex club, especially when witnessed by others who understand the importance of a Daddy to a Boy, is most often followed by an embrace and a slap on the back, even a kiss. There is a reward from the older man to the youngster for having endured his initiation.

There is another level at which the masculinists' philosophy fits in with the experience of the sex clubs. Many of the acts that are performed in these public places—fist-fucking is a good example—require a certain skill. Though the idea of their being spontaneous is appealing and many of the performers try everything to make it appear that they are spontaneous, few people can be expected to perform such exploits without some education. (They also require some preparation. Fist-fucking requires considerable amounts of special lubrication that has to be transported to the site, and it is usually done with the help of drugs that also must be planned for.)

The older man—the initiator—provides this role. He is often seen as a sexually desirable first person to fist-fuck a novice, and he is also the one who will oversee the performance and make sure that it is accomplished safely and correctly. The older man in this instance is passing on the ancient rites of the tribe. He is making sure that the passage into malehood is done appropriately and with ample regard to the rules of the clan. His power is like that of the storyteller; he gains respect for his knowledge of the myths that tell us where we have been and where we should be going.

Although heterosexuals obviously indulge in public sex acts, especially precoital ones such as kissing and holding hands, the public performance of genital sex acts remains much more in the realm of the male homosexual. The question thus comes up, Why does this male homosexual behavior differ from the behavior of heterosexuals?

If, as the masculinists pronounce and even Freudian and Jungian thinkers say less frankly, the male needs a rite of social initiation, obviously the gay man needs it all the more. Since he has been denied access to the more common initiations, and since private acts are too weak to accomplish transformation, no matter who is performing them, the gay man has had to create coming-out scenarios of his own. The political theatre involved in some of these coming-out acts are also weak; though they protest the repression the gay man has experienced, they don't really provide the necessary bridge from adolescence to adulthood.

Rough male sexuality, including public acts of bondage, flagellation, fist-fucking, and cock-sucking, give the supplicant a means to show his tribe that he is ready to become a man. He is willing to endure his initiation rite to join the adults. He often accepts a mentor in the person of a Daddy-figure, a more potent symbol of fatherhood than the man who failed him as biological parent.

The popularity of public sex clubs, even in the face of a deadly AIDS epidemic, prevails because these places represent an arena in which men can publicly undergo these transformations. Their nearly religious music, their reliance on symbolic posturing and clothing, and their ability to define stages of development produce a codification of gay male sexuality against which the applicant can measure himself. There are certainly some men who approach these places for the sake of anonymous sex, but they are not the real actors in this play. The true celebrants are the aspirant and the mentor, the teacher and the student, and the gathering congregation of a tribe of men.

Index

UNIVERSITY PRESS OF NEW ENGLAND publishes books under its own imprint and is the publisher for Brandeis University Press, Brown University Press, University of Connecticut, Dartmouth College, Middlebury College Press, University of New Hampshire, University of Rhode Island, Tufts University, University of Vermont, and Wesleyan University Press.

Library of Congress Cataloging-in-Publication Data

Gender in performance : the presentation of difference in the performing arts / edited by Laurence Senelick.
   p.   cm.
Includes index.
ISBN 0-87451-545-9. — ISBN 0-87451-604-8 (pbk.)
   1. Sex in the performing arts.   I. Senelick, Laurence.
PN1590.S3G46   1992
791—dc20   92-11968

∞